OXFORD HISTORICAL MONOGRAPHS

Editors

J. A. GALLAGHER   N. GIBBS   J. B. OWEN
R. W. SOUTHERN   R. B. WERNHAM

NOTE

Oxford Historical Monographs will consist of books which would formerly have been published in the Oxford Historical Series. As with the previous series, they will be carefully selected studies which have been submitted, or are based upon theses submitted, for higher degrees in this University. The works listed below are those still in print in the Oxford Historical Series.

The Pauper Press

A STUDY IN
WORKING-CLASS RADICALISM
OF THE 1830s

BY
PATRICIA HOLLIS

OXFORD UNIVERSITY PRESS
1970

Oxford University Press, Ely House, London W.1

GLASGOW NEW YORK TORONTO MELBOURNE WELLINGTON
CAPE TOWN SALISBURY IBADAN NAIROBI LUSAKA DAR ES SALAAM ADDIS ABABA
BOMBAY CALCUTTA MADRAS KARACHI LAHORE DACCA
KUALA LUMPUR SINGAPORE HONG KONG TOKYO

PRINTED IN GREAT BRITAIN

FOR
MY FATHER

1539410

'It was not against the respectable Press that this bill was directed, but against a pauper Press, which, administering to the prejudices and the passions of a mob, was converted to the basest purposes, which was an utter stranger to the truth, and only sent forth a continual stream of falsehood and malignity, its virulence and its mischief heightening as it proceeded.'

ELLENBOROUGH, 29 December 1819
(*Hansard*, 1st ser., xli, col. 1591)

Newspaper stamps placed newspapers under the control of respectable men, 'who for their own sakes, would conduct them in a more respectable manner than was likely to be the result of a pauper management'.

CRESSET PELHAM, 20 March 1832
(*Hansard*, 3rd ser., xi, col. 492)

PREFACE

THIS book is about two things, popular journalism and working-class radicalism in the London of the 1830s.

From 1815 newspapers had to carry a fourpenny stamp, a 'tax on knowledge', which effectively and explicitly priced newspapers out of the pockets of the poor. In the autumn of 1830, just three months after the July Revolution in France had recharged popular radicalism in England, illegal unstamped anti-Establishment papers appeared on the streets of London, selling for a penny. Six years later their circulation had far surpassed that of the stamped press, and the duty was reduced to a penny. The Unstamped press then dried up.

In those six years a score of self-employed London printers, coffee-house keepers, and radical freelance journalists deliberately defied the law and put out several hundred Unstamped under such titles as the *Poor Man's Guardian*, the *Slap at the Church*, the *Destructive*, and the *Working Man's Friend*. For selling these papers in the streets some 740 men, women, and children went to prison.

The Unstamped, like the *Penny Magazine* and the crime reporters, were a species of popular journalism. The Unstamped were illegal, and to print and circulate them was one of the leading tasks of working-class radicals in the 1830s. The Unstamped reiterated the right the working man had both to the vote and to the produce of his own labour, and they thereby elaborated working-class radical and socialist theory. For these three reasons the Pauper Press of the 1830s merits a study in some detail.

There have been three main styles of writing about the popular press. The two-volume nineteenth-century histories of the press[1] gave a paper-by-paper, chapter-by-chapter chronicle. They usually devoted half a chapter or so to the

[1] e.g. A. Andrews, *The History of British Journalism*, 2 vols., 1859; J. Amphlett, *The Newspaper Press*, 1860; F. K. Hunt, *The Fourth Estate*, 2 vols., 1850; H. R. Fox-Bourne, *English Newspapers*, 2 vols., 1887.

Unstamped, conceded that the Unstamped had forced the reduction of the stamp duty in 1836, but regretted that these penny papers were not as wholesome as those of Charles Knight or John Cassell. The Unstamped, on this account, were a colourful and strident step towards cheap journalism and cheap literature. Two-and-sixpenny boards rather than the Six Points showed the success of the Unstamped. There was little attempt to set these papers in the context of working-class radicalism, or to assess the claims of working-class journalists that they were out to educate their readers into political and economic self-awareness. The Unstamped were cheap news rather than cheap politics.

With the flood of writings on Chartism that began after the First World War,[1] the Unstamped were incorporated into the intellectual lineage of Chartism. Because these papers regularly denounced Malthus, middlemen, and the Moloch of capital, they were held responsible for exacerbating class hostilities and for creating the working-class consciousness that underpinned Chartism. This account is much more interesting than the first, but for several reasons it is hardly more satisfactory.[2] These authors ignore the technical and contextual problems of the Unstamped, the considerations of profit, sales, circulation, and prosecution which so affected the style of these papers. Worse, they assume that the Unstamped spoke with one voice the spondees of an anglicized pre-Marxian socialism. But a closer study of the Unstamped shows that there were two radical rhetorics, not one. The older was shaped in the years around 1819, and denounced aristocracy, monopoly, taxes, and corruption; the newer was that of Hetherington, Carpenter, and Bronterre O'Brien, and it denounced exploitation, property, and power. The 'socialist' writers tried—and failed—to displace the older language by the new. Place exaggerated the socialism of the Unstamped, and it has been exaggerated ever since. Finally, on this

---

[1] e.g. M. Beer, *The History of British Socialism*, 1914; M. Hovell, *The Chartist Movement*, 1918; R. H. Tawney's edition of William Lovett's *Life and Struggles*, 1920. More recently, E. P. Thompson's *The Making of the English Working Class*, 1963, seems to share this approach. W. Wickwar's *The Struggle for the Freedom of the Press, 1819–1832*, 1928, is an exception.

[2] For more detailed criticism, see below, pp. 285–90.

account of the Unstamped, there is no way of explaining why working-class and middle-class radicals (who also sought to abolish the stamp, for educational ends) were closer allies in 1836 than they were in 1830, an alliance that can be traced through the 1840s into the Association for the Repeal of the Taxes on Knowledge in 1849. If the Unstamped created the sense of class behind Chartism, they also made it possible for Place and Roebuck to assist Lovett in drawing up the Charter.

The third way of writing about the popular press has developed since the 1950s and indicates, perhaps, the current interest in such sociological questions as opinion formation, methods of communication, and patterns of social control. Specifically the press has been studied in three aspects, in its relation to working-class literature and culture, to public opinion, and thirdly to politics and the political structure. R. K. Webb, in his fascinating monograph on the British working-class reader, has shown how press, pamphlets, and cheap literature were used by middle-class educationalists to instruct the working classes in right notions. And this has been followed by detailed studies of street literature, popular fiction, and working-class literary 'culture'.[1]

The second approach has been to examine the provincial press and provincial opinion.[2] The problem here is to assess the effect of a popular press on its community, and to determine whether it shaped or merely reflected current attitudes. It is important to know what a newspaper editor said; it is even more important to know whether what he said carried any weight and had any influence. G. Cranfield, in his book on the early eighteenth-century provincial press, has meticulously documented the structure of the trade, but has outlined the views of their proprietors without in any way attempting to assess them. D. Read has examined

---

[1] R. K. Webb, *The British Working Class Reader, 1790–1848*, 1955; R. D. Altick, *The English Common Reader*, 1957; L. James, *Fiction for the Working Man*, 1963; M. Dalziel, *Popular Fiction a Hundred Years Ago*, 1957; L. Shepard, *The Broadside Ballad*, 1962.

[2] G. Cranfield, *The Development of the Provincial Newspaper, 1700–1760*, 1962; D. Read, *Press and People 1790–1850: Opinion in Three English Cities*, 1961.

the early nineteenth-century press in Manchester, Leeds, and Sheffield. He devotes nearly a hundred pages to the political opinions of their owners, and only eight pages to measuring their influence on local and national affairs. As the main indicator of this influence he employs sales figures. Though this may be a useful measure within a middle-class reading public, it is an unreliable test for a working-class press when so many of the papers were read in public houses, coffee houses, and reading-rooms. Likewise, Professor Aspinall has assured us that *The Times* was increasingly responsive to middle-class opinion, but though he is almost certainly correct, he has not attempted to test this.[1] It is extraordinarily difficult to assess the influence of a paper or a press, because at no point does there exist a control-group against which to measure it. But it is not a problem which dissolves if it is ignored. It must at least be tackled if the press is to be fitted into its community and social and political climate.[2]

Finally, there have been a few attempts to relate the press to politics. The classic work on this has been Professor Aspinall's *Politics and the Press*, which is a quarry for the period. The *History of 'The Times'* asks similar questions of just one paper in the nineteenth and twentieth century. More recently, John Vincent has sketched the way in which a growing provincial press helped to create an authentic rank-and-file Liberalism in the middle of the nineteenth century.[3]

This book differs somewhat from all of these in attempting to relate working-class journalism to working-class politics in the 1830s.[4] It is in two sections. In the first part the Unstamped are looked at from the outside, as a cause of concern to Government, magistrates, and educationalists, seeking to manipulate or eradicate the radical underworld

---

[1] A. Aspinall, *Politics and the Press, 1780–1850*, 1949, pp. 380–1.
[2] See below, pp. 283–92.
[3] Aspinall, op. cit.; J. R. Vincent, *The Formation of the Liberal Party, 1857–1868*, 1965.
[4] S. Coltham, 'The *Beehive* Newspaper: its origins and early struggles', in *Essays in Labour History*, ed. A. Briggs and J. Saville, 1960, and at greater length in 'George Potter and the "Beehive" Newspaper' (Oxford University D.Phil. thesis, 1956) relates the *Beehive* to working-class radicalism in the 1860s.

from which the Unstamped emerged. The middle-class campaign to repeal the taxes on knowledge is studied as a pressure group in its own right, bringing public opinion to bear on a Government that was reluctant to lose £500,000 of revenue and reluctant to admit the validity of such a method of political change.

The second part of this book, and its core, is a study of the Unstamped press, of its sales, its profits, its readers, and its vendors. Because the Unstamped were published mainly in London, their proprietors had to build up an elaborate network of country agents. Because the Unstamped were illegal their proprietors had to distribute them in dummy parcels, in fancy dress, and over the rooftops. Because the quarto radical Unstamped were avowedly 'educational', they provoked rival publications from the Society for the Diffusion of Useful Knowledge. Because the broadsheet Unstamped were profitable, they incurred the wrath of the stamped press, and the duty had to be reduced. The Unstamped was a political activity in an educational world— that was what made it radical journalism. It supported and complemented other political activities, such as the National Union of the Working Classes. And it offered an ideological analysis of the rights due and the wrongs done to the working classes. A study of the Unstamped press, it is hoped, will throw light on London working-class radicalism, on the development (or lack of it) of working-class theory, and on the relations of middle- and working-class radicals in the 1830s.

This book has many limitations. Three of them are deliberate. It is a study of the London Unstamped, even though several of the industrial towns had an Unstamped press of their own. The main reason for this is that a good three-quarters of the penny papers and almost all of the radical ones were published from London, and owed their vitality to the London National Union of the Working Classes and the London Victim Fund. The three or four provincial papers that were important, such as the Birmingham *Pioneer* or Doherty's run of papers in Manchester, are included in the text where they offer points of comparison. Most of the smaller provincial penny papers were ephemeral and derivative.

To have attempted a fully comprehensive study of them would have taken much time and space without substantially affecting the analysis.

The second limitation is that of time. This is a study of the pauper press between 1830 and 1836, and it does not, except for the Introduction to Section Two and the occasional comparison, analyse the radical press of the years around 1819 or the Chartist press of the 1840s. This is because the Unstamped were illegal, and the other waves of journalism were not. The ambitions of, and constraints on, the publishers of the 1830s were very different from those of the earlier and later periods. In any case, W. Wickwar and E. P. Thompson have described the press of the 1819 period. The press of the 1840s is an integral part of Chartist history and requires treatment as such.

The third limitation is that I have concentrated on the radical Unstamped out of all the penny papers. Co-operative magazines, comic sheets, crime reporters, Society for the Diffusion of Useful Knowledge publications, and religious weeklies were all unstamped, and technically all violated the law. But only the radical Unstamped were prosecuted, presented as a threat to public order, and described as a pauper press.

The main source for this has been the Unstamped press itself, together with the Home Office Papers for the early 1830s and the Carlile Papers (held by the Huntington Library, California), neither of which have been extensively used before. I have not been able to track down any Stamp Office Papers, if they should still exist. If they do, the limitations of this book will be clearer still.

NOTE

I WOULD like to thank University College, London, for the use of the Brougham Papers, the Chadwick Papers, and those of the Society for the Diffusion of Useful Knowledge; also the Huntington Library, California, for the use of the Carlile Papers.

I am much indebted to Mr. Michael Brock, Dr. A. Macintyre, and Dr. B. H. Harrison, of Oxford, for their comments and advice; and to one book in particular I owe a vast debt, namely Edward Thompson's *The Making of the English Working Class* (1963).

Many of the footnotes contain several references. These follow the order of the text except where the passage footnoted contains, or ends with, a quotation, in which case the first reference in the footnote is to that quotation.

CONTENTS

ABBREVIATIONS

Add. MSS.	British Museum Additional Manuscripts
BAPCK	British Association for the Promotion of Co-operative Knowledge
Coll.	Collection
FP	*Friend of the People*
GNCTU	Grand National Consolidated Trades Union
HO	Home Office papers, Public Record Office
LWMA	London Working Men's Association
Mepol.	Metropolitan Police Papers, Public Record Office
Midland Rep.	*Midland Representative*
NAPL	National Association for the Protection of Labour
NPU	National Political Union
NS	*Northern Star*
NUWC	National Union of the Working Classes
PMG	*Poor Man's Guardian*
Pol. Letters	*Political Letters*
Pol. Reg.	*Political Register*
PU	Political Union
Red Rep.	*Red Republican*
Rep.	*Republican*
RRA	Radical Reform Association
S.C.	Select Committee
SDUK	Society for the Diffusion of Useful Knowledge
SPCK	Society for the Promotion of Christian Knowledge
T.	Treasury Papers, Public Record Office
n.d.	undated
WMF	*Working Man's Friend*
WPG	*Weekly Police Gazette*

SECTION ONE

THE TAXES ON KNOWLEDGE

THE BLACK ART

The disputes about the Liberty of the Press will one day be read with as much wonder as the disputes about witchcraft. The belief that helpless old hags could ride the winds and dispense sickness, sorrow, and calamity, will not seem less astonishing than the belief that poor scribblers can exercise baneful powers over the public mind, and order at pleasure the rise and fall of institutions. Libel is the black art of modern times; the pen, the broomstick; the press, the cauldron; and the viler the ingredients flung in, of the more fearful potency the charm is supposed to be . . . The dabbler in the black art makes, in words, a likeness of the thing he wishes to injure, and sets it before a blaze of invective, and it wastes away: he sticks sharp charges into it, skewers it with vituperation, and the object of the malice is pierced and destroyed. These are things which our ancestors believed of the body natural; they are now believed of the body politic. To put to the torture an object in representation by words, as formerly in wax, is supposed to destroy it in reality. As no health in the person could withstand the torture of him in effigy, so no virtue in an institution can bear up against its detraction on paper . . .

Our ancestors have not afforded the folly for the completion of the parallel. They did not tax broomsticks, though they knew full well that a broomstick was essential to the movements of a witch, as their descendents know circulation to be necessary to the effect of libel. But there was no stamp-duty on broomsticks, though a fourpenny tax would certainly have taken them out of the hands of the wretchedly poor class of witches—for, favoured as they were with the devil's gifts, riches were not among them, as he gave all his disposable wealth to the church, and would not spare from the bishops a maravedo for the wizards. Our forefathers, doubtless, considered that though it was a shocking thing that witches should run their careers through the sky mounted on broomsticks, yet broomsticks being serviceable to ten thousand honest folks for one witch, it would be inexpedient to put restraints on their use . . . By depriving the petitioners of the modern black art of their broomsticks, our Legislature has driven them to spitting cattle—or, to drop metaphor, by imposing taxes on knowledge, which place them out of the reach of the needy, a contraband trade has been called into existence, and a cheap illicit spirit, ten times above proof, has been hawked among the working classes. The cheap publications of whose alleged inflammatory tendency so much complaint is made, are the off-springs of the Stamp Duties: reduce the price of journals which have some character at stake for truth and knowledge, and this fry would sink in the competition.[1]

[1] A. Fonblanque, *England under Seven Administrations*, 1837, vol. ii, pp. 142–5.

I

POLITICS AND THE UNSTAMPED—THE PROBLEM OF EDUCATION

IN 1830 the stamp duty on newspapers was 4*d*. a copy; *The Times* cost 7*d*. The duty on alamanacs was 15*d*., on pamphlets 3*s*. an edition, and on advertisements 3*s*. 6*d*. an item. The whole, together with the duty on paper, comprised the 'taxes on knowledge'.[1] In 1836, the four-penny stamp on newspapers, the heaviest of these taxes, was reduced to a penny. Two groups in London had campaigned for its repeal. There were the middle-class radicals, who included Place, Hume, Roebuck, Grote, Birkbeck, Bulwer, Wakley, Warburton, and occasionally Brougham, together with the working-class radicals, led by Hetherington, Carpenter, and Cleave. Both groups claimed that an unstamped press was central to informal adult education; both believed that education was the working-class passport to politics. When radicals of both classes and all creeds campaigned for an unstamped press by bringing 'pressure from without' to bear on Parliament, they assumed that politics, property, and education dove-tailed in various ways to structure the political community. Because the Unstamped press was an educational question it was ultimately a political question, and it was for this reason that the radical campaign was opposed.

Each version of the political community under debate in 1832[2] had certain educational implications. The con-

[1] The almanac duty was abolished in 1834; the advertisement duty was reduced to a scale of 1*s*. to 2*s*. an item in 1833 and abolished in 1853; the pamphlet duty was repealed in 1833; the paper duty was abolished in 1861; and the last penny on newspapers was removed in 1855.

[2] See D. C. Moore, 'The Other Face of Reform' in *Victorian Studies*, 1961, and 'Social Structure, Political Structure, and Public Opinion in Mid-Victorian England' in *Ideas and Institutions of Victorian England*, 1967, ed. R. Robson; S. Beer, 'The Representation of Interests. . .' in *American Political Science Review*, 1957; N. McCord, 'Some Difficulties of Parliamentary Reform', in *Historical Journal*, 1967.

servatives[1] believed that Parliament should represent certain
species of property and certain legitimate interests, such as
corporations; and that this property map of interests and the
community map of influence should reflect each other.
The task of a Reform Bill, therefore, was to turn a bundle
of local and competing properties into a homogenous local
'interest'; and these various local interests should have their
claims assessed in parliament. This had a number of consequences. It meant that there could be no legitimate
'pressure from without' for two reasons. If Parliament was
the 'sole arena of serious social contest',[2] the arbiter of
interests, and the only deliberative body, then pressure
groups either infringed on it, intimidated it, or both. The
Quarterly Review as late as 1849 complained of a growth
of 'agitation—that is, *intimidation*'.[3] Such a view squarely
ruled out pledges, instructions, and mandates for parliamentary candidates, a Platform, a crusading popular press,
and all the tactics employed by radicals during the summer
of 1832. Secondly, if Parliament already embraced local
'interests', then all other forms of organized public opinion
were artificial. Canning in 1820 thought that public meetings of a corporate character were legitimate, because
'ancient habits, preconceived attachments, that mutual
respect which makes the eye of a neighbour a security for
each man's good conduct' made their opinions authentic.
But where a mass were brought together 'having no permanent relation to each other, no common tie but what
arises from their concurrence as members of that meeting',
the result would be political mischief.[4] On the very same
grounds, Toulmin Smith, the staunch opponent of Chadwick's Board of Health and of any centralization, favoured
local self-government because it created 'a common feeling
of neighbourhood and of united interests'.

[1] The labels 'conservative' and 'tory' refer to a much wider group than the parliamentary Tory party; in the eyes of the radicals, they included those Whigs who
took issue with radical notions of education and franchise extension. The capital
letter is reserved for the Tory party.

[2] Lord Houghton, 'On the Admission of the Working Classes', in *A Plea for
Democracy*, ed. W. Guttsman, 1967, p. 54. Houghton, of course, used this as an
argument to extend the vote to trades unionists.

[3] *Quarterly Review*, lxxxv, p. 291: 'Democracy'.

[4] Quoted H. Jephson, *The Platform*, 1892, vol. i, pp. 508–10.

None of that unhealthy 'pressure from without', which has of late been so much used to act upon governments . . . is needed when true local self-government exists. Such 'pressure from without' is generally artificial, always suspicious, never healthy. Local self-government gives the constant opportunity for the lawful and peaceful uttering of true and soundly formed Public Opinion on every question that arises.[1]

When Attwood complained to the Birmingham Political Union in May 1832 that if he held no meetings he was ignored, that small meetings were disregarded, and large meetings were considered rebellious,[2] he was missing this second point altogether; by no means, in conservative eyes, could his meetings ever be anything but artificial. Such a view of parliament and such a view of political opinion meant that the propertyless remained outside the political community.

This entailed certain attitudes towards education. Whatever education there was had to be limited, functional, useful in its strictest and narrowest sense, fitting men for their station and their duties in life. Hannah More and Patrick Colquhoun had stated in the opening decade of the nineteenth century that no system of education for the poor should 'pass the bounds of their condition in society' as that would 'confound the ranks of society' on which the happiness of the poor depended.[3] To give men ambitions that could not be fulfilled, aspirations that could not be met, and, as the century progressed, an interest in politics when they were outside the political community, was to make men unhappy and society unstable. Gaskell, in 1833, thought there was no virtue and much political danger in making men dissatisfied with their lot. Samuel Greg, the benevolent patron of model factory villages, provided music, drawing lessons, chess, and evening classes for his factory hands but explicitly dissociated himself from 'those who think that the highest ambition of a working man should be to rise above the station in which Providence has placed him'.[4]

---

[1] J. T. Smith, *Local Self-Government and Centralization*, 1851, p. 43.
[2] Quoted Jephson, op. cit., vol. ii, p. 120.
[3] P. Colquhoun, *A Treatise on Indigence*, 1806, p. 148. For Hannah More, see *Mendip Annals*, ed. The Revd. A. Roberts, 1859, p. 6.
[4] P. Gaskell, *The Manufacturing Population of England* . . ., 1833, p. 272; S. Greg, *Two Letters to Leonard Horner Esq.*, 1840, p. 24.

It was a position with which even Charles Knight at times sympathized:

The object of this general diffusion of knowledge is not to make men discontented with their lot—to make the peasant yearn to become an artizan, or the artizan dream of the honours and riches of a profession—but to give the means of content to those who, for the most part, must necessarily remain in that position which requires great self-denial and great endurance.[1]

Hannah More's decision to teach reading but not writing to the poor was repeated in essence by the Society for the Diffusion of Useful Knowledge and the Mechanics Institutes twenty years later when they decided to teach the elements of chemistry but not the language of politics to their artisans. The content of useful knowledge had expanded; its concepts had not. Not for nothing did Hetherington and Place join to point out that useful knowledge was useless at best and tory at worst. Another twenty years later, and a government inspector, J. D. Morell, attacked those who would limit the schooling available to rural children in order to preserve a 'feudal type of society'.[2] Morell thought that the function of education was to make the children of the poor critical, restless, and mobile. He would educate all classes in order to confound all class distinctions.

The second version of the political community entailing distinctive educational views was that of the middle-class radicals. Place saw politics as a siege of the aristocracy by 'the People'.[3] So the political community must include not

[1] C. Knight, *The Old Printer and the Modern Press*, 1854, p. 307.

[2] J. D. Morell, *The Progress of Society in England, as affected by the Advancement of National Education*, 1859, p. 10.

[3] See G. Wallas, *Life of Francis Place*, 1951 edn., p. 192: 'By the word "people", when as in this letter I use the word in a political sense, I mean those among them who take part in public affairs, by whom the rest *must* be governed'.

Compare Bowring's assessment of James Mill. 'His object was to crush aristocratical influence, whether Whig or Tory, and he saw little distinction between the tactics of either party. Both were equally moved by a passion for place and power, both seemed to claim an hereditary right to govern, and both concurred in the policy of excluding the middle classes and the people from any influence in the legislature, excepting so far as that influence could be made to serve their own purposes . . . the great interests of the people were opposed to the views of the aristocratical sections.' *Autobiographical Recollections of Sir John Bowring*, 1877, p. 69.

The Revd. Miall, editor of the *Nonconformist*, was making the same point when he reported that the Anti-Corn Law agitation 'had now been going on for three years; they had had their meetings, their conferences, their bazaars, and what

merely property but 'the People', and the People were those who were politically active. Those who were *de facto* members of that political community because they read newspapers, belonged to pressure groups, signed petitions, supported the National Political Union, and attended public meetings, should become members by right. They should be given the vote. The franchise should catch up with the effective structure of politics.

As a political philosophy it emphasized that only the People could represent the common interest, and could be trusted to break down sinister influences and monopolies. Like that of the working-class radicals, it was a statement of the greatest happiness of the greatest number, but it was an élitist version of it. Unlike Hetherington, Place did not believe that the greatest number knew where the greatest happiness lay. This sort of knowledge was possessed by the middle classes and the middle-class radicals in particular, whose task, right, and duty it was to educate the working classes into suitable notions. They must do this for two reasons. If the concept of the People was to have any meaning, then Hetherington's sense of class must be smothered, and be replaced by economic and political ideas common to both middle- and working-class radicals. The mechanism for this was inevitably adult education. And if the Whigs were to lose their fears of an extended political community, then education must be seen to bring with it social peace, the end of strikes and rick-burning, the growth of artisan skills, and industrial prosperity.

For working-class radicals, such as Hetherington, politics was a simple affair. The greatest happiness was known by, and accessible to, the greatest number. The consequence of this was not that the politically active must become politically recognized, as it was for Place, but that political notions and political radicalism must be pushed further down the social structure into the lowest levels of the working class. All

effect had they produced upon the aristocracy! Before they did that they must have a broader base to rest upon. They required some stronger lever to move the aristocracy than any they had yet worked, and they could only find that lever by extending the suffrage. .... Neither the middle nor the working classes were sufficiently powerful to carry their point, but by uniting they would break the yoke beneath which they now groaned.' *NS*, 19 Feb. 1842.

who were citizens, who lived under the laws, should be members of the political community. Instead of education turning the politically active into the politically respectable and reliable, as Place hoped, education in Hetherington's eyes would simultaneously make men both politically active and give them political power. On tory theory the political community was limited; for Place it should be enlarged; for Hetherington it was total. The conservatives still spoke the language of orders and interests—when Grey praised the middle classes he was still attributing to them the functions and virtues of an order. Place spoke the language of aristocracy and People, and within the People there could be no division of class. Hetherington spoke the language of class.

Before 1830 the main line of debate had been between whig theories of interest, and more general radical theories which in common drew on Paine, Bentham, and Cobbett. From 1831 a stricter working-class theory, the 'new ideology',[1] gained ground, though it never displaced more generalized radicalism, as the careers of Lowery, Vincent, and even Lovett show. The strength of this new ideology, as it was argued in the columns of the *Poor Man's Guardian*, lay in its definition of the working class as an excluded class. Working men formed a class *because* they were simultaneously excluded both from political and economic power. The gulfs created the class; the class did not create the gulfs. Education was for working men, as it was for all classes, a political tool—not now to maintain a stratified society, not now to maintain even a stable society, but to shape a sense of class consciousness and class power which would allow working men to force open the political community. 'The "pressure from without" ', wrote the *Chartist*, in 1839, 'will carry any question. All power is in the people.'[2]

Education was a political battle; and it was fought out in a dozen and one sectors of the educational world. The arguments for and against the taxes on knowledge were carried over from one sphere of popular education to the next, from

---

[1] For a discussion of the new ideology, see below, Chapter VII.
[2] *Chartist*, 16 Feb. 1839; see also *Notes to the People*, June 1851; G. Edmonds, *An Appeal . . .*, 1836, p. 9.

mechanics institutes to national schools, from cheap newspapers to the hours the British Museum stayed open, from
the availability of factory schools to the desirability of
public libraries. When Roebuck, in a speech on popular
education, insisted that national schools would abolish
rick-burning, sturdy paupers, and all the other ills of
ignorance,[1] he was deploying arguments that could have
come right out of a debate on the Unstamped press. When
the managers of public and working-class libraries refused
to put popular fiction on their shelves, they were deploring
what Place and Charles Knight had long known, namely that
the attractive and the useful seldom coincided in cheap
literature. If the artisan had access to cheap fiction, it was
feared he would 'dissipate' his intellectual resources.[2]
Mechanics Institutes offered an even sharper version of the
debate. The tory clergy on the one side denounced them
as schools of infidelity: 'When we give a working man more
education than what is necessary to read his Bible, we do him
an injury.'[3] Brougham and the masters, on the other,
hoped that the Institutes would teach practical science and
used them to teach political economy. R. J. Richardson
pointed out the class basis of this in his series of articles on
the Handloom Weavers Report of 1840 for the *Northern
Star*. Two groups were always in favour of machinery,
he wrote—the manufacturers and the march-of-intellect
men. The one employed the other by encouraging
'Mechanics Institutes, Arts and Sciences, the works of the
Society for the Diffusion of Useful Knowledge, lecturers
upon Political Economy and Free Trade; by such means
they not only keep up a system devoted to the aggrandise-
ment of wealth, but they pervert the minds of the rising
generation.'[4] When every sector of education was a three-
sided battle between tories, middle-class educationalists,

---

[1] *Hansard*, 3rd ser., xx, col. 143 (30 July 1833). Jevrons as late as 1881 argued
that the cost of public libraries was met by the resulting reduction of poor rates
and government expenditure on crime. Free libraries were 'an engine for operating
upon the poorer portions of the population', quoted R. Altick, *The English Common
Reader*, 1957, p. 230.
[2] E. Baines, *Life of E. Baines*, 2nd edn., 1859, pp. 105–6.
[3] Quoted in M. Tylecote, *The Mechanics Institutes . . .* , 1956, p. 64.
[4] *NS*, 21 Nov. 1840.

and working-class radicals, when Place could assert in good
faith to a Select Committee on Drunkenness that had the
stamp duties on newspapers been removed three years before,
'I have not the smallest doubt there would not have been
a single trades' union either in England or Scotland', then
with good reason did Hetherington, O'Brien, Lovett, and
Ernest Jones insist that *a People's Education is safe only
in a People's own hands . . .* '[1]

The campaign for an Unstamped press was one more
educational struggle with consequences for the political
structure. As a result the methods, hopes, and fears of the
two groups of radicals were sharply distinct.[2] Place disliked and disavowed the unnecessary extravagance of the
Unstamped, Hetherington was properly suspicious of
Place's motives. The middle-class radicals' campaign method
was to introduce motions in Parliament, backed by a
'pressure from without' which they had created by means of
petitions, public meetings, and deputations. They hoped to
persuade Ministers that repealing the stamp duties would
usher in good government, high revenue, free trade, and
social peace. Working-class radicals, however, decided that
the Government was not open to persuasion; that it would
never voluntarily abandon a stamp duty that allowed them
to keep working men ignorant, uncritical, and apathetic.
The law, Hetherington told his faithful National Union
of the Working Classes, would be altered only if it failed,
if it were repeatedly flouted, if prisons were swamped by
defiant and persistent vendors of the Unstamped, if police
were overworked, and if the magistrates eventually refused
to commit. The middle-class radicals tried to change the law,
the working-class radicals to smash it.

The conservatives found both methods of pressure and
both sets of educational ends distasteful. The press, they
argued, already enjoyed as much liberty as was safe and
useful; to remove the stamp duties would flood the country
with seditious papers pandering 'to the basest passions of
the mob'.[3] The country would be reduced to anarchy. But if

[1] *S. C. on Intoxication, 1834*, viii, qu. 2054; *People's Paper*, 3 July 1852.

[2] For the effect this campaign had on middle- and working-class relations, see
below, pp. 300–5.   [3] *Brighton Gazette*, 11 Oct. 1832.

such papers were suppressed, the working people would remain peaceable, contented, and deferential. The middle-class radicals hoped that cheap newspapers would imbue the working classes with truer notions of orderliness, sobriety, and political economy. The working-class radicals expected that cheap working-class newspapers would teach the working man the dignity of his class and the right he had both to the vote and to the products of his own labour. The tories upheld the sanctity of property; the middle-class radicals sought to instill a respect for property as being in the general interest; the working-class radicals argued that such property had been acquired by force or fraud. The tories pointed out that working men would obey the laws from habitual deference; the middle-class radicals hoped that newspapers would teach working men what the laws were and why they should be obeyed; the working-class radicals proclaimed that the laws were bad and must be overturned. The tories wished to maintain the stamp duties because they represented a property to the newspaper proprietors; the middle-class radicals wanted the repeal of the duties to break the monopoly of the existing proprietors and to purify the stamped press by widening its readership; the working-class radicals were interested only in establishing a press of their own.

The radicals believed, where the tories did not, that a free press would ensure social peace, but the middle-class radicals thought that this was because reading inhibited rioting, the working-class radicals because a free press would so transform government that a bloody revolution would no longer be necessary. The tories feared and the radicals hoped that a free press would undermine the aristocratic grip on government. The middle-class men were sure that a cheap press was essential if middle-class ideas were to gain currency among working men. The working-class radicals knew that a cheap press was essential if the working class was to be organized and unified. The tories wished to suppress new doctrine and intellectual notions within the working classes; the middle-class radicals hoped to eradicate 'dangerous' doctrines by opening the market to their own; the working-class radicals wanted to disseminate such doctrines as central to an authentic working-class self-image.

(a) THE MIDDLE-CLASS ARGUMENT[1]

Taxes on newspapers were taxes on knowledge, a sin against principle, for they taxed the free communication of ideas.[2] Such a tax was not only morally wrong, but also highly expensive. Local newspapers, middle-class radicals pointed out, had warned their readers time and again during the winter of 1830 that rick-burning was a capital offence; but barely a quarter of the prisoners taken in Berkshire could read. Had the Dorchester labourers known that oath-taking was illegal, they would never have been transported. Working men who wanted to read newspapers had to go to the public house; were newspapers untaxed, Mechanics Institutes could afford to take them, and working men would be saved from drink. The social cost of ignorance could be calculated quite precisely from the size of prisons, the level of poor rates, the frequency of death sentences, the number of public houses, and the length of strikes.[3]

If the diffusion of knowledge was society's best insurance policy, then newspapers were the most efficient means of informal education. Adults were not going to be disciplined into knowledge like children at school benches. They had to want information, and this sort of information was best found in newspapers, where 'every account of a trial, every examination at Bow Street, every dogma of my lord mayor, had for them not only an interest and an amusement, but

---

[1] No attempt is made to attribute these arguments to particular groups within the middle-class radicals, nor to weigh their occurrence; for by the beginning of 1831 the two great meetings at the City Literary and Scientific Institution, Place's pamphlet and the writings of the *Reviews* (see below, pp. 64–6) had established a common body of argument on which most of the radicals drew most of the time. The appeal to public opinion, however, became more prominent after 1834. This is not to say that the motives of the radicals in supporting the campaign did not differ.

[2] *Examiner*, 20 Mar. 1836; see also NPU resolution of 11 Jan. 1832.

[3] *Hansard*, 3rd ser., xiii, col. 621 (Bulwer, 15 June 1832); 'Taxes on Knowledge', *Westminster Review*, July 1831, p. 245; H. Brougham, 'The Newspaper Tax', *Edinburgh Review*, Apr. 1835, pp. 181–5; *Hansard*, 3rd ser., xxiii, col. 1209 (Roebuck, 22 May 1834); *S.C. on Newspapers*, 1851, xvii, qus. 1034 f. (evidence of Mr. Thomas Hogg).

also a warning and a moral'.[1] The Revd. Thomas Spencer told the Select Committee on Newspaper Stamps in 1851:

If I were a great educator of the people, my first step would be, not in schools, but in the newspaper press; I have not so much opinion of the education of children as some people have; as long as the atmosphere they breathe is so impure, and the fireside where they must spend part of their time is so prejudicial, they will have their characters formed at home, and not at school; but the newspapers will educate the adult population, the young men and the fathers, and if they are right, their children are sure to be right; this, it appears to me, is the shortest way to get at them. . . .[2]

Only the newspapers could teach the poor what the laws were, why they were to be respected, and what would happen if they were broken. As it was, the Government passed nearly 300 Acts a year, and those who were most likely to infringe them were those who were least informed about them. The Government kept the working man blindfolded and then punished him for stumbling.[3]

The working classes were determined to read, and they were determined to discuss politics. Unable to afford the stamped press, which was half a week's wage to many of them, they patronized an unstamped contraband press, selling for a penny or so. The authors of such illegal papers 'could scarcely be well-affected to the law, for they broke the law; they could scarcely be reasonable advisers, for they saw before them the penalty and the prison, and wrote under the angry sense of injustice; they could scarcely be safe teachers, for they were excited by their own passions, and it was to the passions of a half-educated and distressed population that they appealed'.[4] The middle-class radicals admitted that the tories had reason to complain of the rabid sentiments of such a press, but this was because the stamp

---

[1] *Hansard*, 3rd ser., xiii, col. 622 (Bulwer, 15 June 1832); see also W. Hickson, 'Taxes on Knowledge', *London Review*, Jan. 1836, p. 351; *Chadwick MSS.*, Hickson to Chadwick, 14 Aug. 1836; *Examiner*, 23 Jan. 1831.

[2] *S.C. on Newspaper Stamps*, 1851, xvii, qu. 2365.

[3] *Hansard*, 3rd ser., xxx, col. 838 (Bulwer, 21 Aug. 1835); op. cit. xxvii, col. 86 (Brougham, 23 Mar. 1835); Add. MSS. 35149, f. 22, Place to Hume, 12 Jan. 1831.

[4] *Hansard*, 3rd ser., xxiii, col. 1196 (Bulwer, 22 May 1834); see also *Brougham's Evidence before the Select Committee on Libel*, 5 June 1834, p. 3; *British and Foreign Quarterly Review*, July 1835.

duty deterred the honest but not the demogogue from publishing. Were there free trade, then the good could compete with the bad, and the wholesome would drive out the blasphemous. Arnold of Rugby, Dr. Whately of Oxford, the Mills and Grote were all willing to write for the poor, but they would not break the law. 'You have given up the field to those who have sown it with noxious weeds, and prevented the good husbandman from labouring in it.'[1]

If the Government removed the duties, the smugglers would be destroyed. If the Government removed the duties, the radicals could send out cheap, wholesome newspapers, which would educate the labouring men into suitable doctrines of political economy, which would show them that machinery was not their enemy nor trades unions their friends. As it was, safe knowledge was banned, dangerous knowledge was circulated. James Mill summarized these fears when he wrote to Brougham deploring

the illicit cheap publications, in which the doctrines of the right of the labouring people, who say they are the only producers, to all that is produced, is very generally preached. The alarming nature of this you will understand when I inform you that these publications are superseding the Sunday newspapers, and every other channel through which the people might get better information. I am sure it is not good policy to give the power of teaching the people exclusively to persons violating the law, and of such desperate circumstances and character that neither the legal nor the moral sanction has sufficient hold upon them. The only effectual remedy is to remove the tax which gives them this deplorable power.[2]

The tories were more sceptical of the cleansing power of a free trade in knowledge. Steady men would read steady papers, the radical would read the Unstamped; good and bad ideas need never confront each other. Indeed, if the duties were repealed, the whole country would be deluged

---

[1] *Hansard*, 3rd ser., xxx, col. 840 (Bulwer, 21 Aug. 1835); see also 'The Penny Press', *New Monthly Magazine*, xl (1834); C. Westmacott, *Serious Considerations on the Proposed Alteration of the Stamp Duties*, 1836, p. 15 (for the tory view); Add. MSS. 35149, f. 75, Place to Hume, 3 June 31; 35150, f. 114, Place to Grote, n.d. (Mar. 1836); *S.C. on Drunkenness*, 1834, qus. 2056-8.

[2] *Brougham Coll.*, f. 10, 765, Mill to Brougham, 3 Sept. 1832; see also Add. MSS. 35149, f. 122, Place to Mill, 26 Oct. 1831; *Hansard*, 3rd ser., xxiii, col. 1196 (Bulwer, 22 May 1834), xiii, col. 627 (Bulwer, 15 June 1832); P. Gaskell, *The Manufacturing Population*, 1833, pp. 280-1.

with trash which was now kept underground. Bulwer and Place replied that trash had always existed and that the demand for it had always been met; anyone who wanted to read trash was already doing so, and there was no reason to think that the market for it would suddenly increase.[1]

But such publications sowed the seeds of disloyalty, atheism, and rebellion, the tories retorted. Freedom of the press must not be confused with its abuse.

The sublime—the almost sacred cry of 'The Liberty of the Press', is not to be idly raised by every foolish writer, or screamed by every traitorous wretch with the halter round his neck; not to be pleaded in mitigation of damages, by the malicious slanderer or by the reckless libeller; not to be held up as a shield by the political firebrand, or the writer of sedition! . . . Let them . . . distinguish liberty and licentiousness, boldness and recklessness, public principle and mercenary mobserving.

O'Connell retorted that the only definition of licentiousness was the uttering of opinions with which another man disagreed.[2]

Hickson and Mill went further. Even if every fear of the tories were to be realized, and inflammatory journals deluged the unsuspecting peasantry, there was no reason to think this would lead to riot and rick-burning. The more violent the battle of words, Mill wrote, the more faithfully did the press act as a 'safety-valve' for popular protest. Readers were not rioters. The Government would come to no harm merely from being abused. Why should 4*d*. be thought to mark the line of truth and safety? If the Government wanted to purify the press, it should suppress every journal that traded in libel and falsehood, not just the cheap ones, 'merely because their opinions may be extravagant or their language not sufficiently refined'.[3] Indeed, many of the

[1] 'The Penny Press', *New Monthly Magazine*, op. cit.; *Observations on the Duty on Paper*, 1836; *Hansard*, 3rd ser., xxiii, col. 1197 (Bulwer, 22 May 1834); Add. MSS. 35150, f. 114, Place to Grote, n.d. (Mar. 1836).

[2] A. Andrews, *The History of British Journalism*, 1859, vol. ii, p. 193; see also *Hansard*, 3rd ser., iv, col. 421 (Trevor, 28 June 1831); op. cit., col. 423 (O'Connell).

[3] Theta (J. S. Mill), 'Notes on Newspapers', *Monthly Repository*, Apr. 1834, p. 105; Hickson, op. cit., pp. 346–7; see also *Pamphlets for the People*, no. 12, p. 12 (H.S.C., 'Mr. Bulwer's Sham Motion'); E. Bulwer, *England and the English*, 1833, p. 249; Roebuck to the NUWC, n.d. (Apr. 1835) in cutting from the *WPG*, *Place Coll.* Set 70, f. 205.

Unstamped were better conducted and more respectable than their stamped counterparts.

All these middle-class and tory arguments were drawn from a wider debate on popular education. The second line of radical attack was on the nature of the law itself. It was a bad law, difficult to enforce, and in the long run defeating its own ends. The tories were demanding that the honest trader, he who paid the stamp duty, should be protected. The middle-class radicals answered that the law made this impossible. Just as the spirit duty had to be reduced because the smugglers beat the Government and undersold the fair trader, so the stamp duty would have to be repealed because the Government could not suppress cheap knowledge. Every prosecution brought publicity, every howl by the tories increased sales. By 1836 the Chancellor of the Exchequer himself had to admit defeat: 'There had been prosecutions for printing, prosecutions for publishing, prosecutions for selling in the shop, and prosecutions for selling in the street, but all these efforts had failed.' Instead there had been widespread sympathy for the victims and handsome subscriptions to pay their fines. To try to maintain such a law was to bring all law into disrepute.[1]

It was a bad law because it did not work. It was also a bad law, the radicals complained, because it was arbitrary. The same offence could be punished with anything from one week to three months' imprisonment to a fine of £20. Some papers were prosecuted, others allowed to circulate. The *Penny Magazine* was patronized, the *Poor Man's Guardian* proscribed, and all at the whim of the Commissioners of Stamps.[2]

The third set of radical arguments for repealing the stamp duties drew on fiscal policy. The tories asserted that all taxes were in some way or other objectionable, a tax on

[1] H. Brougham, 'Taxes on Knowledge', *Edinburgh Review*, Oct. 1835, p. 131; *Pamphlets for the People*, No. 8, p. 6 (F. Place, 'The Taxes on Knowledge'); J. Crawfurd, *A Financial and Historical Review*, 1836, p. 35; *Hansard*, 3rd ser., xxxiv, col. 629 (Chancellor, 20 June 1836).

[2] Place to Melbourne, Hume to Melbourne, reported *WPG*, 20 Feb. 1836; Add. MSS. 35148, ff. 38–9, Place to Hume, n.d. (Jan. 1830). For a fuller treatment of the law's ambiguity, see below, pp. 156–8 f.

soap could be called a tax on cleanliness, a tax on windows a tax on light. But revenue had to be raised somehow, it was better to tax newspapers than to tax food, and at present the revenue was being defrauded. The radicals replied that the revenue would suffer very little if this tax were repealed, for it raised less than half a million pounds, and the cost of ignorance was bayonets, special commissions, and hangmen. Further, the expense of collecting the duty, and prosecuting those who evaded it, was greater than the sum collected. But if the duty were repealed, circulation figures would shoot up, from their present ratio of one newspaper for every thirty-six people, to a figure comparable with that of America, where there was one paper to every four people. Many new papers would be launched; and the amount collected from the paper duty would increase twentyfold. The price charged by the stamped papers for advertisements would have to fall if there were to be more journals, the number of advertisements would then increase, and so would the Government's revenue from that source. Finally, if the Government were to allow the Post Office to handle this enormously increased circulation by charging a penny postage stamp, the revenue on that alone might be double the revenue the Government at present received from the newspaper stamp. Every argument seemed to suggest that the Government would actually profit by repealing the stamp duty on newspapers.[1]

While the stamp remained, it perpetuated two monopolies,

[1] *Hansard*, 3rd ser., xxii, col. 1287 (Winchilsea, 24 Apr. 1834); 'Taxes on Necessities *versus* Taxes on Knowledge', *New Monthly Magazine*, vol. xliv, 1835; *Hansard*, 3rd ser., xxxiv, col. 613 (Knightly, 20 June 1836), col. 617 (Barclay), col. 636 (Goulburn)—for the tory view.

O'Connell to Melbourne, *WPG*, 20 Feb. 1836; *Hansard*, 3rd ser., xiii, cols. 631–2 (Bulwer, 15 June 1832); *Brougham's Evidence*, 1834, p. 6; *Hansard*, 3rd ser., xxiii, col. 1202 (Bulwer, 22 May 34), xxx, col. 841 (Bulwer, 21 Aug. 1835).

The radicals were in a difficult position about the paper duties; theoretically, the duties were highly objectionable for by inflating the cost of newspapers and books, they impeded popular knowledge. However, if they were totally repealed, a reduced newspaper stamp duty would not produce enough revenue to be attractive to the Government. See J. Crawfurd, op. cit.; and see below, p. 89. As for the postal duties, the radicals tried to have it both ways. They claimed that a penny newspaper stamp was not a fair alternative to a penny postage, because newspapers in bulk were sent by coach; however, they also argued that a penny postage on newspapers would protect the revenue from loss. The Chancellor pointed out this inconsistency, *Hansard*, 3rd ser., xxx, col. 847 (21 Aug. 1835).

one among the stamped press and one among the Unstamped; for the stamp with other costs meant that a daily newspaper required a capital of £40,000, and this gave the existing newspaper proprietors a virtual monopoly. No new newspaper could break into the market at that price. So naturally proprietors were willing to pay a stamp duty when it secured them their market. As a result, the proprietors had only to advocate the interests of a narrow class, their readers. If the stamp were abolished sales would rise and the partial sinister interests of the press would be purified.[1]

Social peace, popular education, good law, increased revenue, and freer trade, the middle-class radicals had argued, would all follow from the repeal of the stamp duties. The final argument was that public opinion demanded it. The tories might doubt the strength of public opinion on this subject, but that was because the London newspapers were interested parties, and deliberately smothered the campaign. Nearly 2,000 people had attended two meetings in the early summer of 1835, one in Southwark and one at the Mechanics Institute, but neither meeting had been reported by the stamped press. Ministers and members of Parliament who took their information from the stamped press were grossly misled. Yet petitions for the repeal of the stamp duty had been signed by more people than those on any subject except the transportation of the Dorchester labourers and the Municipal Corporations Bill.[2] Roebuck gave Melbourne a case from his own city of Bath. A man was charged with selling the Unstamped and was fined by the magistrates; he was taken away by the people to some open ground, exhibited as a victim, speeches were made, his fine collected, and he was set free. Perronet Thompson assured the Prime Minister that no future borough candidates would be elected unless they were pledged to repealing the stamp duty. If the Whigs ignored such pressure from without, they could have no further claim on popular goodwill.[3]

[1] *Hansard*, 3rd ser., xxiii, col. 1195 (Bulwer, 22 May 1834); xiii, col. 639 (Warburton); *Pamphlets for the People*, no. 12, p. 12 (op. cit.); no. 8, p. 2.
[2] *Edinburgh Review*, Oct. 1835, op. cit., p. 127; *Public Ledger*, 20 July 1835; Add. MSS. 35149, f. 227, Hume to Place, 28 July 1835; Hickson, op. cit., p. 340.
[3] Roebuck, etc., in *WPG*, 20 Feb. 1836; Hickson, op. cit., p. 348.

(b) THE WORKING-CLASS ARGUMENT

Man was a rational being, working-class radicals asserted, and each man had an inalienable right to knowledge. It was knowledge that set man above beast. To strive against knowledge was to strive against God, to deny a free press was to wage war against God's providence. No man should dare to set limits to other men's intellects; no class had the right to say that it alone might enjoy knowledge and the power that knowledge brought.[1]

The aristocracy, working-class men claimed, knew that they had to keep the people ignorant if they were to be excluded from politics. 'Ignorance is calculated', wrote Carpenter, the first of the journalists to be imprisoned for publishing an unstamped paper in 1830, '. . . to give stability to corrupt and unjust governments.' What the aristocracy feared was not popular passion but popular reason, not too little sense among the working classes but too much.

> Whereas we royal and aristocratical banditti of robbers and murderers disrelish the *cheap* publications which have recently appeared and been extensively circulated, because they speak the truth and show us up to the Public in our true colours; And whereas these unvarnished publications uttering such unpalateable truths, as a matter of course, tend to bring our swindling government and humbugging Constitution into hatred and contempt; Be it enacted that all honest men who shall dare to expose royal, aristocratical or parliamentary scoundrelism, shall be taxed, fined and imprisoned.[2]

Thoughts and thrones, the aristocracy well knew, could not coexist: the education of the poor was limited, in the interests of the rich.

The tories would deny the people education as far as possible; the middle classes would offer working men and their children an education which, in Cobbett's words, would 'fashion the minds of the people to passive obedience

---

[1] *Voice of the People*, 27 Aug. 1831; Lovett and Proctor, Rotunda, 21 Feb. 1831; T. McConnell in *WMF*, 12 Jan. 1832; T. Parkin, *The Battle of the Fowls of Heaven, against the Rulers of Darkness* (1831); Edward Greenhow, *Kendal Mercury*, 30 May 1835.

[2] *Carpenter's London Journal*, 13 Feb. 1836; *Republican*, 28 May 1831; see also *Gorgon*, 11 Oct. 1820; *PMG*, 3 Nov. 1832; *Medusa*, 1 Jan. 1820.

and submission, be their wrongs or their sufferings what they may'. Schools, Cobbett thundered, were seminaries of slavery; school teachers were government spies; the tracts of the Society for the Diffusion of Useful Knowledge were gingerbread dolls to stop the poor from asking awkward questions.[1] O'Brien, the editor of Hetherington's *Poor Man's Guardian*, and Ernest Jones, the Chartist leader of the early 1850s, again and again denounced an educational system that was controlled by middle-class radicals, infected by middle-class notions, and inspired by middle-class interests. As long as the tuition of the young was entrusted to a class, Ernest Jones wrote, 'we shall have class tuition distorting and warping the young mind'. One of the great needs of Chartism, he felt, was local radical schools, for without them the children of the poor were forced into the schools of the rich, where they were suitably indoctrinated.[2] O'Brien, too, pointed out that whatever was taught by the middle classes would be in the interest of the capitalist, the trader, and the middleman.

Some simpletons talk of knowledge as rendering the working classes more obedient, more dutiful—better servants, better subjects, and so on, which means making them more subservient slaves, and more conducive to the wealth and gratification of idlers of all description. But such knowledge is trash; the only knowledge which is of any service to the working people is that which makes them more dissatisfied, and makes them worse slaves. This is the knowledge we shall give them. . .[3]

Enlightened Whigs had tossed them the *Penny Magazine* and pretended to diffuse useful knowledge by pirated descriptions of tea-growing in China, of the origin of Somerset House, and of the entrance into Fingal's Cave—'dear me, how instructive!—or by telling us how many humps there are on the back of a dromedary: how many transmigrations

[1] *Pol. Reg.*, 9 May 1835, col. 367; see also *Pol. Reg.*, 29 May 1830.
[2] *People's Paper*, 3 July 1852; *Notes for the People*, June 1851.
[3] *Destructive*, 7 June 1834; see also *Mechanics Magazine*, 11 Oct. 1823. One of Harney's many complaints against the LWMA, and one of the *Northern Star*'s many complaints against Lovett's New Move in 1841, was that to encourage working men to seek education rather than the Charter was to preach 'up the doctrine of passive obedience and non-resistance . . .' on the model of Mechanics Institutes. *NS*, 24 Mar. 1838, 24 Apr. 1841.

a caterpillar undergoes from a chrysalis to a butterfly: and how a kangaroo jumps!' This was useless tory frippery, as patronizing as it was hypocritical. The knowledge the people wanted was not to be found in school, nor in school books, and certainly not in the *Penny Magazine*. What the people wanted to know, O'Brien insisted, was their rights as members of society, and the wrongs committed on them by a class government and a corrupt legislature. Dromedaries and kangaroos were all very well, but it was far more important to know why a man who worked all day, and whose father and grandfather did the same, should be poorer than another man who never worked at all, nor his father nor his grandfather before him; why the working man should be denied the vote and a say in the laws, while the idle and the mischievous had the vote; why the most useful classes of society were always the most degraded, and the most useless the most honoured; why the wealth of society should be produced entirely by one class, and why another class, who produced nothing but crime and misery, should possess and enjoy it all; why those who created crime were alone allowed to legislate on crime, and why the religion of the country should be in the hands of those whose acts showed that they believed in no religion at all. 'Now this is the sort of knowledge the people require most.' Charles Knight had explained on behalf of the Society for the Diffusion of Useful Knowledge that the aim of this general diffusion of knowledge was not to disturb men's peace of mind nor to make them discontented with their lot. This was exactly what Hetherington and O'Brien hoped their dangerous doctrines would achieve.[1]

Briton's Rights, or the Unstamped Newspapers

By J. MORGAN[2]

> . . . In every Neighbourhood,
> Where every class resort Sir,
> In every Lane, and Street,
> And almost every Court Sir,

---

[1] *PMG*, 6 Oct. 1832; *Twopenny Dispatch*, 26 Mar. 1836; *PMG*, 30 June 1832.
[2] See *Place Coll.*, Set 70, f. 493.

The Papers you may get,
Without any dread or fear Sir,
And all for Just the Price,
Of a single Pint of Beer sir,

Chorus: Then Britons stand your ground,
We value not their Capers
In Country, and Town
We will sell the Unstamped Papers.

I suppose those great big fools
When young was sent to College
To Learn which way to keep
The Poor from having knowledge,
But the time approaches fast,
When men will be discerning,
And they will wiser grow,
If they will insist on Learning. . . .   [*sic*]

Chorus.

Working men did not want the repeal of the newspaper stamps merely to read the capitalist press at cut rates. Why should they pay even 3*d*. for a bundle of lies? Working men needed a cheap free press of their own, concerned with *their* interests, catering to *their* tastes, guarding *their* rights, demanding *their* entrance to the political community. Up till now the whole of the press had been in the hands of the monied and trading classes to whom the wants, the wishes, and the sufferings of the working man were unknown and unheeded. 'His dress, his person, his hard hands, his unwashed condition, all the consequences of his useful toil, were subjects for unceasing jibes.'[1]

But a free press would hold up a mirror to the working man in which he would see himself as the most useful and most important member of society, raising him in his own estimation

and in the estimate of all rational and intelligent citizens, by proving that usefulness and utility are the only badges which ought to entitle a fellow creature to respect . . . that the scavenger, the chimney sweep, the washerwoman and the spunkmaker, if their behaviour be consistent, are infinitely more worthy of the thanks and respect of society than

[1] *PMG*, 15 Aug. 1835; see also *PMG*, 12 Jan. 1833; *Man*, 18 Aug. 1833; *Trades Newspaper*, 17 July 1825, 11 Dec. 1826; *Official Gazette*, 7 June 1834.

my lord who has nothing to recommend him but the thousands of acres which his birth entitles him to . . .[1]

Knowledge would show working men their true dignity. 'Until we learn to esteem ourselves, we shall never have our rights respected (hear); and to give men a true knowledge of their importance, the unstamped press was of the greatest value (cheers).' Such knowledge would free working men from that servility and deference to empty lords and strutting lordlings which was their besetting sin.[2]

Knowledge was dignity. Knowledge was power. Knowledge would teach working men the political rights that they were being denied, and show them how to attain them. O'Brien reported that Lovett's New Move in 1840 required a cheap periodical to link up its supporters across the country; it could then arouse the masses from apathy and teach them their rights. A free press was 'the portal' through which working men could pass into political society.[3] Knowledge would bring union to working-class movements. The prospectus to the *Voice of the People* stated, 'We shall endeavour to collect their [the working classes'] scattered energies into a common focus, to give them importance and consequence, by acquainting them with their strength.' Knowledge would teach the working classes solidarity, and would show them that they had common interests and common grievances against a common oppressing class. Without knowledge there could be no union, O'Brien told readers of the *Guardian*, without union there could be no strength, and without strength no radical reform. 'Would that the oppressed knew this as well as the oppressors.' The knowledge we want, wrote Benbow, the backstreet book-seller promoting a grand national holiday, was knowledge of ourselves; 'a knowledge of our own power, of our immense might, and of the right we have to employ *in action* that immense power'.[4]

Without this sort of knowledge, without a free press,

---

[1] *Herald to Trades Advocate*, 16 Oct. 1830.
[2] *PMG*, 6 July 1833 (Hetherington at the NUWC); see also *Radical Register*, 20 Feb. 1835; *Radical*, 1 May 1836.
[3] *Southern Star*, 3 May 1840; *Radical*, 3 Sept. 1831.
[4] *Prospectus, Voice of the People*, Dec. 1830; cf. Gaskell's fears, op. cit., p. 272. *PMG*, 22 Dec. 1832; W. Benbow, *The Grand National Holiday* . . ., Jan. 1832.

there could be no organized working-class movement. John Cassell, the cheap-book publisher, told the Select Committee on newspaper stamps in 1851 that any movement —he cited temperance—needed a press. Without a paper in which to record proceedings, to communicate with members, to chide, argue, and exhort, a movement, said Ernest Jones, could only be half a movement. The Press, the *Northern Star* informed its readers, was the cheapest, easiest, and most efficient way of holding a party, a movement, or a pressure group together.[1] An unstamped press would structure working-class opinion and turn it into a political force. An unstamped press would push political notions and an appropriate working-class knowledge down into the a-political masses and out into the non-political rural areas. As a result, 'the "normal schools of agitation" shall be removed from the beershop, the institute, or the field, to the domestic hearth—every family shall be a Working Man's Association—every lodging shall hold a Political Union; and their hearts shall be the register in which their resolutions shall be preserved'.[2]

The publishers of the Unstamped insisted that they would circulate this kind of knowledge at whatever cost and hazard to themselves. Their papers might or might not be classed as newspapers by the Government, and might or might not be prosecuted by the Government. The proprietors knew quite well why the *Penny Magazine*, the *Literary Gazette*, the *National Omnibus*, and the *Athenæum*, all 'useful' knowledge papers, could sell openly; as a correspondent wrote in to the *Guardian*, had Hetherington held Society for the Diffusion of Useful Knowledge attitudes and upheld the *status quo*, he could have published an unstamped paper till kingdom come; he was *really* imprisoned 'for the disseminating of principles which tend to open the eyes of the plundered and oppressed Many'.[3]

The publishers would evade the law if possible; if that was not possible, they would defy it.

[1] *S.C. on Newspaper Stamps*, 1851, xvii, qu. 1306; *People's Paper*, 8 May 1852; *NS*, 2 June 1838, 14 July 1840.   [2] *Chartist*, 2 Feb. 1839.
[3] *Radical*, 8 Oct. 1831; *PMG*, 3 Sept. 1831 (correspondent from Blackburn); see also *Cab*, 31 Mar., 7 Apr. 1832; *Church Examiner*, 15 Sept. 1832; *Ashmodeus*, 13 Oct. 1832; *Reflector*, 15 Dec. 1832.

We begin this paper in a spirit of warfare, and we are not to be scared by informations, or street arrests, or imprisonments. There is a sturdy band of us, not of beggars, but sellers of cheap news and knowledge—who will not be beggars—who will bid defiance to the hypocritical tyranny of whig malice. We will put down stamps here, as our fellow-suffering brethren are putting down tithes in Ireland; we will resist that which is called the law on the subject; . . . *resistance to oppression is the best and only argument to carry conviction with it.*[1]

Vendors of the Unstamped who were imprisoned were martyrs to the sacred name of freedom, not offenders against the law. Hetherington battled for Right against Might, Justice against mere Law.

Were this law self-imposed, the publishers of the Unstamped said they would be morally bound to obey it. But laws were made behind the people's backs, without their consent, kept secret from them, and garbed in unintelligibility. Edward Hancock, one of the leading vendors of the Unstamped, told Alderman Kelly at the Guildhall that, being unrepresented, he was not bound to obey any law. He and Hetherington, however, were prepared to start by disputing the stamp law. 'To defy one is quite enough at a time, we find.'[2] Any law that did not stem from the popular will was illegitimate. Any law that forbade the exercise of that popular will by denying it political knowledge, must be defied. The press was the 'eyes of the Sovereign people', and the people would not allow themselves to be shut up in a world of darkness.[3] If the Government persisted in taxing newspapers, if it severed itself from the popular will, then it made peaceful radical reform impossible and brought closer change of a bloodier sort. Did the Government prefer the March of Intellect, or 'such marches as the French and Belgians have lately made'?[4] That was the choice.

---

[1] *Cosmopolite*, 10 Mar. 1832; see also *Slap at the Church*, 28 Apr. 1832.

[2] Hancock, reported *PMG*, 13 Oct. 1832; Hetherington, *PMG*, 23 July 1831; see also *PMG*, 9 July, 20 Aug. 1831; *Republican*, 4 June 1831; *Bonnet Rouge*, 23 Feb. 1833.

[3] *London Dispatch*, 11 Dec. 1836; Helot to *PMG*, 19 Jan. 1833; Hetherington's speech at the Rotunda in *Political Pamphlet*, 26 Feb. 1831; *Pol. Letters*, 4 Dec. 1830; *WMF*, 12 Jan. 1832.

[4] *Penny Papers*, 2 Oct. 1830; see also *Chronicler of the Times*, 12 Jan. 1833; *New Weekly True Sun*, 16 Jan. 1836.

II

GOVERNMENT AND THE UN-STAMPED—THE PROBLEM OF PUBLIC ORDER

WHEN middle- and working-class radicals demanded an unstamped press, they were demanding that government should be accountable to organized public opinion. The Government, in its turn, could safely ignore the bluster of those radicals in Parliament who claimed to represent widespread popular feeling. What the Government could not ignore, was radical efforts on the platform and through the press to create that popular feeling, for that potentially threatened public order. Both radicals and the Government, therefore, manœuvred around the press. The radicals wanted the Government to free it, to listen to it, and thereby to open up the political community. The Government's task, on the other hand, since the 1790s, was to manage the legitimate press so that it might avoid direct collision with respectable opinion, and to eradicate the illegitimate press, in the name of public order. The line between the two came to be represented by the fourpenny stamp. J. S. Mill and William Hickson were missing the point when they argued[1] that the opinions of the stamped and the Unstamped press were often equally distasteful, equally respectable. The same attitudes, when held by the property-less as well as by the propertied, had totally different social and political implications. The function of the fourpenny stamp was not simply to suppress violently radical papers, but to suppress cheap violently radical papers; not simply to suppress dangerous ideas, but to keep those ideas from the dangerous classes. It was not the opinions themselves but those who held them that created the problem of public order.

[1] See above, p. 15.

The Government handled the established press and the pauper press, therefore, very differently. The established press was exposed to government influence, with subsidies, official advertisements, and early news as the bait. The pauper press was contained by government controls, especially taxes, libel law, and licences.

The Government's treatment of the stamped press seems to have changed in the years around 1819.[1] Both parties had by then appreciated that if a paper was to have moral influence it had to appear independent, and that if it was to be useful it had to have a wide circulation. This meant that to establish an official party paper was both costly and relatively useless. The Whigs, in 1817, failed to set up the *Guardian* to displace the *Morning Chronicle*; the tories in 1830 could not afford to purchase the *Standard* to replace the loss of the *Courier*; when the *Morning Chronicle* was bought by Easthope in 1834, the Whigs encouraged him but did not subsidize him. By 1819 also, most Treasury subsidies to proprietors or to hack journalists seem to have dried up. Instead, the placing of official advertisements and the offering of early news to friendly newspapers became the subtler version of Treasury subsidies in the 1820s. *The Times*, hostile to the tory Government since Peterloo, frequently complained that it was starved of departmental advertisements as a result, even though its circulation was the largest in the country and official advertisements were paid by public and not by party funds.[2] The second bait that Government could offer was information. Palmerston in the 1830s fed the *Morning Chronicle* with foreign news, Brougham fed *The Times* with news of the Cabinet. One of the reasons behind *The Times*'s quarrel with Brougham in 1834 was that official news was being withheld.[3] But the newspapers which were widely read attracted enough advertisements for them not to need government patronage and as they developed their own news services, so they were less dependent on government information. The newspapers the Government would have most liked to manage were those

<hr />

[1] This paragraph draws heavily on A. Aspinall, *Politics and the Press 1780–1850*, 1949.
[2] Aspinall, loc. cit., pp. 128–31.
[3] Loc. cit. pp. 253 f.

most independent of it. So the correspondence of party whips and government Ministers was littered with complaints that even friendly newspapers were unmanageable, were free in their criticisms of government policy, acid in their attacks on government Ministers.[1] The stamped press, for most Ministers, was something that had to be tolerated, not something that could be manipulated in their own interest. Radicals might denounce *The Times* as a prostitute of Government 'who always take care to keep in their pay the most of the papers which are most read by the people' [*sic*].[2] The Government regretted that this was not true.

Subsidies, advertisements, and news were the baits Government could dangle in front of newspapers; on the punitive side, Government retained parliamentary privilege and the law of libel. But here two battles had already been won by 1819. During the 1770s the Wilkes's struggle had established the right of newspapers to report parliamentary debates; and Fox's libel act of 1792 had made juries the judges of libel as well as of the event of its publication. And this meant that it was often difficult for the law officers to obtain a conviction. Daniel Eaton, Hardy, and Tooke were acquitted in the 1790s, Wooler and Hone in 1817, Cobbett in 1831. From the end of the Queen's Affair in 1822 until the resurgence of the reform movement in 1830 there were very few prosecutions for criminal libel. They were deemed 'inexpedient'.

The Government's attitude to the stamped press was therefore necessarily permissive. But towards the Unstamped press it was penal. The Six Acts of 1819 included two that affected the radical press, 60 G3 c8, which defined and controlled more precisely 'Blasphemous and Seditious Libels'; and 60 G3 c9 which specified what was to be considered a newspaper and what must therefore carry the fourpenny stamp. Its preamble declared that

Pamphlets and printed Papers containing Observations upon Public Events and Occurrences, tending to excite Hatred and Contempt of

¹ Loc. cit., pp. 370–3.
² HO 64/11, 23 Nov. 1831 (Hetherington at the Rotunda).

the Government and Constitution of these Realms as by Law established, and also vilifying our holy Religion, have lately been published in great Numbers and at very small Prices; and it is expedient that the same should be restrained. . . .

The first Act punished rash writing after the event; the second sought, quite unambiguously, to price rash writing out of the pockets of the poor. The first Act came within the joint province of the Home Secretary and the Law Officers; the second was a revenue matter, and therefore the business of the Chancellor of the Exchequer in Parliament and the Commissioners of Stamps outside Parliament. The Home Secretary was concerned with the threat to public order, the Chancellor with the threat to public revenue. The Unstamped press was squeezed between the two.

(a) THE HOME OFFICE

When the Home Office scrutinized every poorly printed penny paper in the years around 1819 and in the early 1830s for its seditious content, this was part of their more general concern with 'inflammatory' radicalism which they believed to be dangerous and knew to be infectious, whose headquarters in the early 1830s was the Rotunda and whose loudhailer was the Unstamped press. The *Bonnet Rouge* and the *Republican*, in the eyes of the Government, came out of the turbulent radical underworld of Macerone's *Instructions* for street warfare, threats to kidnap Victoria, plots to assassinate Wellington, runs on the bank, the rioting around the Rotunda in November 1830 which compelled the king to cancel his Guildhall dinner, and the gloomy prophecies of arson and insurrection made by Southey and Wakefield.

Pressure was put on the Home Office for three main reasons. The first was that with the law officers, the Home Office was ultimately responsible for checking the circulation of criminal libels; secondly, the Home Office maintained public order and social peace (and as a result was extremely sensitive about allowing the army to be exposed to 'sedition'); thirdly, the Home Office was ultimately responsible for the punishment of law-breakers, such as the vendors of the

Unstamped, for overseeing the machinery of prosecutions, arrests, and sentences, and for supervising the behaviour of police, informers, and magistrates.[1] The tories pressed the Home Secretary in Parliament on the first; rural justices of the peace, London magistrates, and the public-spirited pressed the Home Office on the second; and the parliamentary radicals, aided by the *True Sun*, questioned and cross-questioned the Home Office on the third.

The first of these responsibilities was to check the spread of criminal libel, that is any writing which tended to a breach of the peace. In the years around 1819 the Government, with and without the help of the Society for the Suppression of Vice, attempted to control the London sales of the *Republican*, *Black Dwarf*, *Deist*, and the writings of Palmer and Paine, by initiating libel trials against their London publishers, Carlile and his shopmen. From 1824, however, the remnants of working-class journalism survived for six years without further libel trials. In the summer of 1830 the political atmosphere changed. In the north, John Doherty, the Irish organizer of the cotton spinners, led the National Association in its demands for an eight-hour day; and working-class restiveness worried Lt.-Colonel Shaw, the military commander stationed in Burnley. So the Stamp Commissioners suppressed Doherty's *United Trades Co-operative Journal* in July 1830. In London, Carlile had acquired the Rotunda, off Blackfriars Bridge, at which the Radical Reform Association, Cobbett, and the Irish Anti-Union Association held their meetings. Their language grew more extravagant as the summer months passed and became openly jubilant as news of the July Revolution in France burst upon London working-class circles. From autumn onwards came reports of rick-burning and Swing's signature in the south; and in London Hetherington, a self-employed printer active in co-operative trading societies, Carpenter, a professional journalist and former editor of the *Trades Newspaper* and various co-operative magazines, and Richard Carlile, the veteran of the struggles of 1819 against

[1] For the mechanics of crime and arrest, see below, pp. 164 f. For a study of the machinery of public order in the 1840s, see F. Mather, *Public Order in the Age of the Chartists*, 1959.

the law of libel,[1] each put out illegal unstamped papers, aggressively demanding working-class rights.

The first Home Office salvo was fired in October 1830. On the 19th Phillipps, the permanent Under-Secretary at the Home Office, sent a copy of Carpenter's *Political Letters* to Maule, the Treasury solicitor, and the law officers, saying that the Home Office had received it from the magistrates, who claimed that it was widely sold, and wondering whether the Home Office should institute proceedings. 'Sir R. Peel desires at the same time that the attention of the law officers may be directed to the general state of the press at this time, which he thinks calls for very serious consideration.'[2] The law officers agreed that the press was 'very licentious', but they doubted whether this could be checked by the Government unless it had Parliament's support. Peel promptly replied that Parliament's opinions had nothing to do with it, that the Government had a clear duty to suppress treason and sedition, and 'I think it is a very serious question—whether there is not greater ultimate danger in the passiveness and apparent indifference of Government—than in an appeal to the law'. He was sure he would have public opinion behind him.[3] Meanwhile, Abinger, the Attorney General, had commenced proceedings against Carpenter, ostensibly to recover the revenue due to the Commissioners of Stamps, though Peel would apparently have preferred a libel trial. A month later Peel was still receiving reports on Carpenter: 'there is in his writings much inflammatory matter—making the lower orders of People discontented with their situation—and setting them against the Rich . . . '. The correspondent attributed the Kent fires to Carpenter's writings. Peel wrote on this anonymous report, 'I think it would be very desirable to keep a vigilant eye upon Carpenter.'[4]

The radical Unstamped had not yet been denounced in Parliament, but Peel continued to search for the dangerous language which it was his duty to prosecute. He received

---

[1] For notes on the publishers of the Unstamped, see Appendix, pp. 307–15.
[2] HO 49/7, f. 405, Phillipps to Maule, 19 Oct. 1830.
[3] HO 79/4, f. 200, Peel to Abinger, 30 Oct. 1830.
[4] HO 64/16, n.d. (Nov. 1830) (see below, p. 39).

reports of the Rotunda meetings from the very first, in which 'Heatherington' [*sic*] and others used 'strong and inflammatory language'. As a precaution, Phillipps wrote to W. B. Gurney, the official reporter to Parliament, at the beginning of November 1830, asking him to send a short-hand reporter to the Rotunda to take correct notes of the meetings 'in order that he may, if required, be enabled to swear to them'. These reports were regularly sent in, at least until March 1833.[1]

Wellington had declared himself opposed to all con-stitutional reform, and the radicals planned a massive demonstration. The king thereupon cancelled his visit to the Guildhall, and a meeting that night at the Rotunda threatened to get out of hand. All Peel's fears seemed to be well founded. A crowd of over 2,000, which Hetherington's *Penny Papers* had encouraged to carry arms, collected outside the Rotunda and planned to enter the city. William Knight, an architect's clerk, who had been at the Rotunda meeting, headed a crowd in Parliament Square, waving aloft the Unstamped. When arrested, he was found to have on him a will bequeathing his body to the barricades if he should fall in the cause of liberty. The magistrates at Union Hall panicked, a hundred special constables were posted at the office, the Lord Mayor was warned that public buildings might be attacked, and Rowan, one of the police com-missioners, and Phillipps stayed up all night exchanging frantic notes.[2] The crowd dispersed next day but not before all parties, including the London radical leaders, had been thoroughly frightened. Peel immediately sent transcribed copies of the Rotunda meeting to the law officers, asking 'whether there is anything of a seditious or illegal nature in the proceedings', and pleaded that the police magistrates were pressing him to take action. By the end of his period in the Home Office, Peel, thought Le Marchant, believed the country 'ripe for revolution'.[3]

[1] HO 61/2, report of Supt. Thomas, 20 Oct. 1830; HO 41/26, f. 44, Phillipps to Maule, 6 Nov. 1830; *PMG*, 9 Mar. 1833.
[2] HO 40/25, 8–9 Nov. 1830; HO 41/26, f. 49, 9 Nov. 1830.
[3] HO 49/7, 10 Nov. 1830; D. Le Marchant, *Memoir of John Charles, Viscount Althorp* . . . 1876, p. 255. For Peel's toughness towards the Unstamped when he briefly resumed office in 1834–5, see *Treasury Papers*, 22/27, f. 84, 13 Feb. 1835;

Melbourne replaced Peel as Home Secretary in the middle of November 1830, but official policy did not change. Place and certain of the middle-class radicals claimed later that it was the Whigs who had initiated a tough policy towards the Unstamped; but on the contrary it was Peel who first employed the shorthand writers, the spies, and libel prosecution. His policies were only just beginning to take effect when he was replaced by Melbourne, who incurred the radical odium. Both Home Secretaries pressed for action; and in both cases it was their law officers, aware of the perils of juries, who counselled discretion. There is no evidence that the law officers ever brought cases of sedition or criminal libel to the attention of the Home Secretary. Carpenter's prosecution was continued by the Whigs, although the trial had to be delayed until the following May as the *subpoena* ran in the name of George IV instead of William IV; but his writing had been cautious so he had to be tried for an infringement of the revenue laws.

Carlile's *Prompter* was less careful, and the Home Office quickly prosecuted him for his paper of 27 November 1830 in which he told the 'insurgent agricultural labourers' that 'were you proved to be incendiaries, you have more just and moral cause for it than any king or faction, that ever made war, had for making war'. In January 1831 Carlile was sentenced by Recorder Knowles to the severest penalty for criminal libel within memory—two years' imprisonment, a fine of £200, and sureties of £500 to guarantee his good behaviour for the next ten years. Melbourne had Althorp's backing; Althorp wrote to Denman, 'If we could succeed in it [the prosecution] I am sure it would be right to do it'; and he was confident that his colleagues agreed.[1]

The Tories, now in opposition, began to denounce the Unstamped in Parliament; the existence of the Unstamped showed what would come of reform; the existence of the Unstamped showed that the Whigs were failing to suppress sedition. Trevor told the House that if the Attorney General

and towards the 'vile trash' circulating in 1842, see F. Mather, 'The Government and the Chartists' in A. Briggs's ed., *Chartist Studies*, 1962 edn., p. 393.

[1] *Brougham Coll.*, f. 14, 913, Althorp to Denman, 1 Jan. 1831; it is not clear to which of the three prosecutions Althorp was referring. See also *Hansard*, 3rd ser., vii, col. 55 (Attorney General, 15 Sept. 1831); *Prompter*, 15 Jan. 1831.

was going to do nothing about Cobbett, who had also defended the rick-burners, then the House should order the Attorney General to take action on its own behalf. Althorp replied that this was a matter for the Attorney General's own discretion. Shortly afterwards the Whigs announced Cobbett's prosecution for criminal libel in his *Political Register* of 11 December 1830.[1] His trial was delayed until Carpenter's had taken place; but where Carpenter was found to have published a newspaper without making the required affidavits and without stamping it, Cobbett's jury on 7 July 1831 could not agree on whether he had published a criminal libel or not, and were consequently discharged.

This did not deter Melbourne from pressing instances of criminal libel upon the law officers for their opinion. In May 1832 he sent them James Acland's *Hull Portfolio* and Lorymer's placard for a *National Convention*, querying whether their publishers were 'liable to a criminal information—and is it expedient?' Not content with this, Melbourne also sent other libellous papers, including the *Hull Portfolio* and the *People's Charter*, to Brougham, asking his opinion as Lord Chancellor. In June the law officers were asked their views of Brook's *People's Charter*, and in July of a placard headed *Military Torture*.[2] Every copy of the *Poor Man's Guardian* was scrutinized, and helpful informers and energetic policemen underlined in red ink the passages which they thought might be construed as criminal libel. Regular reports of the National Union of the Working Classes meetings were sent to the law officers, and always two questions were asked of them—whether the proceedings were libellous and seditious, and (in view of Cobbett's acquittal) whether prosecutions would be sure to succeed.[3]

In very few cases did prosecution follow, presumably

[1] *Hansard*, 3rd ser., i, col. 1213 (16, 17 Dec. 1830); ii, col. 71–8 (23 Dec. 1830).

[2] HO 49/7, ff. 457–8, 24 May 1832; *Brougham Coll.*, f. 43,487, Melbourne to Brougham, 18 June 1832; HO 49/7, ff. 459–60, 9 June; ff. 460–1, 7 July 1832.

[3] e.g. HO 79/4, f. 218, 27 Feb. 1833. For a similarly cautious attitude by the law officers towards eighteenth-century newspapers, see G. Cranfield, *The Development of the Provincial Newspaper, 1700–1760*, Oxford, 1962, pp. 143–7; and at the time of the 1866–7 Hyde Park riots, see R. Harrison, *Before the Socialists*, 1965, p. 88.

because the law officers were more cautious than Melbourne in exposing themselves to the verdict of a jury. All parties agreed that it was more difficult to get a verdict returned for spoken sedition than for written sedition, and that in any case spoken sedition was less influential than written sedition. No meetings were ever prosecuted even when spies reported that Hetherington 'concluded by stating that nothing but force would ever gain the people's rights and the sooner they prepared themselves for resistance the better as he was certain Revolution must come in this country sooner or later'.[1] Both the Home Office and the law officers agreed to prosecute 'Palafox's' letter in the *Guardian* of 25 May 1833,which recommended that working men should bring sharp knives with which to cut their food at subsequent open air meetings.[2] But even here the original trial for criminal libel was later abandoned in favour of a prosecution for publishing unstamped newspapers. The Carpenter method was safer than the Cobbett method.

In Parliament, the Tories pronounced they were much alarmed by the undercurrent of revolutionary activity that seemed to be attaching itself to the reform movement. Denman, the Attorney General, and Althorp, the Chancellor of the Exchequer, minimized both the sales and the violence of the Unstamped, and told the House that the Unstamped were being prosecuted only because they defrauded the revenue and not because they were circulating criminal libel. Melbourne's activity as Home Secretary belied this. Although the law officers usually reported that it was 'inexpedient' to prosecute for criminal libel in London, Melbourne did all he could. To Earl Talbot he recommended 'With respect to the individual who has been selling printed papers, the obvious tendency of which must be to incite riot and disturbance', that he should be tried at the Assizes. He told Earl Harewood that 'Prosecutions should be instituted by the Magistrates' wherever possible.[3] When Wellington complained to him that agricultural labourers

---

[1] HO 40/25, 7 Dec. 1830.   [2] HO 49/7, f. 478, 7 June 1833.
[3] HO 41/8, Melbourne to Talbot, 30 Nov. 1830; HO 41/10, Melbourne to Harewood, 20 June 1831 (Talbot was Lord-Lt. of Staffordshire, Harewood of the West Riding).

around Winchester and Andover had joined political unions in the hope of receiving money when they were unemployed, and that the *Guardian* and Cobbett's *Register* were widely read, Melbourne regretted that he could do nothing while the unions respected the Corresponding Societies' Act.[1] Melbourne was far from being the idle dilettante of his portraits. His energy in chasing sedition was tempered only by the cautious and perhaps more liberal attitudes of his law officers, Denman and Sir John Campbell, and by the lack of a rural police force.

Pressure on the Home Office was at its height in 1831 and 1832. As in the years around 1819 and as in the 1840s, the same groups, justices of the peace, clergy, army officers, and loyal associations denounced the sedition that was undermining the tranquillity of the lower classes and the security of established institutions. W. Waddilove, Esq., of Hexham, sent a typical letter to the Home Office, enclosing an unstamped paper which he had found that morning circulating in the open market and which had been bought 'with great avidity—and before this reaches you, the poison will have infected our retired valleys'. Magistrates sent in copies of new seditious papers as they arrived before the courts. Vigilant citizens complained that the streets were infested with vendors of the Unstamped and shop windows placarded with 'indecent' publications.[2] From 1833 Melbourne showed more restraint and on at least two occasions refused to encourage magistrates in their witchhunting. By then the Chancellor of the Exchequer had become publicly responsible for controlling the Unstamped.

If the first concern of the Home Office was to control the circulation of criminal libel, their second task was the more general one of keeping the peace. The line between the two was blurred, but that the one was an extension of the other was transparently clear to most tories, if not to the rest of Parliament. It was the mark of a tory to believe, in 1819, in 1831, and in 1842 that he was confronted by an under-

[1] Wellington to Melbourne, 7 Nov. 1832, quoted L. Sanders, *Lord Melbourne's Papers*, 1889, pp. 149–50.

[2] HO 40/29, f. 749, n.d. (early Nov. 1831); HO 59/3, Rawlinson to Phillipps, 11 Feb. 1832. HO 59/3, the case of Daniel Jaycock, brought on the information of Downes, 18 May 1832.

ground conspiracy, the more sinister just because it was loose and ill defined, but whose outward and visible signs were treasonable pamphlets, machine-breaking, incendiarism and plug plots, and the oaths and arms of working-class unions. It was also the mark of a tory to believe that every breach of the peace was instigated from the outside, by travelling demagogues or by a travelling radical press, both trading in agitation.[1] Keeping the peace meant taking measures to preserve tranquillity and to pre-empt the libeller's ground. It means damping down the rural or urban 'disaffection' on which the libeller drew. Every prosecution for criminal libel was to that extent a confession of failure by the Home Office.

Keeping the peace in London demanded that the Home Office maintain a careful watch on the organized centres of sedition, the National Union of the Working Classes and, later, the lodges of the trade unions. Keeping the peace in the country meant, in the eyes of the justices of the peace, watching, deploring, and wherever possible, banishing radical orators, radical papers, and radical beershops.

Rural justices of the peace were landowners; and the landowner's wish for an industrious, deferential peasantry was the justice's wish for an orderly, peaceable village. The question put by a member of Parliament, Bankes, in the debates on the Six Acts in 1819, remained just as pertinent in 1832: 'He saw members who were agriculturists'; did they consider it 'desirable' that their labourers should read Paine and the *Black Dwarf*?[2] The landowner, wearing his hat as justice, did his best to eradicate such poison. He had two broad sets of powers. Before 1834 he supervised rural poor relief. He was also the rural magistrate, upholding the

---

[1] The interrelation of these attitudes is clearly shown by Pollock, the Attorney General, in 1842, when he proposed to indict O'Connor together with trade union, chartist, and mob leaders. 'I propose to charge O'Connor as a general conspirator with the others, and not to proceed against him for Libel merely, or for acting as a Delegate, or taking part at the meeting of Delegates—I propose to try him in the same indictment with the worst of the defendants who headed mobs, made seditious speeches, and stopped mills and factories. I shall blend in one accusation the head and the hands—the bludgeon and the pen, and let the jury and the public see in one case the *whole crime*, its *commencement* and its *consequences*. . . .' Pollock to Graham, 9 Oct. 1842, quoted by F. C. Mather in op. cit., pp. 391–2 (my italics). See also Abinger's charge to the Chester Special Commission, *NS.*, 15 Oct. 1842.

[2] *Hansard*, 1st ser., xli, col. 1348 (Bankes, 20 Dec. 1919).

game laws (which were strengthened in 1831), sentencing at petty sessions, licensing preachers (until 1812) and public houses, visiting county jails. Together with the resources the justice had as a landowner, as squire and employer and landlord, as patron of charities and prop of the parson, the justice of the peace possessed a web of powers, defined and ill-defined, with which to preserve his terrain from disaffection.

Sidmouth's Circular Letter of March 1817 had reminded justices that they could arrest persons selling seditious literature as a breach of the peace, though the implication that justices and not juries were the judge of sedition was too controversial for most justices. Justices could punish a hawker for selling pamphlets without a licence; they could go beyond the law and forbid shops to sell radical literature, and not be challenged; and they could revoke the licence of a public house if they chose. Wooler and Cobbett both reported that landlords had had to stop taking the *Black Dwarf* and the *Register* for fear of losing their licences.[1]

On one front, at least, the powers of the rural magistrates had been curtailed by the 1830s. Before 1830 any publican needed two licences, one from the Excise to sell drink, one from the justices to open a public house, and this the justices could grant or refuse at will. The Beer Act of 1830 abolished the need for this second licence. This meant that after 1830 there were whole pockets of working-class activity beyond the scrutiny of rural justices. As the pressure of the justices relaxed, so the demand of the landlord's customers was asserted; and the natural connection between newspapers, especially radical ones, and alehouses was cemented. The village alehouse could become the rural equivalent of London's coffee-houses and reading-rooms. What this meant for the justices and for village life was indicated by Chadwick in 1834:

In the tap of the inn, or the village public-house, the drinkers were, in some degree, under the eye of parlour company, and more sober people, and of the neighbourhood . . . But at the beershops in by-lanes

[1] *Black Dwarf*, 23 Apr., 14 May 1817, 29 Sept. 1819; *Pol. Reg.*, 16 Nov., 21 Dec. 1816. Licences were a very common method of control—they were used to control religious as well as political dissent. Methodist preachers were refused licences by J.P.s in the 1790s, and one of the 'securities' proposed for Catholic Emancipation was to license Catholic priests.

the drinkers are entirely exempted from these checks; in such places, the poacher, the smuggler, and the petty depredator, and the sturdy pauper, who frequently combines all these characteristics, may remain from morning to night free from all inspection or interference.[1]

With good reason Hetherington recommended his Penny Papers as suitable for the 'new beershops'.

Rural magistrates had objected to the publications of the years around 1819 because they were 'infidel' and because they undermined rural order. John Stratford, the Norwich murderer, suitably attributed his ruin to reading Paine and Carlile. In the early 1830s radical papers not only disturbed rural peace, but, in the eyes of the justices, they were responsible for a more heinous crime—that of encouraging the labourers to take economic revenge for their economic ills. Carpenter, Carlile, and Cobbett had obviously incited rick-burning, the smashing of agricultural machinery, and the activities of 'Swing', because their papers had predated the disturbances by only a month or so. In vain did Carlile show that all the copies of the *Prompter* were absorbed by London and the northern manufacturing towns, and that it was impossible for his writings to circulate in Kent and Suffolk. He was sentenced to two years' imprisonment. An anonymous report on Carpenter in November 1830 stated: 'I have a strong belief that all the Fires and mobs in Kent and elsewhere have been caused and planned by such men as Carpenter and others in my own mind I think there is a correspondence between certain disaffected Book-sellers and Printers in every town in the country who do all they can by the circulation of inflammatory papers and writings to create disaffection and mischief. . . .'[2] (*sic*).

The most amazing piece of evidence was the answers from the rural districts to the questions put by the Commissioners of the Poor Law in 1834,[3] when magistrates and overseers were asked to give the Commissioners information 'respect-

---

[1] *S.C. on Intoxication*, 1834, viii, qu. 395.

[2] HO 64/16 n.d. (Nov. 1830); *Quarterly Review*, Jan. 1831, 'The Moral and Political State of the British Empire' (by Southey). Spy reports from the Rotunda told Melbourne that its leaders were not connected in any way with the country riots, though they were delighted by them; but this awkward piece of information was ignored. HO 64/11, 27 Nov. n.d.

[3] *P.P. Reports of the Commissioners of Poor Laws*, 1834, xxxiv.

ing the causes and consequences of the agricultural riots and burnings of 1830 and 1831'. Most replies referred to low wages and 'contagion'; but one answer in nine from the counties that had been affected by Swing reported that 'inflammatory publications' or a 'licentious press' had been the cause. According to Hamppreston of Dorset, it was 'the active dissemination, through the press, of seditious and revolutionary principles, seconded by much distress'; from Gloucester, the Berkeley Division replied, 'None, but an opinion that the villainy of the press, Messrs. Carlile, Cobbett, Taylor etc., who are read in every Country pot-house, and the march of intellect'; Wrotham of Kent ascribed the rioting to the writings of the Carliles and Cobbetts, 'which were taken exclusively, or nearly so, at all the ale and beerhouses, where they were read and commented upon by the lower classes, who frequented these houses, and would allow no publication of a contrary tendency to be brought into the house, so that the baneful poison had its full operation . . . '. West Rainham of Norfolk complained of the 'Vicious Tracts, where the Poor Man is taught to look upon his Master as his oppressor'; and Sir Morris Ximines of the Wargrave Division in Berkshire thundered against 'the violent language of many public speakers, the seditious publications read in every beer and ale house, the facility of concealed drinking in beerhouses, the facility of selling game have undermined the former honest thoughts of the lower classes, made them dissatisfied with the situation Providence has placed them in, and brought all above them in contempt, and engendered a hope of plunder by a convulsion of the State'.

Keeping the peace in London required that the Home Office should scrutinize the National Union of the Working Classes, the centre of organized working-class radicalism and the patron of these seditious working-class papers. Home Office fears now seem widely exaggerated. The NUWC was far from being the vanguard of a London insurrection, and the handful of men who clubbed together to buy an unstamped paper at the East India Company were far from being the 'Secret Society' described by Melbourne. The NUWC was riddled with spies and plain-clothes men who reported not only on the class leaders but also on each other.[1] Hetherington and Lovett, rather than clothing their activities in secrecy, did their best to keep the union transparent, as this they knew would thwart spies and attract members. Though they delighted to flout the law by publishing unstamped papers, this was as far as their law-breaking went. There was no hint of a revolutionary conspiracy among the leaders of the NUWC. Even when Watson and Lovett announced their need of a La Fayette, and wondered whether Carlile would do, spy reporters hastened to assure Melbourne that no 'mischief' was planned.[2]

Yet much of what the NUWC members said and did could be given an ominous interpretation. As in 1839, the Government feared two things—widespread popular arming, and mass demonstrations led by men from the Rotunda; and it was hints of these, rather than 'obnoxious property doctrines', that were marked with red ink on the spies' reports. When Hetherington rashly offered a prize for the best pistol shot among members of the NUWC, the spies affected to take the matter seriously, and two years later the police commissioners could still quote its details.[3] Both Hetherington and Carlile published a cheap edition of Colonel Macerone's *Instructions* for street warfare, which showed how to make lances and construct barricades. The pamphlet was common enough in middle-class radical circles, but very much more alarming in working-class hands. Watson, indeed, used to bring one of Macerone's lances to his class meeting to aid his members' education. He also kept one on display in his shop.[4] A few members

[1] For an analysis of the problems involved in using HO material in the period 1790–1830, see E. P. Thompson, *The Making of the English Working Class*, 1963, pp. 487–93. Throughout, the Government was kept well informed.

[2] HO 79/4, f. 219, 30 Mar. 1833; HO 64/11, 27 Nov. n.d., 5 July 1831. Very many of the spy reports in 1831 and 1832 reported that 'No mischief was afoot' despite incidents apparently to the contrary.

The S.C. on Popay revealed that some twenty men were employed as spies, but whether this figure refers only to the Whigs is unclear. *PMG*, 19 Oct. 1833, the Quarterly Report of the NUWC.

[3] *S.C. on Cold Bath Fields*, Aug. 1833, xiii, qus. 216–17.

[4] Loc. cit., qu. 5161. Napier told Phillipps that Macerone's pamphlet was again circulating in April 1839 (W. Napier, *The Life and Opinions of General Sir Charles Napier*, 1857, vol. ii, p. 16).

(urged on by Popay, the police spy) practised broadsword exercises in a deserted yard, though when the police rushed there the swords turned out to be wooden ones.[1] The 73rd Class called itself the Fighting Class and, according to one police report, a sawyer who was a former member of the union had stated that 'all our class had arms of some kind, most of those who could afford it had spears, others had daggers. . . . A short time ago, I and my fellow workmen sawyed up two 12 foot planks of the very best deal, for pike handles, they were for Mr Williams, a class leader in Theobold's Road. . . .' When the branches of the union were integrated into the NU and replaced by classes, in the autumn of 1831, Benbow would have soldiers as class leaders, 'so that he might learn his Class to march or the use of the Firelock. . . .'[2].

Reports from Theobold's Road during late 1832 and 1833 suggested that speeches were getting bolder, as discontent with the Reform Act and then with the Irish Coercion Bill grew. For, as Hetherington was in prison, and Lovett and Watson had left the NUWC after Benbow's double-dealing over the Fast-day trials, so the Irish and the group around Lee, Mee, Petrie, and Preston had come to dominate the NUWC with their talk of a National Convention. Lee, a young self-employed printer, was reputed at one meeting to have said, 'Your laws be damned', and this found its way into the evidence of the Select Committee on Cold Bath Fields.[3]

The NUWC was thick with spies, as its leaders well knew. Carlile had some justification for pointing out that 'In serious times, all political societies will be worked and managed by the existing government.'[4] Every couple of weeks spies were denounced, though not usually named, with the monotony of warnings against pickpockets in street markets. Popay, a plain-clothes policeman and agent of a shadowy Special Branch, who considered himself an

[1] HO 64/12, 12 Mar. 1832; *PMG*, 31 Mar. 1832.
[2] *S.C.*, op. cit., qu. 214; HO 64/8, police report of 20 May 1833; HO 64/11, 22 Nov. 1831.
[3] *S.C.*, op. cit., qu. 185. For further detail on the development of the NUWC, see below, pp. 263–7.
[4] *Cosmopolite*, 18 May, see also 6 July 1833.

intimate of many of the leaders, sometimes sent in two or three reports a week, either to John Stafford (the chief clerk at Bow Street, who paid Popay's bills and forwarded his reports to Phillipps at the Home Office), or to his immediate police superior, his Superintendent, who then relayed them to the police commissioners, Rowan and Mayne, who would forward the more important ones to the Home Office.[1] Class leaders were seduced into turning informer. Dean, a Spitalfields weaver and the leader of the East End branch of the NUWC, was in their pay, as was Charles Clements, himself a publisher of unstamped papers. Public meetings, class meetings, committee meetings, as well as the gossip of the working-class leaders, all came to Home Office ears. If Hetherington intended to make one sort of defence in court, Stafford knew what it would be. When committee members of the NUWC turned up at Stafford's office to plead for George Pilgrim, an imprisoned vendor, Stafford had been warned of this by Popay. When Hetherington was wanted by the Bow Street runners, Popay gave details of his movements and of the meetings he would attend.[2] The Home Office sourly scribbled on this report that Hetherington should already have been arrested. When Osborne, the secretary of the NUWC, moved the minutes and the committee papers to Cleave's coffee house for safe keeping, the police knew where to find them. When Hetherington toured the north on behalf of his papers and the NU, the Home Office had an itinerary detailed enough to inform their local commanding officers whom he would meet and where he would stay; and asked them to collect enough information to lodge a charge if necessary.[3] For what it was worth, the Home Office knew of Carlile's

---

[1] In the S.C. on Popay, all parties insisted that Popay was a plain-clothes police-man reporting only to his police superiors. There was no mention at all of the Stafford–Phillipps connection with its Special Branch implications, through which most of his reports passed, and from whom he received specific instructions. This connection may have developed out of the job of each chief clerk at the various police offices to handle fines and to pay informers' fees. (See *S.C. on the Police of the Metropolis*, 1834, xvi, qus. 4833 f., 4904.)

[2] HO 64/11 n.d. (July 1831), HO 64/12, 20 Dec. 1832; HO 64/12, 26 July 1832; HO 64/11, 16 and 19 Sept. 1831.

[3] HO 64/12, 2 Apr. 1832; HO 79/4, f. 208, Phillipps to Spooner, 19 Oct. 1832, to Major General Campbell, 25 Oct. 1832, to Foster, 20 Dec. 1832.

quarrels with his wife and sons, of Hetherington's quarrels with Carlile, of feuds within the NUWC, of the profits of the *Guardian* and of the imminent collapse of the *Gauntlet.* The letters of NU leaders Cleave, Osborne, Benbow, and Dios Santos (though not those of Hetherington or Carpenter) were opened by the Government at the height of the Reform agitation, just as Carlile's and Wooler's letters had been opened in August 1819, and as Chartist letters were to be opened eight years later.[1]

Melbourne and Phillipps acted on much of this information. Details of Hetherington's tours were sent to local justices as well as to the Stamp Commissioners. When Popay reported that Lucking, a vendor who was prominent in the NU, worked as a warehouseman for the East India Company, Melbourne wrote to the Chairman of the Directors that Lucking had spread 'Republican Principles—and has by introducing Penny Papers formed a Secret Society amongst men there'. Melbourne thought it only 'right' that the directors should be informed.[2] Lucking was dismissed, and the warehouse doors were placarded with threats of dismissal for anyone found reading seditious literature.

The Home Office treated mass meetings with great seriousness. Working-class men regarded mass meetings and processions as holiday occasions, on which they displayed their strength and self-discipline. The Government saw it rather differently. Recalling the panic of November 1830, and alarmed by Gibbon Wakefield's *Householders in Danger from the Populace*, the Government saw every mass meeting as a potential mob and every procession as a potential riot. Their fears were not lessened by the hopes and claims made for these meetings by the Unstamped. The proposed NU meeting on the Reform Bill at White Conduit Fields in November 1831, which Wakley was to chair, was banned when the Home Office received information that 'intentions of employing force and violence upon this occasion are entertained by many, and as such a meeting may very possibly endanger the public tranquillity'.[3] Working-class

---

[1] HO 79/4, f. 208, 5 Nov. 1831. (This was stopped in Apr. 1832.)
[2] HO 79/4, f. 219, 30 Mar. 1833.
[3] HO 41/26, f. 56, Melbourne to Lord Mayor, 4 Nov. 1831.

leaders, after much self-questioning, called the meeting off. None the less, the Lord Mayor was requested to guard all public buildings, especially prisons (was there some fear that a second Bastille might be stormed?), the Earl of Munster was to order the First Tower Hamlets Militia to protect King's Bench Prison, directors of the East India Company were warned, the Royal Artillery was brought up, and magistrates were ordered to be in attendance.

Four months later the NUWC decided to celebrate Perceval's Fast Day (a day of national humiliation to avert the cholera) with a feast, for which they would acquire an appetite, they thought, by marching round the streets of London. Popay immediately reported, 'There is no organization in us as a body, but many do calculate that on that day we shall have "a good opportunity to do something".' The Government's 'something' was to issue a warning against the procession, though they did not forbid it, and to station some 1,500 troops around London in addition to the police. The procession found the streets blocked by police waving cutlasses; Lovett waved his umbrella back; and after some scuffling the procession dispersed for roast beef and radical music.[1]

In May 1833 Lorymer, Hetherington's editor of the *Radical* and *Republican*, together with Lee and Mee of the NUWC, called a meeting in Cold Bath Fields to discuss ways of forming a National Convention. Melbourne banned it, Hetherington was again in prison and Lovett stayed away, but some 3,000 turned up. The police chiefs and Melbourne were all thoroughly familiar with the writings of the *Guardian*, the *Working Man's Friend*, Lorymer's placards, and the speeches made on the subject in the Rotunda. As they were sure that 'these newspapers exercise a considerable influence over the minds of the persons who read them', they expected an armed working-class riot, and Melbourne 'the disorganization of society'. As Mayne, the police commissioner, put it, 'most of them were men of desperate character holding principles subversive of all existing Institutions and destructive of Property'.[2] In a rehearsal

[1] HO 64/12, 12 Mar. 1832; HO 79/4, f. 214, 15 Mar. 1832.
[2] *S.C.*, op. cit., qus. 184, 186, 191, 4784, 5161, 2235.

for the Bull Ring riots of 1839, the police charged the meeting, swinging their truncheons and battering women and bystanders indiscrimately. The crowd retaliated with stones, staves, and iron railings, and a police constable was killed. The verdict returned at the inquest was an unthinkable 'justifiable homicide' which had to be changed to 'murder by persons unknown'; and a Select Committee sat to investigate the brutality of the New Police.[1]

The fifth and last mobilization by the NUWC was in mid April 1834 when Lovett and Place organized a working-class march to the king to protest against the sentence passed on the Dorchester labourers. The troops were called out, the Lord Mayor warned, and the usual precautions taken.[2] In his *Memoirs* the governor of Cold Bath Fields outlined the additional defences which his prison enjoyed for the occasion. The western boundary wall was swiftly rebuilt, an artillery wagon of small arms was received from the Board of Ordnance, the basement exits were blocked, scaling ladders, ropes, hand-grenades, naval commanders, and justices of the peace were added to the fortifications, and all the prisoners were locked away in their cells. To the governor's gratification Edward Hancock, one of his former prisoners and a leading vendor of the Unstamped, wrote to him that 'Our Council' did *not* intend to storm the prison and set free all the vendors, whatever he might have heard.[3]

This concern for public peace and order meant that the army, the main peacekeeping force outside London, must be thoroughly insulated from sedition. The problem of contamination was always very real: it was for this reason that Pitt had built so many barracks during the 1790s,

---

[1] G. Kitson Clark in *The Making of Victorian England*, 1962, p. 61, has suggested that the London mob were finally beaten and police control established at the battle of Cold Bath Fields. This seems premature. The Sunday trading riots of 1855 and the Hyde Park riots of 1866–7 had much in common with Cold Bath Fields: e.g. the enrolment of street mobs, given to smashing windows, behind radical banners and popular rights; the crowd's deep hostility to the New Police and the direct physical challenge they offered them by occupying public grounds in defiance of government order. (See B. Harrison, 'The Sunday Trading Riots of 1855' in *Historical Journal*, 1965, R. Harrison, op. cit., pp. 88–100.)

[2] Somerville in his *Autobiography* described the revolutionary concoctions brewed around the Tolpuddle affair. *Autobiography*, 1951 edn., pp. 266 f.

[3] G. L. Chesterton, *Revelations of Prison Life*, vol. 1, pp. 199–204.

and that troops stationed in the Luddite areas in 1812 had
had to be regularly moved to stop 'disaffection' spreading
in the ranks.[1] In the years around 1819, Sidmouth was
informed of every sergeant reading the *Black Dwarf*; and
a man was indicted at Hull for selling a copy of Sherwin's
Letter to the Soldiers to a private. Byng told the House of
Commons that at least six attempts had been made to seduce
soldiers from their loyalty by selling them radical publications.[2] Similarly in 1839 Napier took seriously reports of
any soldier attending Chartist meetings, and worried about
the fraternization between soldiers and working men entailed by a system of billets rather than barracks.[3]

Both working- and middle-class radicals took up Alexander
Somerville's case when he was flogged for allegedly writing
to the *Weekly Dispatch* and *Birmingham Journal* at the end
of May 1832 that the Scots Greys would not attack the
people whatever their orders. And the NUWC fussed over
William Simmens when he was, he said, drummed out of
the army for his political opinions. Rawlinson, the Union
Square magistrate, thought the 'worst part' of Costello's
offence in selling the *Guardian* in the 'Quebec Arms',
Bryanston Square, was offering the papers to soldiers.
The *Morning Chronicle* reported that another vendor of the
Unstamped, an immigrant from Argyleshire, was induced
to sell the papers by a soldier of the Guards, who, seeing his
acute poverty, gave him the money to start, and told him
where to buy the papers at trade price. One of Lucking's
many offences was that he was employed by the grenadier
soldiers to drill their recruits, and he took the chance to
discuss politics with them. Popay reported that another
soldier from the Foot Guards told him, 'I often talk to them
[other soldiers] and as I take in the *Guardian* Regularly I
often shew it and read it to those I know and who think as I do.'[4]

---

[1] J. L. and B. Hammond, *The Town Labourer, 1760–1832*, 1919 edn., pp. 83–6;
E. P. Thompson, op. cit., p. 565.

[2] *Black Dwarf*, 11 Oct. 1820; *Register*, 17 July 1819; *Hansard*, 1st ser., xli,
col. 300 (Byng, 24 Nov. 1819).

[3] Napier, op. cit., vol. iii, pp. 1–153; see also F. Mather, *Public Order in the
Age of the Chartists*, 1959, pp. 177–81.

[4] *Cosmopolite*, 28 Sept. 1832; *Morning Chronicle*, 13 Sept. 1832; HO 64/15, 29
Apr. 1833; HO 64/12, 24 Dec. 1832.

The Unstamped began to advertise their impact on the army. In an editorial that must have made alarming reading in the Home Office, the *Guardian* claimed that it was finding its way into many regiments, especially the Grenadier Guards, who were becoming 'thoroughly republicanized'. One soldier, the paper went on, had bought his first *Destructive* from a charwoman at Somerset House and read it under the staircase, knowing that he would be flogged if he were caught. Other soldiers, reading the *Guardian* together, then tore the paper to shreds and chewed them, to make sure they would not be flogged.[1] Carlile had two soldiers regularly writing into the *Gauntlet*, one of whom was paid for circulating it. A travelling union lecturer, Edward Mead, wrote in to the *Gauntlet* that at Norwich ten soldiers were among his audience, and that they borrowed old *Gauntlet*s, *Cosmopolite*s, and *Guardian*s from the Unionists. Commanding officers were having to refuse recruits from the towns, and taking only country lads, because there was so much 'knowledge' circulating in the towns.[2] Such infiltration seemed to be confirmed by a report from Burnley in March 1833, when a local barber, one Robert Ripley, tried to sell the *Guardian* to the non-commissioned officers. To their astonishment he told them they were worse than slaves. One sergeant loyally reported that 'Ripley's conversation was such as to set all us Serjeants astray'. Ripley was quickly brought to trial before the local magistrates.[3] This case went swiftly to Melbourne—an indication, perhaps, of how seriously the incident was taken.

Some of the more prolific and insistent of the Home Office correspondents were former army and navy officers, intent on denouncing the sedition with which they found themselves surrounded in the very streets of London. When a police officer attended a radical meeting at the 'Crown and Anchor' at the beginning of June 1833, he devoted more space in his report to William Simmens, who was hawking the Unstamped, than he did to the speeches themselves.

[1] *PMG*, 9 Mar. 1833.
[2] *Gauntlet*, 11 Aug., 15 Sept., 19 Oct. 1833; 22 June 1833; HO 64/12, 24 Dec. 1832.
[3] HO 40/31, ff. 30–40, 15 and 22 Mar. 1833.

'He stated that there was plenty more left behind in the Regiment of the same opinions as himself, and hinted that not much dependence could be placed on them in case of any collision with the people.'[1] Carlile cashed in on all this when in December 1833 he launched the *Political Soldier*, which Somerville was to edit. Its object was 'to bring the people and the army nearer together, and to a better knowledge of each other's interest'. The paper lasted only a few weeks.[2] Similarly, an important part of the 'Coming Revolution' outlined by the *Chartist* in 1839, was the plan for infiltrating the army 'and shaking its fidelity'. When Hetherington's *Dispatch* went stamped in 1836, it carried a letter from a soldier who had been afraid to write into an unstamped paper. 'I thought that the fact of illegal papers being read by soldiers would have subjected the proprietors to increased oppression.'[3] He was quite right.

None of this, of course, is evidence that the Unstamped *were* widely read by the army. What it does show is how sensitive the Home Office was on the subject, and perhaps how insecure the Government felt its grip to be on public peace and order, even after the Reform agitation had died away. The militia was even more vulnerable than the army to sedition, and for more than one reason, after Lovett and the NU leaders had refused to serve in 1831, the militia was no longer called up.

The Home Office, then, tried to check criminal libel and to maintain public peace and order. The third way in which the Home Office affected the world of the Unstamped was through its judicial powers. The Home Office was ultimately responsible for the number and legality of arrests, sentences, and sojourns in prison.

Vendors of the Unstamped could be arrested by the New Police. More often, they were brought to the police offices by common informers entitled by law to a reward. Statutory rewards, it has been pointed out, were as much part of the process of justice in the eighteenth and early nineteenth

---

[1] e.g. HO 40/31, f. 317, 21 May 1833; HO 61/8, Report of Insp. Maccalieu, 1 June 1833.

[2] *Gauntlet*, 1 Dec. 1833.

[3] *Chartist*, 5 May, 1839; *London Dispatch*, 16 Oct. 1836.

century as statutory punishments.[1] Until the New Police were widely established, rewards offered by government departments, associations of citizens, or private individuals hoping to recover their property; government pardons for criminals turned informer; and statutory fees for persons bringing offenders against various laws to justice, were all expected to supplement the efforts of constables, runners, and night-watchmen, by turning citizens into 'voluntary policemen'.[2] Rewards and fees were paid by law in the 1830s to those who laid information against publicans permitting gambling, for example, against frauds of weight and measure, against infringements of public safety such as the regulations controlling coaches and hackney cabs, and for offences against the revenue, such as hawking without a licence and selling unstamped newspapers.[3] It was a method of payment by results which was thought to keep the police up to scratch: at its worst, it led to blackmail, bribery, protection rackets, and the cooking up of offences. Colley and Currie were two common informers who lived off the vendors of the Unstamped. One of them would trap a stranger into selling the papers, the other would turn him in, and the two informers would then share the £1 reward.[4]

Sir Peter Laurie, a city alderman, was full of praise for the work done by informers, but most magistrates found them distasteful and disliked receiving their self-interested evidence. The Society for the Prevention of Cruelty to Animals, as a result, stopped using informers, politely called inspectors, in 1833; and instead rewarded policemen who arrested offenders against Martin's Act of 1822.[5] By 1834 many of the London magistrates refused to sentence vendors of the Unstamped on the evidence only of an informer; and the Home Office was forced to change its policy towards both vendors and informers.[6]

[1] L. Radzinovicz, *History of Criminal Law*, vol. ii, p. 35. This paragraph draws heavily on his work.

[2] See Henry Goddard, *Memoirs of a Bow Street Runner*, 1956 edn., for the financial rewards of a Runner.

[3] For examples of most of these in just one month, see the *True Sun*, 4, 10, 25 Jan. 1836.   [4] See below, pp. 166–9.

[5] *True Sun*, 25 Jan. 1836; SPCA Annual Report 1833, p. 7 (I owe this reference to the kindness of Dr. B. Harrison of Corpus Christi, Oxford).

[6] See below, pp. 191–3.

It was the Home Office that received petitions against illegal arrests and extra-legal informers. It was the Home Office also that received petitions and complaints about prison conditions, that had to answer the charges made by Hume, Roebuck, Cobbett, and Wakley in the House of Commons to the effect that vendors of the Unstamped were treated as common felons, crowded in with thieves, made to stand shivering in the exercise yards of Cold Bath Fields, denied books, fires, and candles, and forced to have their heads shaved and wear prison dress.[1]

The Home Office and the Treasury together shared responsibility for the punishment meted out to the publishers (though not to the vendors) of the Unstamped, since only the Treasury Lords could remit the fines in lieu of which publishers were imprisoned. Thus the Treasury officials, in December 1831, directed the Commissioners of Stamps to remit Carpenter's penalties, and Doherty applied to them for a stay in proceedings in January 1832.[2] Hethering-ton was imprisoned for twelve months in December 1832; but in June 1833 Phillipps of the Home Office wrote to Maule, the Treasury Solicitor, querying the legality of two consecutive imprisonments of six months each when both offences had been committed on the same day, and asked whether it would have made any difference had the two offences been committed on different days, or if they had been tried on different days.[3] Hetherington, greatly to his surprise, was released. When, at Hetherington's Exchequer trial, the jury, encouraged by Lord Lyndhurst, decided that the *Guardian* was not a newspaper, the Treasury Lords directed the Commissioners of Stamps 'to take measures for the immediate release of any parties now in confinement under circumstances similar'.[4]

The Home Office, then, was active, although careful to stay within the letter of the law. Yet the results were not always as reliable and efficient as the Home Office would

[1] e.g., *Hansard*, 3rd ser., vii, cols. 52–3 (15 Sept. 1831); xv, col. 768 (15 Feb. 1833); xvii, col. 381 (22 Apr. 1833); xxx, col. 202 (10 Aug. 1835); xxxii, col. 331 (15 Mar. 1836); *Mepol.* 1/50, 4 Apr. 1836.

[2] *Treasury* (T.) 22/20, f. 120, 24 Dec. 1831; T. 22/20, f. 153, 9 Jan. 1832.

[3] HO 49/7, f. 478–81, 8 June 1833.

[4] T. 22/26, f. 116, f. 120, 16 and 31 July 1834.

have liked. Melbourne spelt out the problem of employing
informers in a letter to Henry Drummond at the end of
January 1831: 'The danger of employing spies and accom-
plices has always been found to be that, in order to further
their own ends, satisfy their employers, and forward their
own interests and maintain their own credit, they are too
apt, first, to bring forward false accusations; secondly to
excite and encourage to the commission of crimes, in order
that they may have the honour of informing against and
detecting them.' Oliver, he thought, had probably cost the
lives of three men.[1] Popay was used in preference to other
men because the Commissioners thought he was more
reliable; and yet Cobbett's Select Committee on Popay in
the summer of 1833 found that he had been among those
suggesting broadsword exercises, had chaired class meetings
of the NU, had pressed friends to speak out for him as he
was a bad speaker, had tried to persuade Lovett to attend
the Cold Bath Fields meeting, and so on. Cobbett and
O'Connell thought that this made Popay an *agent provocateur*,
and not simply the impartial reporter of public meetings
which Althorp and the police claimed he was.[2] Popay was
dismissed from the force. Those informants who were
reliable disliked the job. Dowling, one of Gurney's short-
hand reporters, complained that the job was physically
dangerous; he dare take only the shortest notes, and had
to rely on his memory for the rest.[3]

So Melbourne sensibly did not prosecute spoken sedition.
Benbow's and Warden's language at NUWC meetings was
far more violent than anything to be found in the Unstamped, yet 'Nothing is so difficult to prove as the utterance
of words, so that it might be very difficult to found a prosecution upon any proof which could now be obtained.'[4] Juries
were notoriously unreliable. To make sure of a conviction,
the major Luddite trials and the Swing riots had had to be
tried by Special Commission. A jury had acquitted Cobbett,
according to Popay, because the foreman was a radical

[1] Sanders, op. cit., Melbourne to Drummond, 23 Jan. 1831, p. 128.
[2] *S.C. on the Petition of Frederick Young and others* . . ., 1833, xiii, qu. 1814;
Hansard, 3rd ser., xviii, col. 1360 (1 July 1833).
[3] HO 59/4, 26 Feb. 1833.
[4] L. Sanders, op. cit., p. 126, Melbourne to T. Sanctuary, 6 Jan. 1831.

from Finsbury who read the *Register*; Cobbett's friends knew that the case would have to be dismissed. A jury had returned that unparalleled verdict of 'justifiable homicide' on the inquest following the Cold Bath Fields meeting. When Lovett, Benbow, and Watson were tried for disturbing the peace with their Fast Day march, the jury found them not guilty. Popay told his superiors that one of the jurymen was a friend of Watson, 'and has a son in Hetherington's employ and he says the jury had nearly all made up their minds to an acquittal in the early part of the case'; some of the jurymen, he added, would have held out for a week.[1] It was a jury in the summer of 1834 who decided that the *Guardian* was not a newspaper and therefore that its vendors could not be prosecuted.

Informers were unreliable and juries were unreliable. The Home Office also found it difficult to obtain witnesses. When the magistrates told Colley and Currie that they would not accept their evidence without an impartial witness, the informers said they could get no one to come forward. Charles Clements had the same difficulty in January 1836 in Birmingham, and in March 1836 in Nottingham. To complicate matters further for the Home Office, the magistrates became increasingly reluctant to commit vendors to prison. Until the summer of 1832 magistrates had relied on their own judgement as to whether a penny paper was a newspaper, but from the autumn they began to demand the presence of a Solicitor of Stamps to prove it.[2]

All of this hampered the efficiency of the Home Office in checking libel and maintaining public order. A further difficulty lay in the very nature of libel itself. As Denman put it, if the evil effect of libel lay in reading it, law cases made numerous readers. To prosecute a libel was to publicize it; to prosecute meetings of the NUWC was to advertise them. Denman frequently warned the Commons of these perils, and added that he did not have the power so often attributed to him, that 'he was a sort of officer going about with an extinguisher, at once to put out all objectionable publications'.

[1] HO 64/11, 11 July 1831; HO 64/12, 22 May 1832.
[2] *True Sun*, 14 Nov. 1832; *London Dispatch*, 11 Dec. 1836. For the position of the magistrates, see below, pp. 169–70.

Papers could only be suppressed by court cases. He was sure libellers 'thirsted for publicity' and that martyrdom had 'its pecuniary advantages'. It was better, he argued, for obscure publications, however offensive, to 'perish in obscurity'.[1] Wetherall ruefully pointed out that it had always been thought that libel and an Attorney General could not coexist; but on Denman's argument, the more atrocious the libel, the safer it was from prosecution.[2] It was Denman, and not Melbourne or the Police Commissioners, who kept a cool head when the tories loudly complained of the licentiousness of the press. As Denman told the House, 'If the whole public were disposed to rush into palaces and mansions and dwellings, and destroy all the rights of property, he was sure that prosecutions would not prevent them.'[3]

The first set of difficulties inhibiting the Home Office was practical; the second lay in the very nature of criminal libel; the third arose from the case for the repeal of the stamp duties advanced by the parliamentary radicals. They turned the stamp on newspapers into a 'popular knowledge' question, to which the Whigs had to pay lip service; and the radicals argued that to prosecute unstamped papers because they disturbed the peace was to turn the problem upside down. The Government should free newspapers from the stamp and allow the radicals to diffuse knowledge.[4]

The only counter-move the Government could make was to change the case for prosecuting unstamped newspapers from a Home Office concern with public peace to a Treasury concern with a defrauding of the revenue. From 1833 this was becoming more practicable, as the Reform agitation was dying away, and with it the extravagance of some of the Unstamped; 1833 was also to see the beginning of the Unstamped broadsheets which not even Melbourne could describe as licentious. So Melbourne now told the Lords that the responsibility for prosecuting the Unstamped lay not with the Home Office but with the Stamp Office.[5]

[1] *Hansard*, 3rd ser., xii, col. 1148 (21 May 1832).   [2] Loc. cit., col. 1156.
[3] *Hansard*, 3rd ser., iv, col. 426 (28 June 1831).   [4] See above, Chapter I.
[5] *Hansard*, 3rd ser., xviii, col. 855 (17 June 1833); xxii, col. 1286 (24 Apr. 1834).

His Whig successor at the Home Office, Russell, never spoke on the subject of unstamped newspapers at all in Parliament; and there is not a reference to them among his papers in the Public Record Office.

(b) THE TREASURY

Stamp duties on newspapers were a piece of fiscal policy. One of the reasons *why* the Home Office under Melbourne had so concerned itself with unstamped newspapers was that Althorp, as Chancellor of the Exchequer, thought the stamp duties were a bad tax; and he was, perhaps, less energetic in using the powers at his disposal than the Home Office would have liked.

Althorp, with his protégé Poulett Thomson, vice-president of the Board of Trade, and their theorist, Henry Parnell, formed a clique of radical Whigs who anticipated others in their party by favouring the ideas of Ricardo and Huskisson on free trade.[1] In 1828 they, with Joseph Hume, had acted together on the Finance Committee which was to abolish the Sinking Fund. The aim of fiscal and budgetary policy, in their view, was to remove all burdens that hampered industry and which thus stopped the country from becoming wealthier. Members of all parties agreed that it was essential for a healthy economy to achieve a surplus (which was attained for every year between 1830 and 1836 except 1832). Most of the tories, however, preferred to put the surplus towards reducing the national debt; whereas Althorp saw the national debt as a running cost. The Whigs were agreed that the surplus should be used to lower taxes, but debate then arose as to whether direct taxes, such as the much-hated assessed taxes, should be reduced, or the indirect taxes, such as those on malt, soap, calico, paper, and glass, which most hampered the expansion of industry or most harmed sectional interests.

The Althorp–Thomson–Parnell group preferred to remove indirect taxes, to abolish such monopolies as the East India Company and the Bank of England, and thus to

---

[1] This paragraph draws heavily on L. Brown, *The Board of Trade and the Free-Trade Movement 1830–1842*, Oxford, 1958, chs. i and iii.

proceed towards freer trade. In this they were supported by the *Westminster Review*, and McCulloch in the *Edinburgh Review*. But only in his first budget of February 1831 did Althorp dare to be doctrinaire enough to act on the principles of Parnell's *On Financial Reform*, published in 1830. In his budget speeches Althorp stated his canons of fiscal orthodoxy. He would reduce taxes where their very heaviness limited consumption and which thus produced less revenue than would a lighter tax; he would reduce those taxes which were partial in their incidence; and he would reduce those which were disproportionately costly to collect. Parnell had added another category of undesirable taxes in his book—those whose heaviness encouraged smuggling.[1]

Many existing taxes could be squeezed into this classification. Althorp (though not Parnell) placed newspapers in the first category; but the implication of this was that though it was legitimate to reduce taxes if revenue would rise as a result, the taxes could not be abolished altogether. This forced the parliamentary radicals either to argue that a total repeal of the duties would be compensated for by the increased revenue from postal and paper duties, thus bringing down on them the ire of Charles Knight and the cheap-book publishers; or they had to change their ground altogether, and argue for the repeal of the stamp duties in the Home Office language of social peace and tranquillity; but this by 1833 was becoming anachronistic. However, as Althorp proposed to remedy any deficit in the budget by a new tax on the transfer of funded property, his budget was so mauled by tories, stamped press, and City, that he abandoned fiscal dogmatism.

In his subsequent budgets Althorp appeared to give up fiscal canons for considerations of trade. Those taxes were abolished which hampered industry (and advertisement duty but not stamp duty affected industry), as were those for which there was most clamour, such as the widely unpopular assessed taxes. Both the *Edinburgh* and the *Westminster* lamented that Althorp should give way to a

---

[1] *Hansard*, 3rd ser., ii, cols. 406–9 (11 Feb. 1831). The objections to smuggling had been the reason for reducing the spirit duties in 1824 and abolishing the silk duties in 1825.

shopkeeper pressure group for, the *Reviews* argued, assessed taxes were direct, cheap to collect, unavoidable, offered no encouragement to smuggling, and did not affect trade.[1] Assessed taxes were, however, partial in their incidence.

Thus the financial arguments pressed on the Chancellor for a repeal of the stamp duties were drawn very much from a common arena of agreed financial orthodoxy; the radicals, among other claims, insisted that the monopoly of the stamped press was bad and the smuggling of the Unstamped undesirable; that dear knowledge hampered trade and industrious workmen; and that a postal duty would compensate for any loss in the revenue. As radicals saw Althorp submitting to public opinion on unpopular taxes, so they mounted their own extra-parliamentary campaign. Althorp held out half hopes of reform, but under other pressures he withdrew them.

Spring Rice's financial policy was much more opportunist. Unlike Althorp, who came to the Chancellorship without any previous financial experience and so was criticized for his inexperience, and as a result, perhaps, turned to the textbook, Spring Rice had served his apprenticeship as Secretary to the Treasury. More to the right of the party than Althorp, he had little sympathy with his fiscal ideas and in 1831 had opposed his funded tax. When Spring Rice defended the Government's financial policy in the *Edinburgh Review* of October 1833,[2] he argued that it was always easy to win cheap popularity by reducing taxes. The Government had resisted repeal of the malt duty, the reduction of the house and window duties, and repeal of the stamp duties; they were therefore accused of being the enemies of the farmers, of disregarding the sufferings of the middle classes, and of impeding the diffusion of knowledge. 'Wherever a demagogue comes forward to frame the indictment, there is no lack of a Tory jury to find a true bill.' Spring Rice then defended the Whig budgets not by any broad statement of policy, but by a piecemeal examination of the

---

[1] *Edinburgh Review*, Apr. 1833; *Westminster Review*, Oct. 1833.
[2] S. Rice, 'Financial Measures of the Government'. Attributed by the *Wellesly Index of Victorian Periodicals* to Spring Rice, possibly with the collaboration of William Empson.

benefits of each tax that had been reduced or repealed. Similarly, when in 1837 Roebuck argued that the Chancellor should repeal taxes on necessities and maintain taxes on luxuries, and that popular education (and therefore news-papers) was a necessity, Spring Rice replied in language very unlike Althorp's that he repealed only the most inconvenient taxes. 'There was scarcely any tax that would stand discussion on its own merits. . . . The question [was] whether it was possible to deal with the question of repeal of taxation except upon the principle of showing the inconvenience felt from one tax in comparison with the inconvenience attending the continuance of another.'[1]

So it was not just sheer cussedness that made Sir Charles Knightly, a former friend of Althorp, and Goulbourn argue in the debates of summer 1836 that it was preferable to reduce the duties on soap rather than the duties on news-papers. The soap duties were widely unpopular, and on this view there was as much reason to reduce that duty as any other. Morpeth, for example, who presented petition after petition for the reduction of the newspaper stamp duties in the five years, had written to Althorp, back in December 1832, that in fighting Yorkshire he had found 'Economy and reduction of taxation speak for themselves. Malt and soap are mentioned most often.'[2]

Where Althorp had stated that the Chancellor had the positive function of freeing trade, Spring Rice's view was that the Chancellor was merely the arbiter between con-flicting vested interests, all of whom had some case for reduction or repeal of the tax that most hurt them; he would conciliate those who made the most clamour. And Spring Rice, unlike Althorp, was subject to the organized pressure of the stamped press from the summer of 1835 on. Even in 1839, his last year as Chancellor, Spring Rice objected to a penny postage scheme as being too rash, yet introduced it into his budget of July 1839 after 320 petitions had been presented on the subject. So when in 1836 Spring Rice reduced the newspaper stamp duty to a penny, he

---

[1] *Hansard*, 3rd ser., xxxvi, col. 1193 (2 Mar. 1837).
[2] Ibid., 3rd ser., xxxiv, cols. 613, 617, 636 (20 June 1836); Le Marchant, op. cit., pp. 447–8, Morpeth to Althorp, 26 Dec. 1832.

was doing as little as he had to and as much as he needed to do, amid the competing pressures of stamped press, cabinet colleagues, parliamentary radicals, Charles Knight, and the Society for the Diffusion of Useful Knowledge.[1]

Up to the end of 1833 or so, it was the Home Office which had been pressed to eradicate the Unstamped. From then on it was the Chancellor who received the petitions and deputations for and against the stamp duties. Melbourne told Eldon in June 1833 that prosecuting unstamped newspapers was not a Home Office matter but the concern of the Stamp Office; however, 'the persons who had been engaged most in violent and seditious libels, were now in prison and indeed had been so some time at the instance of the Stamp Office . . . His Majesty's Government were resolved at all hazards to maintain the supremacy of the law—the supremacy of Parliament—and to repress and punish every species of turbulence which might arise in the country.'[2] The *Guardian* took up the implication. At last it had been acknowledged that the *Guardian* 'has been persecuted on account of its politics'. Althorp had always denied this in the Commons, and insisted that it was a revenue matter, but 'We always scouted this plea as a vile subterfuge, seeing that divers other periodicals, published equally in violation of the stamp laws, were connived at by the Commissioners, who, if it were merely a question of revenue, would have made no distinction.'[3]

Melbourne's statement to Eldon seems to mark the divide. As the panic from Cold Bath Fields died away, and as the Popay investigations brought Home Office methods into disrepute, so the newspaper stamp question came to be argued only in terms of revenue and not in terms of 'turbulence'. Hetherington's trial for seditious libel, fixed for the summer of 1833, was abandoned in favour of a revenue trial in the summer of 1834. When a copy of the *Workman* was sent to him in May 1834 Melbourne agreed it was 'mischievous' but thought a government prosecution was

---

[1] See below, pp. 85–90 f.   [2] *Hansard*, 3rd ser., xviii, col. 855 (17 June 1833).
[3] *PMG*, 22 June 33. For Althorp's denials, see *Hansard*, 3rd ser., xv, col. 769 (15 Feb. 1833), col. 1113 (22 Feb. 1833).

'inexpedient'.[1] Melbourne left the Home Secretaryship when the unstamped papers were already turning themselves into broadsheets, papers that were undeniably respectable but also undeniably newspapers. From 1834 there were few complaints by the Unstamped that prosecution was selective. As each new broadsheet came on the market, so its proprietor was swiftly prosecuted. The old rivals of the Unstamped, such as the *Penny Magazine*, did not turn broadsheet; the new rivals of the Unstamped were the stamped papers, which were interested not at all in social peace but very much in the level of smuggling. Where Melbourne, as Home Secretary, spoke frequently on the subject both of unstamped papers and the stamp duties, Russell was silent; where the Home Office papers of Peel and Melbourne contain dozens of letters from magistrates and citizens complaining of the Unstamped, there is not a single letter on the subject among Russell's papers. Because the Government was able to change its ground, it kept itself free to do nothing. The middle-class arguments on social peace won out; but the radicals had then to restate their case, first as a fiscal measure, finally as a demand by respectable opinion.

Spring Rice defended his Penny Stamp Bill in June 1836 not because it would cheapen newspapers but because it would abolish the financial incentives for illegal ones. A year later he said he had been guided not by financial considerations at all but by the number of criminal prosecutions (*sic*) brought by the Home Office and the magistrates under the stamp duties. In 1840 he told the Bishop of Exeter that his real reason had been that it was legally and physically impossible to put down the Unstamped.[2]

The Home Office and the Treasury's failure to contain the Unstamped explains in part why Russell was so extraordinarily tolerant to Chartism in its opening years. He and his law officers time and again refused to prosecute Oastler, Stephens, and the *Northern Star* for seditious libel. When he was forced to take action, Russell drew the attention of the law officers to the *Northern Star* not for any 'libellous matter against the Government' but because it encouraged

[1] HO 41/12, Phillips to Bruce, 10 May 1834.
[2] *Hansard*, 3rd ser., xxxvii, col. 1166 (13 Apr. 1837); *Southern Star*, 16 Feb. 1840.

its readers to resist the New Poor Law officials. When the Earl of Harewood sent him some of Oastler's writings, he replied, as Melbourne would never have done, but in words very similar to Denman's, 'So long as mere violence of language is employed without effect, it is better, I believe, not to add to the importance of these mob leaders by prosecutions.'[1] Cobbett's acquittal had cast a long shadow.

[1] Russell to Harewood, 18 Sept., 1838, quoted by F. Mather, op. cit., p. 375.

III

THE MIDDLE-CLASS CAMPAIGN

THE Home Office and the Treasury were under pressure from the parliamentary radicals to repeal or reduce the stamp duties. The radicals were not entirely homogeneous, containing within their ranks free traders, educationalists, social missionaries, utilitarians, local government reformers, colonial and post office reformers; yet all wished to see the end of the taxes on knowledge, for cheap newspapers were not only desirable in themselves, but would also be the means by which to publicize any or all of the other radical causes. The problem within the radical ranks, as Place saw it, was that those radicals who wanted cheap newspapers as a means to some other end, rather than as an end in itself, would be satisfied with a penny stamp and would not press for a total repeal of the stamp duties.

The radical campaign was essentially a parliamentary one. Unlike the working-class radicals, the middle-class men sought to change the law, not to make it unworkable. There were three possible ways of doing this. First, they could attempt to rely on their own numbers and their own powers of persuasion, and introduce motions for debate into the Commons. Accordingly Bulwer initiated debates on the stamp duties in June 1832, was persuaded not to do so in July 1833, introduced a second motion in May 1834, and a third motion in August 1835. It is hard to judge the attitude of Parliament to these three motions, as only the leading radicals, the Chancellor, and the Attorney General ever spoke in the debates. The numbers of those voting was always low. Probably most of the reforming members favoured a reduction though not necessarily a repeal of the duty, Whigs and moderate tories were indifferent but ready to retain the stamp revenue if the Chancellor thought it necessary, while only the extreme tories objected to any concession at all. As at their height in the first reformed

Parliament, the radicals did not number more than a hundred or so, they could not hope to carry a measure against both the Whigs and the Tories. When a weakened Whig Ministry returned to office in April 1835, Roebuck suggested that the radicals should bargain with the Government, offering to support the reform of the Municipal Corporations in return for a government-sponsored motion on the stamp duties; but Hume and other radicals were reluctant to use their strength to embarrass the Ministers.

The second way open to radicals was to persuade the Ministers into a change of heart. Hume and Warburton regularly lobbied Cabinet Ministers and sought private meetings with them to demonstrate the latent advantages of repealing the stamp duties, pointing out that, among other things, it would destroy the influence of *The Times*. But Althorp and then Spring Rice vacillated between reduction, repeal, and doing nothing as they listened to radicals, the police commissioners, the stamped press, their colleagues, and Charles Knight in turn.

The third way open to radicals was to lead national public opinion on the subject and from this to argue that Ministers were placing themselves, their seats, and their country in jeopardy by not responding to it. Such a body of public opinion would also refute the ministerial plea that the public were not sufficiently interested in the matter for them to sacrifice some portion of the revenue. The problem, however, was that the public opinion the radicals found was a working-class opinion created by the Unstamped. It was unrespectable, extravagant, and beyond the law. The public opinion the middle-class radicals tried to create from 1835 on was more middle-class, respectable, and constitutional.

In the 1820s middle-class radicals were more concerned with the issue of criminal libel than with that of the newspaper stamps. Place encouraged Hume to keep the newspaper stamps before public opinion by bringing motions before the House in June 1825, December 1826 (when Hume was supported by Brougham), and in May 1827; and to extract from the Commissioners of Stamps a return

of the small publications prosecuted under 60 G3 c9.[1] In
the spring of 1830 the Government made two moves of its
own. The first was an abortive attempt to raise the Irish
stamp duty from twopence to fourpence and to tighten the
application of the stamp duties. This led to the first public
meeting in London for the repeal of the taxes on knowledge.
Southwood Smith chaired the meeting at the City Literary
and Scientific Institution on 20 April 1830 and Chadwick
was its driving force. Significantly, most of the stamped
newspapers ignored it and the proceedings had to be printed
as a pamphlet.[2] The *Westminster Review* debated the subject;
and Place threw himself into his favourite activity, lobbying,
and persuaded Burdett, Hobhouse, and Hume to promise
that they would speak to as many members as possible and
so use this agitation to press for the repeal of the Six Acts.
Nothing was done.[3]

   The second move by the Government was the libel Act
of Scarlett, the Attorney General, which repealed an in-
operative clause of 60 G3 c8, whereby a second offence of
criminal libel brought banishment, but which also tightened
up the securities required of publishers. Place stormed at
Hume and other radicals that this Act was more arbitrary
and inquisitorial than the Act it was replacing, but nothing
was said in Parliament to oppose the Bill. Depressed, Place
thought of starting a daily newspaper, a recurrent radical
dream, and wrote to Burdett about it, but the subject
dropped.[4] From the summer of 1830 Peel at the Home
Office was trying to contain the Unstamped, suppressing
the *United Trades Co-operative Journal*, initiating a prosecution against Carpenter's Political Letters, and trying also
to contain the growing London working-class activity
centred on the Rotunda, which had taken new life from
the July Revolution. But before Peel's efforts could attract

   [1] *Hansard*, 2nd ser., xiii, col. 1276 (22 June 1825); xvi, col. 400 (13 Dec. 1826);
xvii, col. 1063 (31 May 1827); Add. MSS. 35148, f. 38, Place to Hume, n.d. (7 Nov.
1829).
   [2] Hickson, op. cit., p. 347; *Moral and Political Evils of the Taxes on Knowledge*,
1830.
   [3] 'Taxes on Knowledge', *Westminster Review*, Apr. 1830, pp. 416–29; Add.
MSS. 35146, f. 109.
   [4] Add. MSS. 35148, f. 64, Place to Hume, 25 May 1830; Add. MSS. 35146,
f. 113, Place to Burdett, 24 July 1830.

the attention of the parliamentary radicals, Grey replaced Wellington, and the radicals took hope.

For some of the Whig Ministers seemed to favour either a reduction or a repeal of the stamp duties. Three Cabinet Ministers, Brougham, Russell, and Althorp, as well as Durham and Denman, were all members of the Society for the Diffusion of Useful Knowledge. When Morpeth, in July 1830, had presented a petition from the London printers, praying for a reduction of the stamp duties, Spring Rice had supported it. In the middle of November Poulett Thomson, then still in Opposition, had agreed that he would introduce a motion on the stamp duties after Christmas, and he was thought to have the backing of Althorp and Brougham.[1] But holding office changed minds, together, perhaps, with the mounting Tory attacks on the 'poison and venom' that the Government was allowing to circulate. Althorp assured the House that the Attorney General was not unwilling to prosecute, but that this was best left to ministerial discretion.[2] Nothing was done about the stamp duties.

So, at the beginning of January 1831, Hume asked Althorp, Thomson, and the Treasury for their intentions on the subject. He was told that to repeal or reduce the newspaper stamps was a revenue question, and would have to await a more favourable time. Hume was satisfied with this, Place and Bowring were not. So Place wrote his *Letter* to Poulett Thomson in which he argued that cheap newspapers should be costed in terms of social tranquillity and not in terms of the revenue; and Bowring pressed the pamphlet on Thomson's attention.[3] At the end of January 1831 Chadwick repeated his efforts of the previous nine months and organized a meeting at the Literary and Scientific Institution, chaired by Dr. Birkbeck, the members of which turned themselves into a Society for Promoting the Repeal of the Taxes on Knowledge. Place sent them his pamphlet, which they agreed to reprint and circulate.[4]

---

[1] *Hansard*, 2nd ser., xxv, col. 889 (2 July 1830); 3rd ser., i, col. 426 (12 Nov. 1830).

[2] *Hansard*, 3rd ser., ii, col. 71–8 (Trevor, 23 Dec. 1830).

[3] Add. MSS. 27789, f. 239; Add. MSS. 35146, f. 130; Add. MSS. 35149, ff. 22–4.

[4] *Penny Papers*, 4 Feb. 1831; Add. MSS. 27789, f. 240.

If Ministers wished to alter the stamp duties on news-papers, they could do this in one of two ways; they could either repeal the aggravating clauses of 60 G3 C. 9, which was a legislative matter but which would leave newspapers without a legal definition, or they could reduce the stamp duties as part of the budget. As nothing seemed to be happening on the first front, radical hopes centred on the second, the first budget that Althorp as the Whig Chancellor would introduce in February 1831. On 11 February Althorp outlined his proposals; the existing stamp acts would be consolidated, the duty reduced by twopence, but the 20 per cent discount brought to an end. The Society for the Repeal of the Taxes on Knowledge complained to Althorp that this was an effective reduction only of a penny-farthing; Place, sagely, was worried less by this than by the possibility that the Deputation would publicly accept the principle of a penny stamp, which Chadwick already advo-cated and with which Roebuck was coming to agree.[1]

However, the stamped press immediately started com-plaining; and the issue never came to a head. The budget was so mauled by the House of Commons that it collapsed. On 7 March Buller suggested that the stamp duty should be reduced to a halfpenny, and Althorp promised to bring in a Bill to consolidate the stamp duties before 5 July 1831. Hume and Warburton wanted to interview Althorp again to tie him down, but Place advised them to let matters rest until Russell's Reform Bill was through.[2]

Apart from Althorp's budget, two other subjects in the field of popular journalism engrossed the attention of the parliamentary radicals during the first six months of 1831. The first was the trials of Carlile and Cobbett for libel, and of Carpenter and Hetherington for publishing unstamped newspapers. For Cobbett and Carlile the radicals went through the lobbying hoops. Place, early in January 1831, wrote to Colonel Jones on behalf of Carlile, who, through Edward Ellice, recommended him to George Lamb, who in turn promised to lay Place's letter before Melbourne.

[1] *Hansard*, 3rd ser., ii, col. 406–9 (11 Feb. 1831); Add. MSS. 35149, f. 31.

[2] *Hansard*, 3rd ser., iv, col. 113 (7 Mar. 1831); Add. MSS. 35149, ff. 75–6, Place to Hume, 3 June 1831.

None of this affected the outcome of the trial, which delighted Carlile. Cobbett claimed that Hume wrote to Brougham and Denman to persuade them to abandon his trial and, like Carlile, he was delighted that his would-be saviours had failed. The radical efforts for Carpenter and Hetherington included presenting their petitions and broadcasting their complaints.[1]

The other subject to which certain radicals devoted their time was the launching of the *Penny Magazine*. Brougham and the Society for the Diffusion of Useful Knowledge gave Knight and Hill their backing, Place their approval, the Stamp Office its clearance, and the *Magazine* appeared at the end of March 1831.[2] Before long, Place changed his mind. Meanwhile, the quarterlies and the periodicals began again to debate the question of the newspaper stamps, and to unite more of the loosely grouped parliamentary radicals around the Hume–Warburton group. W. J. Fox, in the *Monthly Repository*, urged a national petitioning campaign, and the *Westminster* and the *Examiner* recited the arguments for repealing the stamp duties, which by now were becoming familiar—free trade, national education, social peace.[3] In July a proposal was again revived in radical circles that was to echo through the decade: a daily national radical newspaper. Burdett had objected to it the year before because he thought such a paper would follow rather than lead public opinion; he now changed his mind but the proposal faded away.[4] Meanwhile, the Unstamped became caught up in the cross-fire of Reform; Gordon read excerpts from the Unstamped in the Commons to show the House what it might expect from Reform, and Hume and the *Satirist* rashly assured Peel that one of the authors of the Unstamped, Lorymer, was too radical to be a radical and must therefore be a tory agent provocateur in disguise.[5]

---

[1] Add. MSS. 27789, ff. 236–8; 35146, f. 130; *Pol. Reg.*, 16 July 1831. Hume, for example, presented Carpenter's petitions on 8 Feb. and 15 Sept. 1831.

[2] See below, pp. 138–9.

[3] *Monthly Repository*, N.S. vl, p. 271; *Westminster Review*, July 1831; *Examiner*, 23 Jan. 1831.

[4] Add. MSS. 35146, f. 113.

[5] *Hansard*, 3rd ser., iv, col. 413 (28 June), col. 468 (29 June 1831), col. 588 (1 July 1831); *Satirist*, 3 July, 7, 14 Aug. 1831.

On 15 September 1831 Althorp told the radicals that, but for the business of Reform, he would have introduced a measure affecting the stamp duties: and the radicals again took hope. Bulwer assured readers of the *New Monthly Magazine* that 'immediately after the passing of the Reform Bill . . . Lord Althorp intends immediately to address himself to the reduction of the Newspaper tax'. But by December Lord Althorp had refused to make any promises whatsoever.[1]

Thus, in ten months, the leading Whigs had retreated from being willing to reduce the stamp duties into a tougher line; and as a ministerial change of heart seemed less likely, so radical activity increased outside Parliament. In October 1831 some of the middle-class radicals formed the National Political Union (NPU) to ensure the success of the Reform Bill; the National Union of the Working Classes had been formed the previous April. Within the National Political Union, Place and Detroisier urged that they should broaden their aims to include the repeal of the taxes on knowledge, and this implied that the NPU would continue to exist after Reform had been carried. Burdett, however, saw the NPU as an auxillary wing to the Ministers; any other form of, or reason for, agitating would 'embarrass' the Whigs. By February 1832 the Place line had predominated, a standing subcommittee of Place, Roebuck, Perry, Detroisier, Rainford, Fox, and John Taylor on the stamp duties had been set up, and Roebuck had presented their first report to the General Meeting of 2 February 1832.[2] The NPU had still to resolve its attitude towards the NUWC; both unions deplored the taxes on knowledge, and there was enough overlapping membership to guarantee that the two unions could not peacefully coexist. Burdett censured any interaction between the two unions; Carpenter and Wakley, on the other hand, tried to ensure that half of the Council of the NPU should be working men. Working-class attacks on the NPU mounted, and Place, caught in the cross-fire, sighed wistfully for £150 to float a series of

---

[1] *Hansard*, 3rd ser., vii, col. 56 (15 Sept. 1831); *New Monthly Magazine*, monthly commentary, Nov. 1831; *Hansard*, 3rd ser., ix, col. 104 (7 Dec. 1831).
[2] Add. MSS. 27822, ff. 29–40; 27791, f. 128, f. 218.

tracts which would oust both the *Penny Magazine* and the Unstamped.[1]

In February 1832 the parliamentary radicals again organized a deputation to the Chancellor to urge him to include a reduction of the stamp duty in his budget, but as the Chancellor had no surplus at his disposal, the deputation failed. Place was determined to keep up the pressure and, when the Reform Bill was passed, he fed Bulwer with the material for a motion in the House of Commons. On 15 June 1832 Bulwer asked the Commons to set up 'A Select Committee to consider the propriety of establishing a cheap postage on Newspapers and other publications', and in one classic speech cited all the middle-class radical arguments for the repeal of the taxes on knowledge. Althorp, unlike Bulwer, managed to adduce a new argument—that to repeal the stamp duty would be to tax the provinces for the benefit of London, for provincial readers would now be denied newspapers unless they paid postage for them. With a hint of that antipathy to London which marked so many Victorian pressure groups, Sir Matthew Ridley told the House that a reduced stamp would give 'an advantage to the metropolis over all other parts of the country'. Warburton put in that the lateness of the Session meant that any committee appointed would be inadequate for the task, and preferred Bulwer to bring forward his motion again in the next Session, the first of the reformed Parliament. The motion was withdrawn, though Althorp's sympathy in principle had been obtained.[2]

The National Political Union printed and distributed 5,000 copies of the Debate together with Place's elucidatory remarks; Chadwick wrote it up for the *Examiner*; and it was followed up by a public meeting at the Institution in which O'Connell, Bulwer, Wade, and Bowring shared the platform

---

[1] Add. MSS. 27795, f. 164; 27791, ff. 34–74; 35149, f. 120, Place to Mill, 25 Oct., Place to Perry, 28 Oct. 1831.

[2] *Hansard*, 3rd ser., xiii, cols. 619–34 (Bulwer, 15 June 1832); col. 636 (Althorp); col. 641 (Ridley). For the same antipathy to London, see the *NS*, 19 Dec. 1840, on the effect of the Convention, which had 'dragged London out of the Malthusian mire, and placed it upon the green sod of provincial Radicalism, and from the moment the country battering-ram broke down the old barrier, pure, unsullied and genuine opinion made a rush to the breach . . .'.

with Cleave and the much-abused leaders of the National Union of the Working Classes. Cleave told the meeting that cholera was rife in Cold Bath Fields prison, where some of the vendors of the Unstamped were held, and the next day a deputation, headed by Bulwer and including Hetherington, Benbow, and Cleave, called on Melbourne, who promised to have the matter investigated.[1]

During the recess the question of the newspaper stamps lapsed, as working- and middle-class radicals together sought to return Wakley for Finsbury, circulated pledge sheets and lists of qualified candidates, and worked to make the *True Sun* solvent. Hume, indeed, received a comically rude letter from Colonel Jones for being too friendly with the working-class 'Destructives'.[2] With the return of the new reformed Parliament in January 1833, middle-class radical activity again focused on the House. In November 1832 Erskine Perry had had an interview on the stamp duties with Althorp, who had cross-questioned him on the financial savings of a postage system, and its efficiency in America. Perry, unsure of his ground, contacted Brougham but failed to produce the necessary statistics.[3] Meanwhile Place, Bulwer, and Hume had long been scornful of the *Penny Magazine*, and its failure to treat of those political subjects which most interested working men. So Place, in December 1832, circulated the idea of a Society for the Diffusion of Political and Moral Knowledge, which would launch a penny paper for the people, 'A Penny Political and Moral Magazine'. Place and Roebuck both considered being editor, Hume was president, Warburton vice-president, and Grote treasurer, each contributing £50 for the privilege. Place feared that he could not be editor as he would be liable to prosecution under the stamp duty laws; but Mill told him that he had recently dined with Brougham and other Cabinet members and that the Chancellor had said that the taxes on knowledge must be repealed, that they should go ahead with the scheme, and that they should ignore the question of the revenue. Warburton, it was

---

[1] *Examiner*, 17 June 1832; meeting of 30 June 1832, reported *PMG*, 7 July 1832.
[2] *Brougham Coll.*, Jones to Hume, 7 Jan. 1833, f. 44,932.
[3] Ibid., Perry to Brougham, 19 Nov. 1832, f. 44,147.

agreed, should see the Ministers and explain to them that they wished only to repeal the stamp duties and not to damage the Whigs' legislative programme. Two days later, the radicals met at Place's house and Warburton reported that, though Althorp favoured repeal and the substitution of a small postage, he did not have all the Cabinet behind him; but Warburton thought events looked promising, and that he and Althorp had agreed that Warburton should on the first day of the Session ask the Chancellor what his plans for the newspaper stamp were, and that Althorp would give an unconditional answer representing Cabinet policy.[1] This leaked; *The Times*, the *Globe*, the *Spectator*, and the *New Monthly Magazine*, all reported that Althorp intended to repeal the stamp duties. The radicals agreed that the proposed penny paper should have the benefit of the law, and should wait until the duties were repealed, before being launched.

Place's draft circular left no doubt of the intentions of the paper. It was to counteract the mischievous notions of both stamped and Unstamped press by 'teaching Politics, Political Economy and Morals'. But Brougham's quarrels with *The Times* now cut across all these plans, for Brougham realized (even if *The Times* did not) that a small postage would prop up *The Times* just when he was coming into open conflict with it.[2] On 5 February 1833, the last day of the financial year, Warburton asked Althorp for his proposals; Althorp replied that the question must wait on the state of the country's finances; and on 19 April he devoted his surplus of £1,500,000 to reducing the assessed taxes and the advertisement duty. The 'matter ended here'; and the penny papers had to await Roebuck's publication of 1835. A fortnight later, Spankie presented a petition from Hetherington, praying, *inter alia*, that the *Penny Magazine* might be prosecuted, whereupon Hume asked Althorp when he was going to do anything about the newspaper stamps; but Althorp once again refused to commit himself. A week later Hume asked for a Return of the convictions for selling the Unstamped, and Bulwer told the Government that by

[1] Add. MSS. 35154, ff. 172–3.
[2] Loc. cit.

refusing to repeal the obnoxious laws, they and not the magistrates were responsible for them.[1]

Ministers therefore had refused to respond to lobbying in private and heckling in public; the radicals' pet scheme of a weekly paper had yet again been foiled. But the radicals did not give up. When Hume seconded O'Connell's motion criticizing *The Times* for its biased reporting, Hume followed this up by going over to Althorp and pressing on him the advantages of repeal, suggesting that among other things it would reduce the influence of *The Times*. Althorp now decided, 'I do not think the *people* care about it; and when I mentioned it early in the Session the *members* paid little attention to it.' In relating this to Place, Hume thought another deputation of some seventy or eighty members of Parliament might impress Althorp, and he suggested that Mill should bring pressure on Brougham to change his attitude.[2] There was one other method left open to the radicals, that Bulwer should reintroduce the motion that he had withdrawn in the last session; but 'to my mortification and a little to my surprise' Bulwer was advised by many of the radicals, including Grote, to postpone his motion yet again until the next Session, as time was running out and public interest was flagging. Bulwer gave way and wrote to Place that he hoped 'I did right'. When Place replied some six or eight months later, he told him irritably that any publicity was good publicity, and that Bulwer should stand on his own two feet.[3] The newspaper-stamp question again died away during the summer recess, though Place tried to keep a skeleton interest alive by pressing the issue on the attention of his correspondents.[4] Not until the early summer of 1834 did the middle-class radical agitation again start to move, and this time it spilled out from Parliament into extra-parliamentary activity.

Althorp, in his spring budget of 1834, removed the last

---

[1] *Hansard*, 3rd ser., xv, col. 768 (15 Feb. 1833); col. 1113 (22 Feb. 1833).

[2] Ibid., xx, col. 7 (26 July 1833); Add. MSS. 35149, f. 227, Hume to Place, 28 July 1833.

[3] Bulwer to Place, n.d., *Place Coll.* Set 70, ff. 28–9; Add. MSS. 35149, ff. 273–4, Place to Bulwer, 5 Feb. 1834.

[4] e.g. Add. MSS. 35149, ff. 240–1, Place to Birkbeck, 6 Dec. 1833; f. 269, Place to Young, 8 Jan. 1834.

of the assessed taxes, because they were so 'unpopular', but left the stamp duties untouched. So in May 1834 Bulwer at last introduced his long-promised motion. Althorp again replied that there was not sufficient public interest on the subject to justify sacrificing a portion of the revenue, though Bulwer had pointed to the petitions that had been presented and the pledges that had been extracted as evidence of national opinion. Matthew Hill confessed to the inadequacies of the Society for the Diffusion of Useful Knowledge, and Bulwer pressed the House to divide. Ninety members voted against and fifty-eight for his motion.[1] The next move therefore lay with the radicals, who had to create a public opinion that the Ministers could not ignore, for they would not otherwise improve their voting strength.

O'Connell had proposed an investigation into the law of libel in February 1834, and a month later Campbell, the Solicitor General, had moved for a Select Committee.[2] Brougham gave evidence before it in June 1834, and, with yet another change of opinion, testified that the newspaper stamp was to be deplored. The Society for the Repeal of the Taxes on Knowledge promptly reprinted and circulated some 10,000 copies of his evidence. Behind Brougham's sudden emergence into the lobby of the parliamentary radicals, lay the history of his tangled relations with *The Times*.[3] Brougham and Barnes, its editor, had been close allies from 1830 to 1832. Brougham indeed had more than once fed *The Times* with quasi-confidential material, to the annoyance of the rest of the Cabinet. In August 1831 Brougham had discouraged Althorp from repealing the duties because he thought this would damage *The Times*;

[1] *Hansard*, 3rd ser., xxiii, cols. 1193–1222 (22 May 1834).

[2] Ibid., xxi, col. 468 (18 Feb. 1834); xxii, col. 410 (18 Mar. 1834). The libel committee was provoked by a number of libel cases in 1833—the prosecution of the *Dublin Pilot* for printing some of O'Connell's denunciations of the Irish Coercion Act; the *ex officio* information against the *True Sun* for printing Lorymer's letter recommending people not to pay taxes; and the imprisonment of the editor of the *Brighton Guardian* for pointing out that rick-burning was most common where the magistrates were most severe. The committee of twenty-eight MPs included Peel, Scarlett, Roebuck, Hill, O'Connell, Pepys, and then Campbell, the Solicitor General (see *Commons Journal*, lxxxix, p. 135). The committee did not report, possibly because of the fall of the Whigs.

[3] This account draws heavily on the *History of the Times*, 'The "Thunderer" n the Making', pp. 318–22.

Brougham then decided that a small duty and a postage would benefit *The Times*, but at this point *The Times* was becoming increasingly critical of the Government, the new poor law, and Brougham. By June 1834 Brougham was severing his ties with Barnes; and he saw that with the abolition of the newspaper stamps he could turn the *Penny Magazine* into a cheap newspaper, which would both embarrass *The Times* and undercut its advertising revenue. The *Examiner* told its readers that 'in the circulation of the *Penny Magazine* there is a great publishing interest and its agencies are determined to carry on the newspaper which is to be started in the Chancellor's service as soon as the duties are repealed'.[1]

The radicals were delighted that at last Brougham's relations with *The Times* were working in their favour. Place and Parkes wrote jubilantly to each other that the Chancellor was 'going it!' They decided that Brougham was preparing for a long battle with the House of Lords (the recurrent hope of the radicals and the recurrent fear of the Whigs between 1834 and 1836), by commencing a series of subordinate campaigns, such as that of the newspaper stamps, 'which can and will be usefully worked out of doors'. Place, with some malice, sent a copy of Brougham's Evidence to *The Times*, and Hume alone sent out some 500 or 600 copies.[2] But all now had to wait on the parliamentary manœuverings which resulted in Peel's Ministry. Parliamentary radical activity had to be suspended until April 1835 when the Whigs again returned to office. Meanwhile, the radicals tried to keep Brougham up to the mark, and on 21 November Bulwer addressed to him his *Letter to a Late Cabinet Minister on the Present Crisis*, which went through twenty-one editions in six weeks and had sixteen replies. Bulwer accused Brougham of backsliding on reform, and Brougham was stung into a reply, which was incorporated in the later editions of the *Letter*.[3]

Thus, during the summer of 1834 Bulwer, for the first

[1] *Examiner*, 19 Oct. 1834.

[2] Add. MSS. 35149, f. 308, 7 July 1834; 35149, f. 312, Place to Hume, 9 Sept.; f. 313, Hume to Place, 20 Sept. 1834.

[3] A. Aspinall, *Lord Brougham and the Whig Party*, 1939, p. 209; *Brougham Coll.*, Bulwer to Brougham, 5 Dec. 1834, f. 14,561.

time, had pressed a motion on the newspaper stamps to a division, and Brougham had joined the parliamentary radical lobby. The third event of summer 1834 was the repeal of the almanac duty, which had stood at 15d. since 1815. Charles Knight claimed the credit for this, as he had collected statistics for the Society for the Diffusion of Useful Knowledge, which had then been sent on to the Treasury, showing the discrepancy between the total duty collected (some £27,000) and the enormous numbers of unstamped almanacs on the market. The smugglers' trade had become a 'capital' one.[1] So the Treasury had reduced the advertisement duty, and abolished the almanac duty. They still refused to do anything about the newspaper stamp duty.

The Whigs, headed by Melbourne, returned to office in April 1835, much weakened by the retirement of Althorp from politics, and dependent for their uneasy majority on Irish and radical support. Althorp, as Chancellor of the Exchequer, had been to the left of his party, ready to flirt with the radicals and toy with radical measures. Spring Rice, who, having failed to be elected as Speaker, now replaced Althorp as Chancellor, was much more to the right of his party, more remote from the radicals, more sympathetic to tory critics and the position of the stamped press, probably more subservient to the pronouncements of the Treasury, and, as he himself admitted, more opportunistic in his fiscal policy.[2]

The radicals were in a common enough dilemma. Roebuck argued that they should exploit the weakness of the Ministers in order to secure radical measures, and should bargain their support on Irish and municipal reform for the repeal of the newspaper stamp. Hume, on the other hand, thought that this was just the time not to rock the boat, for the Government was too precariously poised to be able to handle the waves of petitions and public 'stir' that Place envisaged. He told Place that he would see Spring Rice

[1] C. Knight, *Passages of a Working Life* . . ., 1864, vol. ii, p. 65; SDUK Reports I, read 14 Nov. 1833; Minutes of Publication Committee, SDUK Papers, 19 Nov. 1833; H. Mayhew, *London Labour and the London Poor*, 1851 edn., vol. i, p. 271.

[2] Compare Althorp's budget speech of 11 Feb. 1831 with Spring Rice's of 2 Mar. 1837.

and Melbourne privately to find out their plans for the stamp duty 'and until then I am decidedly of opinion that nothing should be done'.[1] He immediately approached Spring Rice and soon afterwards saw Brougham and Normanby; public agitation and radical pressure, he concluded, should be deferred until they had the Ministers behind them. Place was furious and stormed on about 'parliamentary men'. He threw back at Hume the abortive Warburton–Althorp negotiations of February 1833 as evidence that Ministers were not to be trusted, and would never do anything they did not have to do.[2]

At the same time, Brougham wrote to Birkbeck that 'some highly respectable persons in the City' wanted to hold a great public meeting, and that Birkbeck, as a leading educationalist, should be prominent at it. Birkbeck took a couple of days to reply, for, though he agreed that the cause was an extremely important one, he was less sure that a public meeting was the right way to proceed. He thought that perhaps private pressure on Ministers was preferable as they were 'more free from trammels than when formerly in power'.[3] Most radicals, even the Ministerialists such as Hume, still agreed that something must be done about the newspaper stamps, whatever the balance of power in the House and however 'embarrassed' they were by their own strength. But the Ministerialists still hoped to do something the traditional way, by lobbying Ministers privately rather than by confronting them publicly. The less orthodox radicals, including Roebuck, Perronet Thompson, and Wakley, agreed with Place that the Ministers would do nothing without pressure. Such pressure, hallowed in the name of public opinion, would not only work on the Ministers, but would break the stalemate among the radicals and even force the stamped press to give publicity to the cause. Place set to work to create such a public opinion.

The only grass roots public opinion that so far existed, however, was the working-class public opinion created by

[1] *Pamphlets for the People*, No. 9, p. 15 (J. Roebuck, 'Persecution of the Unstamped Press'); Add. MSS. 35150, f. 35, Hume to Place, 24 Apr. 1835.

[2] Add. MSS. 35150, f. 47, Hume to Place, 10 May 1835; 35150, ff. 36–45, Place to Hume, 2 May 1835.

[3] *Brougham Coll.*, Birkbeck to Brougham, 20 Apr. 1835, f. 22,872.

the unrespectable, illegal, Unstamped press. Place had never ignored this opinion. Now that the old entrées into Cabinet circles, through the Birkbeck–Brougham and Warburton–Althorp axes, were closed, Place sought to cultivate and co-opt this working-class public opinion into the service of the middle-class radicals. He did this in two ways: he tried to re-educate the London leaders of the Unstamped, and he tried to build up a classless provincial public opinion, which from the summer of 1835 was fed on Roebuck's *Pamphlets for the People*.

Place and Dr. Black of Kentucky, a middle-aged middle-class pedagogue, grouped round them in London a dozen or so young working-class men who were to serve as clerks for the more middle-class Society for the Promotion of the Repeal of the Stamp Duties. This Society was heir to that for the Promotion of the Repeal of the Taxes on Knowledge, established in January 1831, and, shorn of its middle-class committee, was to become the London Working Men's Association and the sponsor of the *Charter*. The Society's committee members included Birkbeck, Place, Falconer, Chapman, Hickson, and Black, the leading writers of the *Pamphlets for the People*. The working-class members were encouraged to come to Sunday morning discussion groups, where competing versions of political economy were debated, as a result of which, Place fondly hoped, 'true doctrines' would filter down through the Unstamped press. The Unstamped *did* become more respectable, less polemical and controversial, but for the sound business reasons that led them to turn broadsheet rather than because Place's doctrines had acquired fresh appeal and cogency. Place, for his part, was prepared to help Cleave bring out his *Weekly Police Gazette* from prison, and Black possibly did the same for Hetherington's *Dispatch*. The Society organized extensive subscriptions for both men in the spring of 1836, paid off their fines for them in May, and gave them a celebratory dinner in December 1836.[1]

Secondly, this London group, suitably 'tamed', was in turn to build up a classless public opinion in the provinces,

---

[1] *Pamphlets for the People*, No. 29, p. 15 (F. Place, 'A Repeal of the Stamp Duties on Newspapers'); *Twopenny Dispatch*, 7 May, 4 Dec. 1836; *True Sun*, 20 Feb. 1836.

drawing on both working-class and middle-class support. To this end they sent out from their office in Leicester Square 1,600 letters, 4,000 copies of printed petition forms, 10,000 copies of Brougham's Evidence, 1,000 printed extracts from London papers, 124 written petitions ready for signing (with instructions that they should each be signed by 200 to 300 people), procured upwards of 300 petitions to Parliament and 32 known public meetings, listed some 2,000 individuals as provincial correspondents, and in all sent out some 20,000 circulars. As their letters were franked free by members of Parliament, and the clerical work was voluntary, Place claimed that all this was done at a total cost of under £40.[1] Place had hoped that similar Corresponding Societies would develop in all the big northern towns, and he claimed that he had committees at work in Birmingham, Manchester, Glasgow, and Coventry, but there is no evidence for it. Now, as earlier, the campaign for an Unstamped press was a London-based campaign. The petitions and meetings were reported from all those areas where the Unstamped was already strong, the Bath–Bristol–Yeovil triangle, Lancashire, the West Riding, and the Midland belt.[2]

As in 1830, deputations were backed by great public meetings. The 28 April 1835 meeting of the National Union of the Working Classes, at which Roebuck and O'Connell spoke for a free press, was followed by a second meeting of 6 May 1835, from which the Society for Promoting the Repeal of the Stamp Duties deputed Birkbeck, Grote, Roebuck, Rowland Hill, Place, Charles Knight, Bowring, Hume, and its secretary William Hickson, to wait on the Chancellor with its *Memorial*. The interview lasted two hours. Spring Rice agreed that the question was a financial and not a moral one, but that the actual remission of the tax was unlikely 'as far as he could judge of the opinions of others, either by the House of Commons or by the Government'; but he would willingly consider any way that would protect the revenue from loss. He would submit

[1] *Place Coll.* Set 70, f. 304; Add. MSS. 35151, f. 279, Place to Gibson, 29 Sept. 1840. In September 1840 Hansard was still owed £20 of this £40 for printing their circulars.

[2] Add. MSS. 35150, ff. 36–45, Place to Hume, 2 May 35; *Pamphlets for the People*, No. 10, pp. 15–16.

the deputation's suggestions for postal reform to the Treasury. Spring Rice followed this up with a letter to Brougham in which he said he would consult Althorp about the matter as Althorp had at one time intended to repeal the duties.[1] While Spring Rice debated and consulted, radical meetings snow-balled through May and into July; mechanics institutes, coffee houses, and taverns echoed to the familiar radical rhetoric.

All this activity alarmed the stamped press, who were already beginning to feel the squeeze of the unstamped broadsheets. Editorials on the subject began to mount. Into this the *Weekly Dispatch* threw its own private bomb, an announcement that certain printers were going to publish a daily unstamped newspaper. According to Hickson this was originally a hoax to get the Government to take action, but a Mr. Holt, encouraged, of course, by Place, took up the idea, and announced the *Daily National Gazette*, at a cost of threepence. This was to appear two hours after *The Times* and was to be replete with news lifted from the stamped press. Cunningham and Salmon, Cleave's and Carlile's printers, were to print it. Place expected that 'the prosecution of the printers publishers and vendors will be so severe that it will be extinguished in a short time but even then another step will be gained towards the abolition of the Stamp duty on newspapers'. Before it came out another unstamped daily appeared on 17 July 1835 but an official injunction to the printer stopped it on its second number. The day after, the *Gazette* appeared and lasted barely ten days. Its appearance was so 'wretched' that Hickson thought the general turmoil was 'ludicrous'.[2] None the less, *The Times* pertinently asked what would happen to the Chancellor's budget were the stamped papers to come out unstamped. *Bell's Weekly Messenger* begged Spring Rice to protect the stamped papers and to inhibit the appearance of an unstamped daily by lowering the duty to a penny; the *Courier* asked that it should be cut to twopence. The *Morning Post* carried a satirical advertisement for the *Gazette*

---

[1] *The Memorial of Certain Inhabitants of the City of London*, 6 May 1835; *Place Coll.*, Set 70, f. 203; *Brougham Coll.*, f. 10,467, Spring Rice to Brougham, 8 May 1835.
[2] Add. MSS. 35146, f. 138, memo for July 1835; W. E. Hickson, op. cit., pp. 342–3.

requesting scissors-and-paste men to cut out paragraphs from the stamped press. 'Persons appointed will have the most liberal notions on meum-tuum' except towards employers. The *Morning Herald* complained that the Treasury was losing its revenue and the stamped press its intelligence. And the *Weekly Dispatch* repeated the warnings of *The Times*. The stamped press began to organize itself, and to urge the Government that a penny or a twopenny stamp would both bring in revenue to the Government and allow the stamped press to protect their capital. As the *Gazette* put it, 'Their principles are in their pocket—their country means themselves, and the sphere of their monopoly.'[1]

Fearing that the pressure of the stamped press might prove all too successful, the radicals called a meeting on two days' notice at the 'Crown and Anchor' for Saturday, 18 July 1835, to demand the total abolition and not the partial reduction of the stamp duties on newspapers. Brougham was in the chair, and 2,000 attended, among them Hume, Wakley, Roebuck, and O'Connell. Two massive petitions were signed, to be presented to both Houses of Parliament. Even *The Times*, which regularly refused to cover the radical agitation, gave the meeting three columns. The *Courier*, less impartially, reported that 'were the monkeys from the Zoological Gardens brought to exhibit in the same place', the result would have been much the same. 'There was the usual cant about knowledge, the usual abuse of the Press and the Peers, and the usual stuff about a monopoly, which exists nowhere except in the muddy brains of those who make a noise about it.'[2] Excitement continued into August when Hetherington's and Cleave's presses were seized. Roebuck used the opportunity to cross-question the Government on its intentions, and Bulwer asked the Chancellor whether he would name a day for repealing the stamp duties. The Chancellor would not, and Bulwer warned him that the radicals would not accept a compromise measure of a penny stamp.[3]

[1] *The Times*, 4 July; *Bell's Weekly Messenger*, quoted *PMG*, 18 July; *Courier*, 19 July; *Morning Post*, 22 July; *Morning Herald*, 24 July; *Weekly Dispatch*, 2 Aug. 1835; *Gazette*, 11 July 1835, cutting in *Place Coll.*, Set 70, f. 232.

[2] *The Times*, 20 July 1835; *Courier*, 20 July 1835.

[3] *Hansard*, 3rd ser., xxx, col. 202 (10 Aug. 1835).

A few days later, on 14 August 1835, Spring Rice brought forward his budget, in which the stamp duties were untouched. Though he had a surplus of £1,250,000, he claimed that he could not spare the revenue. Hickson, writing six months later, thought the main reason was that the Cabinet were still in disagreement, that Russell was the main obstacle to repeal, and that under pressure of the stamped press Spring Rice had become a convert to a penny stamp.[1] On 17 August Hume brought in a Bill to repeal 60 G3 c9, and hoped that as it was not a fiscal matter, he would have the Government's support. The Chancellor disagreed.

So the radicals were forced to fall back on a third path, a motion on the newspaper stamp. On 21 August Bulwer moved that a committee should investigate the newspaper stamps, and provoked the third great debate on the subject.[2] He emphasized yet again that the issue was a national one, and that the number of petitions on this subject surpassed that of any other. Spring Rice reiterated that he could not spare the revenue. The radicals then made the false move that was to give Spring Rice his ammunition: Bulwer asked that the Chancellor should reduce the duty to twopence, Grote, Baines, and Wakley that he should reduce the duty to a penny. Place commented that it was 'strange' that they should have reversed their position so dramatically from that of the 'Crown and Anchor' meeting. Bulwer, seeing that the House was almost empty and thinking that the radicals had extracted as much from the Ministers as they could, did not press the House to divide. His motion had in any case asked for a Select Committee, and not for the repeal or reduction of the stamp duties. None the less, for some reason Bulwer's failure to press the motion to a division entered radical historiography as one of the great betrayals. Hume and Place were disgusted. Chapman wrote that as

---

[1] *Hansard*, 3rd ser., xxx, col. 514 (14 Aug. 1835); W. E. Hickson, op. cit., p. 343. Yet Russell did write to Brougham on reading his Evidence of June 1834, 'I agree in your views of the matter, almost entirely . . . ' *Brougham Coll.*, f. 14,414, Russell to Brougham, 29 Aug. 1834.

[2] *Hansard*, 3rd ser., xxx, col. 623 (17 Aug. 1835); col. 835 (21 Aug. 1835). The other two great debates were in June 1832 (see above, pp. 68–9), and in May 1834 (p. 73).

the newspaper stamp issue had taken Bulwer as far as he could hope, Bulwer then abandoned it. Brougham, in the *Edinburgh Review*, described his action as 'mortifying' and 'inexplicable'.[1] Place, four years later, was sure that had Bulwer forced the House to divide, the duty would have been totally repealed. William Hickson told the Select Committee of 1851 that Bulwer had compromised the question with the Government, Collet thought that total repeal had been delayed for twenty years, and Holyoake long afterwards claimed that Bulwer obtained his baronetcy for his tactful behaviour.[2]

All parliamentary tactics had failed. The Ministers had ignored meetings and deputations, private lobbying, budget amendments, and hostile motions. But the Session of 1835 had seen at least one long-cherished scheme launched. The Society for the Diffusion of Political and Moral Knowledge had been unable to publish its projected cheap paper in the spring of 1833 because Althorp had declined to do anything about the stamp duties. The Society had had to turn to publishing radical tracts and reprints from the quarterlies. Now, as an arm to the extra-parliamentary activity being mounted by Place and Black in the spring and summer of 1835, the reorganized Society put out a series of *Pamphlets for the People* in June 1835, edited by Roebuck. Chapman, Falconer, Hickson, and Place were among the main contributors. Each paper, following the stratagem of Carpenter's *Letters* of 1830–1, was separate and undated. Though patently illegal, weekly, and containing parliamentary news, they were never prosecuted. Roebuck continued them for thirty-six issues, and ended the series at the beginning of the next Session. Each pamphlet was entered at the Stamp Office, and its advertisement duty accepted; the British Museum demanded and received its copies. Each issue contained one or two main articles, on such

---

[1] *Pamphlets for the People*, No. 29, p. 15 (op. cit.); *Spectator*, 5 Sept. 1835; *Pamphlets for the People*, No. 12, p. 11 (H.S.C., 'Mr. Bulwer's Sham Motion'); *Edinburgh Review*, Oct. 1835, op. cit., p. 129.

[2] Add. MSS. 35151, f. 279, Place to Gibson, 29 Sept. 1840; *S.C. on Newspaper Stamps*, 1851, xvii, qu. 3183; C. D. Collet, *A History of the Taxes on Knowledge*, 1933 edn., p. 28; G. J. Holyoake, *Sixty Years of an Agitator's Life*, 1892, vol. i, p. 293.

topics as the aristocracy, trades unions, the ballot, municipal reform. In about every alternate issue there was an article on the taxes on knowledge. The papers soon reached a circulation of 10,000 (that is, a quarter of the circulation of Cleave's *Gazette*), but by July 1835 they needed a subsidy of £200 and by the following January were some £150 in debt.[1]

The extra-parliamentary campaign, extended by Roebuck's *Pamphlets*, hardened the positions of all groups. Crawfurd added to his writings in the *Pamphlets* by publishing two pamphlets on the newspaper stamp question, which provoked hostile replies.[2] Place redoubled his efforts. The *Morning Herald* accused 'Mr. Celibacy Place . . . [and] Radical Roebuck [of] . . . going about, here and there and everywhere, for these three long wearisome years now last past, by night and by day, in season and out of season, in highways and byways and upon the house tops, vowing and declaring, and protecting and proclaiming that "THE PEOPLE" were everywhere unanimous in calling for the instant and total abolition of the Newspaper Stamp duty. . . .' Lovett wrote that he was 'much gratified to hear of your renewed exertions in our *holy cause*', and praised his contributions to the *Pamphlets*.[3] Meetings followed each other in quick succession. Bulwer, Wakley, and Watson shared a platform at the Finsbury Mechanics Institute, Harvey and O'Connor appeared together at the old National Union of the Working Classes meeting-place, the Borough Chapel. A meeting of the Common Council on 3 March was followed by a public meeting of over 5,000 people at the Guildhall five days later, chaired by the Lord Mayor. *The Times* ignored it. Every public holiday had its great open-air meeting, Easter Day at Primrose Hill, Whit Monday at White Conduit Fields, and each had an estimated

---

[1] *Pamphlets for the People*, No. 30, pp. 15–16 (Chapman, 'The Crusade against the Unstamped').

[2] J. Crawfurd, *A Financial and Historical Review of the Taxes which Impede the Education of the People*, 1836; J. Crawfurd, *The Newspaper Stamp and Newspaper Postage Compared*, 1836; Anon., *Observations on the Duty on Paper*, 1836; Charles Knight, *The Newspaper Stamp and the Duty on Paper . . .*, 1836.

[3] *Morning Herald*, 27 Feb. 1836; *Place Coll.*, Set 70, f. 305, Lovett to Place, 5 Jan. 1836.

audience of 3,000. In all, there were at least fourteen meetings in London in the spring of 1836, and perhaps some forty meetings in the provinces, many presided over by local mayors and bailiffs.[1] Whether Place's hopes were indeed realized, how broadly based all this activity was, is difficult to say. In Manchester, as in London, working-class men held their own meetings. But more commonly members of Parliament shared platforms with labourers and mechanics. The London co-operation between Place, Hume, and Cleave, for example, had its provincial counter-part in Nottingham, where a local middle-class radical, John Clayton, took up the case of a prosecuted agent of the Unstamped, John Smith, and wrote on his behalf both to his London friends and to the Chancellor of the Exchequer. A month later Clayton called a meeting, chaired by Notting-ham's mayor, against the taxes on knowledge.[2]

Some of these meetings gave rise to deputations. Until now, deputations to the Chancellor had been of a more private nature, the effort of a handful of radicals determined to lobby every available Cabinet Member. Now these deputations became more public, and were more expressly the delegations of public meetings. Where the members of a deputation had formerly argued that the repeal of the stamp duties was in the interests of social prudence and free trade, now delegates more freely cited the onward march of demo-cracy and the divine right of popular sovereignty, and more ostentatiously invoked the spirit of the times. On 11 Feb-ruary 1836 Birkbeck, Thompson, Hume, Place, and others called on Melbourne. Melbourne told them that he had listened to all their arguments, moral, political, statistical, financial, and even personal, and admitted that the duty could not be defended on 'so mean a foundation' as the state of the revenue.[3]

What, then, was left of Spring Rice's position, who, after all, was shortly to introduce his budget? Spring Rice abruptly changed his ground, though not his intentions. Total repeal was impossible, he told a deputation from the

---

[1] This estimate is based on Place's newspaper cuttings in *Place Coll.*, Set 70, supplemented by local provincial papers.

[2] *Place Coll.*, Set 70, ff. 321–4, 359.   [3] *WPG*, 20 Feb. 1836.

Primrose Hill meeting of Easter Monday, because the House would not pass it. On 7 March 1836 Spring Rice gave notice in the Commons that he would bring forward a Bill to consolidate the stamp duties. A week later a circular was issued from the Home Office, calling a meeting of all reform members in the Foreign Office for the following day. There Spring Rice announced that he would reduce the stamp duty to a penny. There was little enthusiasm among the radicals who, a year before, had professed themselves satisfied with a penny stamp. Wakley, who had already given notice that he intended to bring in a Bill to repeal the stamp duty, now withdrew his motion, agreeing with Hume that it made better tactical sense to amend a Ministerial Bill in committee than have the Ministers amend his. Spring Rice's Bill was introduced into the House on 15 March, and tied a reduction of the stamp duty to a more rigorous system of Stamp Office controls;[1] his Bill would take almost all of his projected budget surplus.

Place, who had for a long time feared just this move, tried to galvanize Grote, wrote and published three papers in March and April, supplied notes for Duncombe's and Wakley's speeches, tried in vain to stir Hume into active opposition, and in late April rallied the radicals into forming deputations to both Spring Rice and Melbourne to point out the evils of a penny stamp. Spring Rice told them that the House would never pass total repeal, that it was not his job to propose a measure he knew would be defeated, and that in any case his Bill gave all that Bulwer's motion of the previous year had asked for. 'The interview was characterized by a stronger display of feeling than on any former occasion. . . . Several of the members observed to each other that the object would only be accomplished by supporting an Unstamped press, since arguments, petitions and remonstrances were alike disregarded.'[2]

Spring Rice had finally decided to reduce the newspaper stamp to a penny, after six years of parliamentary debate.

[1] *True Sun*, 5 Apr. 1836; T. Wakley, *A Letter to the People of England; WPG*, 26 Mar. 1836.
[2] Add. MSS. 35150, f. 114, Place to Grote, n.d. (Mar. 1836); cutting in the *Place Coll.*, Set 70, f. 495.

Why now? The timing of his move seems to have been dictated by the success of the unstamped broadsheets. He admitted in Parliament that their circulation was enormous and their respectability undoubted. No longer could the Government argue that the Unstamped were so licentious that they must be suppressed in the national interest, nor that they were publicly abhorred, since their readership was far larger than that of the established stamped newspapers.[1] The Stamp Office policy of imprisoning vendors had been expensive, unpopular with the magistrates, and a failure. Worse, perhaps, radical members of Parliament were working closely with the proprietors of the Unstamped, and the subscription lists for Hetherington and Cleave had reached the dimensions traditionally reserved for national monuments. The Unstamped had always proclaimed that the law was unworkable. The Chancellor seemed at last to believe them. As Walter of *The Times* put it, the question was not whether the tax should be repealed but by whom it should be repealed, the 'Representatives of the People', or 'a secret junta, who had long been encouraging the people to set the Government and laws at defiance'. The law must catch up with its use.[2]

Given that the law must be changed, the Chancellor's choice of a penny stamp seems to have been dictated by two other sources, the stamped press and Charles Knight. His own Cabinet, according to Mill, were divided on the subject; Poulett Thomson, Melbourne, Russell, and Howick, Mill thought, favoured the total abolition of the duty, Lansdowne and Palmerston objected to it, but the ultimate decision lay with the Chancellor.[3] Individual proprietors of stamped newspapers had been urging a penny stamp on Spring Rice ever since the scare of a daily Unstamped the previous July. On 4 March 1836, 150 newspaper dealers held a meeting at the 'Crown and Anchor', and agreed that a penny stamp was preferable to any postal scheme in lieu of it. They presented a petition, and set up a committee to watch their interests.[4]

---

[1] *Hansard*, 3rd ser., xxxiv, col. 627 (20 June 1836). For their readership, see below, pp. 123–4.

[2] *Hansard*, 3rd ser., xxxiv, col. 660 (20 June 1836).

[3] Theta, 'Manifesto of the Chancellor of the Exchequer . . .', *Monthly Repository*, x (1836), pp. 259–60.　　　　　　　　　　　　[4] *The Times*, 5 Mar. 1836.

Provincial news-dealers did the same. Early in March the proprietors of the London stamped press came formally together. By the second week in May they had held ten general meetings at the Somerset Coffee House in the Strand, had 'several interviews with the Chancellor of the Exchequer', and had a committee, comprising Delane of *The Times*, Baldwin of the *Standard*, Young of the *Sun*, Westmacott (their chairman) of the *Age*, Anderson of the *Advertizer*, Stewart of the *Courier*, Stevens of the *Ledger*, and Shaw of the *Marklane Express*; that is, of six daily and three weekly papers. Proprietors of the daily *Herald*, *Post*, *Globe*, and *True Sun*, and fifteen weekly papers, attended most of the meetings: the notable absentees were the *Morning Chronicle*, the *Examiner*, and the *Spectator*. Beaumont of the *Radical* attended as a saboteur.[1]

Wakley had early suspected that the stamped press were manipulating Spring Rice, but he appreciated enough of their case to think that they would be entitled to compensation if the stamp was totally repealed. Roebuck, on the other hand, appeared to be waging a personal vendetta against the stamped press. Only Wakley, Roebuck (who was in bad health), and Place, among the middle-class radicals, continued to fight. Wakley entered the ring on 16 April 1836 with a *Letter to the People of England* denouncing the Bill; he urged, with the *True Sun*, that people should petition while there was still time. This *Letter* he turned into a six-week series of pamphlets, *A Voice from the Commons*, which he hoped would continue the pattern of Roebuck's *Pamphlets*. Like Roebuck, he claimed that each paper was separate and distinct, but Place told Hume that he thought the series was illegal, and the papers were stopped when their vendors ran into trouble.[2] Wakley complained that the 'gagging clauses' in the Bill were punitively stiff, and that the proposed penny stamp was there not because the Cabinet wanted it, but because the stamped press did. He quoted from the *Morning Advertiser* of 28 April 1836.

It is but right that the public should know that what have been termed the 'gagging clauses' in the Bill about to be considered

[1] *Radical*, 14 May 1836.
[2] Add. MSS. 35150, f. 118, Place to Hume, 10 Apr. 1836.

tomorrow, are not *clauses thought of, or proposed by the Chancellor of the Exchequer, but clauses suggested to and urged upon him by the whole of the metropolitan press,* with the solitary exceptions of the Morning Chronicle, Spectator and Examiner, and therefore if there be anything improper or unconstitutional in the clauses, the cause is *not* to be found in the right honourable gentleman to whom the financial concerns of the country are entrusted, but in the proprietors and editors of the existing newspapers, who have justly felt that they have been greatly injured and seriously robbed by the printing, publishing and smuggling of unstamped and illegal publications.

The *Morning Advertizer* repeated this statement on 11 May, and, according to Wakley, it was never contradicted.¹ The penny stamp, the stamped press argued, would lower the cost of their papers from 7*d.* to 5*d.*, and increase their sales and advertisements. A penny stamp would have the opposite effect on the present unstamped broadsheets; their proprietors would need considerable capital to cover the cost of the stamp, prices would have to go up from 2*d.* to 3½*d.* as a result, and this would put the papers beyond the pockets of most of their present readers. To a penny stamp must be tied controls stringent enough to prevent any new wave of unstamped papers; but a penny stamp, unlike the present fourpenny stamp, was too low to encourage 'smuggling'.² According to this argument, the stamped press had everything to gain and nothing to lose from a penny stamp.

Charles Knight was the other source of pressure on the Chancellor advocating a penny stamp. For most of the last six years he had objected to all the taxes on knowledge, though for himself he had preferred to stay within the pale of the law and diffuse knowledge, rather than flout the law. Until 1834 or so, the apparent success of the *Penny Magazine* seemed to justify this approach. But, as Matthew Hill had

¹ *Voice from the Commons*, 8, 22 May 1836. There is some confirmation of this in the Chancellor's remarks, *Hansard*, 3rd ser., xxxiv, col. 628, 20 June 1836. Harney subsequently explained the penny stamp in the same way, in his review of Hunt's *Fourth Estate*, *Red Rep.*, 19 Oct. 1850.

² See the complaints of the former Unstamped, e.g. *London Dispatch*, 17 Sept. 1836. The stamped press did quarrel amongst themselves over the proposed maximum size of a newsheet, 1,530 sq. in., which would benefit the Whig *Morning Chronicle*, the largest single sheet in London, but disadvantage *The Times* which used a smaller sheet but made up for it by frequently employing a double sheet. Under the Bill a double sheet would have to be doubly stamped.

confessed to the Commons, it was becoming increasingly clear that the *Penny Magazine* was not reaching the audience it was intended for; and from 1834 and the rise of the broadsheets, the *Penny Magazine* was being outpaced. William Hickson wrote to Place in July 1836, 'Charles Knight has been our greatest enemy. He told me that penny newspapers would interfere with the *Penny Magazine* and has (as you now see) published a pamphlet in favour of a penny stamp. He has I declare the ear of Spring Rice. Both of them should have their ears cut off.'[1] Knight himself gave three reasons in his *Memoirs* for preferring a penny stamp to the total repeal of the stamp duties, of which only the last is probably true. He said he feared first that 'cheap newspapers would involve the degradation of journalism'; secondly, that a penny postage in lieu of a penny stamp would destroy national papers and preserve the petty and local papers; and thirdly, that if the newspaper stamp were repealed he could not hope that the paper duty would be reduced. Knight seems to have been unfavourably impressed by the radicals' argument that what would be lost by a repeal of the newspaper stamp would be more than compensated for by a penny postage and the increased consumption of paper, stamped at threepence a pound. William Henry Ord, he wrote, was working on the Stamp Consolidation Bill.

In the spring of 1836, I frequently saw him. We had many conversations on the subject of the newspaper stamp duties and the paper duties. I fancied that if the government consented to abolish the newspaper stamp, they would retain the high Paper duty. Mr. Ord and I came to the conclusion that the safest and the best course would be to lower both imposts. I wrote a pamphlet advocating this policy, which was circulated amongst members of both Houses. Whether it had any effect upon the settlement of the question is not for me to judge. At any rate, the reduction of the Paper Duty was to me a matter of vital importance.[2]

Knight, after all, was the greatest producer of cheap books of his time. He also boasted that he met Russell, Spring Rice,

---

[1] *Hansard*, 3rd ser., xxiii, col. 1216 (22 May 1834); *Place. Coll.*, Set 70, f. 561, Hickson to Place, n.d.

[2] C. Knight, *Passages of a Working Life . . .*, 1864, vol. ii, pp. 250–1; p. 131; C. Knight, *The Newspaper Stamp and the Duty on Paper . . .*, 1836.

Althorp, Denman, and Parnell regularly at the monthly dinners of the Society for the Diffusion of Useful Knowledge.

Spring Rice introduced his Bill in the Commons on 15 March 1836, its second reading was moved on 11 April, and it went into committee on 20 June. Roebuck was absent from most of the debate because of his ill health; and only Wakley, together with certain of the tories (Goulburn, Sir Charles Knightley, and Trevor) consistently opposed the Bill, attempting to amend it or introduce hostile clauses to nullify its meaning. Wakley proposed a total repeal of the duties, the tories that the duty on soap should be repealed instead. The moderate tories stayed silent. After 15 March, Buller, Hume, and Grote spoke only once against the Bill, the other radicals not at all. It had its third reading on 25 July and passed by 55 votes to 7. Bowring and Warburton voted for it, while only Wakley and Perronet Thompson of the radicals voted against it. Hume, Roebuck, the Bulwers, Duncombe, Grote, Molesworth, and O'Connell did not vote at all.[1] Place was angry and disgusted. Those members of Parliament who had formed deputation after deputation, who had agreed among themselves that the last penny would be the worst penny, that the 'gagging clauses' were far too stiff, and that the aim of the Bill was to destroy cheap newspapers, those very members of Parliament had either voted for the measure or stayed at home. Place was going to cut himself off from all of them save Roebuck.

The parliamentary radicals had accepted as final Spring Rice's decision of 15 March. Place did not accept this as final even after the passing of the Bill by the Commons. For, when the Bill was taken to the Lords, the Tory leader Lyndhurst (who, two years before, had suggested to a jury that the *Guardian* was too paltry a thing to be a newspaper), asked Melbourne why he did not take off the final penny. Place wrote to Hume that 'means were privately used' to persuade the Cabinet to take off the penny stamp when the Bill was returned from the Lords, but that the Chancellor had refused to budge.[2] Hume, presumably, could not have been among those exerting pressure. The Bill became

---

[1] *Hansard*, 3rd ser., xxxv, cols. 566–8 (25 July 1836).
[2] Add. MSS. 35150, f. 134; 35150, f. 189, Place to Hume, 3 Jan. 1837.

effective on 15 September 1836. Even then Place did not give up; he told his numerous correspondents that the final penny could not last long. Hume, with belated concern, promised him that at the beginning of January 1837 he would give notice to the House that he would move 'the *total repeal of the laws against the Press*', as long as he could get Wakley out of the way. Place told Parkes three weeks later that it was now believed that Peel would agree to repeal the penny stamp and working men were forming deputations to him; if so, Place would 'shout at the top of my voice for the Tories'. Finally, in the middle of April 1837 Roebuck introduced a motion to set up a Committee to consider the propriety of repealing the penny stamp.[1]

This was the last of the debates of the decade on the newspaper stamps. Roebuck insisted that it was a matter of educating the poor, Wakley that it was an issue of trust between radicals and Whigs, and Hume pleaded with Peel to vote with them. Even Bulwer, who had welcomed a penny stamp, now confessed that there had been little improvement in the state of the press. Roebuck lost his motion by 81 votes to 42; Peel was in the same lobby as the Whigs. Ironically, for the first and last time all the radicals found themselves in one lobby objecting to the penny stamp. Six months before they had abstained from voting on it. Six months before that many of them had welcomed that penny. Place's six years of prophesying the seductiveness of a penny stamp had been well founded. Roebuck, Hume, and Perronet Thompson lost their seats in the summer general election, though Hume was back in the House by December 1837 by courtesy of O'Connell. And from this point the stamp-duty question for the working-class radicals became absorbed in the wider ends of the London Working Men's Association, and middle-class radical agitation turned increasingly to the issues of ballot and corn laws. But opposition to the penny stamp still remained a bond of sympathy between middle- and working-class radicals during the years of Chartism and its aftermath.

---

[1] Add. MSS. 35150, f. 207, Hume to Place, 5 Jan. 1837; f. 233, Place to Parkes, 27 Jan. 1837; f. 191, Place to Hume, 3 Jan. 1837; *Hansard*, 3rd ser., xxxvii, col. 1162 (13 Apr. 1837).

If the reduction of the stamp duty was due to the success of the Unstamped in flouting the law, as Spring Rice and the middle-class radicals themselves admitted, then what had the middle-class parliamentary and extra-parliamentary campaigns managed to achieve? They had kept up a continuous pressure on the Front Bench, yet, at the beginning of six years of agitation, the Chancellor was already closer to reducing the duties than at any time again until the spring of 1836. The radicals had aroused public opinion, yet the Ministers, particularly Spring Rice, never suggested that they felt they had to respond to it. The radicals had rehearsed yet again all the arguments for educating a people that possessed the vote and lived under the laws—arguments that were repeated in debates over national schools, public libraries, and mechanics institutes—yet the Whig Front Bench were already professed adherents of such views, and the only possible convert could have been Peel. Although few of the middle-class radicals would have agreed, perhaps their greatest success was to create a more sympathetic and tolerant climate towards the Unstamped, their street sellers, and their proprietors. By questions in Parliament, private lobbying, public petitions, platform speeches, and articles in the Reviews, the middle-class radicals made sure that no one forgot the number of street sellers who were imprisoned for a crime created by law, the selective and arbitrary prosecutions brought by the Stamp Office, or the punitive fines and illegal seizures suffered by Hetherington and Cleave. When, from the spring of 1835 middle-class radicals, in and out of Parliament, began openly to identify themselves with the working-class agitation, they created a public opinion too tolerant of the Unstamped for the Government to be able to suppress them. In Nottingham in the spring of 1836, for example, not one person in a population of 40,000 could be found to testify against the leading agent of the Unstamped; two or three years earlier, the Stamp Office would have had no such difficulty. As a result the stamp duty was reduced.

SECTION TWO

THE UNSTAMPED PRESS

GENTLEMEN OF THE BENCH—I appear at your request, to state to you why I took upon myself to break what you are pleased to call the law. I was induced to publish the *Voice of the West Riding,* because a paper was wanted to support the rights and interests of the order and class to which it is my pride to belong, it being notorious that their just privileges were not only left unadvocated, but absolutely denied. The object of the paper was to teach the productive classes the means by which they might extricate themselves from their degraded state of thraldom, and place society upon a basis where every individual member of the social brotherhood should enjoy his just rights and no more. Its object was also the exposure and reformation of local as well as national abuse. To drag the tyrant and hypocrite from their den of infamy, and to show up the hideous monsters to the gaze and virtuous indignation of every good man in the community—to teach the sanctified knaves they could not with impunity practise those vices which they affect so loudly to condemn—to learn the oppressors of the poor that though they might for a time pass unnoticed, and be allowed to practise their unholy deeds unmolested, yet there was a point which they could not pass, when the Argus eyes of the great moral corrector should be directed upon them, and every movement and action of their lives watched and noted for adoption by others if virtuous, or rejection if vicious. I contend, further, that the printing and publishing such a paper, is not a violation of any moral principle, but, on the contrary, one of the most virtuous actions that man can do, that of doing good to his species.

The speech of Joshua Hobson of Huddersfield, 6 August 1833, reported in *Man,* 18 August 1833

INTRODUCTION

BETWEEN 1830 and 1836 several hundred unstamped papers were floated. There was nothing new about working-class papers as such, for in the years around 1819 Cobbett, Carlile, Wooler, Davidson, and Wade had dedicated their papers to 'the ragged Radicals', had lectured them on their miseries, their interests, and their political rights, and had attempted to project this sort of knowledge 'into every village, hamlet and workshop in the kingdom'.[1]

This New Move had come in November 1816, when Cobbett reprinted his leading articles from his shilling-halfpenny *Register* as a series of twopenny Addresses, his 'trash' for working men. The first, an *Address to Journeymen and Labourers*, said what Cobbett had always said, at least in recent years, that the people's wrongs were the other side of borough-mongering privilege, and that taxes were the warp and weft of Old Corruption. What was new was the price. Working men could now buy the *Register* and not merely read it at the publican's pleasure. The *Address*, Cobbett said, proceeded to occupy 'the conversation of three-quarters of all the active men in the kingdom. The labouring classes seemed, as if they had never heard a word on politics before . . .'.[2] Within a fortnight he had sold 20,000 copies, within a year 200,000 copies of the first *Address*. And sales of the *Twopenny Trash* settled down at 20,000–30,000 weekly.

Almost immediately, Cobbett was opposed. Established booksellers were reluctant to handle papers that were both radical and cheap. Magistrates quickly put pressure on publicans, news-vendors, and hawkers to check its sales. And the Government determined to write Cobbett down and so financed various small Establishment pamphlets, though without much success.[3] In spring 1817, after a winter of radical pamphlets, Spenceans and Spa Fields, and

---

[1] *Medusa*, 11 Dec. 1819, 1 Jan. 1820; *Gorgon*, 16 Jan. 1819.
[2] *Pol. Reg.* 2, 16 Nov., 2 Aug. 1817.   [3] See below, p. 136.

Hampden Club conventions, the Government suspended habeas corpus, and Cobbett fled the country.

Meanwhile, Thomas Wooler, a London printer, had started the *Black Dwarf* in January 1817, and in it he detailed Major Cartwright's schemes for constitutional reform, reprinted Bentham, criticized the Spenceans for their plotting, Cobbett for his flight, and praised the newly formed discussion-circles of Political Protestants as the soundest way of spreading knowledge. In May 1818 John Wade's *Gorgon* joined the *Dwarf* in denouncing oppression and high taxes, and in 1819 Thomas Davidson's *Medusa*, James Griffin's *Cap of Liberty*, and Carlile's *Republican* (formerly Sherwin's *Register*) went out to do battle with borough-mongering. Together, these papers formulated the attack on Old Corruption, naming it, placing it, and putting it on public view.[1]

These papers, if they contained nothing seditious, could be sold by established booksellers. The *Gorgon*, the *Cap*, and *Medusa* circulated mainly in London and Manchester; the *Dwarf*, the *Republican*, and the *Register* broke through to a national circulation. The *Dwarf* relied on orthodox outlets, but Cobbett and Carlile encouraged their readers to take sales into their own hands. Cobbett showed that a thousand *Registers* would bring in a profit of nearly £3 a week to their retailer, and he offered free posters for display. Carlile, on acquiring Sherwin's *Register* set about establishing a network of outlets. 'I want agents that will go round the country in their neighbourhood, to the extent of ten or a dozen miles, and plant the scions of liberty and sound principles with a bold masterful hand: bidding defiance to persecution . . .', and he asked that sympathizers should buy and sell his papers rather than send him money.[2]

Holmes, Carlile's Sheffield agent, showed how a career could develop within the world of the radical press. As one of Carlile's shopmen he was imprisoned in 1822. On his

---

[1] For their ideology, see below, pp. 204–6; for comments on Carlile's business organization, see below pp. 128; 135. W. Wickwar, *The Struggle for the Freedom of the Press*, 1929, is a study of the radical press of 1819. E. P. Thompson, op. cit., has much fascinating material on it.

[2] *Rep.*, 13 June 1823; see also *Pol. Reg.*, 16 Nov. 1816; *Rep.*, 17 Sept. 1819, 29 Dec. 1820, 4 Jan. 1822; Carlile MSS., Carlile to Turton, 23 June 1823.

release Carlile persuaded him to go to Sheffield in 1824, where he was set up as a news-vendor by some of Carlile's friends. He sold the papers part-time, hawking them at local fairs, while he worked as a shoemaker, and gradually enlarged his area. He added books, newspapers, roasted corn, and steel knives to his stock. In nine months he had started negotiating for a wooden press, had hired a journey-man compositor to teach him, and added printing to his skills.[1]

Despite their efforts, distribution remained a problem. The agents on whom Carlile and Cobbett had to rely were often untrustworthy and failed, for example, to send money back to London. Vendors, where they could be found, hesitated to sell cheap papers when the customary 25 per cent retail margin brought in such a low rate of profit. For this reason, the *Gorgon* had to push its price up from 1*d.* to 1½*d.* in order to keep its retailers. Printers and stationers were unwilling to extend much credit to publishers so obviously on the financial borderline. As Carlile was in prison for most of the 1820s, his organization remained haphazard, and he had to close the *Republican*, temporarily in 1821, and finally in 1826, partly because he lacked vendors and country outlets, and could not tour the country to find them. Even Cobbett's distribution system became so erratic in the 1820s, that villages went unsupplied, towns received copies a fortnight old, and parcels got lost in their travels. So in 1827 he turned his sixpenny pamphlet into a sevenpenny newspaper, so that he could send the *Register* through the post instead of by coach parcel.[2]

Until the summer of 1819 there was nothing systematic about the repression of these papers. But a few months after Peterloo the Government passed the Six Acts and brought cheap radical papers within the scope of the law.

Two clauses of the Six Acts affected the radical press. The first was 60 G3 c9, which tightened up the definition of a newspaper. This meant that radical papers had either to conform to the requirements of a newspaper, carry a fourpenny stamp, and, like *The Times*, retail at sevenpence,

---

[1] Carlile MSS. Carlile to Holmes, 1, 16 Jan., 24 Aug., 6 Oct. 1824, 14 June 1825.
[2] *Pol. Reg.*, 1 Dec. 1827.

or conform to the requirements of a pamphlet, and appear only monthly, at an enlarged size or at a price above six-pence. Only the *Black Dwarf*, the *Republican*, and the *Register* survived the Six Acts, and they all turned pamphlet and doubled their price. The Queen's Affair helped the *Dwarf* to linger on till 1824, the *Republican*, selling at under a thousand copies lasted until 1826, and Cobbett's *Register*, which became a newspaper in 1827, died with him in 1835.

Secondly, the Six Acts tightened up the definition of, and penalties for, criminal libel—that is, writing which was likely to cause a breach of the peace. To abuse established institutions could be construed as criminal libel, if a jury so wished. It was in defiance of this clause of the Six Acts, and for selling Paine, Palmer, and certain dubious issues of the *Republican*, that Carlile was imprisoned in November 1819. The sales of the *Republican* thereupon reached their all time high of 15,000. The following year six of his shop-men, and his wife, were imprisoned; and they were followed in 1821 by his sister, in 1822 by another four shopmen, and in 1823 by three shopmen (whose charges were brought at the instance of the Society for the Suppression of Vice). A final eight shopmen were imprisoned in 1824. Carlile's own fines were eventually remitted in 1825.[1]

Carlile was supported by popular subscription, his shop-men were supported by Carlile. During the 1820s Carlile received several thousand pounds in relief. For a few years after Peterloo, relief funds were set up in the larger towns, Manchester, Birmingham, and Nottingham, to aid all political prisoners, including radical publishers, and to spread subscriptions more evenly and systematically. But these funds dried up in 1823, as they became increasingly diverted to Hunt's Great Northern Union, and subscriptions became very much more sporadic.[2]

In many ways, therefore, the working-class press of 1819 and that of 1832 had the same problems. They both faced difficulties of organization and distribution; they were both concerned with the rights and dignity of working men. Yet in two important ways these papers differed.

---

[1] For details of all these cases, see W. Wickwar, op. cit.
[2] See below, pp. 194–5.

The papers of 1819 were legal; those of 1832 were not. Where the publishers of 1819 supplemented established outlets with their own, the publishers of 1832 had to rely entirely on their own unorthodox agencies. Though the papers of 1819 might be burked, they were not illegal until a jury pronounced them seditious. The papers of 1832 were illegal unstamped penny newspapers, within the meaning and the range of the Six Acts.

The second difference between 1819 and 1832 was one of location. At both times, if a radical paper was to survive it had to be published in London, and then be fanned out to the provinces. In 1819 the strength of the reform movement was largely provincial; in 1832 London had its own working-class radicalism organized around the National Union of the Working Classes. The Hampden clubs of 1816, the Political Protestants of 1818, the Great Northern Union of 1821 were all based on the provinces. Most of Carlile's sales, shopmen, and subscriptions were provincial. London possessed only the Westminster Committee on the one hand (which was about as relevant to working-class radicalism as was the National Political Union in 1832, and for the same reasons), and the Spenceans, with their airy conspiracies, on the other. London journalists in 1819 were not rooted in London working-class radicalism, they had not come from a background of trade union activity, and for many of them radical journalism was their first—and their last—plunge into radical politics. As a result, Carlile, Davidson, Griffin, and even Wooler, were the theoreticians and not the leaders of an increasingly articulate working class. What national reform movement there was gained dimension, much of its language, and some of its direction from the radical press of 1819; but these papers did not themselves lead a working class into battle. They stood on the side-lines and passed comment.

Each paper was a separate piece of journalism. There was no sense of a common crusade. Only Carlile's struggle against the law of criminal libel had something of the nature of a political movement about it, and even that was a highly individualistic piece of protest. His writings, indeed, attacking universal kingcraft, priestcraft, and lordcraft were almost independent of time, place, and politics. O'Brien in 1832 was just as willing as Carlile to theorize, but O'Brien worked outwards from the here-and-now of radical struggles in the parish of Marylebone, in the Manchester mill, in the west of England woollen village. Carlile, slashing away at his priestly phantoms in prison, lacked O'Brien's sense of the concrete. There is a gap between the roots and the writings of radicalism in the years around 1819, that was closed in 1832, because the writers and publishers of 1832 were politically engaged in London radicalism in a way foreign to the earlier generation of writers.

By the end of 1826 the pamphlet literature of the years around 1819 had died away; and with them collapsed the network of radical agencies and provincial relief funds which had sustained them since Peterloo. When Carlile came to start the *Prompter* in 1830, he had to start again from scratch.

If a paper was not a pamphlet, registered as such at the Stamp Office, it had, by law, to carry the fourpenny newspaper stamp. The *Trades Newspaper*, started in 1825 to consolidate the position of the unions after the repeal of the Combination Acts, was a stamped but working-class newspaper, perhaps the first 'newspaper of their own', to put 'the views, the interests and the wishes of the working part of the community'.[1] It was financed by joint stock, controlled by a committee of the London trades (including metal workers, silkweavers, hatters, carpenters, sawyers, and shipwrights), inspired by John Gast, leader of the shipwrights, and for its first six months edited by Robertson, editor of the *Mechanics Magazine*. In 1828, with a circulation well under a thousand, it merged with the *London Free Press*, to become the *Weekly Free Press*, and William Carpenter, one of the first to put out an unstamped newspaper in 1830, became its editor. The *Trades Newspaper* was a working-class trades union newspaper. The new *Weekly Free Press* was a co-operative and less strictly working-class newspaper. From 1829 it carried increasingly full reports of the British Association for the Promotion of Co-operative Knowledge, whose members, Lovett,

[1] *Trades Newspaper*, 17 July 1825, 29 July 1827.

Hetherington, Watson, Hibbert, and Petrie, were to become leaders of the National Union of the Working Classes and the Unstamped.

The *Trades Newspaper* was one working-class paper which spanned the years between 1825 and 1830. It was both legal and stamped—and expensive. It seldom sold above a thousand copies, and most of its sales were confined to London. The second type of working-class periodical during these years was legal but unstamped—namely the co-operative and the mechanics-institutes' magazines, selling for upwards of a penny. The London *Mechanics Magazine* was one of these. Originally a useful-knowledge type of review, it was from 1824 the organ of the London Mechanics' Institute, which had been founded in the early part of that year. It was edited by Robertson and Thomas Hodgskin, and the result did not always please Lord Brougham. So like the *Gorgon* before it, and the *Trades Newspaper* after it, less orthodox sentiments on political economy gave way to the more orthodox. All three ideological shifts seem to have owed something to the hidden hand of Francis Place. If so, Place failed to get an adequate grip on the *Mechanics Magazine*, forced it into the role of critic of the London Mechanics Institute, and displaced it as the official voice of the Institute by the *London Mechanics Register*.

More important than either the *Trades Newspaper* or the *Mechanics Magazine* were the co-operative periodicals. Dr. King started his *Brighton Co-operator* in May 1828, and brought back into penny journalism some of the vigour and polemic of Cobbett's *Twopenny Trash* of 1816 and 1817.[1] The first London Co-operative Trading Society launched the *Associate* six months later, and this was followed by a small army of co-operative chronicles, magazines, and miscellanies in the midlands and north. Together they encouraged working men to see themselves as the wealth producers, the industrious classes, the stamina of society; and to found and support trading schemes so that the labourer might retain the produce of his labour.

Like the papers of 1819 and 1832, the co-operative magazines were papers for working men which were often

[1] See below, p. 216.

by working men. But in other ways they were very different. At no point were they illegal: they never crossed the legal rubicons between social criticism and sedition, or between pamphlet and newspaper. They were not prosecuted. The co-operative magazines span the late 1820s, but in no manner do they bridge them. They did not carry forward the analyses of 1819. Competition was not an additional feature of Old Corruption; it was a total and alternative theory. The vote might well be desirable, if only for the sake of dignity, but it was not exactly necessary. Political radicalism was to be rediscovered for the press in late 1830; the ideology of the Unstamped, as well as its distribution and support, had to be built up anew. Finally, the co-operative magazines, unlike the papers of 1819 or 1832, and unlike the *Trades Newspaper*, were essentially local, provincial, and limited. They were no part of London journalism; they did not lead a national reform movement. They may well have created the *Guardian*'s readers for it, but they did not attempt to do what the *Guardian* did—create a unified working class.

From 1826, therefore, there had been a thin trickle of working-class writing which, by 1829, was mainly co-operative. The one exception—and in terms of sales not a very signal exception—was Carlile's *Lion*, which he launched in 1828 as a pamphlet in the tradition of the *Republican*. Most of its writing was theological, much of it eulogizing the Revd. Robert Taylor, though it carried occasional and acid reports of the British Association for the Promotion of Co-operative Knowledge and the Radical Reform Association (RRA). Carlile closed the *Lion* in 1829. For five years or so the press laws had been respected by working-class radicals.

The BAPCK and the RRA had both emerged in 1829 as the most important of the working-class associations which foreshadowed the National Union of the Working Classes and shaped the working-class reform movement in London. The RRA had developed out of the Civil and Religious Liberty Association of Irish and English radicals pressing for Catholic emancipation, and survived under Hunt's patronage until the spring of 1831, when its members came over into the NUWC. Its leaders, Hetherington, Lovett, Watson, Cleave, Hibbert, and Warden also belonged to the BAPCK which had grown out of the First London Cooperative Society of the mid 1820s, in an attempt to provide intellectual and practical headquarters to the mushrooming co-operative movement. Like the RRA, the BAPCK folded up in the summer of 1831, torn between the more political and the more Owenite of its members. Before it did so, however, Hetherington, Warden, and Foskett had, under BAPCK auspices, encouraged an embryro trade and benefit society of carpenters to expand, first into a general union of all trade and benefit societies, and then into a political union of RRA radicals, Irish, co-operators, and the more middle-class radicals of parish politics. The whole was the NUWC.

Both the BAPCK and the RRA found that without outlets in the press their influence was limited to London, and that the *Weekly Free Press*, the one sympathetic radical paper, was too expensive to be efficient. Carlile had meanwhile been fretting, in the later issues of the *Republican* and the *Lion*, that he could not print the sort of news and commentary, classed as 'intelligence', that his readers wanted. So at the beginning of 1830 he decided to test 'the real state of liberty of the press in this country'. He would publish a *Journal*. But the Stamp Office warned him that any pamphlet which served the functions of a newspaper would be prosecuted, so he withdrew.[1] Three months later John Doherty's National Association for the Protection of Labour published the Lancashire *United Trades Co-operative Journal*. Unlike the orthodox co-operative magazines, this one carried news and comments on news, as well as harmless exhortations to knowledge and to unity. The Government, afraid that the paper was stirring up labour unrest, suppressed the *Journal* in July, while allowing other less-offensive co-operative journals to circulate without trouble.[2]

Carpenter, who was by now no longer the editor of the old *Trades Newspaper*, was sufficiently angry at this piece of selective repression, and sufficiently unemployed, to

---

[1] *Carlile's Journal for 1830*, 2 Jan.: Letter to J. Timm; 16 Jan.: Liberty of the Press.

[2] HO 40/27, 3 July 1830; Carpenter's *Pol. Letters*, 14 May 1831.

decide to try the law and aid the cause by issuing a series of fourpenny *Political Letters*, ostensibly independent of each other. Both the RRA and the BAPCK could supply him with news and with sales. And he encouraged Hetherington to bring out a series of more-or-less daily *Penny Papers*. These were launched in October 1830, and in November Carlile published the *Prompter*. They had started the Un-stamped, and a New Move in radical journalism.

All three men, together with William Cobbett, were prosecuted, Carpenter in the October, Carlile in the November, Cobbett in December, and Hetherington in the following June. Carlile and Cobbett were prosecuted for the old offence of seditious libel, Carpenter and Hetherington for the new offence of publishing an unstamped newspaper.

The proprietors of the Unstamped soon found that the regular news-vendors would not sell papers for which they might be brought to court, so they were forced to develop their own outlet, the London street vendors. The expansion of the Unstamped went hand in hand with the growth of the NUWC, which had been formally established in May 1831, and both with the Reform crisis. In the summer of 1831 Russell introduced the second Reform Bill; the *Radical* entered the battlefield and Hetherington's *Penny Papers*, still edited by Thomas Mayhew, became the *Poor Man's Guardian*, the most powerful and the longest-lived of the Unstamped. At the same time, the Unstamped began to be fanned out into the provinces where they were handled by a newly established network of country agents and bought and studied by a network of newly formed political unions on the model of the NUWC. In London, Lovett and Hibbert cajoled the NUWC into setting up a Victim Fund to aid all vendors and publishers of the pauper press.

Every major prosecution brought its NUWC meeting, its petition, its subscriptions, and its letters from country readers. As the Reform crisis mounted in the autumn of 1831, with the rejection of the Reform Bill by the Lords, the prorogation of Parliament, and the formation of Place's National Political Union, so sales of the Unstamped rose, the number of country agents increased and with them the

regional coverage of the Unstamped. By the spring of
1832 the Reform crisis was coming to a head, culminating
in the Days of May. A handful of new papers had been
launched, including the *Slap at the Church*, *Figaro*, *Crisis*,
and the vendors' *Cosmopolite*. Arrests of vendors were at
their height, sales of the *Guardian* stayed steady at over
16,000 copies a week, and the NUWC membership had
doubled to some 2,000.

For eighteen months the leading Unstamped held this
level; at the end of 1832 they were joined by the *Working
Man's Friend*, the *Destructive*, and the *Gauntlet*; and in
July 1833 by the *Man*. The struggle over the Irish Coercion
Bill replaced the Reform struggle in keeping up sales. But
from the summer of 1833, sales fell slowly away, as the
Irish crisis ended. The NUWC collapsed, the Victim Fund
dried up, and government prosecutions for a time stopped.
Co-operative and trades union news replaced reports of
NUWC class meetings in the columns of the Unstamped,
but that too came to an end with the smashing of the unions
during 1834.

The final blow to the small penny papers was a develop-
ment within the trade of the Unstamped itself. The quarto
Unstamped were systematically replaced by unstamped
broadsheets, the size of *The Times*, headed by the *Twopenny
Dispatch*, the *Weekly Police Gazette*, and the *People's
Hue and Cry*. By 1836 they included the *New Weekly
True Sun*, the *Weekly Herald*, and the *Police Register*.
Journals of opinion had given way to popular newspapers,
which now came increasingly into competition with the
stamped press. Where a reasonable circulation for a quarto
Unstamped had been 5,000 or so, the broadsheets circulated
at 15,000 to 20,000, outselling the stamped press. The
quarto Unstamped had been sold on the streets. The broadsheet Unstamped were sold from the shops of working-
class radicals, for they had became a 'respectable' trade. The
Government accordingly changed its forms of attack. It
prosecuted every proprietor, and in August 1835 tried to
ruin Hetherington's and Cleave's businesses by impounding
their presses; but it stopped making martyrs of the street
sellers. Instead, the police office runners were empowered

to seize bundles of the Unstamped as they were taken from printer to publisher to shopman. But the trade was too profitable, too well organized, and had too much public support to be suppressed. Middle- and working-class radicals were openly collaborating in a mass agitation against the stamp duties. In September 1836 the fourpenny stamp was reduced to a penny.

The Unstamped had to fulfil four functions, and the following chapters will examine each of them in turn. First, the Unstamped served as newspapers, and they had to succeed by the customary canons of the trade. They had to circulate, show profit, provide attractive material, and out-pace their rivals, especially the middle-class *Penny Magazine* (Chapter IV). Secondly, the Unstamped were not only newspapers: they were illegal newspapers. Their publishers had to avoid informers and police, find compliant printers and cloak them in pseudonyms, recruit and support vendors, and find glory as well as profit in martyrdom (Chapter V). Thirdly, the leading Unstamped, the *Guardian* and *Destructive*, *Man*, and the *Gauntlet* were avowedly didactic, preaching the right of the working man to the vote and to the products of his labour. Some of the Unstamped reiterated strands of social and political criticism formulated a decade before. O'Brien and Carpenter developed a systematic critique of the established order and its magic circle of law, property, and economic power, which deliberately confronted many of the premisses of the middle-class political economists (Chapters VI and VII). Finally, the Unstamped was the voice of London working-class movements. At a time when the Corresponding Societies Act was still in force, the Unstamped (especially the *Guardian*) attempted to tie together the various working-class threads: political radicalism, unionism, co-operation, and parochial reform, and to act as a medium of information and as a call to action (Chapter VIII).

IV

ORGANIZATION

I F the Unstamped were to mould opinion, they had to
sell. Most of the difficulties arose because the papers
were illegal, but some of the problems were more technical and due to the structure of the trade. Any paper,
stamped or unstamped, needed editors, capital, presses, and
offices. Any paper would have to show enough profit to
survive. Any paper would have to build up a stable circulation and, if it wanted national influence, penetrate into the
provinces and extend its sales. Any paper would need to
outpace its competitors and hold a loyal readership. The
toughest problem of all these was undoubtedly distribution,
for newspapers, unlike books, dated quickly. The eighteenth-
century travelling newsman had been supplemented in the
early nineteenth century by coach routes and coach parcels;
but the breakthrough in distribution did not come until the
late 1830s, when the railways cut the news lag between
London and the provinces from four days to twelve hours,
and the costs of distribution down by 80 per cent. Only
then was a daily radical or provincial press feasible.[1]

Problems of finance, sales, and circulation were complicated for the Unstamped because they were illegal—an
entirely new network of agencies had to be built up, for
example, because established booksellers would not handle
the Unstamped—but for the most part they were problems
common to the newspaper trade, to *The Times*, the *Leeds
Mercury*, and the *Penny Magazine*, as well as to the *Poor
Man's Guardian*.

The provincial press shared just these problems of the
trade. They too were bedevilled by a lack of ready money
(since most of their readers were subscribers), found it
difficult to circulate their papers outside their home town

---

[1] G. Cranfield, op. cit., pp. 192–3; *S.C. on Newspaper, Stamps* 1851, qus. 2595,
2598 (evidence of Abel Heywood), qus. 2813, 2820 (evidence of W. H. Smith).

and into villages off the coach routes, were restricted by the low literacy rates of rural areas, and shadowed by fears of libel and sedition. For the same reasons as the Unstamped, the provincial press had to remain a weekly press. And like the Unstamped the provincial press deliberately educated its readers into a public opinion on issues of national importance. Both saw their task as political education.[1] The parallels between the two are striking, but perhaps hardly surprising. For the pauper press *was* a provincial press, catering intellectually if not geographically for a class of reader beyond the impact of the London stamped press.

A working-class press, almost by definition, found its trade problems aggravated. Wooler's, Cobbett's, and Carlile's papers, though registered as pamphlets with the Stamp Office, were burked and bothered. Similarly, when O'Brien started the *Southern Star* in 1840, the Stamp Office refused his sureties and he found it difficult to arrange regular printing and distributing. In the 1850s, Harney found that printers refused to touch a paper with the title of *Red Republican*, and newsagents refused to sell it. In many country towns he could not find a single agent for it.[2]

In the 1830s, the Unstamped faced greater problems than did either the radical papers of 1819 or the Chartist papers of 1840. None the less, they survived, they sold, they circulated, and, immodestly, they boasted of their success.

(a) DISTRIBUTION

Between 1830 and 1836 there were several hundred Unstamped, most of them lasting only a month or two. They included literary papers, co-operative journals, Christian magazines, and crime reporters, as well as the seventy-odd radical papers which, as a class, were prosecuted. Some two-thirds of these radical Unstamped were put out by half a dozen men in London. From 1831 these papers began to find their way into the provinces, and from 1832 some of them could boast of a national readership. Many other large towns produced 'safe' Unstamped, containing Useful

---

[1] D. Read, op. cit., pp. 205–7; *PMG*, 9 July, 24 Sept. 1831, among a host of references.
[2] *Southern Star*, 9 Feb. 1840; *Red Rep.*, 10, 31 Aug. 1850.

Knowledge, whose circulation was confined to the home town; Manchester, Leeds, Birmingham, Liverpool, and Glasgow produced radical Unstamped similar to those prosecuted in London. Their appeal and most of their coverage were local, however, and their circulation confined to neighbouring towns. Joshua Hobson, later publisher of the *Northern Star*, put out his *Voice of the West Riding* in the summer of 1833, and it survived until April 1834, but sold only in Huddersfield, Bradford, Leeds, Halifax, and Barnsley. Doherty of the National Association for the Protection of Labour produced a succession of working-class papers in Manchester, the *United Trades Co-operative Journal* in 1830, the *Voice of the People* in 1831, the *Poor Man's Advocate* in 1832, and the *Herald of the Rights of Industry* in 1834. In September 1831 he tried to shift the *Voice of the People* to London, for, he said, no country paper could attract enough advertisements, it lacked general news, and, above all, it could not reach other provincial towns before its news was stale. So sales stuck at 2,000 or 3,000 a week.[1] The one local paper to break through into a national circulation, the *Pioneer*, was printed both in Birmingham and in London, and it drew on the well-established London network of agencies.

London news-vendors and booksellers early refused to sell Hetherington's *Penny Papers*. Readers complained they could not persuade any news-vendor to take their order. Carpenter's fourpenny *Letters* had better success at first, but when the Attorney-General announced his prosecution, Carpenter found that the stamped press refused his advertisements, police pulled down his placards, and strangers were sent to newsagents to 'persuade' them not to sell his papers. In Manchester, too, Doherty found that the 'threats and contrivances of the cotton lords, parsons, lawyers, and other "professional" men' frightened away all but four of the booksellers of the *Advocate*.[2] By default, then, the

---

[1] *Voice of the People*, 24 Sept. 1831. See also *Chambers Edinburgh Journal*, 28 Apr., 16 June 1832, for similar complaints. Chambers met the problem by printing both in London and in Edinburgh.

[2] *Penny Papers*, 6 Oct., 10, 23 Nov. 1830; *Pol. Letters*, 29 Oct. 1830; *Poor Man's Advocate*, 28 Apr. 1832. See also *Red Rep.*, 31 Aug. 1850. Thomas Cooper adopted similar methods and vastly improved the sales of his *Illuminator* when 'men, who had no work, took it into the villages'. *Life of Thomas Cooper*, 1872, p. 148.

Unstamped had to develop its own outlets and recruit its own sellers, the street vendors, to supplement the shops of the proprietors.

At first the Unstamped were confined to London. However, James Watson, a Huddersfield man who had come to London as one of Carlile's shopmen in 1824, early in 1830 visited the West Riding woollen towns as a missionary of the British Association for the Promotion of Co-operative Knowledge. And from November 1830 he sent them the halfpenny fly-sheets that Hetherington and Carpenter published to advertize their papers. Popay, the police spy, found out from Baume, the proprietor of the radical Optimist Chapel, that they cleared a considerable profit for 'many Thousands are sent Weekly to the Largest Towns in most parts of the North of England by Watson'.[1] The breakthrough in distribution came in May 1831, when a paragraph appeared in the *Guardian*: 'We have hitherto confined our papers to the metropolis itself, but arrangments are making [*sic*] for circulating them in the country, *when* we hope to have the whole of the working classes under our *guardianship*. . . .'[2] The NUWC had been founded the previous month and there were now two reasons for formalizing this provincial circulation of the Unstamped. The Unstamped would both co-ordinate and be a medium of communication between the political unions; and they in turn would be a captive readership for the Unstamped.[3] From July to September 1831, and again in April and November 1832 and January 1833, Hetherington toured the north, avoiding Bow Street runners in pursuit of him, speaking at working-class meetings and founding agencies for the *Guardian* and branches of the NUWC impartially. He told a Coventry audience, for example, to join the NU, sell the *Guardian* and 'remain firm for universal suffrage'.[4] Carlile, Cleave, Doherty, and James Morrison of the *Pioneer* copied his methods and used his agents.

By 1832 this network was established. Hetherington had agencies in Yeovil, Bath, and Bristol, along the south coast centred on Brighton, in the midlands belt stretching from

---

[1] HO 64/11, 13 Nov. 1830.   [2] *PMG*, 13 May 1831.
[3] See below, p. 269.   [4] *PMG*, 30 July 1831.

Worcester up to King's Lynn, in Lancashire and the woollen towns of Yorkshire, and finally in Newcastle, serving the north-east. A late agency was established in Newport, but Wales, the south-west, Cambridge, Suffolk, and the north were thinly served.[1] While Lee, the printer-proprietor of the *Man*, used Hetherington's agents, Carlile, where possible, used different agents in the same towns. The *Penny Magazine* had much the same pattern, since it followed the large towns—though it was stronger in the west country, and of course was sold by regular news-vendors. Like the Unstamped, the SDUK sent out its missionaries to broaden the basis of its sales.[2]

Rural apathy worried the London proprietors. Part of it was due to the bad communications which had inhibited Cobbett's sales five years before; still more was due to the lower level of literacy in the country; but some of it was also due to the non-political cast of mind with which Chartist missionaries had to battle in the 1840s.[3] 'The agricultural districts more especially require the attention of those who are wishful to extend the benefits of intellectual improvement among the destitute labourers', wrote Watson, and he and Lee (like Harney nearly twenty years later), recommended that readers should send extra copies to their country friends. Lovett, campaigning for two causes at once with his usual economy, told readers of the *Guardian* that he spent the money saved by temperance on sending out copies of the Unstamped to Land's End. The cost of a glass of gin a day would cover the *Weekly True Sun*, the *Guardian*, the *Working Man's Friend*, the *Destructive*, the *Crisis*, Paine's Political Works, Owen's Lectures 'and seven shillings to the Victim Fund'.[4] Other and more colourful suggestions were made at NUWC meetings for publicizing the

---

[1] See map (facing p. 336). The map only *indicates* distribution; it may have been far wider, as only a few letters were published in the Unstamped. The *Penny Magazine*'s coverage was probably more thorough than the map suggests, as it printed only the lists of its agents, and carried no subscriptions, correspondence, or local news to fill in this organizational skeleton. It would be rash to compare the patterns of distribution on such sketchy evidence. See also below, pp. 119–20.

[2] See below, p. 138.

[3] *Pol. Reg.*, 1 Dec. 1827; *Hansard*, 3rd ser., xiii (Bulwer, 15 June 1832); *NS*, 23, 30 Apr. 1842; *Weekly Record*, 25 Oct. 1856.

[4] *WMF*, 3 Aug. 1833; *Man*, 25 Aug. 1833; *FP*, 29 Mar. 1851; *PMG*, 23 Feb. 1833.

Unstamped in London. Plummer told members that they should march in procession with the *Guardian* in their hands. Mee would have the National Union visit the West End promenades with their families on a Sunday, carrying the Unstamped, and thus defying Agnew and their 'tyrants' simultaneously.[1]

The provincial agents recruited for the Unstamped were men for the most part new to journalism. They were brought into the trade by a flying visit from a London publisher, or urged on by their local political union.[2] Occasionally, someone was sent out from London to open up an agency. Holmes was sent to Sheffield in 1824; two vendors, Hancock and Pilgrim, went into the country; George Baker, one of Carlile's shopmen, went to Worcester; the Wastneys were encouraged to move from Sheffield to open an agency in Newcastle, and when they were imprisoned, David France, another of Carlile's shopmen, took their place. David France, in turn, was the brother-in-law of the Bolton agent. One of Carlile's sons went down to the west country, and when a Plymouth agent was accidentally arrested, Carlile smelt again the battles of the 1820s and sent another son to replace him.[3]

As sales went up and profits with them, so there was more competition to sell the Unstamped. Carlile 'received applications from all quarters'. Most agencies began as part-time businesses. Carlile's agents in 1824 included James Mann, a cropper at Leeds; Holmes, a shoemaker at Sheffield; Penny, a Huddersfield weaver; Barling, a shoemaker at Salisbury; Roberts, a singer in Dorchester; and Joseph Swann, a Macclesfield hatter. In the 1830s, Robert Ripley, who was prosecuted for selling the Unstamped to the soldiers of Burnley Barracks, and John Mark of Exeter, were hairdressers; Cogswell of Bath was a shoemaker; the Yarmouth agent was a cobbler; Benjamin Hackett of Salford, John Knight of Oldham, and Harrison of Bath were schoolteachers. In London part-time, but regular, sellers of the

---

[1] *PMG*, 9 Feb., 20 Apr. 1833.
[2] *Weekly Record*, 5 July 1856. The main exception was Lancashire, where Hetherington's agents had very often sold the *United Trades Co-operative Journal* in summer 1830.
[3] *Cosmopolite*, 22 Dec. 1832; *Gauntlet*, 17 June 1833, 16 Feb., 16 Mar. 1834.

Unstamped included Lucking, a warehouseman; Buck and Boreham, who were silkweavers; Caffyn, a cabinet maker; Grindon who was a publican; and Underwood, who kept a 'low Shell and Fried Fish shop in Moorfields'.[1] Charles Clements, the informer, found the Unstamped sold in Birmingham in beershops and barbers' shops; and he listed six sellers of the Unstamped in the small towns round Manchester as a barber, a shopkeeper, a landlady (Mary Hobson, the mother of Joshua Hobson), a painter, and a stationer. Other agents, such as Bready of Sheffield, added books and stamped newspapers to their stock and gradually became full-time agents, as Holmes had done for Carlile before. James Guest, the main Birmingham dealer in the Unstamped, had a shop in 1836 'well stocked with stationery, cutlery, books, pamphlets' as well as stamped and unstamped newspapers.[2] Some of the agencies became so well established that they survived into the 1850s—among them the Heywoods of Manchester, the Wastneys of Newcastle, Ibbotson of Bradford, the Manns of Leeds, Robinson of Edinburgh, and, on a small scale, Wright of Leicester, Yates of Coventry, and Baker of Worcester.

The bigger agents acted also as wholesalers. Heywood (still in his early twenties and soon to dominate the Manchester periodical trade), subcontracted agencies to the smaller towns within some twenty miles—to Joseph Swann, for example—and supplied a host of streetsellers, making a penny a dozen from selling to the trade. Some of these men were already in the centre of local politics, Heywood and Hobson on the Short Time Committees, Doherty in the National Association for the Protection of Labour. Knight and Gleave of Manchester were both veterans and both had sold Doherty's *United Trades Co-operative Journal*. James Watling, the Norwich agent, had, ten years earlier, organized funds for Carlile. Others extended their activity. Benjamin Hackett of Salford put out his own *Salford Patriot*; Bible Aked of Keighley published the *Weaver's Complaint*. Thomas Perry and John Seal in Leicester, Blanchard of

---

[1] *Gauntlet*, 27 Oct. 1833; HO 40/31, 22 Mar. 1833 (Bouverie to Phillipps); HO 64/15, 20 Apr. 1834.
[2] Charles Clements' Memorandum Book, quoted *London Dispatch*, 4 Dec. 1836.

Hull, and Bready in Sheffield, opened reading-rooms. In London, Lucking lectured the Grenadier Guards and organized a local republican society. Buck was secretary to a Spitalfields Burial and Trade Society, Caffyn organized a Cabinet Maker's Union, James Catchpool was secretary of the Southwark Radical Association, Thomas Heins of the Civil and Religious Society, while Haggett and Hussell started a Westminster Society for the Diffusion of *Really* Useful Knowledge. Over half of these provincial agents, some twenty-five out of forty, were imprisoned, and defied their local magistrates in speeches that were circulated round the country.[1]

Hetherington sent coach parcels direct to his agents. Lee and Carlile, both in the 1820s and in the 1830s, used intermediary agents in London to forward some of their parcels, until they grew disgusted with the interminable quarrels of forwarding agent and country retailer over the division of profits.[2] The agencies paid the carriage, which was $1\frac{1}{2}d.$ a pound for large parcels carried over a hundred miles; the postage for some 2,000 of the quarto Unstamped would cost 11*s.*

With the parcels went books, scribbled notes, the enclosures of other publishers, and the usual placards and bills, on which Hetherington was reputed to economize. George Baker of Worcester wrote to Lee:

Sir—to give publicity to any publication, it is quite necessary that country agents, in particular, should have bills or placards of it to expose. I have been in the habit of taking a few numbers of the *Man* every week; and I have applied to Mr H.—almost as frequently for a bill, but without success. I have not a doubt but that, with the help of a couple of bills every week, I shall make the sale of the *Man* in this town worth your notice.[3]

Placards and bills were carried by street vendors, posted in windows, stuck on walls and public houses, and formed part of the street literature which kept rusty reading skills alive. Cobbett had recognized their importance. When the Revd.

---

[1] *S.C. on Newspaper Stamps*, 1851, qu. 2595. For the speeches of Swann, see *PMG*, 12 Nov. 1831, for the Wastneys, *PMG*, 1 Feb. 1834, for Hobson, *Man*, 18 Aug. 1833.

[2] *Gauntlet*, 12 May 1833, compare *Rep.*, 24 Feb. 1826. Cobbett in 1822 had caused confusion by taking 'the wholesale trade into his own hands' which meant that mixed parcels of periodicals could no longer be forwarded. *Rep.*, 23 Dec. 1825.

[3] *Man*, 27 Oct. 1833; W. Hickson, *Fox's Monthly Repository*, Apr. 1836.

Robert Taylor was imprisoned for blasphemy, Carlile wrote to him, 'Several hundred placards (good ones) are crying murder on the walls.' When Hetherington was prosecuted in the summer of 1831, he printed large placards attacking the Whigs 'which are thickly posted around London and he is determined still to proceed in printing and publishing them'.[1] Meetings at the Rotunda took 200 placards to advertise them. The White Conduit Fields Meeting of November 1831 was cancelled by 800 placards, of which a quarter went to Spitalfields alone. When Carlile feared, in January 1831, that the Government was about to suppress all political writing and pamphlets, he threatened to 'Placard London and the Country calling the people to Arms at once . . .'.[2] Lee advertised the *Man* by posting bills on the walls of Cold Bath Fields prison, as well as on various public houses, and in August 1834 he printed tricolour placards against 'Despotic Governments' which could be had free from vendors of the Unstamped. The Home Office Papers are full of such bills advertising Walker's *Political Touchwood*, Hetherington's 'WANTED some hundreds of POORMEN', Hobson's fury at the seizure of Hetherington's and Cleave's presses in 1835, and Lorymer's National Convention.[3]

Clean, unsold copies of the Unstamped were usually received back within a month of their date, although, as papers reached the financial subsistence line, this was tightened to four days, and for the *Man*, *Gauntlet*, and *Cosmopolite* finally abolished. Carlile insisted on monthly returns from his country agents, weekly returns from his town agents. Both Hetherington and Carlile regularly overprinted, and in 1839 Carlile was still selling sets of the *Republican*, *Lion*, *Isis*, and *Newgate Magazine*.[4]

The papers were sent off from London every Thursday

---

[1] R. K. Webb, *The British Working Class Reader*, 1955, p. 24, points out that heavy advertising duty helped to drive advertisements into the street. *Pol. Reg.*, 16 Nov. 1816; Carlile MSS., Carlile to Taylor, 16 July 1831; HO 64/11, 24 June 1831.

[2] HO 64/11, 31 May, 6 Nov. 1831; n.d. (Jan. 1831).

[3] *Man*, 28 July 1833; HO 64/15 and HO 64/17.

[4] *Gauntlet*, 8 Dec. 1833, 5 Jan. 1834. Full sets of the *Republican* cost £6, of the *Political Register* £50. Carlile to Turton, 22 Mar., 22 Dec. 1839 (Carlile MSS.).

evening, to arrive by Saturday morning. When the Stamp Office, in the winter of 1835, began to seize the Unstamped, bundles for the longer journeys were sent off on Wednesday —this meant that they carried no news of events after Tuesday mid-day. Coaches left from half a dozen main yards in London: the 'Belle Sauvage', on Ludgate Hill, for East Anglia; 'Blossom's Inn' for Brighton; the 'Bull and Mouth', in St. Martin Le Grand, for the midlands and the west country; and the 'Swan with Two Necks', in Lad Lane, for Lancashire. It was at these yards that the Runners were able to impound the Unstamped in the winter of 1835.[1] Robert Lowery, later a temperance lecturer, who sold the Unstamped in Newcastle for a few months when the Wastneys were imprisoned, wrote that the readers of the working class papers of 1819, had been

worthy men of mental powers and peculiar intellect superior to the masses and standing apart from them rather than acting upon them; but the whole multitude seemed to be roused to interest in the matter of unstamped papers and their collateral subjects. Even those who could not themselves read often became subscribers with others who would read to them. The parcels generally arrived by the London coaches on Saturday afternoon, and I have frequently seen a crowd waiting their arrival, and if by any mishap the newspaper parcel did not arrive they would evidently be much disappointed. The women, too, would often be waiting with their children in their arms, and when any apology was offered and a hope that it would come, perhaps next mail, would say, 'Yes, yes, but I like to get it on Saturday and then he doesn't go to the public house after he's done his work, but stops at home and reads it.'[2]

(b) SALES

Some three dozen of the Unstamped lasted more than three months, but sales were erratic. Hetherington did 'very well' by the *Penny Papers* in November 1830, but when he started them again in December he could barely sell 500. In October 1831 Popay reported that the sales of the *Guardian* had fallen to 2,200, and that the last issue was late 'for want of means'.[3] When Hetherington defended Hunt, sales

[1] H. Mayhew, *Life and Labour* . . . , 1864 edn., vol. ii, p. 118.
[2] *WR*, 5 July 1856; however, compare *Pol. Reg.*, 2 Aug. 1817.
[3] HO 64/11, n.d. (early Jan. 1831); 27 Oct. 1831.

fell by 500; a meeting for the repeal of the taxes on knowledge raised sales by 500. O'Brien mentioned in the *Northern
Star* that the *Guardian* lost 1,500 subscribers in a fortnight
when he attacked O'Connell; and many of his Catholic
vendors 'refused to sell it from an honest but deplorable
belief that to attack O'Connell was to attack the Catholic
religion. . . '.[1] Every time a popular vendor was arrested,
sales went up; and in the first month of prosecutions the
sales of the *Republican* trebled. When Hetherington himself
was arrested, the paper sold out. Wakley's *Ballot* reported
that the *Guardian*'s sales had for a long time been steady at
3,000. The Saturday following Hetherington's arrest, 5,000
were sold before 9 o'clock in the morning. 'The work could
not be struck off sufficiently fast to answer the demand, the
office was crowded throughout the day, and at night not a
copy of the *Poor Man's Guardian* could be obtained.'[2] Sales
rose to an estimated 10,000. Popay reported Hetherington's
reasoning to his superiors: He stated that

he had received a Summons to attend at Bow Street on Friday for
publishing the *Guardian* and expected to go to prison. He says he will
be damned if the Whigs shall have a penny from him fine him what
they will, that he is not sorry that he is again prosecuted for it will do
both him and the cause good, that the Whigs are only making a Rod
for their own backs and the more they prosecute the more he will
go on and he is sure he shall get supported by the People . . .[3]

Sales of Carlile's *Republican* had leapt from below 10,000
to above 15,000 during his trial in 1819—'The Attorney
General has been the chief agent in the extensive circulation
of the *Republican*.' And in 1840 he sadly told a friend that
'the cessation of prosecution was my political death'.
According to Abel Heywood, the *Destructive* was saved by
prosecution, as was the sickly *Voice of the West Riding*:
'Our bitter enemies, in the excess of their hostility, have
not only lent us crutches but stilts.'[4]

¹ *PMG*, 31 Oct., 7, 14 July 1832; *NS*, 10 Feb. 1838.
² HO 64/18: MSS. note from Abram Fletcher, Insp., pinned to *Rep.*, 27 July
1831. *Ballot*, 10 July 1831; see also *Midland Rep.*, 6 Aug. 1831.
³ HO 64/12, 20 Dec. 1832.
⁴ *Rep.*, 30 Dec. 1819, 18 Feb. 1820. Carlile to Turton, 12 Feb. 1840 (Carlile
MSS.); *S.C. on Newspaper Stamps*, 1851, qu. 2584; *Voice of the West Riding*,
17 Aug. 1833.

The Government knew that publishers had sound financial reasons for wanting martyrdom. Denman told a sceptical House of Commons that he regularly received anonymous letters, abusing property and established institutions, which their authors hoped would provoke him into a kiss of life prosecution. Conversely, when White, the magistrate of Queen Square, with sudden scrupulousness, refused to convict vendors without the evidence of an impartial witness, this

had the effect of increasing the sale of the Guardian to upwards of 4000 or 5000 numbers in one week. Last Saturday afternoon after the usual number of Guardians were printed, I could not obtain a copy at any of the places where they are sold. And I was informed by very good authority that they had to begin printing on Sunday afternoon.

In the summer of 1835, when Hetherington's and Cleave's presses were seized, Macconnell, a radical lecturer, told a meeting at the Borough Chapel that demand had 'greatly increased', sales had doubled, and that on Sunday supply could not keep pace with demand.[1]

For most of 1832 and 1833 the *Guardian* sold between 12,000 and 15,000 copies, but from then on sales fell away slowly to 3,000 or so in its final year. The *Destructive* at best sold between 7,000 and 8,000 copies, the *Gauntlet* and the *Cosmopolite* never more than 5,000 and more usually around 3,500, and the *Working Man's Friend* seems to have had a similar circulation. *Man* reached 10,000 in its first year, though 5,000–7,000 was its later sale. *Slap at the Church* claimed to have sold 7,000 of its first number and to have a readership of 300,000.[2]

The *Guardian*'s sales were surpassed by only two radical papers in the early nineteenth century, the *Register* and the

[1] HO 64/16, report of P. C. Ewart, 5 Nov. 1832; *Hansard*, 3rd ser., iv, col. 425 (Denman, 28 June 1831); cutting in the *Place Coll.*, Set 70, 10 Aug. 1835.

[2] *PMG*, 26 May 1832, 21 Sept. 1833; *Destructive*, 6 July 1833; *Gauntlet*, 23 May 1834; *Cosmopolite*, 6 Oct. 1832; *PMG*, 1 Dec. 1833; *Man*, 25 Aug. 1833; *Slap*, 28 Jan., 3 Mar. 1832. Gifford's statement in the *Standard* (10 Sept. 1833) that the *Gauntlet* sold 22,000 was obvious nonsense; a quarter of that figure would have pleased Carlile immensely. Yet it is accepted by D. Read (op. cit., p. 97). Altick gives the circulation of the *Gauntlet* as 16,000 and the *Voice of the People* as 30,000 (op. cit., pp. 391–3) and Thompson repeats his figures (op. cit., p. 719); Doherty himself complained that the *Voice* sold only 2,000–3,000 a week (*Voice of the People*, 24 Sept. 1831). Nor did the *PMG* sell 20,000, as I. James suggests (op. cit., p. 13)— that was the *Dispatch*.

Northern Star, neither of which was illegal. After the Six Acts, Carlile's *Republican* never sold above 1,000; and the Home Office estimated—and certainly exaggerated—the sales of the *Black Dwarf* at 12,000 in September 1819, the *Cap of Liberty* at 6,000, and Cobbett's *Register* at upwards of 20,000 in 1817. With the exception of the *Northern Star*, later papers did far worse. The *Charter* reached 5,000 in 1839; the *Southern Star* started with a sales of 2,000 and found it hard to improve on it. Ernest Jones's *People's Paper* seldom sold above 3,000 in the early 1850s. The *Beehive*'s ceiling was 8,000 in the 1860s and its usual sales were between 3,000 and 5,000.[1]

Readership far exceeded sales, perhaps by twenty times. Hetherington put the readers of the *Guardian* and the *Destructive* at a conservative 50,000, most of whom would have heard the Unstamped read in their workshops or read the Unstamped in public houses, coffee- and reading-rooms. Members of the National Union used to meet at Benbow's coffee shop on Sunday mornings to read and discuss the Unstamped; others shared the Unstamped at their class meetings. The East End publicans were so dependent on their radical clientele that the weavers could control the papers they took, and used exclusive dealing to increase the sales of Wakley's *Ballot* and Bell's *True Sun*. Lovett knew one publican who spent £5 a week on periodicals.[2]

London sales alone could keep the *Prompter* or *Penny Papers* afloat at under 2,000 to 3,000; and London sales, more sensitive to events than those of the provinces, accounted for the *Guardian*'s fluctuations of up to 1,000 copies. But the steady increase in the circulation of the London Unstamped from the end of 1831, and of the broadsheets during the winter of 1835, was absorbed by the provinces. Cleave and Hetherington, on tour in the midlands, wrote back for a thousand copies each of the *Guardian* but such is the sale for them in London and the lately increased Orders

---

[1] Carlile to Turton, 9 July 1840, Carlile MSS.; *Rep.*, 22 Feb. 1822. For the *Black Dwarf* and the *Cap of Liberty* see Wickwar, op. cit., pp. 57, 64. *Southern Star*, 23 Feb., 22 Mar. 1840. For the *People's Paper*, Saville, op. cit., p. 51; for the *Beehive*, see S. Coltham, 'George Potter and the "Beehive" Newspaper' (Oxford Univ. D.Phil. thesis 1956).

[2] *New Monthly Magazine*, xliv (1835); Webb, op. cit., p. 32; *S.C. on Public Libraries*, xvii (1849), qus. 2773, 2779; HO 64/12, 15, 17 Feb. 1832.

for them in many parts of the Country that though 15000 was printed from Friday to Sunday morning last that no more could be had by 12 o'clock on Sunday and they will be kept in Print until (this) Tuesday evening.[1] [*sic*]

Lancashire alone took a third of Carlile's publications. It came out at Carlile's trial that he printed a thousand copies of his threepenny *Prompter*. Of these, 400 were sold over the counter and 400 wholesale, of which Manchester took 100, the Lancashire towns 50, the Yorkshire towns 50, the Scottish towns 25, Nottingham 25, and 150 were sold by metropolitan vendors. In March 1833 he was sending 1,250 copies of the *Gauntlet* to Lancashire 'and a hundred to each of the other principal towns'. Some two-thirds of Carlile's shopmen had come from Lancashire and it remained his 'first county for support'. Carlile's grip on the provinces is reflected in the names of his 3,000 volunteers to cut taxes in 1833, of whom only 675 came from London. Massey, one of his agents, sent him 630 names from Birmingham where the threepenny *Gauntlet* sold only 25 copies; the discrepancy perhaps illustrates the influence of an Unstamped paper beyond its sales.[2]

At least half, and probably two-thirds, of the well-established Unstamped were sold to the provinces. As late as March 1834, when sales were falling away, General Bouverie reported:

Lord Melbourne is perhaps not aware of the extent to which unstamped Papers are circulated in Manchester, and indeed throughout the whole of the Manufacturing district . . . I believe that the numbers may be pretty accurately stated as follows, for the town of Manchester and Salford, being read almost entirely in Clubs and at the meetings of the Unions, viz.

Guardian	1200 copies weekly	Conservative 400
Gauntlet 150		Rights of Industry 800 (Doherty)
the total 2550.		

These are the principal, but there are several others.[3]

---

[1] HO 64/12, 30 Oct. 1832.

[2] *State Trials N.S.* 11. 610; Carlile to Turton, 8 Mar. 1833 (Carlile MSS.); Carlile to Holmes, 5 May 1824 (Carlile MSS.); *Rep.*, 12 Aug. 1823, cf. *Prompter*, 2 July 1831; *Gauntlet*, 5 May 33.

[3] HO 40/32, ff. 97–104 (Bouverie to Phillips). *Chambers Edinburgh Journal* had 14,000 copies printed in London, of which 7,000 sold in London, 2,000 to Manchester, 1,400 to Liverpool, 700 Leeds, 375 Birmingham, 250 Nottingham and Hull, 175 Norwich, 75 Bath and Derby, 50 Bristol and York: 1 Feb. 1834.

The London proprietors worked hard to cultivate this new readership. Hetherington boasted of every new agency, and encouraged his agents to act as collectors of local news. He printed provincial letters, to the exclusion of London ones—'We are pleased to learn from a friend that the insertion of the Dudley article has given great satisfaction in that vicinity'—and tried to maintain something of a balance between areas. Readers were quick to complain of any bias.

Mr. Hunt has forwarded to us a letter (addressed to him by the chairman of a meeting recently held in Manchester) in which the writer complains of the difficulty of getting communications from that town inserted in the *Guardian* ... There is not another town in the kingdom, which we are always so happy to accommodate in this way as Manchester, because there is not another in which genuine Radicalism more abounds, nor in which the *Poor Man's Guardian* has found so many able and warmhearted supporters ... Our Preston friends will find their case fully set forth in today's *Destructive*. ...

Oastler, when he was invited to write for the *Twopenny Dispatch* in the autumn of 1835, warned O'Brien that the paper might lose readers because of his ultra-toryism and O'Brien himself complained that his strictures on Methodism, Catholicism, and trade unionism lost sales. Hetherington and Carlile were certainly ready to push unpopular causes; but, like any other proprietors of a newspaper, they tried to draw on provincial news and cater for sectional interests.[1]

The big concession to public opinion came in June 1833, when the *Destructive* agreed, at the request of correspondents, to devote far more space to police reports (at the cost of cutting down on Useful Knowledge). The *Man*, which was started a month later, devoted three of its eight pages to police news, poetry, cuttings, and 'scraps of everything'. At the beginning of 1834 the *Destructive* again changed its style to become 'a comprehensive vehicle of news ... the grand secret of journalism, as in everything else being to combine the *utile* and *dolci* ... '. When in the summer the

[1] *PMG*, 6 July, 23 Nov. 1833, *Twopenny Dispatch*, 3 Oct. 1835. For a further treatment, see below, pp. 269-75. One of the strengths of the *Northern Star* was its local coverage, on which it spent £500 a year even in 1841 when sales were falling. See D. Read, op. cit., p. 100; and compare *NS*, 9 Jan. 1841.

Destructive became the broadsheet *Twopenny Dispatch*, Hetherington went the rest of the way and promised his readers that it would

henceforward be a repository of all the gems and treasures, and fun and frolic and 'news and occurrences' of the week. It shall abound in Police Intelligence, in Murders, Rapes, Suicides, Burnings, Maimings, Theatricals, Races, Pugilism, and all manner of moving 'accidents by flood and field'. In short, it will be stuffed with every sort of devilment that will make it sell . . . Our object is not to make money, but to beat the Government.[1]

Tribune had given way to *Punch*, and both to the *News of the World*. Hetherington had travelled a long way from the austerity of the early *Guardian*.

The older Unstamped were occasionally octavo, usually quarto, and rarely folio. With good reason, Lord Lyndhurst suggested to the jury of Hetherington's Exchequer trial in June 1834 that the *Guardian* was too puny to be called a newspaper. The great divide in the content, costs, and sales of the Unstamped came when the quarto papers were replaced by broadsheets the size of *The Times*. Charles Penny, a wholesale stationer, put out the *People's Police Gazette* in the summer of 1833, on the model of the London police force's *Gazette*, and by January 1834 it was selling 20,000. Cleave copied him and brought out the *Weekly Police Gazette*, while Lee and Richard Carlile jun. turned the *Man* into a broadsheet and added the *People's Hue and Cry*. In the summer of 1834 Hetherington followed with the *Twopenny Dispatch*, and Cousins soon joined the trend. The quarto papers collapsed. Hetherington declared, in the dying *Guardian*, that the battle was now to be fought with the larger papers and Charles Knight said they killed off the smaller ones.[2]

Where the quarto papers had been as much pamphlet and tract as newspaper, these broadsheets were by any account newspapers.[3] Where the quarto papers had sought

---

[1] *Destructive*, 15 June 1833, 25 Jan., 7 June 1834.

[2] *PMG*, 21 June 1834; *Scourge*, 25 Oct. 1834; *PMG*, 26 Dec. 1835; Charles Knight, *The Newspaper-Stamp and the Duty on Paper*, 1836.

[3] S. Coltham in his thesis on the *Beehive* (op. cit.) shows that the *Beehive* went through a reverse process. It started as a general newspaper with a fair coverage of police cases, rapes, and murders, but increased its coverage of working-class affairs at the expense of general news, until by 1868 it had become 'a journal of opinion'.

to create a provincial and essentially working-class readership,[1] the broadsheets appear to have tapped a middle-class
radical readership as well. Most commentators noted how
respectable the broadsheets had become, free of slander and
'well-conducted', their opinions 'no more strong than other
papers'. And it was their respectability, not their radicalism,
which threatened the stamped press.[2]

Circulations rose. Buckingham told the House of Commons, in the summer of 1834, that he had recently toured
the country and there was not a town of 20,000 inhabitants
that did not have three or four cheap publications. *Penny's
Police Gazette* was reckoned to have a circulation of 12,000
in November 1833. The *Weekly Police Gazette* and the
Dispatch soon stood at 20,000. In May 1835 a Memorial
of the City of London gave the circulation of the *Weekly
Police Gazette* as 32,000, the *Twopenny Dispatch* as 27,000,
the vendors *Weekly Police Gazette* as 10,000, the vendors
Dispatch as 8,000, Cousins's *Police Register* as 6,000, and
others as 15,000, bringing the total to 100,000 a week.[3]
The relative circulations are probably reflected in an account
page in the Carlile MSS. (though whether they were for
his own sale or whether to be sent as a parcel is unclear).
The entry for 15 May (1835) reads: 100 *Police Gazettes*,
88 *Dispatches*, 30 *Police Registers*, 18 *Guardians*, 13 *Shep-
herds*, 2 *Moral Worlds*, 2 *Doctors*, 1 *Figaro*, 1 Cobbett's
Political Register, and 6 newspapers. The entries for 22 and
29 May were virtually the same. If the *Guardian* was selling
about 4,000, this would put the *Gazette* at 22,000–25,000,
and the *Dispatch* around 20,000.

The average country newspaper sold under a thousand
copies; *The Times* had a circulation of around 10,000,
the *Morning Herald* 7,000, and the *Chronicle*, the *Standard*,
the *Morning Post* and *Morning Advertizer* all circulated at

---

[1] O'Brien estimated that only 3,000 or so of the *Guardian*'s readers were middle
class, though half of the *Destructive*'s readers were probably middle class. *PMG*,
17 Aug. 1833.
[2] J. Crawfurd, *A Financial and Historical Review* . . . , 1836, p. 38; *Pamphlets
for the People*, No. 12, p. 12 (H.S.C., 'Mr. Bulwer's Sham Notion'); Knight, op. cit.
[3] *Hansard*, 3rd ser., xxiii col. 1219 (Buckingham, 22 May 1834); *Cosmopolite*
16 Nov. 1833; *Memorial of Certain Inhabitants of the City of London*, 6 May
1835, *Place Coll.*, Set 70, f. 203.

under 5,000.[1] By the beginning of 1836 Cleave's *Gazette* was thought to have a circulation of 40,000, and this from Place who was helping Cleave to edit his papers from prison. The *Weekly Times* claimed similar sales in August 1836 and estimated that the leading six Unstamped had a combined circulation of 200,000 a week. Chapman, a middle-class radical, reckoned that Birmingham alone took 8,000 a week, Clements, the informer, put the figure at nearer 10,000 and commented that they were 'as openly offered for sale as bread or any other commodity'.[2] Place wrote in Roebuck's pamphlets, themselves selling at 10,000 a week, that one broadsheet sold more in a day than *The Times* did all the week, and that another one did almost as well. Cousins's *Weekly Herald* boasted in July 1836 that in Bath its circulation was ten times that of the stamped. 'A stamped paper now indeed is regarded as a curiosity, in Bath, Birmingham, Manchester, Liverpool, Newcastle, Hull, Portsmouth etc.' George Edmonds wrote that the readers of the Unstamped, rapidly increasing in number, 'are even now four millions, or ten times the number of the political readers of the stamped papers, with tenfold the energy of the opposing, rich, lazy, timid, ignorant classes . . . '.[3]

(c) BUSINESS[4]

Editors, printers, and publisher-proprietors joined to put out the Unstamped. Few of the leading figures were all three. Hetherington and Cousins printed and published, but did not write their papers. Thomas Mayhew, a young law student, possibly Phipps, formerly editor and proprietor of the *News*, and then O'Brien, edited the *Guardian* (and

---

[1] J. Grant, *The Newspaper Press*, 1871, vol. ii, p. 4; vol. i, pp. 324, 282, 399; vol. ii, p. 59, 109.

[2] Add. MSS. 35150, f. 49, Place to Hume, 12 May 1835; *Weekly Times*, 14, 28 Aug. 1836; *Pamphlets for the People*, No. 8, p. 12 (H. Chapman, 'Victims of the Unstamped Press'); *London Dispatch*, 4 Dec. 1836.

[3] *Pamphlets for the People*, No. 8, p. 10 (F. Place, 'The Taxes on Knowledge'); *Weekly Herald*, 3 July 1836; G. Edmonds, *Appeal to the Labourers of England*, 1836.

[4] For biographical notes on publishers and authors, see Appendix, p. 307.

later the *Destructive*), and Lorymer the *Republican* and
Radical.[1] Carlile wrote and published but did not print his
papers. Only Lee for six months carried all three jobs.
What was important was to stamp a paper with the imprint
of one man, as Cobbett, Hetherington, Carlile, Lee, and
Morrison knew well. None of Hetherington's editors was
imprisoned, possibly because they had been carefully
instructed to keep out of the limelight; except for Lorymer,
who created his own republican milieu, they rarely spoke
at public meetings. It was Hetherington who was known
as the '*Guardian*', Hetherington who made the speeches,
went to prison, ate the public dinners, and took the applause.
The *Cosmopolite*, the joint stock concern of a group of
vendors, never won the loyalty and eulogy bestowed on the
Guardian; and the *Working Man's Friend*, which had the
same air of anonymity, was never prominent. Similarly
the *Charter*, just before it folded up in 1840, attributed its
failure to being a joint-stock paper.[2]

A few, like Hetherington, Lee, Cowie, and Cousins,
started as professional printers. Hetherington had been
apprenticed in his youth to Luke Hansard. In the 1830s he
employed an indoor apprentice, Thomas Stevens (whose
indentures were broken by the magistrates when he refused
to set up the Unstamped); a shopman (in the summer of
1834 one John Murray, whom Carlile had dismissed for
theft and who turned out to be a spy; subsequently Henry
Robinson, a vendor who went on to develop the 'periodical
trade' in Edinburgh; and finally George Julian Harney);
and probably two journeymen compositors, one of whom,
Samuel Taylor, eventually set up on his own. His wife and
two sons occasionally served behind the counter. In 1839
he still employed two men and a boy.[3]

Until April 1834 Hetherington published from 13

[1] *Scourge*, 8 Nov. 1834. It was Thomas, not Edward (as Linton claimed) nor
Henry Mayhew (as Cole stated); see Appendix p. 313. Phipps was subscribing towards
the imprisoned vendors of the early 1820s (*Black Dwarf*, 13 Nov. 1822) and spoke
at the Cooperative Conference of 1830.
[2] *Charter*, 1 Mar. 1840.
[3] *PMG*, 4, 18 Jan. 1834; *Scourge*, 25 Oct. 1834; *PMG*, 1 Nov. 1834; *Red Rep.*,
28 Sept. 1850; J. Bertram, *Some Memories of Books, Authors and Events*, 1893,
p. 138; J. F. Wilson, *A Few Personal Recollections by an Old Printer*, 1896, p. 19;
Cowie's *Pocket Manual*, 1839.

Kingsgate Street (where Southampton Row now runs), an eight-roomed house that cost him £55 a year in rent: in his early days he printed there as well, but from the end of 1831 he appears to have had separate printing works. Until the end of 1832 the *Guardian* was printed on the common Stanhope hand-press, capable of printing 250 impressions an hour and costing perhaps £30; Hetherington had two of these presses going 'all the time' to meet demand. From the spring of 1833 the early editions of the *Guardian* were sent out to a machine (possibly that of the *True Sun*) though not to a steam press, while the *Destructive* and the London edition of the *Guardian* were printed on the Stanhope. From the summer of 1834 the broadsheet *Twopenny Dispatch* had to be printed by machine as it was too large for the Stanhope platen; and at some point Hetherington used Hibbert's legacy of 450 guineas to buy his own Napier press, worked by two men and capable of producing 2,500 impressions an hour.[1] In 1834 Hetherington moved to 126 Strand. His stock included some sixty or so periodicals (among them the maligned Christian ones), Paine, Voltaire, and Shelley, *Moral Physiology*, cookery books, grammars, romances, and cottage economies. He used Watson's new premises in City Road for printing his papers, a separation of printing and publishing offices that continued at least until 1840.[2]

Richard Lee, who was still in his teens, used a hand-press when most other printers had gone over to a machine, and printed and published the *Man* from 31 Marylebone Street. In 1839 he was described as a printer in the Post Office Directory, but was not classed as a master printer in Cowie's Manual. Cousins's business was larger even than Hetherington's. Working from 18 Duke Street, Lincoln's Inn Fields, he printed and published the London edition of the *Pioneer*, the *New Moral World*, and the *Shepherd*, as well as his own *Political Register*, the *People's Weekly Police Gazette*, and the *Weekly Herald*, all broadsheets, for which he needed a machine at least the size of the Napier. To this he added a shop, according to Frost at one time one of the 'chief depots of the literature of unbelief'. In 1839 he employed five men and five boys.[1]

A second group were the professional writers, who might serve as editors to radical proprietors, like O'Brien, or who might set up on their own, employing a jobbing printer for the run of a publication. Carpenter, for example, between editing the *Weekly Free Press and Trades Newspaper* in the late 1820s, and sub-editing the *True Sun* from 1832 on, launched his *Political Letters* from Carlile's offices at 1 Bouverie Street; when these were required by the *Prompter*, he moved to Strange's offices at 21 Paternoster Row. He and Cleave collaborated on the *Slap at the Church* and the *Church Examiner*, but Strange and Cowie were its publishers, and W. Johnston of Liverpool Street, Bishopsgate, its printer. Henry Berthold had put out his tricolour *National Guardian* in the summer of 1830; a year later he produced his *Political Handkerchief*, which was printed and published both by Carlile at 1 Bouverie Street, and by Cousins in Duke Street. James Baden Lorymer, a youthful former barrister whose apocalyptic radicalism made the columns of *Hansard*, edited over six years a profusion of *Radicals*, *Republicans*, and *Reformers*, adding or subtracting papers as they caught his fancy.[2] For a time Hetherington was his printer and publisher, taking any profits while Lorymer took the losses. Lorymer next acquired his own printers, publishing from the office of the *True Sun* at 336 Strand, then from Lee's 5 Brydge Street, and finally from 378 Strand. Lorymer collected mishaps: one copy of the first number of the *Bonnet Rouge*, due to appear on 2 February 1832, had a manuscript note interleaved:

this number was never issued to the public, 200 were struck off but all immediately destroyed with the exception of some two or three. Application was made to several printers to print this number but they refused owing to its being strong destructive principles, it was ultimately printed by a man living in a Garret in Holywell St. who was drunk

---

[1] *Man*, 25 Aug. 1833; T. Frost, *Forty Years Recollections*, 1880, p. 84.
[2] HO 64/11, 2, 4, 7 July 1831; *Rep.*, 2 July, 13 Aug. 1831; *Satirist*, 3 July, 7 Aug. 1831; Lorymer to Carlile, 19 July 1831 (Carlile MSS.).

at the time which may account for the misplacing of the pages. [*sic*]¹

The third group in the world of the Unstamped were those radical booksellers and publishers who acquired printing skills or floated a periodical, whichever best served the radical cause and offered profits. They included Carlile, Cleave, and Watson, and the less-prominent booksellers, Strange, Berger, Purkess, and Steill (who had been Wooler's publisher in 1819).

Carlile wrote most of the material in his papers, though contributions came from Thomas Turton, his Sheffield friend who made steel knives; the Revd. Robert Taylor who, dressed as the Archbishop of Canterbury, informed his Rotunda audience that Jesus Christ was yet one more sun god; and 'T. P.' (possibly Thomas Perry, Carlile's Leicester agent). Carlile was usually his own editor, though Julian St. John edited the *Republican* for him in 1819–20. He never printed his papers, and, though registered as a printer, never had a press. Sherwin, himself a radical journalist, was his first printer; Moses, a professional printer, was his second; James Watson and Richard Hassell, his shopmen, for a time helped out as compositors. The *Prompter* seems to have been printed by Cunningham and Salmon, a professional printing firm, who later printed Carlile's *Gauntlet* and *Scourge*. Julian Hibbert, the wealthy young Greek scholar who kept the Rotunda open and sustained the Victim Fund, helped Carlile with the bills. Both Moses and Salmon exercised a veto over what they printed; Moses, possibly because Carlile was invariably £150 in his debt, printed at his own speed, and Salmon vetoed some of Robert Taylor's love letters. Steill, Cousins, and Holmes of Sheffield did some casual printing for him. He published his papers at 64 Fleet Street, which flanked on to the printing premises of 1 Bouverie Street. The seizure of Hetherington's and Cleave's presses in August 1835 brought difficulties for other proprietors of the Unstamped. Carlile wrote to Turton 'I am at work on another periodical, but the state of things is that no regular printer

---

¹ *Bonnet Rouge*, 2 Feb. 1832 (*Cole Coll.*, Nuffield College, Oxford). Harney had the same problem, *Red Rep.*, 10 Aug. 1850.

will venture to print an unstamped paper and I, having no types and presses, suffer for want of a printer and not for want of credit. . . .'[1]

Watson had been licensed as a printer back in 1818, when he stood in for Carlile, and learnt to be a compositor in 1825, but, save for a few months' work for Hibbert, he did not practise his skill. In 1830 he became a bookseller in two rooms at 33 Windmill Street, and in 1831 Hibbert gave him his types and presses, which were duly registered, and these he used between customers and after hours.[2] In the spring of 1834 he moved into the Hall of Science, City Road, as its custodian, lent some of his new-found space to Hetherington, and published for Carlile, but his printing business was always on a small scale and subsidiary to bookselling.

Cleave owned a coffee shop on Snow Hill, was a small-time printer in 1831, and worked with Carpenter, Watson, and Penny on various papers. In January 1834 he registered a press of his own,[3] but the 'registration' seems to have been nothing more than a gesture of legal responsibility for what was about to appear under his name, the *Weekly Police Gazette*. Cunningham and Salmon seem to have been his printers, for when questioned by the Solicitor of Stamps in the summer of 1834, they told Timm that Cleave hired one of their machines, he 'being a licensed Printer' and 'That it is the common and ordinary practice of the Trade for a Paper to be composed and set up at one place, and brought to your Memorialists, and to others who keep similar Machines, to print the same . . . the most respectable Printers in London have been engaged in printing similar publications without supposing thereby they were acting illegally . . . '.[4] They promised not to print any other unstamped papers. What happened then? Did they continue to print for Cleave as later they printed the unstamped

[1] Carlile to Turton, 10 Dec. 1835; see also Carlile to Holmes, 24 Aug., 6 Oct. 1824; Carlile to Taylor, 16 July 1831; Carlile to Holmes, 8 Nov. 1822, 9 Dec. 1823, 16 Sept. 1824; Carlile to Taylor, 17 July 1831; Carlile to Turton, 19 July 1840 (Carlile MSS.); *PMG*, 1 Nov. 1834.

[2] Printers' Certificates, Corporation of London Record Office, 14 Dec. 1818; Printers' Certificates, Middlesex C.R.O., 24 Jan. 1831.

[3] Printers' Certificates, Corporation of London R.O., 3 Jan. 1834.

[4] Memorial, copy in *Place Coll.*, Set 70, ff. 198.

Daily National Gazette? When Cleave's press was seized on 1 August 1835, he told his readers that it took place at the 'printer's premises' (not printing premises), and that the presses had not been 'entered'. This would suggest that this was not the hypothetical press for which he registered in January 1834, nor a press belonging to a commercial printer. A John Chappell claimed the goods as his own.[1] Subsequently T. Wakelin, of Cleave's address in Shoe Lane, was named as the printer of the *Weekly Police Gazette*; but he was never registered. Hetherington, on the other hand, did register the press he acquired after the seizure. So if Wakelin was not one of Cleave's shopmen, was it a pseudonym for Cleave himself? Or was it all bogus, and was Cleave continuing to send his papers to be printed elsewhere? The *Gazette* could not be printed on the machine used by the *Dispatch*, for their joint circulations were too high. Richard Moore, a young woodcarver who was Watson's brother-in-law, registered a press on 31 August 1835 at 13 Newcastle Street (now Kean Street), Strand. Moore never put out a paper of his own, nor was he named as the printer of any. Lovett witnessed both Hetherington's registration and Moore's registration. Could Moore have been the registered and ostensible owner of the presses Cleave was using?[2]

There is also some mystery about Hetherington's business arrangements. Lovett claimed to be the owner of Hetherington's 350 guinea press, but almost certainly Hetherington had made it over to him so that the authorities could not seize it in lieu of Hetherington's fines.[3] Hetherington, on 6 August 1835, registered a press, presumably to replace the press that had been seized. Where did he get the money? Hibbert had died in January 1834 leaving Watson

---

[1] *WPG*, 15 Aug. 1835. There are three John Chappells classified in the *Post Office Directory* of 1839 as Printers; no John Chappell registered his presses.

[2] Printers' Certificates, Middlesex C.R.O., 31 Aug. 1835.

[3] Hetherington talked of a 'transfer of property' (*Twopenny Dispatch*, 8 Aug. 1835); Lovett claimed in his Memorial to have *paid* 350 guineas for the press. The whole affair is ignored in his autobiography. Hetherington repeated the manœuvre in 1841 when he was prosecuted for selling *Haslam's Letters* (W. Linton, *Three Score Years and Ten*, p. 80). When the authorities realized that the presses did not legally belong to Hetherington and Cleave they invoked an obsolete clause that the owner and not the user must be registered.

and Hetherington 450 guineas each, though according to Carlile the will was not cleared until the following year. Watson spent his money on bringing out foreign works. If Hetherington had used his money, or an advance on it, to buy the 350 guinea press which was made over to Lovett between the summer of 1834 (when the broadsheet *Two-penny Dispatch* came out) and August 1835 when the press was seized, then he could not have spent the money a second time buying a replacement (which was Cooper's version of the incident).[1] On 3 September 1836 Hetherington advertised a Napier press for sale, seen at work. Which of four possible presses was this? O'Brien, according to his own account, stopped working for Hetherington a week after the 'sham-Radicals' had given Hetherington back his press and stock, but he was writing for the *London Dispatch* of 17 September. It could hardly be Cleave's press as the *Gazette* and *Dispatch* did not merge till October.[2]

(d) PROFITS

An unstamped paper could, with care, be made the basis of a flourishing business. Its costs were mainly paper and labour. Sheets came in various sizes, from single crown (20 × 15 in.) to the double demy (35 × 22½ in.) of newspapers, and were folded once to produce a four-page folio, twice to produce an eight-page quarto, and so on. A quarto of double demy would be almost as large as a sheet of single crown. Some 500 sheets comprised a ream, which would weigh between 16 lb. and 35 lb., and cost between 15s. and 35s. according to the size of the sheet and the quality of the paper. Paper for the *Penny Magazine* cost £1 a ream, each sheet of which would make two copies. Hetherington was certainly using paper of the thinnest and flimsiest sort and it probably cost him no more than 15s. a ream, including the 3d. a lb. duty, from which he would produce a thousand copies of the *Guardian*. Thus, on a circulation of 10,000, paper would cost Hetherington about £8.[3] He hired his type (usually the most expensive capital cost for a printer)

---

[1] *Scourge*, 21 Feb. 1835; Cooper's *Eloge* (*Reasoner*, 1849, vol. x).
[2] *London Mercury*, 9 Apr., 28 May 1837.
[3] *Man*, 25 Aug. 1833; *Cosmopolite*, 5 Oct. 1833.

from James Savage, the Marylebone radical, and used long primer for his editorials, brevier for his secondary articles, and minion for his reports. Each paper contained about 90,000 'ens', which at 7*d*. a thousand together with the 2*s*. 6*d*. charged for mixed type, would bring Hetherington's composing costs to about £3, or 45 man hours of composing at the standard speed.[1] Press work on the Stanhope cost 1*s*. 6*d*. for 500 copies, and would make his press costs £1. 10*s*. Thus his piecework costs for composing and printing would be about £4. 10*s*., which, on the standard flat rate, would pay for two journeymen and one or two boys.[2] Ink, porters, placards, the hire of type and printing premises, and the occasional woodcut by Seymour at 25*s*. a time, would bring his total costs to about £14 for 10,000 copies. This figure excludes his overheads of rates, shopboy, and the wages of an editor.

If Hetherington sold 1,000 copies over the counter and 9,000 to the trade at 8*d*. for 13, this would bring him in about £24, less any unsold copies. Advertisements would not bring in any revenue, as charges were low (between 2*d*. and 9*d*. a line in most of the Unstamped), Good Causes were inserted free, and Hetherington in turn had to place his own advertisements. So before he paid his overheads (which were shared by the *Destructive*, as well as by his bookshop and his freelance printing) Hetherington would make £9 to £10 a week from the *Guardian* alone on a circulation of 10,000, and the paper would break even at 2,500 copies. When the *Guardian* folded with sales around 3,000–4,000, Hetherington assured readers that that was 'amply sufficient to pay costs'.[3] Hetherington had his papers edited for him. Thomas Mayhew was never paid: 'our time and our labour is free'. Lorymer, according to spy reports, 'on his first writing for Hetherington he agreed with him to do so gratuitously, and said that if any profit came of the

[1] *PMG*, 8 Aug. 1835; T. Hansard, *Treatises on Printing and Type Founding*, 1841, pp. 166 f., 90–1.

[2] *Hansard*, op. cit., p. 108; E. Howe and H. E. Waite, *The London Society of Compositors*, 1948, p. 125. Carlile's printer, Moses, charged him £2 for composing a sheet of the *Republican* in small pica, and £1 for presswork for a thousand sheets. Carlile to Holmes, 2 Aug. 1824 (Carlile MSS.). The *Republican* was twice the size of the *Guardian*.

[3] *Slap*, 17 Mar. 1832 (Seymour's costs). Popay thought the papers would break even at 2,000, HO 64/11, n.d. (Jan. 1831); *PMG*, 19 Dec. 1835.

work if he would print it he should have it and if not he
would see he lost nothing by it he has done do . . .' [*sic*]
Alexander Somerville had the reverse arrangement with
Carlile, whereby Somerville would take half the profits and
none of the losses of the *Political Soldier*. O'Brien was paid
only irregularly; he edited the *Destructive* within six months
of joining the *Guardian* and may also have kept on his legal
work. James Cooke, Hetherington's editor of the *Oddfellow*,
wrote that he and Hetherington never worried about
money until Saturday night when Hetherington worked
out his profit, and paid Cooke what he could afford.[1]

Lee gave a partial breakdown of the expenses he had to
meet when he printed and published four issues of Benbow's
Tribune, which sold for twopence: 10,000 prospectuses
came to £2; bills announcing the first number were 9*s*.;
the expenses (excluding paper) of each issue were £4. 6*s*.
As receipts had not yet met half of Lee's total costs, and as
his credit with the stationer had expired, Lee brought the
Tribune to an end.[2] It is unlikely that any of Lorymer's
papers paid their way. Within six months of launching the
Republican in May 1831 it had to become a monthly; by
December old copies were being given away free, and back
numbers of another paper he edited, the *Radical* (started in
August 1831), were being sold at half-price, the proceeds
going to the Victim Fund. 'The sale though extensive has
not equalled the expenditure once . . . it labours under the
disadvantage of being sold but by a very few publishers. . . .'
A month later Popay reported that the *Republican* was
'unsaleable', and in 1833 Lorymer was complaining that
'the publication of unstamped Newspapers is a very hazard-
ous and fluctuating business'. None the less as late as April
1834 his circulation was being estimated at around 5,000.[3]

These papers were all individually financed. The

---

[1] *Penny Papers*, 20 Nov. 1830; HO 64/11, 2 July 1831; *Political Soldier*, 14 Dec.
1833; *PMG*, 10 Oct. 1835. O'Brien said he paid £60 p.a. for Chambers in an Inn
of Court. *Oddfellow*, 26 Dec. 1840.

[2] R. Lee, *Benbowism or Victimization Unmasked*, 1832.

[3] *Radical Reformer*, 31 Dec. 1831, 5 Jan. 1832; HO 64/12, 6 Feb. 1832; *PMG*,
21 Dec. 1833; HO 64/15, 28 Apr. 1834. James Acland was reputed to make £1,000
p.a. from the *Hull Portfolio* (F. Adams, *Eyes for the Blind*, Hull, 1832). Harney and
Ernest Jones both lost money on their papers of the early 1850s (*F.P.*, 21 July 1851;
Saville, op. cit., p. 51.)

alternative method was to finance them by joint stock. The *Trades Newspaper* in 1825 was financed by £5 shares, the *Northern Star* by £1 shares, and the *Beehive* by 5s. shares. The *Cosmopolite* was launched in March 1832 by eight vendors, including Hancock, Pilgrim, Knight, and Walker, who counted up twenty-four imprisonments between them. Its capital, like that of the *Midland Representative* and the *Voice of the People* was to be raised by £1 shares, held either individually or jointly, and each share entitled its holder to be a delegate on the committee of management. An almanac was included in the first number, and sales were 'beyond all expectation'. Not enough capital was raised, however, and within a few numbers the vendors were £8 to £10 in debt to the printer; none the less from May 1832 they claimed to be able to pay a competent editor, possibly Rowland Detroisier. From July 1832 the paper came under the patronage of the Carliles, but still scarcely paid the journeymen's wages. In October it had to raise its price to 1½d. as it had not yet met its costs or sold above 5,000; it relied by then on an 'irregular kind of filling up'. Six months later it passed totally into the hands of the Carliles, who spent £100 on the paper without making it solvent, and at the end of the year it merged with the *Man*.[1]

The big broadsheets selling at twopence needed a circulation of some 10,000 to cover costs;[2] none the less profits doubled or trebled. Penny's *Police Gazette* was worth over £20 a week in November 1833. According to Lee, a rival printer, Cleave's *Police Gazette* was worth some £20 to £30 a week within a month or two of being launched, and it was worth probably twice that by the following year.

---

[1] *Cosmopolite*, 17 Mar. 1832; *Gauntlet*, 1 Dec. 1833; *Cosmopolite*, 5 May 1832.

[2] When some of these broadsheets went stamped, extra capital was required. The *London Dispatch* selling at 3½d. required a circulation of 16,000 (*London Dispatch*, 17 Sept. 1836). The *Northern Star* selling at 4½d. broke even at about 6,000 (see D. Read, op. cit., pp. 98–102).

The problem that emerged in 1834 and became acute after 1836 was the relation of price to size and sales. O'Brien's *Southern Star* was originally 6d. and sold 2,000; the price was reduced to 4d. and the size went from folio to broadsheet; it still failed to break even, so O'Brien raised the price to 5d. and doubled its reporting. *Southern Star*, 5 Apr., 26 Apr. 1840. When the *Northern Star* complained, 'All our best endeavours are but a poor substitute for the Unstamped', this was a comment on the ratio of finance to sales, not on ideology (*NS*, 2 June 1838).

In 1836 O'Brien reckoned that Hetherington and Cleave had an income of £40 to £60 a week, and in 1839 Carlile repeated what he never tired of saying, 'The revenue case of the stamp on the newspaper was perseveringly because profitably worked by Hetherington and Cleave.'[1] Carpenter was supposed to have lost £100 on his *Political Letters*, and Carlile himself seems to have made little money from his papers. The spy reports always described Carlile as desperately poor, though willing to spend his last shilling to 'disseminate knowledge'.[2] Carlile's fortunes fluctuated wildly. His stock was always worth £2,000 and sometimes as much as £5,000; while in prison he received about £400 a year in subscriptions, and by 1834 he had received £4,000 in subscriptions, two sizeable legacies and perhaps £7,000 in aid from Julian Hibbert. And he owned a house worth, at his own estimation, some £3,000 to £5,000.[3] But the *Republican* lost money from 1820 onwards; and he had to support not only his family, but a number of shopmen, the Revd. Robert Taylor and 'Isis', as well as subsidizing such papers as the *Isis*, *Cosmopolite*, *Political Soldier*, *Union*, and possibly the *Man*. A month before he died, when he was extremely ill and living from one sovereign to the next, he managed to sell 300 copies of Paine's theological works, and the £15 'will enable me to start another periodical'.[4]

Hetherington, it was thought, could have been a rich man, had he devoted more time to his business and less to working-class projects. In 1837 O'Brien estimated that Hetherington possessed £5,000 of stock, a press worth £1,500, and a business bringing in £1,000 a year. But Hetherington died so poor in 1849, leaving only £200 of 'goods and chattels' that Watson and Whittaker, his executors, had difficulty meeting the claims on his estate.[5] Most of these men had

---

[1] *Cosmopolite*, 16 Nov. 1833; *Man*, 13 Apr. 1834, see also *Scourge*, 25 Oct. 1834; *London Mercury*, 4 June 1837; Carlile's *Pol. Reg.*, 7 Dec. 1839.

[2] *Political Anecdotist*, 9 July 1831; *Pol. Letter*, 13 Aug. 1831; HO 64/11, n.d. (27 Nov. 1830).

[3] *Rep.*, 19 Nov., 17 Dec. 1819, 22 Feb. 1822, 21 Feb., 23 May 1823, 9 Apr. 1824, 9 June 1826; *Prompter*, 7 May 1831; *Scourge*, 29 Nov. 1834; T. C. Campbell, *The Life of Richard Carlile*, 1899, p. 249.

[4] *Rep.* 23, 30 May 1823; Carlile MSS., notes of a letter to Turton, 6 Jan. 1843.

[5] *London Mercury*, 4 June 1837; Hetherington's Will, Somerset House, proved 19 Dec. 1849.

some supplementary source of income which would help sustain the papers through lean times. Hetherington, the Carliles, Cleave, and Watson ran bookshops; Lovett and Cleave had coffee and reading-rooms; Lee and Cousins were freelance printers; and most of them could count on generous subscriptions when they were in prison. The Unstamped, therefore, could be profitable, though they often were not; they could be the basis of a business as well as a style of life.

(e) RIVALS

The Government did not allow the Radical papers to go unopposed. Sidmouth in 1816, according to Cobbett, decided that Cobbett 'must be written down'. Norwich, Oxford, and Ramsey produced cheap government papers, Birmingham a tribe of *Job Notts* and in London Gifford, Southey, and Canning brought out an '*Anti-Cobbett*' at a cost of £20,000 and some 200,000 bills, which asked men of influence to circulate the paper if they wished to prevent 'a bloody revolution'.[1] Wooler's *Black Dwarf* was met by Merle's *White Dwarf* which expounded the tory Social Contract. But as Sidmouth failed to pick up the bills, the paper ended in some acrimony in April 1818. Merle next brought out the *True Briton*. Shadgett, backed by Kenyon (the Bishop of London), and the Society for the Suppression of Vice, published in the spring of 1818 his *Weekly Review of Cobbett, Wooler, Sherwin and Other Democratical and Infidel Writers*, for 'the best Governments must fall, if such publications as Sherwin's are permitted to be circulated through the country unopposed and uncontradicted'. He boasted that he reduced the circulation of the seditious papers from as many thousands to as many hundreds, but according to Carlile, none of these government papers ever sold, but had to be distributed free to all coffee shops, taverns, and alehouses to get them into circulation.[2]

This was overt counter-propaganda. In the 1830s the tactics were usually more subtle, and direct confrontation was side-stepped. The Home Office and the Society for the

[1] *Pol. Reg.*, 2 Aug. 1817.
[2] *Shadgett's Weekly Review*, 1 Feb. 1818; *Rep.*, 8 Dec. 1820.

Suppression of Vice were, significantly, replaced by the efforts of the Society for the Diffusion of Useful Knowledge. Charles Knight, editing the *Plain Englishman* from 1820 to 1822, had employed the diversionary tactics which he and Chambers were to employ in the 1830s. Bad opinions were to be met not by good opinions but by good literature.

Chambers' Journal was the first in the field. Observing the 'worthless and ephemeral' papers that were popular, Chambers decided he would lead public taste, 'if possible in a proper direction; let me endeavour to elevate and instruct, independent of mere passing amusement'. He decided to avoid any political or religious controversy. His 'grand leading principle' was to offer to the humblest labourer 'a meal of healthful, useful and agreeable mental instruction'. Like Carlile, he felt the power of the press by which he could 'instil the most pernicious opinions on almost any subject, into the minds of three millions of human beings. But I see the straight path of moral responsibility before me.'[1]

Within a year sales were steady at 50,000 of which Scotland accounted for some 30,000. Chambers claimed that the *Journal* was read by all classes, in cottages and in Glasgow factories; it was aimed primarily at the working classes, but whether it was read by any working men outside Scotland is hard to estimate as the *Journal* printed no letters and no 'ephemeral' comment. Chambers shared no agents with the radical Unstamped, and his readership was probably very similar to that of the *Penny Magazine*; but he offered somewhat tougher intellectual fare than the *Penny Magazine* (though leavened by a weekly short story) and with deadly accuracy criticized the SDUK publications:

Ignorance being the bane which these respectable and well-meaning persons wished to eradicate, they appear to have, in most instances, assumed that knowledge which in ordinary language stands as the opposite of ignorance, was the one simple and direct thing which they were called upon to cultivate. They have accordingly spent several years in the happy dream that, by communicating information respecting various natural and artificial objects and the more familial departments of science, they were regenerating the race—a hostile

[1] W. Chambers, *The Story of a Long and Busy Life*, 1882, p. 30; *Chambers' Edinburgh Journal*, 4 Feb. 1832; compare *Rep.*, 22 Feb. 1822.

class of thinkers being equally convinced that this information was likely to raise the people in a universal rebellion against their ordinary duties and customary mode of life. To an unconcerned party, it must appear incomprehensible that either good or evil should proceed from being acquainted with the silk manufacture or the height of Rouen cathedral. The error appears to us to consist in an imperfect view of human faculties . . . [*Chamber's Journal*] . . . has addressed itself to the whole moral and intellectual nature of its readers. While conveying information, where formerly was ignorance, it has also endeavoured to arouse reflection and kindle sentiment.[1]

None the less, the resulting mixture was not so very different from that of the *Penny Magazine*. This paper, even more than *Chambers' Journal*, was launched to wipe out the Unstamped. M. D. Hill and Charles Knight, walking into town one morning in February 1832, discussed those 'cheap and offensive publications . . . nearly all dangerous and coarse in degree' which 'abounded' in London. So Knight saw Brougham and showed him nine weekly papers which were 'morally, scandalous and obscene; religiously not simply infidel, but scoffing and ribald; politically preaching anarchy, hardly even confined to the crazy dreams of socialism'. The *Penny Magazine*, Brougham claimed, drove these 'vile publications' out of existence.[2]

Hill proposed a weekly paper, and an SDUK subcommittee on the subject reported that the sale of some of the Unstamped was nearly 30,000. 'These are precisely the circumstances in which . . . the Society ought to interpose in order to direct the taste for reading into proper channels.' Coates, the secretary of the SDUK, cleared the prospective *Penny Magazine* with Timm, the solicitor of the Stamp Office, and the first number came out on 31 March 1832.[3] Thomas Cahussac went on tour to place the *Magazine* with booksellers. 'In such places as Oxford and

[1] *Chambers' Edinburgh Journal*, 30 Jan. 1836; see also 31 Jan. 1835.

[2] C. Knight, *Passages of a Working Life*, 1864, vol. ii, p. 180; H. Brougham, *Cheap Literature for the People*, an Address to the National Association for the Promotion of Social Science, 12 Oct. 1858.

[3] *SDUK Papers*, SDUK General Committee Minutes, 22 Feb. 1832; SDUK Penny Publication Committee, 8 Mar. 1832; SDUK Letter Book 2, Coates to Timm, 19 Mar. 1832; SDUK Letters 1832, Timm to Coates, 20 Mar. 1832.

Reading', he wrote back to Knight in April 1832, 'it is quite evident from what I learnt that it had already had the desired effect of checking the progress and the sale of many of the shameful publications at the same price which preceded it.' In July he wrote to Coates:

The interest excited everywhere by the *Penny Magazine* is quite extraordinary; its sale in almost every town I visited is daily increasing; and I have had the gratification to learn from several booksellers, that in proportion to its increased circulation has the demand for other publications (many of them of a pernicious tendency) in the same shape declined.[1]

The sales of the two papers must have reached 200,000, and encouraged a host of imitators, penny doctors, penny lawyers, and in 1835 Thomas Walker's *Original*, which offered 'an alternative diet of sound and comfortable doctrines blended with innocuous amusement'. They had some loyal readers: 'The contents of the *Penny Magazine* when once read and treasured up in the mind can never be lost', wrote Josiah Riddle of Hoxton New Town. Christopher Thompson went without sugar in his tea to buy the *Magazine*; and Chambers related that five poor Cambridgeshire boys walked seven miles and shared a copy between them for ten years— most satisfactorily two had become headmasters, one a clergyman, another a builder, and the last a sheep-farmer in New Zealand.[2]

Yet their rivalry with the radical Unstamped must have been a shadow thing, if Hickson's comment to the Select Committee of 1851, that 'I never did know of a poor man taking in the *Penny Magazine*', was widely true. *Chambers*, he thought, was read mainly by small shopkeepers. Collett, secretary of the Association for the Repeal of the Taxes on Knowledge, agreed with him. Chambers himself admitted in 1840 that the benefits supposedly conferred by cheap publications were overrated; he was read by the respectable of the working class, the labour aristocracy, but by very few below this. Gaskell, studying the manufacturing districts

---

[1] SDUK Letters, 1832, Cahussac to Knight, 27 Apr. 1832, Cahussac to Coates, 12 July 1832.
[2] The *Original*, 20 May 1835 (Walker was a London police magistrate); SDUK Letters, 1832, Riddle to Coates, 23 May 1832; C. Thompson, *The Autobiography of a Working Man*, 1847, p. 319; W. Chambers, op. cit., p. 34.

in 1833, reported that the weekly magazines were 'being taken by the middle classes of society'; the working classes preferred

sectarian and political tracts, which, by their exciting nature seem to harmonize better with the depraved taste existing amongst them. Very little interest or curiosity is shewn by this class of the community for the generality of subjects discussed and illustrated by the weekly periodicals. They do not come home sufficiently to their feelings and situations—they do not apply themselves sufficiently closely to their peculiar passions and wants, and they are, in consequence, neglected by them.[1]

The Manchester Statistical Society in 1835 surveyed the cheap publications that were selling in Manchester; these included 900 radical Unstamped, 400 humorous papers, and 1,600 of the *Penny Magazine*, *Saturday Magazine*, *Chamber's Journal*, and *Dublin Penny Journal*, but it added ominously, 'it is impossible to tell what number of these [the latter] are distributed among the working classes.' Street vendors told inquisitive magistrates that there was no sale for these papers in the streets.[2] Brougham was far from correct when he claimed that the *Penny Magazine* wiped out the Unstamped. Bulwer in 1834 charged the SDUK with offering only the 'rattle and hobbyhorse of education' and Matthew Hill sadly replied:

'He wished that he could admit that the Society for the Diffusion of Useful Knowledge had penetrated deeply into the masses of the people. It had not, nor would the exertions of that or any other society be able to do so, unless their works carried with them the stimulant of news and politics'. The SDUK had done what it had done 'by honest means . . . taking the law as it was, had availed itself of all the advantages it could command'. . .[3]

Their failure led to a second venture in competing with the Unstamped. Brougham in 1825 had argued that 'the peace

---

[1] *S.C. on Newspaper Stamps*, 1851, xvii, qus. 3238–51 (Hickson), qus. 923–4 (Collet); *Chambers' Journal*, 25 Jan. 1840; P. Gaskell, *The Manufacturing Population of England . . .*, 1833, p. 280.

See also R. M. Martin's evidence to the S.C. on the Handloom Weavers Petition 1834 and his description of the scurrilous press as 'intellectual dram drinking' (qus. 3988–90).

[2] T. Ashton, *Economic and Social Investigations in Manchester . . .*, 1934, pp. 18–19. For the street vendors, see below, pp. 171–93.

[3] *Hansard*, 3rd ser., xxiii, cols. 1216–17 (22 May 1834).

of the country and the stability of government' demanded cheap tracts on politics and political economy. These subjects were necessarily excluded from the *Penny Magazine* and *Chambers* if they were to avoid charges that they were a newspaper. Charles Knight did persuade the SDUK to give its imprimatur in 1830 and 1831 to tracts on machinery, and on capital and labour.[1] A monthly paper, however, could carry politics and political economy without being stamped. So Chambers launched his *Historical Newspaper* in November 1832, as a monthly commentary on news; within two months it had a circulation of 28,000, of which 18,000 were sold in Scotland. Three months later Brougham and Knight started the *Companion to the Newspaper*, 'a repository of FACTS', a guide to legislation, and a means of diffusing political economy for the 'correction of popular error and the advance of general happiness'.[2] In the summer of 1834 a Society for the Diffusion of Political Knowledge formed around the *Companion*, and it undertook to publish a second work, the *Citizen*, to discuss politics and political rights. Both papers, its sponsors promised, would appeal to all sections of society 'but especially the working class'. The Whig element, so strong on the SDUK committee, was replaced by Ewart and Grote, James Mill, Chadwick, Nassau Senior, and Sir Henry Parnell. But the Stamp Act of 1836 seems to have killed the *Companion* as it did the Unstamped, and the *Citizen* was never published at all.[3] Knight never gave the *Companion's* circulation nor made any claims for its 'utility'; and as the Unstamped seldom referred to it, it is hard to judge whether it represented a serious threat to the Unstamped.

The third group of papers sent out to compete with the radical Unstamped were 'anti-infidel' tracts in the tradition of Hannah More. Evangelicals, Methodists, Roman Catholics, all circulated tracts; their best-sellers, such as the *Dairy Man's Daughter*, over the years acquired a circulation of nearly a million. The Society for the Promotion of Christian

[1] The *Chartist* was tackling its premises as late as 1839 (*Chartist*, 16 June 1839), and finding itself in agreement with many of them.
[2] H. Brougham, *Practical Observations* . . ., 3rd edn., 1825, p. 5; *Companion to the Newspaper*, 1 Mar. 1833.
[3] *Companion*, 1 Aug. 1834.

Knowledge (SPCK) met the challenge of 1819 with half a million tracts; within ten years this figure had risen to 1½ million tracts a year; and by the late 1860s the SPCK sent over 8 million tracts into circulation. These tracts were circulated; they could not be sold. The poor of Lancashire and London were reluctant to read them, newsmen were reluctant to stock them. Local auxiliary societies had to tuck them into baskets, push them out at coach and railway stations, and bestow them on such captive groups as the hospital sick, school children, and the prison poor.

Cobbett remarked that the hope of the SPCK was to prevent the people from reading and thinking politics. Priests with a new sense of urgency stood outside Carlile's shop, and even at his counter, pressing tracts upon customers who only shrugged them off. 'These sort of things', wrote Carlile with some satisfaction, 'have been so long crammed down the throats of people that they have taken a surfeit of them'. He kept a pocketful of tracts 'to wipe my lens, light a candle, to remove dirt wherever they are applicable'.[1] By the 1830s success was even further away. Henry Dunn, questioned by the Select Committee on Education in 1835, said that the *Guardian*, a mischievous penny publication, was extensively circulated.

Qu. 84. 'And with a pernicious effect?' 'A very pernicious effect.'
    85. 'Are they bought or distributed gratis?' 'Bought.'
    86. 'Is there any circulation of tracts?' 'The tracts of the Religious Tract Society are circulated by the agents of the Christian Instruction Society; but there is not the same taste for them; men generally read greedily anything that tells them they are injured and illtreated. . . .'[2]

Street sellers who found it difficult to sell the *Penny Magazine*, found that religious tracts were so much waste paper. A young London pickpocket, interviewed by Mayhew in the late 1840s, told him that tracts were brought to the lodging houses where they were used to light pipes. 'Tracts won't fill your belly. Tracts is no good, except to a person that has a home; at the lodging houses they're laughed at.'[3]

---

[1] *Pol. Reg.*, 6 Sept. 1817; *Rep.*, 3 Mar. 1820; *Prompter*, 19 Feb. 1831.
[2] *S.C. on Education*, 1835, vii.   [3] Mayhew, op. cit., vol. i, p. 45.

The SPCK did bring its methods somewhat in line with those of the SDUK by launching its *Saturday Magazine*, which acquired an estimated circulation of 20,000; and together with the nonconformist *Christian's Penny Magazine*, the *Methodist Evangelical Penny Magazine and Bible Illustrator*, and the *Halfpenny Magazine or Witness*, restyled religious literature. But their readership was probably middle class and converted.

The Unstamped affected to take such unsubtle competition seriously. They abused the useful knowledge papers —'for children of a larger growth', a 'sneaking paltry canting attempt to make the labourer contented with his lot', 'a penny imposter', or, in Lorymer's choice verdict on the *National Omnibus*, 'a water closet' magazine. *Figaro in London* repeated the accusations that were frequently heard in 1819 when it complained that Secret Service money was being spent on the *Penny Magazine*, and that Treasury 'subs' were being sent through London with a few pence to purchase and puff the work, and thus persuade shopkeepers that it was 'an excellent selling publication', on which it would be 'safe to speculate'.[1] Sometimes abuse was met by abuse. The *Bristol Job Nott* warned its west country readers that Hetherington and Carlile in their 'poison shops' offered that 'black draught' which brought down on its victim 'discontent, sulkiness, sabbath-breaking, scoffing, hatred of the law, of kings, magistrates, and all superiors'.[2]

Occasionally the *Guardian*, the *Gauntlet* and the *Destructive* deigned to challenge the premises of the *Penny Magazine*, joined with critics in scorning 'kangaroos and dromedaries', and argued that there were two competing versions of 'useful knowledge'. The *Penny Magazine*, O'Brien complained, insinuates 'the most poisonous doctrines in company with the most fascinating information'. A labourer from Poplar wrote in 'to caution the readers of the Guardian against the base and insidious intentions' of the Society for the Diffusion of Useful Knowledge—

Useful knowledge, indeed, would that be to those who live idly on our skill and industry, which would cajole us into an apathetic

[1] *PMG*, 14 Apr. 1832; *Cosmopolite*, 11 Aug. 1832; *PMG*, 7 Apr. 1832; *Figaro*, 22 June 1833.   [2] *Bristol Job Nott*, 26 Jan. 1832.

resignation to their iron sway, or induce us to waste the energy and skill of man for them all day, and seek relaxation of an evening in the puerile stories or recreations of childhood. . . . This first number of their Penny Magazine, insinuates that poor men are not qualified to understand the measures of government. 'Every man is deeply interested in all the questions of government. Every man, however, may not be qualified to understand them.' My fellow-countrymen, I beseech you now do be modest, do be very diffident,—pray do distrust the evidence of your reasons—submit implicitly to the *dicta* of your betters![1]

The SPCK came in for even tougher criticism. The Society aimed to prop up the 'present cannibal order of things' by reconciling the poor to poverty. O'Brien felt it degrading even to comment on their dirty productions. But for some reason 'the canting vagabonds who circulate them have, by their hypocritical pretensions to religion, got such a hold on weak minds, that it is really more difficult to break through their slimy meshes' than it was to demolish the armoury of the villainous stamped press.[2]

At one point Hetherington and Watson tried to stop their agents from selling these papers, but as they sold them themselves, they had little success. The Unstamped had two strong weapons—the profit they offered vendors[3] and the diversity of material they offered readers. Retailers received 5*d*. in the shilling on the *Guardian*, but only 3*d*. in the shilling on the *Penny Magazine*; and the Unstamped carried parliamentary news and police reports, both of which were denied to the *Penny* and *Saturday Magazines*.[4] The *Guardian* and *Slap*, however, to their cost, had to follow the *Penny Magazine* in offering woodcuts.

If the main rivals of the quarto Unstamped were the 'useful knowledge' papers, the broadsheets were in competition with the regular stamped press. Until the summer of 1835 the Unstamped were largely ignored by the stamped press. Vendors were reported as police news along with

---

[1] *PMG*, 14 Apr. 1832; see also *PMG*, 21 Apr. 1833, *Gauntlet*, 15 Dec. 1833.

[2] *PMG*, 2 Feb. 1833.

[3] Wade had recognized the importance of the profit level in extending sales, *Gorgon*, 26 Sept. 1818.

[4] D. Read, op. cit., has shown the importance of a balanced paper, strong in news as well as editorials, if it was to outdistance provincial rivals (p. 204).

thieves and prostitutes and were thought to have something of the same 'colour'. Occasionally an editorial would denounce the authorities for allowing an unstamped press to continue, but the tone was unworried and detached. It was a comment on the machinery of law and the disrespect in which it was held. This changed in 1835. The stamped press objected to the new wave of broadsheets, were indignant when Holt, encouraged by Place, brought out a daily Unstamped in July 1835, the *Daily National Gazette*, and became really alarmed when the sales of the unstamped broadsheets soared after the seizures of Hetherington's and Cleave's presses in August 1835. From then on most of the proprietors of the stamped press urged Spring Rice to reduce the stamp duty to a penny to destroy the demand for a smuggled press while tightening up the law against vendors and printers of the Unstamped.[1]

How real was the competition? F. K. Hunt, writing in 1850, voiced the current orthodoxy, that the cheap papers made 'considerable inroads' upon the circulation of the stamped.[2] Certainly the sales of the unstamped broadsheets were phenomenally high compared to those of the stamped press, and much of their readership must have been middle-class. But Chapman, in one of Roebuck's *Pamphlets*, demonstrated that between January 1834 and June 1835 the sales of the stamped press had risen by 5 per cent, and this, he thought, showed that the Unstamped had created their own readership. Sales of *The Times*, *Examiner*, and *Morning Herald* had fallen off for independent reasons, that of the *Morning Chronicle* had increased, and only the *True Sun* might be thought to have suffered from the Unstamped. According to Cousins, the Unstamped never won very much advertising revenue away from the stamped press. Crawfurd, however, suggested that though the Unstamped might not have diminished the circulation of the stamped, they might account for its lack of growth.[3]

---

[1] Add. MSS. 25146, f. 138; W. Hickson, op. cit., *London Review*, 1 Jan. 1836, pp. 342–3.

[2] F. K. Hunt, *The Fourth Estate*, 1850, vol. ii, p. 72.

[3] *Pamphlets for the People*, no. 20; *Pol. Reg.*, 15 Aug. 1835; J. Crawfurd, *A Financial Review . . .*, 1836.

This lack of growth was nothing new. Newspapers for many years had barely kept pace with the increase in population. In 1821 some 25 million stamped papers were read by a British (that is, excluding Ireland) population of 14 million, a *per capita* consumption of 1·8 newspapers a year. In 1831 some 33½ million newspapers were absorbed by a population of 16½ million, a *per capita* consumption of just over two newspapers for the year of the Reform crisis. In 1834 and 1835 some 31 million newspapers were read by a population of around 17½ million, a fall to a *per capita* consumption of 1·8. In 1837, the first year after the reduction of the stamp duty and the fall in price of stamped newspapers from 7*d*. to 5*d*., 48,600,000 stamps were issued; by 1851 85 million stamped papers were read by a population of 21 million, a *per capita* consumption of four newspapers a year.[1] So it would seem that it was the price of newspapers rather than the intermittent competition of the Unstamped that inhibited the sales of the stamped press. Whitty, a Liverpool newspaper proprietor, told the Select Committee of 1851 that when he published a 'high price newspaper' its sale was 2,700; in 1846 he reduced the price to 3*d*. and the paper sold 10,000.[2]

Contemporaries congratulated themselves on the implications of the statistics. Certainly the total consumption of stamped newspapers soared, but for two reasons which were not quite so directly related to the decrease in their price. The first was that some of the great Unstamped, in particular Hetherington's *Dispatch* and Cousins's *Weekly Chronicle*, now went stamped and helped swell the statistics. The second was that hundreds of new papers were started, for their proprietors required less ready capital (though heavier securities) than before, and the market for medium-priced newspapers seemed ripe for exploitation. In 1832 London had around 70 stamped papers, 6 of which discontinued or merged with other papers in the course of the year; in 1839 it had 154 papers; in the country as a whole the number of newspapers went up from 397 in 1836 to 493 in 1840.[3]

¹ *Accounts and Papers*, 1831–2, xxxiv; 1842, xxvi; 1851, xvii Appendix 4.
² *S.C. on Newspaper Stamps*, 1851, xvii, qu. 576.
³ *Accounts and Papers*, 1833 (610), xxxii; 1840 (524), xxix.

If, however, the increase in sales of stamped papers that circulated both before and after the reduction of the stamp duty is calculated, the story is rather different. Thirty political and semi-political newspapers were published in London both in 1832 and in 1839; their combined sales for 1832 were 16,250,000, for 1839 a little over 19 million, an increase of only 18 per cent; if *The Times* is excluded, the increase was only 13 per cent; that is, it just surpassed population growth. For the country as a whole the total sales of stamped newspapers went up by 66 per cent.[1]

It would seem, therefore, that though the Unstamped had not been taking away readers from the stamped press, neither had their sales been as depressed by the fourpenny stamp as contemporaries believed. The verdict of a recent study, that 'The fact that heavy taxation was the most important cause of the restricted sales of newspapers is amply proved by the statistics', does not indeed seem fully proven.[2] It is also unlikely that the total increase in news-paper sales was due to a wider readership, for in that case the sales of individual well-established newspapers would have risen. Presumably people were taking two papers where formerly they had taken only one, adding a local country paper, perhaps, to a London one. Newspaper sales in the two 'capital' cities, London and Manchester, rose very little in 1837; the 'provincial' papers of Leeds and Sheffield, however, increased their sales by upwards of 50 per cent.[3]

Between the Unstamped themselves, all was not sweetness and light. There were, of course, ideological differences at stake between the trade union *Pioneer* and the political-radical *Guardian*; between the hand-pressed *Advocate* and

---

[1] *Loc. cit.* These calculations are taken from the accounts for Jan. 1832–June 1833, and for Jan. 1839–Dec. 1839, as these break sales down by individual news-paper. But as there are no accounts for 1832 alone, I have had to use those for the eighteen months; as the total sales of newspapers in each year were about the same, I have divided the figures by two-thirds to arrive at an estimated circulation for these thirty London newspapers for the year of 1832. If there is any error, this will have underestimated the sales for 1832, and have overestimated the percentage increase in newspaper sales between 1832 and 1839; to correct for this error would strengthen the argument.

[2] A. Aspinall, op. cit., p. 23.

[3] For the sales of these papers, see D. Read, op. cit., pp. 209–19.

all papers printed by machinery; between Carlile who distrusted unions of any sort and the leaders of the National Union of the Working Class; between the Owenites and the parliamentarians; between Benbow's style of direct action and more orthodox co-operators.[1] For the most part, these differences were discussed and aired in civil unemotional language. The spitting and the claws came out in personal squabbles and commercial jealousies. In 1817 to 1820 Wooler and Carlile, Wooler and Cobbett, Sherwin and Cobbett, had all been estranged at various times, and Hunt quarrelled with everyone.[2] In the 1830s Carlile broke with Taylor, Hetherington and Carlile refused to speak to each other, Benbow and Lee abused each other, Benbow and the Hetherington circle were less than friendly, and eventually O'Brien and Hetherington denounced each other from public platforms and attempted to burke each other's newspapers.[3]

The big quarrel was between Carlile and Hetherington. Popay reported back in 1830 that Hetherington, Hunt, and Carlile nearly came to blows on the hustings and had to be forcibly separated. When Hetherington defended the first Mrs. Carlile, Carlile reminded him 'of a species of polecat of which I have read'; Hetherington, according to Carlile, had been a 'secret, hypocritical and villainous enemy' for upwards of six years.[4] There *were* real differences of conviction; but the acrimony seemed to have spilt over from the great Carlile–Hunt quarrels of the 1820s on to Hetherington's subsequent friendship with Hunt. There was also the displacement of one popular hero by another, and some commercial jealousy—Carlile claimed that Hetherington's papers were a blackleg undercut job, Hetherington that Carlile's prices were 'aristocratical'.

[1] See below, pp. 250–1, 234, 268.

[2] *Rep.*, 22 Feb. 1822; compare Carlile MSS., Ferrar to Turton, 21 June 1863, 'During the time that you and I have known the theological and political world it is amazing the amount of Discord we have witnessed among the Leaders— Cobbett & Hunt, Hunt & Carlile, Carlile & Cobbett, Carlile & Taylor, Holyoake & Cooper (Robert, afterwards reconciled), Holyoake & Southwell—Barker & Bradlaugh—Barker & Watts. . . .'

[3] *London Mercury*, 11 June 1837.

[4] HO 64/11, 16 Nov. 1830; *PMG*, 1 Nov. 1834; *Scourge*, 8 Nov. 1834. Hibbert to Carlile, 9 Aug. 1833 (Carlile MSS.).

Where Carlile offered his retailers 25 per cent, Hetherington and his friends allowed 33 per cent. Carlile still felt bitter about being called a 'money-grubber' in 1839, and in 1837 he had refused to allow Heywood to act as a peace-maker between them. 'I could not endure it. My quarrels with men are for life.'[1]

Benbow's quarrels with the Hetherington circle were less complex, and were the result of feuds within the NUWC being aired in the field of journalism. Lee's version was that Benbow claimed that he suffered from designing enemies, 'Messrs Cleave, Hetherington and others, who, according to his statement, have made it their business to prejudice him in the eyes of his paper merchant, and in other ways contribute to his injury by spoiling his credit'. Lee, for his too-willing sympathy with Benbow, was left with a bill for £11 and a warrant against him in Marlborough Street for selling copies of the *Tribune* without Benbow's permission. Lee, when he first started, according to Carlile, 'came to me to say that he would war to the knife against Hetherington and Cleave. At that time in 1831 I advised him not to do so. He took my advice, but he soon joined the gang to make war upon me!' Then in the spring of 1834 Lee floated the *People's Hue and Cry*, a penny broadsheet, where the *Gazette* and the *Dispatch* sold for 2*d*. According to Lee, Cleave persuaded the booksellers not to distribute either Lee's *Man* or the *Hue and Cry*, and Lee in despair 'throws himself on the public in the face of such a monopoly'.[2]

The quarto Unstamped argued with each other and sometimes squabbled with each other. The broadsheets copied each other and thus tried to acquire one another's circulation. Cleave was the culprit in another piece of sharp practice. In the autumn of 1833 he worked to promote Penny's *People's Police Gazette* until its sales mounted to 20,000 and Cleave's slice of them to 3,000; then, without

---

[1] *Scourge*, 11 Oct. 1834; *PMG*, 1 Nov. 1834; Carlile to Turton, 22 Dec. 1839, 22 Nov. 1837 (Carlile MSS.). Carlile's letters are sick with strictures on his enemies—Carpenter kept a prostitute, Cleave's wife was to be placed in an asylum so Cleave could sleep with her servant, Hetherington was being bought by the tories, Watson was spreading rumours that the Rotunda was a brothel, etc.

[2] Lee, *Benbowism* . . .; Carlile to Turton, 16 June 1840 (Carlile MSS.); *Man*, 3 Apr. 1834.

warning to Penny, Cleave put out his *Weekly Police Gazette*
in the spring of 1834, substituted the one for the other,
and drove Penny out of the field.[1] George Johnson was the
printer and publisher of the *Weekly Times*; 'discharged for
embezzlement', he produced a second *Weekly Times*. The
Entertaining Press was duplicated by the *New Entertaining
Press*, Cleave's *Weekly Police Gazette* by the *People's
Weekly Police Gazette*, Hetherington's *Twopenny Dispatch*
by the *People's Twopenny Dispatch*.[2] When the stamped
Weekly Dispatch claimed that Hetherington had taken its
title and its news, O'Brien replied that the *Twopenny Dispatch*
went to the press several days before the stamped *Dispatch*;
but 'Our title had been stolen—a fraudulent imitation of this
paper was got up—an imitation so exact that at first sight
no eye could distinguish between the counterfeit and the
genuine. . . . Of piracy in the ordinary sense, we cannot
complain; but in a sense much worse than the ordinary one,
we have deep and frequent cause to complain. Our articles
have been ransacked and garbled extracts made from them
into stamped newspapers.' In July 1836 the *True Sun*
denied that it was connected with the unstamped *Weekly
True Sun*, put out by John Bell, a former editor of the *True
Sun*. 'This is the second piratical attempt, under the same
false colours, to injure our property.'[3]

At its worst, the rivalry between the broadsheet Unstamped led to one turning informer on the other. According
to the *Weekly Times*, one of the proprietors of an unstamped
paper was himself an informer against 'his more favoured
contemporaries. We can clearly trace to him informations
by which several enormous seizures were made.' It did
not name him. Cousins's *Weekly Herald*, a few months later,
charged an ex-vendor with being an informer, selling
obscene books and committing offences with 'boys of bad
character'. One of these was possibly Charles Clements,
the former publisher of Cobbett's *Political Register*, whom
George Pilgrim thought to be a spy back in August 1835,

[1] *Scourge*, 25 Oct. 1834; *People's Police Gazette*, 3 May 1834.
[2] *Weekly Times*, 20 Mar., 8 May 1836; Memorial of Certain Inhabitants of the
City of London, 1835, *Place Coll.*, Set 70, f. 203.
[3] *Twopenny Dispatch*, n.d. but probably mid May 1836, cutting in *Place Coll.*,
Set 70, f. 521; *True Sun*, 13 July 1836.

who was known to be employed by the Stamp Office in
February 1836, but who was not finally denounced by
Hetherington and Cleave until December 1836.[1]

Yet the surprising thing is that there was so little cut-
throat competition: Hetherington was even known to
collect subscriptions for Carlile. Five things checked it.
The first was that Hetherington, Carlile, and Cousins
dominated the market. Each was the proprietor of several
papers, which advertised each other and made for a more
economical use of material. Carlile put material he could not
use in the *Gauntlet* into the *Cosmopolite*, and used the one to
explain his doings in the other; Hetherington did the same
with the *Guardian* and the *Destructive*, printing Davenport's
letter in one and answering it in the other, starting an
article on universal suffrage in the *Guardian* which was
'resumed' in the *Destructive*. But he ran into trouble for
it: newsmen were reluctant to stock both papers and
Hetherington had to reply. 'We have heard it prevail that
the two papers contain the same material. This is a great
error and calculated to do us great injury. . . . Our correspondent must allow us to reply in either vehicle.'[2]

A second and more subtle check on competition lay in
the way empires were built up. At the end of 1833, for
example, the Carliles were publicly identified with the
Gauntlet, they published the *Man*, though Lee was still its
editor, and were the anonymous publishers, writers, and
proprietors of the *Cosmopolite*. Carlile could use the *Scourge*
to denounce Hetherington and Cleave, but in those papers
in which he had an interest but did not control, the verbal
warfare had to be moderated. Readers would not tolerate a
change of line overnight; and there would be other influences
to balance Carlile's. Former owners stayed on as editors,
former printers continued to print for the new owner,
two papers might merge, and some balance of opinion
have to be struck. Lee's *Man* was friendly to both Hetherington and Carlile; so was the *Cosmopolite*. When Carlile acquired

---

[1] *Weekly Times*, 22 May 1836; *Weekly Herald*, 14 Aug. 1836; *London Dispatch*,
4 Dec. 1836.
[2] *Destructive*, 2 Mar. 1833; see also *Gauntlet*, 26 May 1833; *Destructive*, 24
Aug. 1833; *PMG*, 6 July 1833.

an interest in the *Cosmopolite*, it became even friendlier towards Carlile without becoming cool to Hetherington. *Man* changed publishers but Lee remained as editor and the paper's stance stayed much the same. The two papers then merged, again without radical consequences, and a few months later Lee resigned from Carlile's Volunteers and regained control of his old paper. Leading vendors, such as Pilgrim and Hancock, offered their allegiance to both groups, Carlile and Hetherington; Lee served as something of a buffer; and Davenport, Petrie, Edmonds, and Lorymer wrote for several papers. All this blurred the edges of competition.

The third influence that checked competition was the superb mutual aid noted by Lowery.[1] Papers carried generous 'puffs' of each other; the *Cosmopolite* described the *Pioneer* as 'a pretty little publication'.[2] In an emergency, presses and types were shared. When one man was in prison, others rallied round. Carlile in 1819 had been much helped by Sherwin and Davidson; in the early 1830s, Julian Hibbert gave both Carlile and Hetherington his time and money; when Lee was sentenced in June 1834 his friend George Petrie quickly organized a committee of aid, extracted funds from the Charlotte Street Institution, and opened new offices at 145 Fetter Lane, while Baume found the paper a new editor and a new printer.[3] When the Attorney-General announced Carpenter's prosecution, Cleave, Watson, and Baume 'have already Volunteered their services should that be the case to stand forward in his place and publish it for him at all risks'. When Hetherington was away, Cleave, Watson, and Lovett were 'to continue' the *Poor Man's Guardian* and the *Republican* for him 'in his absence';[4] when on tour themselves they did their best to advertise and sell the paper. When eventually Watson and Cleave put out their own paper, the *Working Man's Friend*, they took great care not to compete with the *Guardian*. As Dr. Wade told the NUWC, 'It was a publication not in the most remote

[1] *Weekly Record*, 5 July 1856.   [2] *Cosmopolite*, 23 Nov. 1833.
[3] *Rep.*, 19 Nov. 1819, 21 Jan. 1820, 22 Feb. 1822; *People's Hue and Cry*, 10 Aug. 1834.
[4] HO 64/11, 13 Nov. 1830; HO 64/11, 26 July 1831.

manner interfering with Mr. Hetherington's *Penny Paper*.' They scrupulously avoided carrying identical reports.

Our friend at Wigan should not be so sore about the omission of the Open air meeting knowing that the *Poor Man's Guardian* has prepared a long and able report: we purposely avoided clashing with that paper, as it has been and will be, our study to strengthen the hands of friend Hetherington.[1]

Similarly, the *Guardian* said very little about the Fast Day trials because Watson was 'getting it up as a 6*d.* work', and the profits were to be divided among them.[2] This cooperation was recalled at Hetherington's funeral in 1849 when Watson testified 'with evident emotion' that though they were two booksellers there was never between them 'the smallest degree of rivalry which was so commonly found, and which degraded trade into a low, a disingenuous, a selfish and a miserable contest . . . their single friendship never knew two interests.'[3]

Fourthly, outside pressure checked competition. The Unstamped tried to show something of a united front towards a prosecuting government and a hostile middle-class press. With the notable exception of Carlile, who scorned all associations for the common end of removing the newspaper stamp, proprietors shared public platforms, came together in committee rooms, worked for the relief of victims, signed joint petitions, and lobbied alongside middle-class radicals.[4] Most of these men came out of a shared background of radical working-class societies and co-operative groups; very many of them were old allies in other causes, and they continued to be allies in new ones.

Finally, the concept of the rational debate checked mud-slinging and *ad hominem* vitriol. The two slogans of the Unstamped were that knowledge was power, and that union was power. Only a united working-class effort would bring the New Society, but that union must be informed, not artificial, and based on discussion and debate, which must be rational, unemotional, impersonal, and conciliatory.

---

[1] *WMF*, 26 Jan. 1833; *WMF*, 30 Mar. 1833.
[2] HO 64/12, 22 May 1832.
[3] Reported, Cooper's Eloge, *Reasoner*, 1849, vol. x.
[4] See below, Chapter VIII.

When the *Charter*, for example, in 1840 was merged into the *New Statesman*, its proprietors thought fit to state that they would never appeal to passion or popular indignation. 'They would address the reason.' Men must be persuaded by ideas and not by other men. When the *Guardian* deplored the evils of 'party spirit', it gave its readers credit,

each of you, the meanest of you, for the ability of thinking for your-selves... so far as you agree with us, respect our opinions—but, without ill feeling, we beseech you to differ from us as to the remainder; so long as you think us worthy of your support, do not withhold it,— and, the instant you think otherwise, do not quarrel with us, but, though you cease to keep company with us, let us part friends. . . .

Even to air differences was to begin to reconcile them. So the debate was almost always courteous and was open to all.[1] Watson advised Holyoake in 1846 when he was about to launch the *Reasoner*, 'But admit what you might into your columns, whether *ultra* or *otherwise* in its advocacy, its manner should be argumentative and calm in its tone; and deviation from this rule should be a ground of exclusion, no matter which side of the question it advocated.'[2] Similarly, when Collins and O'Neill argued in the *Northern Star* that any middle-class radical who accepted Chartist principles should be allowed to enrol under the Chartist banner, they appealed to the concept of the open and rational debate. 'On the method of advocating much depends. Always distinguish between vituperation and argument; remember that insult and animadversion are not conviction, and never for a moment conceive that a swaggering Billingsgate, is either dignity or determination.'[3]

The whole philosophy was summarized by one of Carlile's correspondents.

Sir—although our opinions respecting the best plan of bringing about the reform we both desire differ very widely, it is at least evident that we are agreed on one point, viz. the paramount necessity of 'Free Inquiry'. So long as this is the watchword, I care not whether any opponents be Orthodox or Infidel, Deist, Demonist or Atheist, Whig, Radical or Tory, because there is an obvious *desire* for truth.

---

[1] *Charter*, 1 Mar. 1840; *PMG*, 10 Dec. 1831.
[2] Watson to Holyoake, 27 Feb. 1846 (*Holyoake Coll.*).
[3] *NS*, 20 Feb. 1841.

But where the advocates of a cause would enforce their tenets in holes or corners, or give them to the world without listening to or allowing others to listen to the opposite side of the question, must there not be a fear regarding the unsoundness of such hole and corner doctrines?[1]

[1] Neville Wood to Carlile, 21 June 1839 (Carlile MSS.).

V

PROSECUTION

THE several hundred Unstamped that were launched between 1830 and 1836 were of a dozen kinds. There were the radical political papers, the *Guardian*, the *Gauntlet*, and the *Cosmopolite*, some of which became the radical broadsheet newspapers of 1834–6, Cleave's *Weekly Police Gazette*, Hetherington's *Dispatch*, and the *Weekly Times*; those papers critical of the Church Establishment, the *Slap at the Church* and the *Christian Corrector*; the trade union and Owenite papers, the *Pioneer*, the *Crisis*, and the *New Moral World*; the co-operative journals, the *Magazine of Useful Knowledge*, the *Lancashire Co-operator*; a few parliamentary papers, including the *People's Press*; many political humorous papers, among them *Figaro*, *Cab*, the *Whig Dresser*, and the *Weekly Show Up*; the humorous ones, *Paddy Kelly's Budget*, *Dibdin's Penny Trumpet*; crime reporters, for instance the *Newgate Calender*, the *Annals of Crime*; the literary and theatrical papers, such as the *Weekly Visitor*, the *Stage*, *Wanderer*, the *Sketch Writer*; the useful knowledge papers, the *Weekly Miscellany*, the *Penny Doctor*, the *Penny Lawyer*, and above all the *Penny Magazine*; and finally the religious papers, the *Witness* and the *Saturday Magazine*.

Now a newspaper, according to the Six Acts (60 G3 c9), was any paper which contained public news, intelligence, or occurrences, any comments thereon or on matters of Church and State; and which was printed for sale and published periodically within twenty-six days; and which was no larger than two sheets and sold for less than 6*d.* exclusive of the duty.[1] What lawyers did not resolve was what each individual clause entailed, and whether a newspaper was defined by all these clauses or only by any one of them.

When Timms, the solicitor to the Board of Inland Revenue, was pressed to define a newspaper by Milner

[1] See below, p. 165.

Gibson in 1851, he could not state how much news a paper could contain before it became a newspaper, or when occurrences became past history, the grounds on which the *Annual Register* went unstamped. He thought a bound volume would not be a newspaper though *The Times* in boards would be; that a monthly and even a bi-monthly publication would be a newspaper but not a tri-monthly one; that the Queen's speech, if reprinted, was news but that that of the Chancellor of the Exchequer was not; that if a court trial was reprinted by the *West Riding Examiner* that was news, but if reprinted by the *Legal Observer* it was not. Yet he insisted that he had never found himself 'in great practical difficulties over deciding what was a newspaper'.[1]

The second problem was whether a paper was a newspaper if it infringed one of the clauses of 60 G3 c9, or only if it infringed all of them, that is whether these clauses were meant to be conjunctive or disjunctive. If infringing any of these clauses made a paper a newspaper, then all of the Unstamped were newspapers. If all the clauses defined a newspaper, and therefore if all had to be infringed before a paper was a newspaper, then some of the monthly co-operative journals, and the humorous papers which did not carry 'intelligence', were pamphlets and not newspapers. But on either account of the law, the great majority of the Unstamped were newspapers.

None the less the Commissioner of Stamps decided which paper contained 'intelligence' and which did not. The *Harlequin* of the late 1820s contained only theatrical news but was suppressed; its successor, the *Tatler*, which had a broader range of interests, was not. The *Penny Magazine*'s articles on dromedaries, cathedrals, and rock-formation, did not constitute 'intelligence', neither did the *Penny Doctor*'s remedies for cholera and palsy, nor the morally uplifting columns of the religious periodicals. The *Bristol Job Nott* could criticize the doctrines of the *Guardian*, and that was not considered 'intelligence'; but the doctrines of the *Guardian* were. Of the twelve categories of Unstamped, only the first three, the radical papers, the broadsheets,

[1] *S.C. on Newspaper Stamps*, 1851, qus. 58, 105–235.

and the anti-clerical papers, were prosecuted. When Cowie appealed against the prosecution of the *Church Examiner*, which he published, Alley, the Stamp Office lawyer, was supposed to have admitted

there are many works, such as the *Penny Magazine*, the *Literary Gazette*, the *Crisis*, the *Figaro* and others you have exhibited, all of which infringe upon the letter of the law, at least equally with the *Church Examiner*, but then as they are either merely or harmlessly amusing, or more really instructive, we should be very reluctant to enforce the law against them.[1]

As late as 1840 there was an exchange in the House of Lords between Spring Rice, former Chancellor of the Exchequer and now Lord Monteagle, and the Bishop of Exeter, who wanted to know why the *New Moral World* was allowed to circulate without being classed as a newspaper by the acts of 1819 and 1836. Spring Rice's reply was that if he had followed the law too literally, then the Bishop's *Saturday Magazine* would have had to have been banned.[2]

Even when the magistrates imprisoned vendors for obstructing the highway rather than for selling an unstamped newspaper, vendors selling the *Omnibus* or *Figaro* were dismissed.[3] Only the radical Unstamped were thought to impede free passage in the streets.

(a) PUBLISHERS AND PROPRIETORS

Because these papers were illegal, their proprietors faced problems beyond that of sales and distribution and profit. They had to build up their own network of outlets, recruit and support their printers and vendors, and protect their businesses from the ravages of government attacks.

Sidmouth's Circular of spring 1817 had suggested[4] that magistrates should hold vendors for selling pamphlets without a licence, but there was neither the wholesale selling nor the wholesale arrests that there were in the 1830s. However, local pressure was put on the agents of Radical papers. 'A respectable man' who employed a vendor

---

[1] *True Sun*, 1 Sept. 1832; see also Dyer's remarks, *The Times*, 19 Mar. 1832.
[2] Reported in *Southern Star*, 16 Feb. 1840.
[3] *The Times*, 3, 7 Sept. 1831 (case of Pavey).   [4] See above, p. 38.

to hawk the periodicals on Henley's market day was illegally fined £80, but he recovered £100 in damages from the Reverend magistrate. Booksellers were reluctant to sell and publicans reluctant to take the *Black Dwarf* and the *Register*. In Birmingham a landlord and his wife burnt the *Black Dwarf*, so the radicals withdrew their custom. Hawkers were taken into custody in Wolverhampton, Coventry, Plymouth, and Exeter; at Oxford the Vice-Chancellor described Sherwin's *Political Register* as 'a scandalous, wicked and seditious libel', and an old man of seventy-two was discharged from the Clarendon Press.[1] Occasionally vendors took alarm, but for the most part the counter-attack was sporadic, ineffective, and local in its origins.[2]

The Unstamped of the 1830s, like the journals of the 1850s, met with similar random gestures of hostility. Booksellers who did sell Carpenter's *Letters* or the *Slap* were visited by clergymen. The *Guardian* and the *Destructive* were denounced from a Macclesfield pulpit as 'the Poor Man's Poison' and the 'People's Destruction'.[3] Hethering-ton was offered all the printing he could undertake if he gave up the Unstamped; Carpenter and Cleave were sent bribes. Men were occasionally dismissed from work for selling or reading the Unstamped. Tufnell, one of the Factory Commissioners, reported that a certain Charles Aberdeen, a regular and reliable workman, was dismissed by the managing partner because he sold Carlile's pamphlets and occasionally wrote in to the Unstamped.[4] And in the autumn of 1831 Carpenter warned that the police were about to raid all coffee shops and public houses, and wherever they found political pamphlets, to take the owner of the house before the magistrates. Bills were torn down; one parson was supposed to have hired two men for three days at two shillings a day to tear down the placards of the Unstamped; one of them was caught at Lambeth and ducked in a horsepond.[5]

---

[1] *Black Dwarf*, 29 Sept. 1819; *Pol. Reg.*, 1 Feb. 1817; *Rep.*, 17 Sept., 1 Oct. 1819.
[2] *Rep.*, 30 May 1822; *Medusa*, 11 Dec. 1819.
[3] *Slap*, 3 Mar. 1832; *PMG*, 7 Sept. 1833.
[4] W. Lovett, *Life and Struggles . . .*, 1920 edn., vol. i, p. 61; *Slap*, 10 Mar. 1832; *Gauntlet*, 12 Jan. 1834; *Report of the Factory Commissioners*, 1833, xx, pp. 838–9, 867.
[5] Carpenter's *Political Magazine*, Sept. 1831; *Slap*, 7 Apr. 1832.

Stamped newspapers refused their advertisements. A respectable Newcastle bookseller, who wrote in to order copies of the *Slap at the Church* from Whitakers, the booksellers of Stationer's Court, had his invoice returned with 'sale illegal'.[1] Missionaries for the *Penny Magazine* tried not only to extend its sale but also to cut back that of the Unstamped. The Home Office received dozens of letters complaining of the proliferation of the poison, and offering to prosecute if the Home Office would foot the bill. But all this was too casual to be really effective. What mattered was the energy of the Stamp Office, under pressure from the Home Office, and the acquiescence of magistrates; and magistrates were only too happy to award the maximum sentence to a publisher, while allowing the vendors to escape lightly.

Publishers had various methods of protecting themselves against imprisonment. The first way was to produce an Unstamped paper which, it could be argued in court, was not a newspaper at all but a pamphlet. Cleave argued that as his papers did not include notices of bankruptcies and stocks they did not have the function of a newspaper. Carpenter tried to prove that his papers were not newspapers because they contained no news; Berthold tried to prove that his papers were not newspapers because they contained no paper. His calico fourpenny *Political Handkerchief* told readers:

> Your wives and daughters may become moving monuments of political knowledge. One shall be dressed in a description of kingcraft, another in a description of priestcraft, a third in a description of lordcraft, or general aristocracy. . . . The nakedness of mankind shall be covered both as to body and mind.[2]

As an afterthought, he added that if the ink washed out, he would buy them back and reprint them. This became a popular and highly profitable gimmick. Richard Carlile junior sold cotton almanacs until he was lectured by the Stamp Office, whereupon he recanted, to the disgust of his father, for 'he saw no fun in going to prison'. Cousins likewise pro-

---

[1] *Slap*, 28 Jan. 1832, 28 Apr. 1832.

[2] Berthold's *Political Handkerchief*, 5 Sept. 1831; see also *Destructive*, 26 Apr. 1834. G. Cranfield has shown that certain protective devices, such as irregular printing, or the binding of a weekly parts edition of the Bible with a cover on which was printed news, went back into the eighteenth century (op. cit., pp. 241–2).

duced a *Duster for the Whigs*, with an almanac printed on one side and news on the other. He brought out some twenty issues of it, and defended them in court as 'printed calico' in the best Lancashire style.[1] Walker and Willis, two leading vendors, put out the *Political Touchwood*, a sheet of shaving thin plywood, as 'a profession of faith calculated to ignite the human understanding'. Rawlinson, with unconscious humour, described it as 'a Seditious and Inflammatory Publication'.[2] The *Comet*, launched by Falvey of Liverpool, gave present news in the shape of future prophecies. Cowie argued that the *Church Examiner* was religious in character and therefore exempt from duties. Hunt and Hetherington argued that their papers were not newspapers because they were published irregularly.[3] But all these were ruses designed more to give the proprietors scope for arguing with the Stamp Office than to evade its hand altogether. The *Guardian*, after all, carried a column unnecessarily headed 'Public news, intelligence or occurences', the *Cosmopolite* described itself as a 'London weekly newspaper', the *Gauntlet* as 'a sound republican newspaper', and Lorymer's *Reformer* of spring 1833 as 'a daily evening newspaper'.

The second way to avoid trouble was for the proprietors to protect their businesses as far as possible. Most of the publishers who were printers made sure their presses were registered—Berthold, Penny, Watson, Walker, and Knight of the *Cosmopolite*, Cowie, Cleave, and Hetherington; and in August 1835 Cousins and Lee quickly registered. It must have pleased their sense of mockery solemnly to admit to having a printing press 'which I require to be entered . . . [according to 39 G3 c.79] an Act for the more effectual Suppression of Societies established for Seditious and Treasonable Purposes; and for better preventing Treasonable and Seditious Practises'.[4] Cousins and Lorymer went further and used pseudonyms to protect themselves; both chose 'Benjamin Franklin'. Cousins also hid behind another

---

[1] HO 64/11, 26 Dec. 1831; A. Heywood, *Three Papers on English Printed Almanacs*, 1904, p. 21.

[2] HO 59/3 contains what seems to be the only extant copy of the *Touchwood*; Rawlinson to Phillips, 11 Feb. 1832.

[3] *Comet*, 4 Aug. 1832; *The Times*, 27 June 1832.

[4] Printers Certificates, Corporation of London R.O., Middlesex C.R.O.

printer, Thomas Wilson, of Great Wild Street, who registered in August 1835.[1] Cleave possibly was using 'T. Wakelin' in a similar way. Carlile published the *Union* as one John Smith, though this was more to cover up his inconsistency in supporting unions than to remain disguised from the Stamp Office. Certain vendors, such as George Pilgrim, William Evans, James Reeve, and the former soldiers Alexander Somerville and William Simmens, allowed themselves to be named as the ostensible printers and publishers of a paper. Sometimes publishers gave their own names as the printers, rather than reveal where the presses might be found.

Hetherington boasted he would never stoop to using pseudonyms and would display his name on all his publications: however, in 1834–5 he took the precaution of making over his bookselling stock to Watson and his press to Lovett, so that his goods could not be seized in lieu of fines. He was prepared to leave London if necessary, and his northern tours kept him out of the hands of the London police: in June 1834 he seems to have toyed with the idea of avoiding his forthcoming Exchequer trial altogether. 'Him and Cleave was determined to avoid the law and had gone to France to do so.' 'I find also that Watson who was last week convicted for selling the *Conservative* had gone to Jersey to avoid being taken [*sic*]'[2]. Hetherington returned within a week, and Watson within a month. For much of 1835 Hetherington lived as an anonymous Mr. Williams in Pinner, a village on the outskirts of London. He dressed up his friends in his clothes, who were then hauled off to Bow Street, while he himself entered his shop disguised as a wagoner, a costermonger, or (his favourite garb) as a Quaker, passing through the ranks of watching policemen with 'all the proverbial meekness and child-like simplicity of a member of the Society of Friends. If spoken to, he used the thou and thee with an accuracy that would have deceived any of the body.'[3]

[1] Printers Certificates, Middlesex C.R.O., 5 Aug. 1835. His witness was George Mudie. In 1839 Wilson and Mudie were stationers in Wigmore Street.

[2] HO 64/15, n.d. (9 June 1834 ?), 3 July 1834.

[3] J. Grant, *The Newspaper Press*, 1871, vol. ii, p. 305.

Thirdly, publishers could be cautious in what they sold and to whom they sold it. In July 1831 there was 'a good deal of anxiety' among those who sold Hetherington's papers. Watson

is determined not to stop the sale of them and to go to prison rather than pay any penalties . . . he is to attend at Bow Street office this day to hear Hethrington's [sic] case, and if he finds that a seizure of Goods or Property follows conviction he means to remove most of his from his premises as he has been told seventeen Sellers of these works are marked out for prosecution.[1]

Six months later Watson would sell the cotton almanacs only to people he knew, and Mrs. Hetherington refused to sell them altogether. Carlile sent Abel Heywood six cotton almanacs on the strict understanding that they would be given to a few friends 'as a suppressed curiosity' and not sold over the counter. According to his wife, Watson circulated his own illegal *Working Man's Almanac* privately; 'gentlemen would call and purchase a quantity and dispose of them among their private friends.' By April 1834 Watson was not selling Lorymer's *Republican*, presumably because it was too much of a risk.[2] Dean, the inspector of licences, complained that publishers sold only to those whom they knew or who were recommended as 'Safe customers'. Another informer, whose face was too well known, hired labourers to buy papers for him. In May 1833 a policeman was put in 'coloured clothes' and given some radical papers to make him appear 'an itinerant dealer in such things'. He bought papers at Lee and Lorymer's shop in Brydges Street, and was directed to make other purchases; but there was 'a great difficulty in getting at two or three shops they deny having any though I believed they have [sic]'.[3] Publishers with their own shops had ways of selling papers while remaining anonymous, which were denied to the street vendor. Papers fell down through holes in the ceiling, swung forth on a basket, came through a tiny aperture in the window. Lowery at Newcastle pushed them out through

---

[1] HO 64/11, n.d. (July 1831).
[2] HO 64/11, 26 Dec. 1831; A. Heywood, *Three Printed Papers*, op. cit., pp. 18, 24 f.; HO 64/15, 20 Apr. 1834.
[3] HO 61/8, 11 May 1833; see also *True Sun*, 28 Nov. 1833.

basement gratings; James Acland of Hull placed a revolving box in front of his shop window.[1] And publishers benefited from the more cumbersome process of arrest.

When faced by imprisonment, publishers responded in very different ways. Carlile wanted martyr's robes, and became angry when Place tried to intervene through Colonel Jones on his behalf. Hetherington seems not to have objected to prison, provided he had had suitable publicity and preferably had given the Bow Street runners a cross-country chase at public expense. Watson was less sure of his taste for prison, but he never paid any of his fines and took imprisonment stolidly when it came. Cleave, on at least two occasions, paid his fines rather than go to prison, though when Sir Peter Laurie in May 1834 tried to persuade him to pay up rather than go to jail, his wife intervened and told Laurie not to bother as Cleave was determined to go. Cousins was prepared to lie his way out of trouble, on one occasion swearing that his shop now belonged to 'a person named Franklin', on another that he was no longer connected with the Unstamped.[2]

(b) THE MACHINERY OF ARREST

Proprietors and vendors of the radical Unstamped could be prosecuted on one of three charges: that their papers were seditious, that their papers were newspapers, or that they were selling papers in the street without a hawker's licence. Seditious libel was defined in Common Law as any writing which tended to a breach of the peace.[3] In the years around 1819 the Government tried to control the radical press by trials for seditious libel, prosecuting not the authors of the libel, but the publishers of it—that is, any shopmen or any vendor.[4] By the 1830s charges of seditious libel were reserved only for the proprietors of the papers in which

[1] *Weekly Record*, 5 July 1856; *Hull Advertizer*, 12 Sept. 1834.
[2] Add. MSS. 35146, f. 130; HO 64/12, 20 Dec. 1832; *Man*, 18 May 1834; *The Times*, 22 Apr. 1835, 18 Mar. 1836.
[3] For a full exposition of the law of criminal libel see Wickwar, op. cit., ch. 1.
[4] Carlile was prosecuted not for writing in the *Republican*, but for selling it; Davidson, not for writing anything in the *Medusa* but for selling the *Deist* and the *Republican*. Both men thought the Attorney-General was deliberately casting his net wide. *Rep.*, 19 May 1820; *Medusa*, 11 Dec. 1819.

they appeared; the Government had other methods by which to control the vendors of the radical Unstamped.

Prosecutions for seditious libel were instigated by the Home Office, which directed the Treasury Solicitor to inquire of the law officers whether a piece of writing was libellous and whether its prosecution was 'expedient'.[1] Local prosecutions could be brought either by the law officers, or by magistrates with or without government aid, augmented in the years around 1819 by the Society for the Suppression of Vice. There were two methods of proceeding: either by Indictment (in which case a Grand Jury had to find a True Bill—that is, sufficient grounds for proceeding with a prosecution), the method used against Cobbett and Carlile in 1831; or by an *ex officio* information filed by the Attorney-General. On either method suspected offenders could be arrested on warrant and held for trial, a course of action which Melbourne was advising local justices and lord lieutenants to employ in 1830–1.[2]

Prosecutions for selling unstamped newspapers were a phenomenon of the 1830s, and were brought for infringing 60 G3 c9, that clause in the Six Acts which defined a newspaper, and forbade the selling of a newspaper not duly stamped.

That from and after Ten Days after the passing of this Act, all Pamphlets and Papers containing any Public News, Intelligence or Occurrences, or any Remarks or Observations thereon, or upon any Matter of Church or State, printed in any Part of the United Kingdom for Sale, and published periodically, or in Parts or Numbers, at Intervals not exceeding Twenty six Days between the Publication of any Two such Pamphlets or Papers, Parts or Numbers respectively, shall not exceed Two Sheets, or shall be published for Sale for a less Sum than Sixpence, exclusive of the Duty by this Act imposed thereon, shall be deemed and taken to be Newspapers . . . and be subject to such and the same Duties of Stamps. . . .

Infringements of 60 G3 c9 were heard by two magistrates in the police courts, and carried a maximum penalty of £20 for each offence, which could be mitigated by the magistrates to £5. If the defendant refused to pay, he was sentenced

---

[1] See above, pp. 34 f.

[2] HO 41/8, Melbourne to Earl Talbot, 30 Nov. 1830; HO 41/10, Melbourne to Lord Harewood, 20 June 1831.

to six months' imprisonment in lieu of each fine, but could appeal to Quarter Sessions. However, only the Attorney-General or the Solicitor of Stamps could bring the charge and prove that the paper sold was a newspaper; and the defendant had to be summoned, not arrested. This was a lengthy and cumbersome process which came to be reserved for those publishers of the Unstamped who sold from their shops.

A second law, 38 G3 c78, demanded that affidavits should be filed naming the printer and proprietor of a newspaper, together with their addresses, on pain of £100; prosecutions would be filed by the Attorney-General in the Court of Exchequer before a special jury. But this law appears to have been invoked only twice, against Hetherington and Cleave in June 1834, and against Cleave in February 1836.

The third offence in the world of radical publications was to sell these papers in the streets. 16 G2 c26 forbade any hawker to

sell, hawk, carry about, utter or expose to Sale, any News Paper, or any Book, Pamphlet, or Paper deemed or construed to be a News Paper, within the Intention and Meaning of any of the Acts of Parliament relating to the Stamp Duties now in Force, not being stampt or marked.

This Act had been in abeyance in the years around 1819, though Sidmouth, in his circular of 1817, had suggested that magistrates might care to invoke it. But in the 1830s, when street selling became one of the main outlets for the Unstamped, and a New Police was available to arrest street sellers, this Act was employed to imprison hundreds of street vendors. Any hawker[1] could be arrested on the street by an informer, taken before one magistrate and sentenced to a maximum of three months without hard labour, from which there was no right of appeal. The Stamp Office did not need to prosecute; pamphlets, however, had still to be shown to be newspapers. But magistrates imprisoned vendors for selling pamphlets which were defined as newspapers not by 'the Stamp Duties now in Force' laid down by 16 G2 c26 but by the later Six Acts, 60 G3 c9. The *True Sun* pointed out that this was illegal, but that did not deter the magistrates.

---

[1] Magistrates did insist that hawkers should have sold a paper, not merely carried it about for sale. This policy was changed in 1835.

This method was much simpler and speedier than prosecuting the publisher-proprietors of the Unstamped; it was also more profitable for the informer. He was paid 6s. a day by the Stamp Office to acquire evidence against booksellers by buying papers in their shops; but he was entitled to £1 reward for every committal obtained against a street hawker. And as street vendors lacked the array of protective devices possessed by the publishers,[1] it was they who bore the brunt of the attack against the Unstamped.

Publishers and street vendors alike were brought before the nine stipendiary magistrates courts[2] and the Aldermen of the City and Southwark. Each court had attached to it some plain-clothes Runners (who were to be employed in the winter of 1835–6 impounding bundles of the Unstamped); each had its own catchment area of crime, and each sent offenders to certain houses of correction—the City Courts to the Bridewell (and occasionally Giltspur Street Compter); Queen Square and Union Hall to Kingston, the Surrey House of Correction; and the Middlesex police courts to Cold Bath Fields House of Correction. If a sentence exceeded three months the Middlesex magistrates had to sentence to a criminal prison, usually Clerkenwell, sometimes King's Bench.

Until March 1832 street arrests were made by policemen. Two of them, Colley and Currie, were so assiduous that they told Minshull of Bow Street that they had the Stamp Office authority to arrest vendors of *Figaro in London*, a political humorous paper. Caught perjuring, they were dismissed from the police force, and turned common informer, tacitly employed by the Stamp Office from whom they got daily 'instructions' as to which papers and which issues were legal or not. Between them that year they made £300 to £400 from the £1 reward attached to committals.[3] In June 1832 the *Cosmopolite* warned its readers that Colley and Currie were trapping men, usually country immigrants, into selling the Unstamped, so that they could quickly

---

[1] See above, pp. 161–3.

[2] Bow Street, Hatton Garden, Marylebone, Great Marlborough Street, Queen Square, Whitechapel (later Lambeth Street), Union Hall, Worship Street, and the Thames P.O.

[3] *True Sun*, 27 Mar. 1832; *Cosmopolite*, 8 Sept. 1832; *WMF*, 12 Jan. 1833.

arrest them; they would sympathize with his 'plain clothes', treat him at a cook shop or a public house, pass themselves off as publishers of the Unstamped, and give the man some papers to sell. A dozen vendors had already been trapped this way. Carpenter and the National Political Union collected evidence on their behaviour from July 1832, but the magistrates ignored it. Thomas Harris, a leading vendor, in September offered to prove to the Middlesex Sessions that Colley and Currie were entrapping men, but his evidence was deemed inadmissible; copies were then forwarded to all the police courts and to the Commissioners of Stamps.[1] Colley and Currie still continued to act for the Stamp Office, and magistrates still professed to believe them. Only Rawlinson of Marylebone Police Office bothered to question their credentials, though Conant did ask Colley not to take his reward. Colley promised, improbably, that he would give it to the poor. Mayhew, during his interviews for London *Life and Labour*, talked to a street ballad-singer who at the age of thirteen had been turned out into the streets by his stepmother. He slept in Covent Garden, in shutter boxes, on doorsteps, living off street refuse, cabbage stumps, and orange peel. 'Well, Sir, I was green then and one of the Stamp Office spies got me to sell some of the Poor Man's Guardians . . . so that this fellow spy might take me up. This he did, and I had a month in Cold Bath Fields for the business.'[2] He was then fourteen.

The conspiracy finally broke at the beginning of 1833 when Alderman Ansley set two Runners to follow Colley and Currie. It seems that the informers went unpunished. They may perhaps have affected Commissioner Mayne's recommendation to the Select Committee on the London Police in 1834, that the power of laying information should be confined to constables, or to the aggrieved parties, since 'informers do not take, nor wish to take measures to prevent parties infringing the law, but merely to entrap them in order to get the penalty . . .' .[3] This did not stop Colley

[1] *Cosmopolite*, 16 June 1832; *Ballot*, 22 July 1832; *PMG*, 12 Jan. 1833; *Church Examiner*, 15 Sept. 1832.

[2] *PMG*, 15 Sept. 1832; *True Sun*, 1 Nov. 1832; Mayhew, op. cit., vol. iii, p. 205 (1864 edn.).

[3] *The Times*, 3 Jan. 1833; *S.C. on the Metropolitan Police*, 1834, xvi, qu. 6252.

being employed by the Stamp Office again from the spring
of 1834, along with Dean, as a licensed informer, and at the
end of the year they were joined by Currie. The *True Sun*
did not even comment on it. Magistrates, however, were
regularly refusing to commit vendors on their evidence;
so for this reason among others the Stamp Office changed its
policy in the winter of 1835, and runners were sent out to
seize papers rather than vendors.

Selling the Unstamped was seen as a threat to revenue and
to public order. The Stamp Office was interested in the first,
the magistrates in the second. If they could charge a man
with obstructing the highway or breaking the sabbath,
they would do so rather than pay £1 into the informer's
pocket.[1] From October 1832 the magistrates were increasingly restless, and increasingly reluctant to commit. They
complained that the vendors were the smaller fry, and
that those responsible for the Unstamped, the publisher-
proprietors, were not being arrested. They complained that
the informers were self-interested and brought no witnesses;
White, of Queen Square, refused to punish Denman and
Smith unless Currie brought a witness, Rawlinson of Marylebone refused to sign Currie's certificate, which would
entitle him to the £1 reward; and Alderman Thorpe would
not accept Colley's word that he was employed by the
Stamp Office.[2] The magistrates complained that not all the
Unstamped papers being prosecuted were newspapers, and
that they were being 'used' by the Stamp Office. Rawlinson
made Currie prove that the *Guardian* was a newspaper,
Halls of Bow Street required that a piece of news be pointed
out to him, and added that if the Stamp Office considered
'these publications deserving of prosecution' they should
take care to provide better evidence; he would deal with
offenders as leniently as possible, for 'the Magistrates are
not to be made tools of'.[3]

None the less, despite their misgivings, magistrates

[1] *True Sun,* 20 Nov. 1832.

[2] *PMG,* 3 Nov. 1832; *True Sun,* 13 Sept., 30 Oct., 14 Nov. 1832; *PMG,*
12 May, 11 Oct. 1832. Colley and Currie hired labourers to act as their
witnesses.

[3] *True Sun,* 20 Nov. 1832; *Cosmopolite,* 8 Sept. 1832; *True Sun,* 25 Sept.
1832.

continued to commit vendors to prison. Indeed, the Unstamped complained that they were sacrificing their judgement to that of the Stamp Office. 'Nothing is more common
than for the magistrate to state openly, that they find some
difficulty in the way of a conviction, and that they must
therefore consult the wise men of Somerset House!' The
magistrates were taking the opinion of the prosecutors
whether they might convict.[1] The Unstamped did embarrass
the relations of Home Office, magistracy, and the Stamp
Office, as the Public Record Office files show. The Unstamped were less successful in their ambition to make the
law grind to a halt. The *Cosmopolite* had hoped that we 'shall
occupy all the time of the Police Magistrates, fill all the
prisons of the metropolis, and put the authorities at a
stand still with all other businesses for want of time and
space in which to confine the offenders. In each prison we
shall be a formidable body acting in concert . . . '. Hetherington boasted to the inaugural meeting of the Midland
Union of the Working Classes that 'they kept the police and
magistrates in pretty constant work'.[2] But overwork was
something about which the magistrates did not complain.
Even in 1832, at the height of offences, only 174 of Great
Marlborough Street's 4,900 police cases were to do with
the Unstamped, 22 of Bow Street's 2,900, 28 of Hatton
Garden's 3,500, 44 of Queen Square's 3,000, and 44 of
Marylebone's 2,800. About 70 cases a day came before
the police courts of London, and on average, in 1832,
only one of these would be for selling the Unstamped;
in 1834 the number would have fallen to one case every
other day.

Sentences between the police courts were reasonably even
and seldom vindictive, although magistrates varied in their
bent for moralizing. Vending carried a maximum penalty
of three months, but half the sentences were for a fortnight
or less, and less than a quarter were for more than a month,
and these were reserved for the repeated offenders and
speechmakers.

---

[1] *Church Examiner*, 14 July 1832; see also *True Sun*, 2, 3 Sept. 1833.
[2] *Cosmopolite*, 24 Mar. 1832; *PMG*, 3 Nov. 1832.

	2 weeks	Up to 1 month	Up to 2 months	2 months+	Total
1831	40	11	2	29	82
1832	150	159	40	33	382
1833	47	28	13	17	105
1834	67	38	11	11	127
1835	43	21	5	7	76
1836	18	14	6	5	43
Totals	365 (45%)	271 (33%)	77 (9%)	102 (13%)	815 (100%)

The *True Sun* acted as self-appointed invigilator of the police courts and was quick to point out any inconsistencies of sentencing, but though it despised Laing's nastiness and described him as a former negro-driver from Jamaica, and Minshull's moralizing, the *True Sun* found little to fault with the magistrates, though much with the law. When they did praise White of Queen Square, the Home Office was provoked into one of its rare reproofs: 'I am persuaded you will feel ashamed at being praised by so infamous a Paper.'[2]

(c) THE VENDORS

Between 1830 and 1836 there were at least 1,130 cases before the London magistrates of selling unstamped periodicals, and there is information on 1,092 of these cases.[3]

[1] This excludes all dismissals, those where the sentence is not known, and cases which are met by payment of a fine.

[2] HO 60/2, f. 243, Phillips to White, 13 Dec. 1832.

[3] The main sources are the Police Court returns, printed in *Accounts and Papers* (see Bibliography). These are very incomplete and record only 700 London cases. Other sources include prison records (the commitment files of Borough Compter, the jail delivery book of Coldbath Fields for 1832, the records of Surrey House of Correction); police reports in the stamped press (*The Times, Morning Chronicle, True Sun,* and *Radical* are the most valuable): the Unstamped press (NUWC reports, police cases, the balance sheets of the Victim Fund, letters and petitions), and some scattered material in the *Home Office* papers and the *Place* collection. These figures include the sale of illegal almanacs as well as of the radical Unstamped. The returns usually fail to distinguish between the two and for three good reasons: some of the Unstamped were also almanacs (e.g. *Cosmopolite,* the cotton papers), many of the almanacs were radical and conveyed disguised political commentary (e.g. Watson's), and the street vendors sold both and it was a matter of chance for which they were arrested. The police appear to have turned a blind eye to the harmless unstamped almanacs; there were only one or two arrests for selling *Old Moore's.* The almanac duty was repealed in 1834.

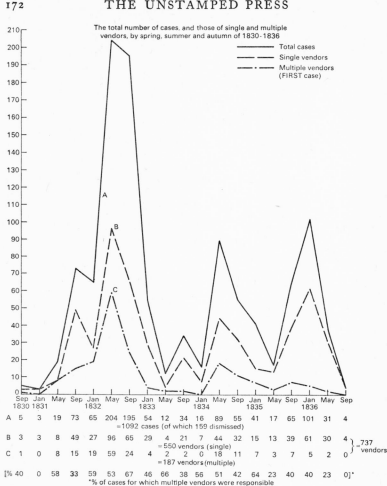

The total number of cases, and those of single and multiple vendors, by spring, summer and autumn of 1830-1836

——— Total cases
— — — Single vendors
—·—·— Multiple vendors (FIRST case)

	Sep 1830	Jan 1831	May	Sep	Jan 1832	May	Sep	Jan 1833	May	Sep	Jan 1834	May	Sep	Jan 1835	May	Sep	Jan 1836	May	Sep	
A	5	3	19	73	65	204	195	54	12	34	16	89	55	41	17	65	101	31	4	
						=1092 cases (of which 159 dismissed)														
B	3	3	8	49	27	96	65	29	4	21	7	44	32	15	13	39	61	30	4	} =550 vendors (single)
C	1	0	8	15	19	59	24	4	2	2	0	18	11	7	3	7	5	2	0	=187 vendors (multiple)
[%	40	0	58	**33**	59	53	67	46	66	38	56	51	42	64	23	40	40	23	0]*	

} =737 vendors

*% of cases for which multiple vendors were responsible

One hundred and fifty-nine of these cases were dismissed.[1] Seven hundred and thirty-seven vendors seem to have been responsible for the 1,092 cases.[2] Other vendors may have

---

[1] Seventy-four of 159 dismissals were for portering; the rest were usually for such semi-technical reasons as the lack of a witness, but occasionally on compassionate grounds

[2] The number of vendors is a little uncertain since fourteen offences were committed by five or six or seven William Smiths. Henry Sizer was also Henry Sisam also Henry Sishum also Henry Seysham. But was George Robinson also George Robertson?

been brought up before the courts in the last year of the Unstamped for portering offences only to be dismissed, but of these there are no further record. Three-quarters (550) of these vendors were arrested only once, the 'single vendors'; the other one-quarter (188) were 'multiple vendors' who accounted for half the cases. Within this second category there was an élite of hard 'core vendors', thirty-six of them, who committed at least three offences (up to John Herbert's nine) and who sold the Unstamped for at least eighteen months. Vendors are assigned to one of these three categories only by their number of offences and the length of time they were associated with the Unstamped.[1] Sorted in this way, the three groups of single vendor, multiple vendor, and core vendor show remarkably different characteristics.

For all 737 vendors, the police office from which they were committed, and the date and length of sentence, is known; and there is uneven biographical detail on 399 of these vendors, of whom 196 were single vendors.[2]

Single vendors, unlike multiple and core vendors, came from all age-groups.

AGES[3]

	−14 years	14–21 years	21–30 years	30–45 years	45 years+	Total
Single	18	25	33	11	19	106
Multiple	1	23	33	5	7	69
Core	2	2	12	12	1	29

Single vendors included young boys sent out into the street by their parents, women (at least ten) whose husbands were ill, skilled men out of employ, and old men unable to work and anxious to avoid the work-house. Over three-quarters of the fifty-two vendors whose appearance was described, were ragged and distressed. William Bray, an unemployed brush maker was a 'wretched looking man', Patrick Donovan

[1] The only exceptions are one or two publishers, Berthold, Cousins, and Watson who were imprisoned only twice, but whose importance justifies their inclusion among core vendors.

[2] The biographical detail is found in the press reports, prison records, the Unstamped, and the Home Office material.

[3] The exact age of a vendor is often given. When it is not, I have classified by description: a child as −14 years, a lad as 14–21 years, a young man with 4 children as 21–30 years, and so on.

a 'poor emaciated Irishman', George Lunts a 'miserable looking lad'. Thirteen were respectable (also worth a comment), including William Smith, a middle-aged man from Stockport, 'genteely dressed'.[1] The trades they gave included a brushmaker, two waiters, two booksellers, two printers, a stationer, a lithographer, four news-vendors of stamped papers, two hatters, a porter, a mechanic, a tailor, two clerks, one clerk 'in a respectable house', a mop and sieve maker, four weavers, two street sellers (one of whom, William Morgan, usually sold oranges), a woodcutter and a labourer.

This was a more respectable group than the multiple vendors, for its twenty- and thirty-year-olds contained many more skilled and semi-skilled men. Those with trades came from two groups: on the one hand the predictably distressed, such as the weavers; the hatter whose hands were injured; or the crippled Joseph Forster; and, on the other hand, those professionally associated with the press, who get bitten once but not a second time, such as the young Richard Carlile, Puttick the publisher, and John Clements the bookseller. These men usually refused to say anything during their cases.

PLEAS[2]

	Promise not to sell again	Ignorant of the law	Led astray	Poor: un-employed	Just cause	Total pleaders
Single vendor	23 (36%)	16	4	44 (52%)	6 (7%)	84
Multiple vendor	5 (16%)	16	3	39 (49%)	22 (27%)	80
Core vendor	2 (13%)	0	0	10 (40%)	22 (92%)	25

Thus nearly half of all the vendors pleaded that they were poor and out of work, and many of them that they had families to support. Poverty would be both the most obvious reason for selling papers in the street, and one which could be expected to arouse the sympathy of magistrates. Edward

[1] *The Times*, 17 Nov. 1835, 25 Dec. 1832; *Cosmopolite*, 16 June 1832: *PMG*, 29 Dec. 1832.

[2] Where a vendor gave two reasons for selling the Unstamped, these are entered separately; thus the total number of pleas is higher than the total number of pleaders. Where possible, the pleas of the first case of multiple and core vendors are entered.

Dixon, for example, was an unemployed printer who had wandered the streets for several nights as he had no money to buy a night's lodging. James Richards, who sold the *Slap at the Church*, 'said he was in great distress, and that he had no other way of obtaining a living than by selling cheap publications. Mr. Dyer expressed his regret that the defendant was in such distress, but said that he must be aware that such publications were illegal. On account of his distress he would only commit him to prison for six weeks instead of three months.' William Bishop, brought to Queen Square for selling the *Guardian*, said he had no work; he must either starve, beg, or steal if he did not earn 'a trifle' by selling these papers. Marriot sourly remarked that all the vendors told him the same story and sentenced him to two weeks in the Kingston House of Correction.[1] Some of the children claimed they had been 'led astray' by their elders; when a young boy was brought before Alderman Lucas by Colley and Currie, the magistrate said that if he allowed the age of the boy to mitigate the punishment, the papers 'would be wholly carried on through little boys'. He therefore had to sentence him to the full three months.[2]

A third of the single vendors promised not to sell the papers again, but rather surprisingly only a fifth of them pleaded that they did not know they were breaking the law. John Ashton was in a public house when he heard that selling the Unstamped provided a living. He told Roe of Bow Street that he little thought that selling them would bring him to prison.[3] Very few single vendors pleaded the morality of what they were doing. Of the six who did so, two (Parker and Little) were tried with a core vendor, Hancock, and copied his mock-heroic stance; two were clerks, a fourth was a little boy whose mother was abusive and defiant on his behalf, and the last was Rooks, the injured hatter, whose persuasiveness won him the help of a kindly alderman.

These single vendors hoped to earn a living by selling the Unstamped; selling papers was merely one of the more

---

[1] *Cosmopolite*, 29 Sept. 1832; *Slap at the Church*, 24 Mar. 1832; *The Times*, 30 Oct. 1832; see also *The Times*, 29 Oct. 1832.
[2] *PMG*, 28 Apr. 1832. (The sentence was harsh, but the magistrate was right!)
[3] *True Sun*, 12 Aug. 1834; cf. also *PMG*, 9 June 1832.

profitable of the street selling trades, and one which required less capital than selling books or ginger beer. Popay appreciated this; he emphasized that the rate of profit on penny papers was 'greater than on most things sold by even hawkers of any goods and is a great inducement to persons to speculate, of whom perhaps there was never so many seen as at present in different parts of London, at all events in such articles as these'.[1] A magistrate asked John Martin, 'a baldheaded old man', why he did not sell less obnoxious papers. He replied, 'We get 5d. profit in every shilling for the sale of the *Guardian*, but in the other publications the profit is not sufficient to keep a man whose dealings are in a small way alive'. He tried to sell religious tracts and the *Penny Magazine* but found them unsaleable. John Johnson pledged his coat to buy papers; another 'having heard that there was a good profit allowed on this publication' pawned his child's frock for 1s. 6d. to raise some stock money, but 'I had scarcely offered one for sale when the police constable took me into custody'. James Kavanagh was asked by Alderman Ansley why he sold the *Guardian*. 'Faith, your honour, they are the things for which we get the readiest sale; in truth, everyone we can get, we are sure to sell and we can't get anything better to live by!'[2]

Many of the street sellers could not have moved on to other work even if they had wanted to, for they could not have scraped together enough capital to start another street trade, nor were they 'respectable' enough to leave the streets altogether. One fifteen-year-old boy, 'covered only by a few rags', was brought to Marlborough Street for selling the *Cosmopolite* and the *Guardian*. He could do nothing else, he said since 'he could not get into any employ, on account of his having no decent clothes. He was never in custody before, and having obtained eightpence by begging, he purchased a dozen of the publications.'[3] He was sentenced to a week in the House of Correction.

These single vendors did not refer to the Victim Fund in court, nor apparently did they expect to receive help from

[1] HO 64/11, 13 Nov. 1830.
[2] *PMG*, 27 Oct. 1832; *The Times*, 5 Nov. 1833; *PMG*, 20 Oct. 1832.
[3] *Morning Chronicle*, quoted *PMG*, 8 Sept. 1832.

it, though some did. They sold the Unstamped because the papers were profitable enough to offer a living.

'Multiple vendors'[1] were almost all lads and young men (over four-fifths were between fifteen and twenty-five years old), unmarried, without skills, and singularly unworried by imprisonment. Where single vendors sold the Unstamped to earn a living, multiple vendors sold the Unstamped to receive cash from the Victim Fund. Of those who received money from the Victim Fund, it would seem that two-thirds committed a second offence, and at least two-thirds of all the multiple vendors received money from the fund while it lasted.[2] They stayed with the Unstamped just as long as the fund paid out, boasted to the magistrates of the money they would be paid,[3] and even pleaded with policemen to be imprisoned so that they might be able to claim from the fund on their release. Thomas Thurgood (*sic*) and John Barnes were brought before Ansley in January 1832 for selling the *Guardian*. *The Times* began its report:

> Latterly some poor creatures, to whom the diet and shelter afforded by Bridewell are, at this inclement season, really desirable, and who have also an eye to participating in the fund which has been raised for sufferers of this class, have begged the officers to take them into custody. . . . The prisoners offered no defence.[4]

Richard Butler and John Chapman chaunted the *Reformers Catechism* very close to the Clerkenwell Station House. To the mirth of an 'immense mob', and the exasperation of the police sergeant, they solemnly questioned each other:

Butler asked: 'What is your name?'
Chapman replied: 'A Radical'.
                          'Who gave you that name?'
                          'Public opinion, and the enlightened age, when I was made a member of reformation, a child of the people, and an inheritor of the land of locusts. . .'
Response: 'Britons arouse, and keep this law.'[5]

[1] There is biographical detail on 103 of the 151 multiple vendors. For core vendors, see below, p. 180.
[2] The balance sheets of the fund are incomplete. See below, p. 199.
[3] *The Times*, 1 Nov. 1832. White of Queen Sq. collected information on the health of the fund.
[4] *The Times*, 19 Jan. 1832.   [5] *The Times*, 19 July 1832.

This was not the activity of men trying to avoid the police. Multiple vendors were not only anxious to claim the 5s. a week offered by the Victim Fund, but some of them were prepared to come to terms with informers for the £1 reward. Policemen who were not entitled to claim the reward, and journalists who were spectators, reported that informer and vendor often divided the spoils between them. Carpenter told the National Political Union that Strickland and Lecomber had been given £1 as a bargain with the Stamp Office men to break the law. Hetherington recommended that a vendor who saw a policeman approach another vendor should beat the policeman to it, and claim the reward. Carlile suggested that if the vendors were in great distress they should agree to turn each other in, for the sake of the money. The *Cosmopolite* told its readers that when summer came, imprisonment would be no hardship to 20,000 unemployed men.

Now it will be well that we become our own police officers, and take our own cases to the magistrates, if the regular officers do not go on fast enough; for then we take to ourselves the whole of the reward. In two cases the regular officers have shared the reward with the victims, agreeable to previous arrangement. If the bargain can be made for ten or twelve shillings with the officer, it may be as well done. If not, let us try to keep the whole reward of information in our own hands.[1]

Very few (6 per cent) of these multiple vendors promised the magistrates that they would stop selling the penny papers, where almost a third of the single vendors did. Almost half of the multiple vendors pleaded that they were poor or without work, but where only 6 (7 per cent) of the single vendors claimed that it was a good thing to sell these papers, 22 (27 per cent) of the multiple vendors did. William and Mary Smith, she nursing a baby, were brought before Gregorie at Queen Square by the ubiquitous Colley and Currie for selling the *Guardian* and the *Cosmopolite*. The husband said he could get no work, and was sentenced to a month;

---

[1] *Cosmopolite*, 24 Mar. 1832; see also *Ballot*, 22 July 1832: *PMG*, 27 Aug. 1831; *Figaro in London*, 20 Oct. 1832.

the wife was discharged as being 'under the influence of her husband' whereupon she told the magistrate that 'she would purchase still more papers and sell them'. George Strickland, 'a youth of decent appearance', was brought before Laing, who doubled his punishment when he learnt that this was his second offence. Strickland replied, 'I don't care, I shall be in the same spot afterwards.' Thomas Hansbury's defence was even more dramatic. In September 1832 Colley brought him before Gregorie for selling the *Guardian* at Astley's Theatre.

> Mr. Gregorie was looking at . . . the papers when the prisoner said to him 'I am glad to see it in your hands, for the first time, a newspaper of the true sort'. The Magistrate asked him whether he had any defence at all to make? Prisoner, 'None in the world; as long as that paper is published he would sell it, let the consequences be what they may. He thought proper to do so, and would, in spite of every obstacle'.[1]

He was sentenced to six weeks. Many other multiple vendors must have played down their opinions on the subject and played up their poverty. Henry Bennet, for example, was arrested in February 1835; 'on the road the prisoner bawled out, "Success to cheap knowledge", "No taxes", "Liberty, and sent forth other ebullitions that left no doubt but he was a thorough Radical Reformer.' When questioned by Laing at the police court, however, Bennet simply said that 'he thought there was no harm in selling a few publications of the sort to get a trifling living'.[2]

Of the few trades stated by this group, there was one butcher, one baker, two regular news-vendors, an attorney's clerk, a tradesman, a musician, a pauper tailor, and a watchman. Of these nine, the butcher, the baker, the musician, and the tailor were in their late thirties and forties. Only one multiple vendor pleaded he had a family to support. So, unlike single vendors, the multiple vendors were young, unskilled, and unmarried. This would seem to be the group that Hetherington tried to round up in the fourth number of the *Guardian*:

---

[1] *Cosmopolite*, 17 Nov. 1832 (Wm. and Mary Smith); 28 Apr. 1832 (Strickland); 29 Sept. 1832 (Hansbury).
[2] *The Times*, 24 Feb. 1835.

WANTED

some hundreds of POOR MEN out of employ, *who have* NOTHING TO RISK, some of those *unfortunate wretches* to whom DISTRESS has made a PRISON a desirable HOME.

An HONEST and moral way of finding *head* and *gaol shelter*, and moreover, of EARNING THE THANKS OF THEIR FELLOW-COUNTRYMEN, now presents itself to such *patriotic* ENGLISHMEN. . . .[1]

and the class that Watson hoped to recruit as volunteers, when outlining the charms of prison as early as the British Association for the Promotion of Co-operative Knowledge meeting of November 1830.

Those who engaged in this work must be volunteers who would not be easily frightened into acquiescence, or tortured into submission by charges of imaginary offences, or by groundless threats. He considered young men who were unencumbered by domestic connections, as especially fitted for this warfare. . . . They should remember the conduct of the youths of the French polytechnic. . . .[2]

The third class of sellers were the 'core vendors', thirty-six men and boys, most of whom were respectable and many of whom were prosperous. A third of these were the printers and publishers of the Unstamped, usually family men and householders in their thirties and forties; a handful were respectable young artisans who for ideological reasons found jobs within the Unstamped—Edward Hancock, in turn silk-weaver, shoemaker, entertainer, and school-teacher; John Williams, who told Currie he was a 'martyr to the Cause'; Joseph Walker, mechanic, self-styled inventor, and owner of an illicit still; John Brown, mechanic; George Payne 'of decent exterior'; John Willis, of the National Union of the Working Classes, who, with Walker, put out the *Political Touchwood*; and the ubiquitous but elusive James Reeve, a goldchaser and publisher of the *London Star*. A half-dozen core vendors were booksellers with their own shops, who became increasingly prominent as the broadsheets displaced the quarto Unstamped; George Nichols, anxious to emigrate to Australia; Thomas Gamble, father of four children; Thomas Heins, who set

---

[1] *PMG*, 30 July 1831; see also *Gauntlet*, 10 Nov. 1833.
[2] *Pol. Letters*, 6 Nov. 1830. Popay described them as 'youths and men of the lowest class' (HO 64/11, 13 Nov. 1830).

up his own Radical Reading Room, published the *People's Hue and Cry* in 1834, and was one of the props of the NUWC in 1835; twenty-year-old Thomas Harriss, busy enough to employ a shopman; George Gee, the radical baker who celebrated Perceval's Fast Day with a roast-beef dinner, a tricolour flag, and a band; and William Fagnoit, who advertised that he would continue to sell the Unstamped 'in defiance of Sir F. A. Roe and Billy Guelph'.[1] The final dozen or so were street sellers who, young, wretched, and jobless, would come into the category of multiple vendor but for their pertinacity and high number of offences. Among them were the Aberfield brothers, eleven and fourteen, themselves sons of a former policeman, who pelted any constable foolish enough to arrest them with mud, stones, and abuse; John Herbert, Surrey's Billy Barlow, 'a destitute half-crazed individual' who answered nine charges in an enormous seedy coat; William Jones, 'a miserable looking fellow', who on being sentenced for the third time 'appeared quite unconcerned', and John Wilson, 'a poor-looking fellow, in threadbare black, with his waistcoat pinned to his neck to conceal the want of a shirt'.[2]

These street sellers may have been freelance, as the multiple vendors were, but they may also have been regularly employed by the publishers as street shopmen. Fifteen-year-old John Jones was charged with selling the *Guardian*, and told the magistrate that selling these papers was no crime; the policeman put in, 'It is the practice of the persons interested in the sale of this and similar publications to hire men of the prisoner's description at 5s. 6d. a week, in order to dispose of them in the streets.'[3]

These four groups, publishers, artisans, booksellers with their own shops, and tenacious street sellers, were the backbone of the London vendors. When caught, their pleading was remarkable. Yates, Lee, Watson, and occasionally Hetherington, preferred not to turn up for trial at all; the Aberfield brothers kept their protests to outside the police office. But of the twenty-five whose pleading is

---

[1] *Man*, 18 May 1834.   [2] *The Times*, 7 Nov. 1832, 19 Jan. 1836.
[3] *The Times*, 1 Jan. 1833. It is possible the policeman was confusing this with the Victim Fund, but 5s. 6d. is a precise figure, the Victim Fund never paid more than 5s. and by January 1833 this had fallen to 1s. a week. See below, p. 197.

recorded, only ten pleaded their poverty, and twenty-two argued that the papers were good and useful ones which they would continue to sell. John Herbert said he sold the Unstamped 'to show that the liberty of the press should not be shackled; as long as the people would buy an unstamped publication, and he could sell one, he was determined to do it'. George Pilgrim, before being bundled off to the City Bridewell, remarked that the law must have been made 'by a set of jolterheads'. Murray of Union Hall told Owen Davis that the *Guardian* and the *Cosmopolite* were 'calculated to inflame the minds of the lower orders, by lessening in their estimation many of the great institutions of the country', and sentenced him to three months. Davis replied, 'I don't care for that; send me as often as you like, and as long as you please.' He left the office in custody, laughing.[1] Edward Hancock chose to turn his trial into a lecture on the first principles of government. Noah Flood, brought before Alderman Thorpe of Southwark, said, 'So long as he saw starvation among mankind, he should not flinch from selling Unstamped publications.' On his release he would return to the same spot and sell them.[2] These were brave words when they meant that magistrates would impose the full three months; 13 per cent of all the cases were sentenced to three months, but 45 per cent (20 of 51 vendors) of those who pleaded the justice of what they were doing, got the full sentence.[3]

Such men as these mocked their way to prison. John Herbert, arrested for the eighth time, gave his name as John Guelph, King of the Unstamped. Joseph Walker, arrested for the third time, in August 1831, suddenly decided he did not know his name.

Gregorie: 'Very well, we can do without it.'
Defendant: 'I say I don't know my name. My father told me, my name, he believed, was Josiah Walker, but that he very much suspected I was changed in my infancy.'

---

[1] *The Times*, 20 May 1834 (Herbert); *PMG*, 17 Sept. 1831 (Pilgrim); *PMG*, 24 Mar. 1832 (Davis). [2] *PMG*, 28 Apr. 1832.
[3] Of the 51 vendors who defended the papers, 7 (they included women and porters) were dismissed; 16 were sentenced to a month or less, but 6 of these combined their plea with that of poverty or lack of work, 2 were women, and a further 4 were sentenced in 1836, when all sentences were lighter; 8 vendors received 6 weeks or 2 months, and 20 the full 3 months.

He was charged, and the constable produced a placard headed 'Taxes on knowledge, the tyrant's only resource.' Gregorie asked to see the papers but the constable ruefully admitted that they had been snatched away by someone else. Walker commented, 'You have properly made a "muff" of it this time. Here is a pretty fellow for a public guardian.' The prisoner was then searched but nothing found on him but some bills headed, 'Wanted, some poor men to sell the "Poor Man's Guardian".'

Defendant: 'That bill you ought to have stuck up in your office.'
Mr. Gregorie: 'What have you to say to the charge?'
Defendant: 'There is no charge against me that I know of. I am, however, proud of the honour of going to prison for selling the Poor Man's Guardian. . . .' The defendant was about commencing a speech when he was removed.[1]

Joseph Seare (sic) was brought to Hatton Garden for selling the Guardian. Asked for his defence, he said he was walking up the High Street, 'with my packet of useful books', and, seeing the policeman, whom he knew was fond of him, said, 'Good morning; dull weather.' The policeman agreed and asked him what he had got there. Seare handed him a Guardian but at that very moment a woman came up, slipped a penny into Seare's hand, 'for which I was much obliged', and took the Guardian from the policeman.

'Now, I don't know what your worship thinks, but I think the policeman ought to stand here, and I be evidence against him; for although I can't swear that woman gave him a penny, I can swear he gave her a Poor Man's Guardian' (laughter).

Mr. Rogers, 'I think you're a very impudent fellow; if I laugh, its no reason you should.'[2]

Once in prison these men did their very best to make themselves nuisances. Cold Bath Fields, which held a thousand prisoners, was the healthiest and the largest of the prisons, and Chesterton one of the most enlightened prison governers. No vendors ever complained of their treatment there. The 'martyrs' interested Chesterton and he personally delivered one of Walker's letters to his 'Dear Guardy'

---

[1] The Times, 19 Jan. 1836 (Herbert); 21 Aug. 1831 (Walker).
[2] PMG, 17 Nov. 1832.

in order to meet Hetherington. He was impressed by the 'Radical magnate, who was a man of considerable ability and of pleasing address'; in return, he received 'a most flattering notice' in the *Guardian*, where he was depicted as the 'model gaoler'. In any case, he would take 'good care to avoid the unwise course of irritating a numerous political party, who could if necessity required it, command many advocates and defenders, both in the press, and in the House of Commons'.[1] Other governors cared less for public opinion. The City Bridewell, for example, administered by the Lord Mayor and Aldermen of the City, provoked many complaints. Its hundred cells were cramped, it lacked exercise yards, and it was exposed to the dangerous miasma of the nearby cemetery. Joseph Walker described men as spitting blood, and fighting for mice to eat. Across the Thames, both the Borough Compter for Southwark and the Surrey House of Correction at Kingston were very small, with cells for some forty or fifty people, and without exercise yards.

Few of the vendors grumbled about their loss of liberty; all complained about the food, which was mainly soup and bread, from which Cleave contracted scrofula; and all complained about the tiny cells which lacked glass in the windows, fires in the grates, were always damp, and were without tables to write on and candles to see by; the restrictions on visiting; and the ubiquitous filth, slops, and vermin.[2] But by far the worst thing about prison was the other prisoners. Only Cold Bath Fields classified its prisoners and maintained a silent system. Berthold begged Owen to liberate him from Kingston Palace. 'Here I am languishing not only in a prison—but tortured near to death by the refuse of society who are with me thrown in this wretched place. . . .' Hetherington wrote to Birnie, one of the Bow Street magistrates who had sentenced him, that 'I am compelled to pass my time with from thirty to fifty of the most depraved characters in the metropolis.' His books and linen

---

[1] G. L. Chesterton, *Revelations of Prison Life*, 1856, vol. 1, pp. 195–8; see also H. Mayhew and J. Binney, *The Great World of London*, 1862, pp. 274 f.

[2] *PMG*, 8 Oct. 1831. No one complained that their health was injured, though two vendors who entered prison ill, died while there. Lovett in 1840 was much weakened by prison and Ernest Jones in 1850 could scarcely crawl across the floor of his cell.

were pilfered, and when a kindly turnkey fixed him a lock, the visiting magistrates ordered it to be removed.[1] Smith, the publisher of the *Reformer*, wrote from Clerkenwell,

> I who had never before been inducted within the walls of a prison, was thus compelled to mingle with this indiscriminate and degraded mass. . . . There are between forty and fifty unfortunate wretches confined in the same yard as myself, the majority of whom are reputed thieves, pickpockets, costermongers and mendicants . . . whose language, manners and obscenity are disgusting to the ears and sight of one endowed with common decency.[2]

Yet these men went back to prison again and again. Morale was high. Core vendors managed to measure their cells to the nearest half-inch and to weigh their bread to the nearest half-ounce before complaining; and when they joined forces in Kingston and the Bridewell they obtained their separate rooms, books and papers, their candles, their visitors, and their eating utensils. Some refused to mount the treadmill. Walker and Willis would not go to chapel and Hetherington, for one, lectured the chaplain on the barbarity of the notion of original sin, matching text with text. When George Pilgrim was joined by other vendors in the Bridewell, they pressed for a separate room and 'after much fuss' something like a separate system was introduced for all prisoners.[3] When one of the Home Office spies, who was looking after Watson's business for him, visited Hetherington and Watson in Clerkenwell in March 1833, he found that 'they are not at all displeased at their situation and mean to continue business as usual. . . . They are now both engaged in writing a New Penny Pamphlet which they mean to bring out shortly on the Obscene and Immoral parts of the Bible and on the Absurdity of all Religions.'[4] These men lectured their fellow prisoners on politics. They complained to the governor about the wardens, to the visiting magistrates about the governor, and to members of Parliament about the governor, surgeon, chaplain, and magistrates. They sent forth a stream of letters, petitions, and memorials. When

---

[1] Berthold to Owen, 24 Dec. 1831, *Owen Coll.*, f. 347; *PMG*, 8 Oct. 1831 (no. 14). See also O'Brien's petition on prison conditions, *NS*, 1 Aug. 1840.
[2] *PMG*, 28 Dec. 1833; see also *PMG*, 17 Dec. 1831 for Hancock's complaints.
[3] *PMG*, 10 Oct. 1832; *Ballot*, 18 Dec. 1831.   [4] HO 64/12, 8 Mar. 1833.

Hetherington left prison, in March 1832, he boasted to the Brighton Political Union that the governor had begged him not to return 'as you really require so much attention and waiting on'.[1] This was triumph, this was beating the system at its own game.

The Chartist prisoners of the 1840s likewise kept up the pressure on prison conditions. Lovett and Collins, in 1839, forced the prison authorities to replace their infested blankets with coarse sheets that could be washed, and fought for their regulation meat allowance. Ernest Jones would not pick oakum. Holyoake in 1842 refused to attend prison chapel at Cheltenham, or to wear prison dress. The only Bible he would condescend to accept from the chaplain was one in calf with marginal references, worth half a guinea. He scorned the tenpenny productions of the Society for the Promotion of Christian Knowledge. Thomas Cooper at Stafford Jail smashed windows and screamed at the chaplain that he was being starved to death; he got better food. He badgered the governor and the surgeon, refused to go to prison chapel, and sent petitions out to Duncombe for books, letters, and papers. ' "I admire your pluck, Cooper", said the dear old governor. . . .' (!)[2] One consequence of imprisoning the articulate and the politically conscious, whether vendors of the Unstamped in the 1830s, Chartists in the 1840s, suffragettes in the 1910s, or disarmers in the 1950s, was to spotlight and to some extent improve prison life.

Vendors of the Unstamped fall into three groups: single vendors, multiple vendors, and core vendors; and this suggests that the grass-roots structure of London radicalism in the early 1830s fits quite closely the structure of Chartism revealed by local studies of the 1840s.[3] Within most Chartist centres were to be found four distinct groups: a hard core of experienced Radical reformers, a second group of new recruits who were often young men, a third group of 'loyal supporters' ready to sign petitions and join in Chartist life,

[1] *Brighton Herald*, 13 Oct. 1832; see also HO 40/29, f. 435.
[2] Lovett, op. cit., vol. i, ch. xii; Holyoake, *60 Years*, vol. i, p. 168 (1906 edn.); T. Cooper, *Life*, 1872 edn., pp. 237–55.
[3] A. Briggs, 'National Bearings', in *Chartist Studies* (Papermac edn., 1962), p. 292.

and a fluctuating rank-and-file who might or might not be stirred into activity. The equivalent groups, within the world of the Unstamped, centred on the professionals, men like Hetherington and Cleave, who spanned co-operation in the 1820s and Chartism in the 1840s; and they co-opted as core vendors a number of young artisans and shopmen, for most of whom the Unstamped was their first venture in radical politics. The campaign was backed by two wings of 'loyal supporters'—the multiple vendors on the one hand, and those active in the National Union of the Working Classes on the other, furnishing sub-scriptions, resolutions, and readers to the cause. The fourth element in the Chartist model had much in common with the single vendors, the street sellers, who were radical in much the same vague way as Mayhew found most of the costermongers to be Chartists in the late 1840s.

Vendors have been classed as single, multiple, and core, according to their number of offences and the length of time they stayed with the Unstamped. The analogy with Professor Briggs's model breaks down, of course, if this classification is totally arbitrary, if it reflects the eyesight of the police rather than the intentions of the vendor. For any one vendor, it might well be a matter of chance whether he was arrested two or three times by an informer, or even whether he was caught at all. But the mechanism for arrest-ing street vendors, when the Home Office wanted them arrested, was reasonably thorough. The policeman was expected to know by sight all the people living on his beat and to patrol it every ten or fifteen minutes.[1] Street selling was conspicuous, especially if the street seller chaunted his wares, strawed them (that is, sold the straw and gave the paper away with it),[2] or carried the usual bill board. Once a policeman had arrested a man, his face would be familiar, and in very many cases police or Stamp Office agents were able to tell the court, apparently from memory, that this was a second or a third offence. Some vendors did roam all over London to sell their papers, but very many of them

---

[1] James Grant, *Sketches of London*, 1838, ch. xii (The New Police).
[2] *Pol. Letters*, 8 Nov. 1830; Mayhew, op. cit., vol. iii, p. 240. His informant estimated that twenty men strawed papers in London 1832–6.

were arrested repeatedly in the same place. John Herbert was arrested four times in the New Cut; James Cahuac and Thomas Thurgood twice in the same street; John Cull and James Conlin kept to the neighbouring parishes of St. George's and St. Saviour's respectively, and William Jones was found first in Blackfriars Road and then in York Road which led off it. The police knew very well that most papers would be sold on Saturday and Sunday, and sold in places where there were people—the Saturday night street markets in New Cut (and Union Street and Cornwall Street which led off it); the markets in Leather Lane, Farringdon, Whitechapel High Street, Clare Market, Newport Market, and around Covent Garden; the stationers' stalls around St. Paul's Churchyard; Westminster and Blackfriars bridges (where an almanac vendor told Mayhew he could sell fourteen dozen in an evening),[1] and roads like Tooley Street and Parliament Street which led on to them; and the main thoroughfares, Tottenham Court Road, Oxford Street, Holborn, and Cheapside. About three-quarters of all the arrests were made in these areas. The police could visit working-class public houses, watch Hetherington's and Cousins's shops, and follow vendors who bought a bundle of the Unstamped.

Even if a vendor changed his round, this did not protect him. Colley, Currie, and later Josiah Dean roved all over London and brought hundreds of vendors before magistrates. James Kavanagh was brought before three police offices, Southwark Town Hall, Marylebone, and Queen Square, George Pilgrim was taken to the Guildhall and Bow Street, Henry Sisam to Marylebone and to Queen Square. Many vendors, according to Lovett, turned informer on the movements of others, hoping for a place in the police.[2] So, if the Home Office or the Stamp Commissioners wanted to commit vendors, their net was quite a fine one. If a vendor sold in the streets for a month or so, the odds were that he would be caught. Very many vendors said they had been selling for less than a fortnight before they were arrested; for many of them their first sale was to Colley and Currie. 'On Saturday a poor fellow purchased at the Repository of Cheap

---

[1] Mayhew, op. cit., vol. i (1851 edn.), p. 271.   [2] Lovett, op. cit., vol. i, p. 65.

Knowledge opposite Somerset House, a dozen of the *Working Man's Friend*. . . . He had not been long in the streets, when one of the lazy blue soldiers, who had been tiger like, watching for an opportunity to seize his prey, took him off to Bow Street. . . .'[1] A young girl, Fanny Le Dieu, was caught the first day her father sent her out with Cleave's *Police Gazette*, instead of the inoffensive *Penny Magazine*; Matthew Bird, an unemployed baker, had sold the *Guardian* for three weeks when he was arrested; Daniel Curran for less than a fortnight; William Jones and John Hatt were taken by Colley just two or three days after they had come out from prison, also for selling the *Guardian* and *Cosmopolite*; Frederick Grant, 'a strong hearty fellow', was arrested the morning he came out of prison; sixteen-year-old Peter Green was free for just three days. Richard Price was imprisoned three times in four months, James Prince was sentenced to a fortnight from 26 September 1831, another fortnight from 31 October 1831, three months from the beginning of December 1831, and for a further two months from the beginning of March 1832. There were many cases like this.

There obviously *were* vendors who passed in and out of the movement very quickly, and without being caught went on to other work. But the number is unlikely to be very large. The Unstamped were so profitable and the street sellers so poor that vendors were likely to continue selling the Unstamped until they were caught. Those who were less likely to be arrested were not street sellers but those who sold at working-class meetings in the Rotunda or Theobold's Road, those who sold papers in coffee houses and public houses, and those who either sold from their homes while carrying on some other trade or who sold from their shops full time. But selling at meetings was a status activity usually restricted to those who had already been imprisoned;[2] selling from a shop meant that the vendor was a professional and very often a core vendor; and those, like George Gee or William Caffyn, who sold from their homes, usually had to obtain custom by advertising in the Unstamped. Colley and Currie were as competent as the customers in locating

[1] *WMF*, 27 Apr. 1833.   [2] HO 64/11, 22 Nov. 1831.

such a vendor. None the less, selling off the streets was much safer than selling on the streets, if only because police and informers preferred the simpler and more profitable arrest of street vendors.[1]

This, of course, is to suppose that vendors always avoided arrest. Single vendors might; but multiple vendors anxious to earn money from the Victim Fund or to share in the £1 reward to which informers were entitled, and publishers anxious for martyrdom, had an interest in being sent to prison. These vendors sold papers under the noses of police-men, and, when arrested, came quietly. Only when the Victim Fund dried up, in the spring of 1833, did multiple vendors start to brawl with the police. The Aberfield brothers encouraged a crowd to throw stones at the police. Another young boy, Maurice Dunn, was eventually charged not with selling the Unstamped but with causing a riot in Whitechapel; he had been bundled into a coach by an officer, had screamed that that he was being murdered, and attracted a crowd of '700 to a 1000' who rescued him from the coach; the officer had to drive away for his own safety. When Henry Bennet was taken into custody he 'made a most desperate resistance, repeatedly exclaimed "The b——y police crew have turned informers"; "Down with the blue devils"; "No Peelers"; and made use of other violent language to incite the mob to violence, and to rescue him from his custody'.[2] When Dean tried to arrest Burrell, a former butcher, by giving him into the custody of a constable, 'the prisoner made a signal' and some twenty or thirty men attacked them; the prisoner escaped, Dean had to take refuge in a neighbour's garden till help came, and the policeman had to flee over the top of the house. Frances Hawkins, with her mother, 'made use of the most opprobious terms' and attempted to start a riot. Reeve hit one policeman in the face, and on another occasion was rescued by the mechanics of Maudsley's factory in Westminster Road, who pelted the runners for him with stones and mud.[3] Among other

---

[1] See above, pp. 166–7.

[2] *The Times*, 12 Apr. 1836 (Aberfields); *Weekly Times*, 6 Mar. 1836 (M. Dunn); *The Times*, 24 Feb. 1835 (Bennet).

[3] *The Times*, 3 Dec. 1835 (Burrell); *Public Ledger*, 12 Jan. 1836 (F. Hawkins); *Place Coll.*, Set 70, f. 296, 22 Dec. 1835 (Reeve).

things, this suggests that being arrested was no longer profitable.

Some men were never caught; these included a few of the publishers who were on the fringe of radical journalism, Berger, Purkess, and Steill, and some part-time but regular sellers, among them the NUWC silk weavers, Boreham, Buck, and Charles Neesom. The advertisements in the Unstamped suggest that about two dozen men sold papers without being arrested. The Home Office certainly knew about them;[1] possibly they were not prominent enough to justify the elaborate process of information and summons.

From the autumn of 1835 the pattern of arrest changed and the lines between single, multiple, and core vendor blurred. The magistrates, since the autumn of 1832, had been pressing the Stamp Office to arrest publishers rather than the street sellers of the Unstamped; since then the sales of the broadsheet Unstamped had risen to five or six times those of the quarto Unstamped. When Currie brought Martin Robinson to Bow Street in September 1835, Hall found it 'very painful' to send a poor man to prison for selling the Unstamped when it was 'notorious' that they were exhibited in shops all over the town; in future he would refuse to convict, as the offence was being 'connived at' in others.[2] A month later Grove of Worship Street asked Dean, the Stamp Office agent, why he was not arresting the publishers rather than the street sellers of the Unstamped. Dean replied that since the seizure of Hetherington's and Cleave's presses in August, and the refusal of the regular printers to hire out their machinery to proprietors of the Unstamped, the parties concerned had their papers printed in the country, and used their own cabriolets to bring them into London and to distribute them; 'no expense or trouble had been spared' but all the Stamp Office could do was to arrest those carrying the papers about for sale; they could not reach the bigger men.[3]

Pressure from the magistrates to arrest publishers rather than vendors, pressure from the stamped press who were more and more alarmed at the mounting sales of the

---

[1] See the spy reports on these men in the HO 64 series.
[2] *Pamphlets for the People*, No. 18.   [3] *The Times*, 27 Oct. 1835.

Unstamped and the hint of a daily Unstamped, and who were threatening to come out Unstamped themselves, presumably pressure from the Treasury to cut the expense of informers' rewards,[1] and perhaps worry at the unpopularity the police were acquiring, together brought a change of policy. On 10 December 1835 Charles Pressley, on behalf of the Stamp Office, sent instructions to the magistrates, 'that in future a certain number of officers attached to the various Establishments shall on every Saturday and Sunday use their best exertions to put down the existing evil, by seizing all the Unstamped carried about for sale by the itinerant traders . . .'.[2] For the first time the runners were used. They were to seize the Unstamped, take the name and address of the porter, and release him; they would not have to witness any sale. The police were not to intervene unless there was a breach of the peace.

So the runners, Goddard, Fletcher, Ruthven, and Shackell, haunted the streets around the publishing and printing offices in Fleet Street, Strand, and Blackfriars on the Wednesday, and patrolled the coach offices from which the parcels were sent to the country on the Thursday. Papers were extricated from bags and sacks,[3] tall hats and waistcoats; they were disguised as laundry parcels 'neatly papered up', as stamped papers, as 'a bundle of old clothes'; they were found in a butter basket, under apples and eggs, 'packed with shoes and chests of tea', and carried in servant girls' bonnet boxes. They were seized from cabs, coaches, and packet offices after races through the streets of London. The *Radical* sourly commented they would be searching pregnant women next. Anguished notes from publishers to retailers were read out in court: 'we have been horribly harassed by the informing thieves this week', or, this one from Cousins to Joshua Hobson of Leeds: 'Cash! cash!! cash!!! . . . the thieves are out and we are obliged to send

---

[1] *Weekly Times*, 27 Dec. 1835.

[2] *Pamphlets for the People*, No. 30, p. 14 (H. Chapman, 'Crusade against the Unstamped').

[3] Accounts of these devices are to be found in the press reports, and also in W. J. Linton, *Three Score Years and Ten*, 1894 edn.; *A. Heywood and Sons*, 1832–99; H. Vizetelly, *Glances back through Seventy Years*, 1893; J. Grant, *The Newspaper Press*, 1871.

the parcels by another coach. We can't send all now, but will make it up next week.'[1]

Some of Hetherington's and Cleave's expedients entered the folklore of radicalism. Dummy parcels were sent out with apparent stealth to draw off the runners, porters would battle with them heroically, while the Unstamped were smuggled out of the back door to safety. Hetherington shifted his papers by night, over roof tops into empty houses and grimy attics, from which they were scattered round the metropolis.[2] The offices of the *True Sun* and possibly the *Radical* were used as fronts. Cleave's *tour de force* was to persuade a local radical undertaker to construct him some plain deal coffins. These they filled at night with the *Weekly Police Gazette*; houses round the town received them with lowered blinds, and from there they went off to the most convenient coach or railway station. The coffins were returned the following night to the undertaker. But the neighbours became alarmed at the movement of so many coffins, feared an epidemic, and called in the parish authorities. Cleave's distribution system collapsed.[3]

How damaging was all this? Except for a bad spell in March and early May 1836, Hetherington and Cleave managed to come off lightly. Hetherington must have lost about 15,000 papers in the nine months (that is, less than a week's circulation) and Cleave probably less than 10,000. The *Weekly Times*, *Weekly Herald*, and *New Weekly True Sun* suffered more, and in the summer of 1836 put a half-penny on their price to cover losses. 'We have used ingenious devices. But our house is literally surrounded by these patriotic finishers of the law for three days out of seven. None but ourselves can divine how we get our parcels off—in fact it seems somewhat marvellous and miraculous.'[4] Cousins said that he had lost more in one week than he made from four weeks 'undisturbed trading'; for the past six weeks he had been losing 200 quires a week, perhaps a quarter or so of his total circulation.

[1] *Radical*, 1 May 1836; *True Sun*, 2, 6 Aug. 1836 (Cousins to Hobson).
[2] Vizetelly, op. cit., p. 93.   [3] J. Grant, op. cit., p. 306.
[4] *Weekly Herald*, 21 Aug. 1836; see also 28 Aug. 1836; *Weekly Times*, 21, 28 Aug. 1836.

(d) THE VICTIM FUND

Vendors were recruited by word of mouth among street sellers (experienced core vendors would often induct a new vendor by selling with him), by advertisement in the Unstamped itself, with the promise of high profits and relief money, and at working-class meetings. Cleave, like a less-benevolent Dr. Barnardo, toured the rookeries of Smithfield rescuing 'poor starving boys', many of whom must have become vendors of the Unstamped.[1] Once recruited, they were supported by the Victim Fund.

The years around 1819 had seen no comparable mass arrest of street vendors. Those arrested in London were the leading publishers of the radical press and their shopmen. Carlile took financial responsibility for his shopmen, and he and Moses, his printer, arranged to pay them 5s. a week, which was later increased to 7s. 6d. The shopmen also received gifts of food and subscriptions which totalled from £50 each downwards. Carlile himself received from £300 to £500 a year in subscriptions alone.[2] Those more likely to suffer and be ignored were the country vendors, whose families were often forced into the workhouse. The *Black Dwarf* suggested that around each imprisoned vendor should be organized a Society of Friends to support him. Nottingham, Manchester, and Birmingham formed relief funds, which in two years collected and distributed nearly £200. Manchester, for example, was divided into twenty-four districts, each with a class of twenty members who contributed a penny a week. Every person imprisoned was to receive 5s. a week for himself, 3s. for his wife and 2s. for any child under ten. Within six weeks the Society had distributed £38, but the names of the recipients were withheld 'from a sense of delicacy'. Nottingham collected and distributed £98 in a year, Birmingham spent £22 first on local vendors and then on men imprisoned elsewhere. In November 1823 Birmingham was supporting Swann,

---

[1] Lovett, op. cit., vol. i, p. 61.
[2] Carlile MSS., Carlile to Holmes, 23 Mar., 8 Nov. 1822; *Rep.*, 4 Aug. 1826, 9 Apr. 1824.

Mrs. Wright of Nottingham, and Mary Anne Carlile.[1]
However, Hunt's Great Northern Union founded in
October 1821 to return Hunt to Parliament, cut across such
societies, and though it was prepared to use some of its
funds to support prisoners, organized relief dried up.[2]

These relief societies were generalized funds for the
relief of all political prisoners as well as vendors; and they
were based on the provinces. Although a sizeable proportion
of Carlile's personal subscriptions came from London,
London did not apparently establish a similar relief fund;
nor did Carlile give these funds any publicity; nor was relief
money ever used as an inducement to recruit vendors. On
all these points the Victim Fund was very different—it
was essentially a London fund, it was for vendors only (separate funds were floated for trade unions, for example),
and it was designed to attract and keep street vendors.

The Victim Fund was established in July 1831. Lovett
at a meeting of the British Association for the Promotion
of Co-operative Knowledge early in July suggested a relief
fund for Carpenter, and for Hetherington if necessary.
By the end of the month the fund had been broadened to
aid all vendors of the Unstamped. The same number
of the *Guardian* that called for mass volunteers advertised
the Victim Fund. The original committee members were
James Tucker of the BAPCK, Watson, Warden (co-founder
of the Metropolitan Trades Union), Petrie, Molineux
(who soon dropped out), and Lovett. They were later joined
by Cleave, Hibbert, Russell (the NUWC secretary), Mansell
(an NU class leader), and W. D. Saull, the radical wine
merchant.[3] Hibbert was treasurer and Lovett secretary.
£73 had been collected by November 1831, £132 by March
1832, £175 by June, £252 by October, £281 by the beginning of 1833, £362 by July 1833. The fund then dried
up. By March 1834 only 30s. had been added to it, and

---

[1] *Black Dwarf*, 28 Feb., 11, 18 Apr., 21 Mar., 23 May, 21 Nov. 1821, 17 July,
1 Aug. 1822, 5 Feb., 5 Nov. 1823. Wickwar, op. cit., does not mention these funds
at all.

[2] *Black Dwarf*, 10 Oct., 14, 21 Nov. 1821. Just as Carlile's network of provincial
radical agents collapsed in the late 1820s, so did these sources of relief. Both had
to be built from scratch in the early 1830s.

[3] *PMG*, 30 July 1831; *Pol. Letters*, 30 July 1831; Lovett, op. cit., vol. i, p. 61.

when James Reeve was imprisoned in April 1834 a separate subscription was floated for him.[1] The fund effectively lasted two years.

Who subscribed? About a third of the money was collected at London NUWC meetings—'64th class [Watson's] 2/6d'. Another quarter or third came from political unions, or through newsagents outside London; 'The Midland Union collected at a dinner to celebrate the birth of Washington, 6/-'; the 'Tribute of a Few Friends to the Freedom of the Press, and Haters of Oppression, in Bury St Edmunds, by J. Tipple, an ultra-radical, now called a Destructive and a Revolutionist: 10/-.' Boxes, placed strategically at coffee and newspaper shops, brought in a few shillings more. Cleave would stand at the door of the Rotunda shaking a box at members. W. D. Saull gave any profits from his natural science lectures to the fund; Wade printed one of his sermons and gave the profits to the fund; Thomas Haberfield a plumber, painter, and glazier, advertised that 10 per cent of his proceeds would go to the vendors.[2] The rest came from individual subscriptions. 'J. H' [Hibbert] 21st subscription, 2s. 6d.; 'G. E. one hour labour note, 6d'; 'a sponge to wipe off the slave mark 1/3d'; 'M. L. not the marquis of Londonderry 6d'; 'a persecuted Radical for 25 years, 4s'; 'T. E. an enemy to Kingcraft 6d'; 'a few brushmakers near the Barbican 1/3d'. The vendor-proprietors of the *Cosmopolite*, in a splendid gesture, willed their bodies for dissection if they should die in prison, and profits to the Victim Fund; and the Female Society suitably contributed their shilling 'churching' fees.[3]

From the moment the fund was projected, the Home Office knew its details.

I was informed at Mr. Heatheringtons [*sic*] that it is the intention of the principals to employ a number of persons to vend the annexed publications and if sent to prison to allow them 1/0 per day during the time they are in confinement and a reward of 10/0 on the day of their

---

[1] *PMG*, 19 Nov. 1831, 31 Mar., 23 June, 27 Oct. 1832., 19 Jan., 27 July 1833, 1 Mar. 1834.

[2] *PMG*, 24 Nov. 1832, 28 Sept. 1833; *WMF*, 12 Jan. 1833; HO 64/11, 26 Aug. 1831.

[3] *PMG*, 24 Nov. 1832, 16 Feb., 9 Mar. 1833; *Cosmopolite*, 9 June 1832; *PMG*, 1 Dec. 1832.

liberation and let them continue ever such a number they will furnish a fresh supply.[1]

By the beginning of September 1831 Popay reported that most of the vendors and the coffee shops displayed collecting-boxes. The proprietors had already collected enough to allow 3s. a week, which they paid to the wives of the married men; if the men were unmarried and not able to buy food in prison 'the whole is to be paid them on their coming out as an encouragement for them to sell again'.[2] By the autumn the Victim Fund was paying what came to be considered the standard rate of 5s. a week. Hancock, Knight, and Lefevre, for example, received £3 for three months; James Knight £1 for one month. From March 1832, as the number of offences increased and the amount in the fund did not, money was given out with more regard to need, and those with a family received more. Edward Parker, who died in prison, received £4. 10s. in October 1832 for his two-month sentence, while in November another vendor received only 8s. for a three-month sentence. The standard rate fell to 1s., though vendors continued to believe it stood at five shillings. Cox and Saich, two 'destitute' young men, 'declared in the lock-up room that imprisonment had no terror' since they received 5s. a week from the National Union of the Working Class. They thought it 'a matter of favour' to be sent to the House of Correction.[3] When Owen Davis was sent to jail, the policeman attributed his scornful mood to the Victim Fund 'raised by readers of the *Poor Man's Guardian*'. Joseph Hyde, a boy just out of prison for selling the *Guardian*, was charged a second time.

The prisoner was closely questioned as to how he got these publications, and by whom he was encouraged; and from his answers, which he gave with extreme reluctance, it appeared that whenever a person has undergone a punishment for this offence, he goes from the prison to a gentleman named Cleaver [*sic*], at some coffee-shop in Cow-Lane, who gives him 5s. to start afresh with, and he is referred to a shop in Kingsgate Street, Holborn, to purchase copies of the *Poor Man's Guardian*, and he then retails them in the streets. None but persons

---

[1] HO 64/18, report of 27 July 1831, by Abram Fletcher, Inspector.

[2] HO 64/11, 2 Sept. 1831.

[3] *The Times*, 1 Nov. 1832; see also the case of Gee, *The Times*, 8 June 1832.

of the most destitute condition are so employed, and if they are committed to prison, they are sure of their 5*s.* at the expiration of their
confinement.[1]

From a *de jure* sum, relief became tied to need. From the
autumn of 1832, when the fund was nearly £10 in debt to
Hibbert, relief was given only to those who continued to
sell. Lovett hinted at this in his account of the NUWC,
which he wrote for Place; assistance was given 'in trifles at
a time' to some of the families, 'and to those who on the
expiration of their imprisonment needed the means of
purchasing the papers for sale, thus keeping up a perpetual
warfare with the Government'. As early as Christmas 1831,
one lad, John Jones, on being released was 'again to sell
the *Guardian,* and they had given him a trifle' for just this
purpose. Popay described the method in some detail.
Cleave's house was the rendezvous for victims

where he sells Coffee and other Refreshments . . . every Victim after
his release, applys there, and his name is registered with his term of
Imprisonment, and if his release takes place before the Committee
Night he is provided with Tea, Coffee etc. and with Lodgings at
Sixpence per Night. When the Committee meet he is (or perhaps
three or four of them) called upstairs from the Coffee Room and told
that the Funds will not at present admit of paying them their Five
Shillings per week, but if they like instead of being paid up for their
confinement—allow Cleave's bill and take 2 or 3 dozen Guardians,
Cosmopolites, Church Examiners etc they may sell them (they are
charged eightpence for thirteen of them) they the Committee hope
when they come out again to pay them up. They are then provided
with a few Shillings and as I have often stated being a set of ill-
principled, ignorant and in poverty take the 'Gentlemen of the Committee's' words proceed again on the same principle as to selling those
things and which I know are often brought by 13 to the dozen by
Hethrington, Cleave and Watson at Cleave's house for this purpose on
Committee Nights. [*sic*][2]

As a result, wrote Lovett, Cleave lost the best part of his
coffee-house customers, who were put off by ragged and
dirty victims. John Marshall, a pauper tailor, was brought
to the Town Hall, Southwark, for selling the *Guardian.*
This was his second offence, and he should, he said, have

---

[1] *PMG*, 24 Mar. 1832 (Davis); *The Times*, 9 Oct. 1832 (Hyde).
[2] HO 64/12, 4 Sept. 1832; Add. MSS. 27791, f. 249; HO 64/11, 23 Dec. 1831.

received 5s. a week from the NUWC, but when he applied
to Hetherington for it he was told that 'he must take out
the sum due to him, amounting to £1. 5s., in the publication
in question'. The alderman, needless to say, commented
on the injustice of forcing a man to commit a second offence
to receive payment for the first.[1] Hetherington was furious
at this 'Flagitious Lie', but a similar incident occurred
when Cleave, suspecting an Irishman would sell no more
of the Unstamped, refused him relief unless he showed a
(hypothetical) certificate of conviction.[2]

Who, then, received relief? Balance sheets were published
for August to December 1831, and from May 1832 until
March 1833, when the fund dried up.[3] The accounts for
the first six months of 1832 were not published. Cleave told
the NUWC in 1832 that so far there had been 200 victims
and that the society 'had afforded to each of the poor victims
a helping hand'. According to Lovett, nearly 300 vendors
were 'relieved', though his figure may refer to the number of
payments made rather than to the number of vendors helped.
The existing accounts record 202 payments to 154 vendors;
some two-fifths or so of the single vendors and over four-
fifths of the multiple vendors were helped. Only eleven
multiple vendors of nearly 100 who were selling during the
period the fund was available, did *not* receive money from it.
Vendors were eligible, if they sold political papers, though
in practise relief was usually given to sellers of the *Cosmopolite* and Hetherington's papers, less frequently for Watson's
and Carpenter's papers, and not for Carlile's papers at all.
And where in its opening months the Victim Fund had
given relief to all vendors, as money became scarce so relief
was reserved for multiple vendors and those who would
continue to sell the Unstamped.[4]

One possible explanation of this is that the Victim Fund
turned itself into an insurance scheme, which only the multiple vendors would be likely to join. In the middle of March
1832 'proprietors, publishers and friends of Unstamped

1 Lovett, op. cit., vol. i, pp. 65–6; *The Times*, 30 Aug. 1832 (Marshall).
2 *PMG*, 1 Sept. 1832; *The Times*, 1 Jan. 1833.
3 *PMG*, 25 Dec. 1831, 13 Oct. 1832, 6 Apr. 1833.
4 *True Sun*, 4 July 1832; Add. MSS. 27791, f. 249; *PMG*, 4 May 1833.

Publications' met to discuss the taxes on knowledge; they met a couple of times in April and by June they had become the Society for the Mutual Protection and Assistance of Booksellers. Carpenter was treasurer, subscriptions were 6*d.* a week and were received by Watson, Strange, Purkess, and Cowie; all London and country booksellers were eligible to join. In July Carpenter suggested that men who had been trapped into selling the Unstamped should report to this Society; and then nothing is heard of it for two years.[1]

It was presumably an insurance scheme. No record of its finances were included in the balance sheets of the Victim Fund, and most of the core vendors continued to receive money from the Victim Fund. Perhaps it was spent on legal aid; probably the Society just died a natural death. One curious case, however, suggests that it might have been alive in October 1832. Thomas Jones was brought to Queen Square for selling the *Guardian*. White, the magistrate, asked him whether he did not receive 5*s.* a week during his imprisonment. Jones replied that he had been imprisoned before for selling the *Guardian* but he had not been given any relief; 'many did, but he did not belong to that society and was therefore not entitled to it'. On further questioning he said the victims went to 'some place on Snow-Hill, where a committee met who managed the funds of the society'.[2] What was this society? There was never any other suggestion that a vendor might have to belong to the NUWC to qualify for relief: yet the Snow Hill committee was Cleave's, not Carpenter's. If the Society was not the Booksellers' Society, then why was Jones, a reliable multiple vendor, not entitled to relief?

In April 1834 this Society was apparently refounded. At a meeting of booksellers and vendors 'of cheap periodicals', chaired by Hetherington, it was agreed 'that a Society be now formed', the Society for the Protection of Booksellers, which would 'render mutual assistance in cases of oppression on the part of the Government, and to afford the best legal and pecuniary aid in all cases of prosecution for infringment of the Stamp Laws'. The contribution was 6*d.* a week,

---

[1] *Ballot*, 25 Mar. 1832; *PMG*, 7 July 1832; *Political Unionist*, 7 July 1832.
[2] *The Times*, 31 Oct. 1832.

Purkess was treasurer, Clements secretary, and Strange, Sharp, Watson, Cleave, Purkess, Hetherington, Lee, Watkins, Penny, Davies, and Cowie would receive enrolments and subscriptions. A month later it was agreed that no one should receive any benefits until he had paid at least four weeks' subscriptions. General meetings were to be held every second Tuesday of the month; 'every member imprisoned for selling Unstamped publications shall receive five shillings per week while funds last'.[1]

This Society was doing what the Victim Fund had done, aiding vendors and their families. But the ethos was very different. The Victim Fund was open to all, and imprisonment was supposed to be the only criterion for it, even when relief became nothing but a bundle of unstamped papers to be sold on the streets. But with the decline of the NUWC, its classes and country branches, and the death of Julian Hibbert in February 1834, the main supply of money for the Victim Fund had dried up. Vendors had no alternative but to acquire relief funds from among themselves. The result was a Friendly Society, a prudential association, and a closing of the ranks. Perhaps it was also a recognition that with the coming of the broadsheets, the distressed casual multiple vendor was no longer being recruited, and that sellers were leaving the streets for shops, a process reinforced from December 1835 when runners were employed. Selling the Unstamped had become a far more deliberate act. Vendors were expected to be regular, careful, and cautious, and to shun the publicity of arrest and martyrdom. Much more was spent on legal aid. By the end of 1833 eleven cases had been defended by an attorney, half of which had been between July and December 1831, the first six months of the *Guardian*. From the summer of 1834 on, twenty-five cases were defended with legal aid, and this was presumably paid for by the Society. At a public meeting in July 1834 Cleave said that any vendor who 'got into difficulties' would receive '*legal* or pecuniary assistance' if he obtained 'a recommendation to the society, even though funds were not overflowing'.[2] Like earlier statements of Cleave's on

---

[1] *PMG*, 19 Apr., 24 May, 14 June 1834.
[2] *People's Hue and Cry*, 10 Aug. 1834 (copy in HO 64/15) (my italics).

behalf of the Victim Fund, this would seem to have been a public relations gesture and far from true.

Meanwhile a second (and presumably rival) society, the 'London Union of Vendors of Useful Knowledge, Male and Female', was established in May. Hancock, the old core vendor, was its secretary, and Cousins, Stallwood, Cook, and Nichols were among its leading members. At the end of May Dr. Wade chaired its meeting 'to adopt measures for the protection of each other against the sanguinary prosecution of the Unstamped, and to aid the wives and families of all martyrs to an independent Unstamped press'.[1] The committees of the Booksellers Protection Society and of the London Union did not overlap; and the formation of the London Union might have owed something to what Carlile obscurely described as a Hetherington–Cleave combination to cut down the profits of the remaining street sellers to 25 per cent.[2] Yet why should this rival society have met in the offices of the *Man*, when Lee was on the committee of the original society? This second society appears to have existed at least until the autumn of 1835 for when William Smart was arrested, he scribbled a note to Cousins, 'as secretary to some society', asking for help for his family.[3] By 1836 only the Booksellers' Society was in existence, giving out aid, raising funds by performing Southey's *Wat Tyler*, and in August 1836 dissolving itself.[4]

[1] *Pioneer*, 17, 24 May 1834.   [2] *Scourge*, 11 Oct. 1834.
[3] *The Times*, 27 Oct. 1835.
[4] *Weekly Times*, 15 May 1836; *Twopenny Dispatch*, 20 Aug. 1836.

VI

IDEOLOGY—THE OLD ANALYSES[1]

THE London Unstamped were radical, clamorous, and competitive. They all drew on Paine and Spence, most of them consulted Colquhoun and Cobbett, some of them quoted Owen, and a few of them invoked Hall and Hodgskin. Paine and later Cartwright had stated the right to representative government. Paine and Cobbett together had put taxation to the forefront of economic evils, and had exposed borough-mongering as the source of political ills. Colquhoun's statistics had shown how the unproductive classes lived off the productive classes. George Mudie, speaking for Owen, had posed an alternative society to that of Malthus and the political economists. Charles Hall had used the idea of an original theft of the land to underpin a theory of exploitation. And in the mid 1820s Hodgskin, Thompson, and to a lesser extent Grey had demonstrated the mechanics of exploitation in an industrial setting.

All these ideas were well circulated. Texts, such as those of Paine, Colquhoun, Spence, and Hodgskin, were sold by Carlile, Hetherington, and Watson, and together with the current numbers of the Unstamped were to be found in dozens of small libraries attached to radical reading-rooms, coffee houses, and public houses. These books were discussed paragraph by paragraph in the classes of the National Union of the Working Classes[2] and quoted in editorial after editorial in the Unstamped. Hodgskin for a while lectured at the Mechanics Institute, Thompson at Co-operative Congresses, and Mudie formed his own discussion circle in the mid 1820s. Yet the effect was oddly non-cumulative. O'Brien and Carpenter did weave most of this material into a coherent critique, and 'Agrarius'

---

[1] This is not meant to be a survey of radical thought from Paine to O'Brien, but a survey of the sources on which the writers of the Unstamped drew.
[2] Add. MSS. 27791, f. 270.

(George Petrie) offered half a dozen different theories of society in half a dozen leading articles in the *Man*. The other writers stopped short along the way. Carlile in 1834 was still denouncing priestcraft with Paine; Lorymer and Lee were still arguing for a Spencean system of land nationalization for physiocratic reasons; and dozens of minor publicists were repeating the indictments of Cobbett in more or less colourful language and with more or less respect for property, king, and country. The working-class debate in the 1830s was a debate not between current alternative theories of society, but between those who invoked the older rhetoric of 1819 and those who innovated on it. The older rhetoric by 1832 seems stale, theatrical, and increasingly irrelevant, an artificial radical language into which new events and experiences have to be fitted. O'Brien and Hetherington were the innovators. Provoked by political economy, they worked the Hall–Hodgskin theme of economic exploitation into existing political radicalism.[1] And yet this seemingly more appropriate analysis was rejected in the NUWC debates, in lectures by Chartist missionaries, and in the columns of the *Northern Star*, in favour of the less appropriate but more traditional analysis. Any socialist patina was always very thin.

The writers of 1819 and of 1832 both saw the poor as distressed and oppressed. The writers of 1819, however, thought that the wealth of the poor was taken away in taxes rather than in the economic process itself. Their analyses therefore by-passed Charles Hall[2] who had shown that the poor were dependent upon the rich because they had been dispossessed of the land; and were exploited because they consumed only a small portion of what they produced. Instead, the old rhetoric was woven from Paine's demand for universal suffrage, Colquhoun's 'labour theory of value', and Cobbett's Old Corruption. Paine phrased the language of abstract rights, in which, for example, the NUWC's Declaration of the Rights of Man, and the Radical Association's preamble were written, and which echoed through the

---

[1] See below, Chapter VII.
[2] Charles Hall, *The Effects of Civilization on the People in European States*, 1805.

speeches of Hetherington and the writings of Benbow:
'We bow to the Sovereign majesty of the *people*; we acknowledge no other power. The people are state and church:
the people are the law.'[1] Colquhoun, unlike Hall, was interested not in the network of power, but in the distribution
of wealth, and his figures[2] showed that one-fifth of the community consumed one-third of its produce; and that the
producers (which included manufacturers) maintained a
non-productive class, some of whom were useful but most
of whom were indolent. Paine and Cobbett showed how this
wealth was redistributed in favour of the rich and idle.
Government taxes on food, drink, clothes, and houses kept
the producers poor while they propped up an idle class of
pensioners, spies, borough-mongers, and standing armies.
Most wrongs would therefore be righted if taxes were
greatly reduced, and this would come from radical reform
and universal suffrage.

This was the raw material of the rhetoric of 1819.
Wooler of the *Black Dwarf* asked only that the poor should
not be taxed, Davidson in the *Medusa* that the poor should
have some say in the laws which released 'the all devouring
monster taxation'. John Wade, who had studied Ricardo,
offered a three-tier society, of upper classes, middling classes
('the active working journeymen of Corruption'), and 'Opposed to this phalanx, with interests quite distinct and even
incompatible, . . . the PRODUCTIVE CLASSES of society.'
But manufacturers were among the productive classes;
so although Wade saw, like Hodgskin, the significance of
Ricardo's wage fund in which wages and profits were
inversely related, he could only conclude that the real
burden on industry was government 'duties', just as the
'whole boroughmongering fabric' depended on the Government's ability 'to levy taxes'.[3] Colquhoun's categories
(which included manufacturers among the producers) had
inhibited any frontal attack on political economy.

[1] Wm. Benbow, *The Trial of Wm. Benbow and others*. 1832.
[2] P. Colquhoun, *Treatise on the Wealth, Power and Resources of the British
Empire*, 1814 edn. Owen's 'industrious but non-productive classes' comes from
Colquhoun.
[3] *Black Dwarf*, 20 Aug. 1818; *Medusa*, 3 July, 23 Oct., 13 Nov. 1819; *Gorgon*,
1, 8 Aug., 12 Sept. 1818 (Wade).

Davidson, Wooler, and Wade were effective as working-class publicists for only a few years. Carlile, another of the men of 1819, spanned two decades: with Cobbett he dominated the 1820s, and he was second only to Hetherington and O'Brien in the 1830s. Yet in those twenty years his writings never advanced beyond those of 1819. Carlile went back to Paine and the *Age of Reason* for his description of Old Corruption as kingcraft, lordcraft, and priestcraft, Other writers, he claimed, failed to get to the root of the matter; they thought that taxes were the source and mainstay of corruption, and that universal suffrage was the remedy. Carlile scorned this as 'humbug and hotchpotch', which 'preserved all the dolls for the national nursery and merely [took] away their costly dresses'.[1] Only republicanism and the end of priestly power would free the people from the burden of Old Corruption; taxes would then disappear.

Priests were the chief buttress of Old Corruption, for not only did priests, like lords, live off the financial manipulations of Old Corruption, its rates and its tithes and its taxes, but they persuaded the people to acquiesce in it. 'The Priests are as much a political body as a standing army, the former are kept up to keep your mind in awe, the latter your body. . . .' Consequently they were 'the main prop of all that is politically corrupt in this country; and I see that no reform can take place without beginning at that end'. Fifteen years later his preface to the *Gauntlet* was: 'I challenge the world to make a good moral defence of kingcraft and priestcraft.'[2] The list of debates in the Rotunda—Church property, tithes, parliamentary debt, high taxation, poor rates, bad laws made to support Church and aristocracy, general corruption—advertised in his *Prompter* in 1831 could have formed his editorials in 1819.

As a critique of the priesthood, it was to have a long history. Thomas Parkin made the same points in the *Christian Corrector*. Watson's *Poor Man's Book of the Church*, published at the end of 1831, aimed to expose 'the injustice and evils of law-Church establishments'; and Benbow in

---

[1] *Rep.*, 24 May 1822, cf. *Prompter*, 13 Nov. 1830; *Rep.*, 22 Feb. 1822, 14 July 1826.

[2] *Rep.*, 22 Feb. 1822; *Lion*, 23 Oct. 1829; *Gauntlet*, 10 Feb. 1833.

his prospectus for the *Agitator and Political Anatomist* wished to show up 'the corruptions and oppressions of the Church and the profligacy and crimes of the clergy. . .'. Carpenter and Cleave in the *Slap at the Church*, Hetherington and O'Brien in the *Guardian*, and Harney in the *Friend of the People*, echoed Carlile's criticisms of the 'politico-religious establishment'.[1]

The Unstamped, like Carlile in 1819, had two main objections to the Established Religion. The first was that the Church was financially part of Old Corruption. Priests, pensioners, and aristocrats were all denounced in the same breath. Priests were the tools and the fellow conspirators of the parasite class, living off lands that belonged to the poor, maintaining their buildings by taxing the poor. Like pickpockets, the priests took what did not belong to them, like highwaymen they took it by force, and like libertines they spent it in criminal voluptuousness. If they met with any opposition, 'they bid the constable seize, and the soldiers shoot . . . and the hangmen hang. . .'.[2]

Secondly, the Church was the intellectual arm of the Established Order. W. Cooke Taylor, touring Lancashire in 1842, noted that the bad times had turned many to religion. The Bible was often the last item to be pawned. 'If any man doubted the benefits which Christianity has conferred upon mankind, he would be cured of his scepticism by witnessing its soothing influence on the distress and suffering of Lancashire.' This, the radicals thought, was to preach slavery and call it peace. In language reminiscent of Carlile's, O'Brien wrote that

the grand object of superstition is to reconcile the poor to the enormities of the rich, by inculcating the belief that all our evils are but so many dispensations of God's providence, or else the results of our own innate corruption, for which we are indebted to the priest's theory of 'original sin'.[3]

If the Church had any place in society, it first needed

---

[1] *Agitator*, 16 Nov. 1833; *Slap*, 21 Jan. 1832; *FP*, 26 July 1851.
[2] *PMG*, 25 Apr. 1835; see also *Penny Papers*, 10 Oct. 1830; *Slap*, 3 Mar. 1832; *Midland Rep.* 14 May 1831.
[3] W. Cooke Taylor, *Notes of a Tour in the Manufacturing Districts*, 1842, p. 298; *PMG*, 31 Aug. 1833. See also *PMG*, 2 May 1835; *Poor Man's Advocate*, 28 June 1832.

disestablishment and reform. *Slap at the Church* wrote mockingly:

> The Saviour lived and died *for* man
> To live *upon* him is the Bishops' plan.[1]

Carlile had a third objection to religion—it made men socially irresponsible. While men believed they could acquire pardons above, they need not reform themselves or society below. Religion was superstition, 'the knowledge of ignorance', a disease, which only reason could destroy. And reason was best diffused by the press, by pamphlets and newspapers, since trade and political clubs became the scene of petty squabbling and rivalries. 'Be you assured', he wrote to Hunt, 'that it is pamphlet vending that is destined to work the great necessary moral and political change among mankind. The Printing Press may be strictly denominated a Multiplication Table, as applicable to the mind of man. . . . Pamphlet vendors are the most important springs in the machinery of Reform. . . .'[2]

In 1819 Carlile's attack on religion was the preliminary to republicanism; by 1830 it had become an end in itself. In 1819 Carlile had expanded the vocabulary of political radicalism, but by 1830 his kingcraft, lordcraft, priestcraft formula had become a straitjacket, excluding any hint of Colquhoun and any such phrase as 'productive classes' or 'wealth-producers'. Sometimes Carlile justified his stance as the 'necessary preliminary' to equal rights and equal laws, and 'more equality in labour, profit and property'. Just occasionally he translated current concerns into his own language. In an article on trade unions, for example, he allowed that the accumulation of property had become oppressive.

Man and citizen have been sunk into the distinctions of lord and labourer, squire and peasant, priest and pauper, in each case the first generating the second evil. O.P.Q. means precisely what I mean, when I talk of putting down kings, priests and lords. The king talks about his private property and vested rights, the priest talks about his sacred interest in the land and ceremonial prerequisites, the lord lays

[1] *Slap*, 18 Feb. 1832.
[2] *Rep.*, 22 Feb. 1822; see also *Prompter*, 11 June, 2 July 1831; *Gauntlet*, 3 Mar. 1833.

claim to rights derived from the king's power, to grant what the people never gave as property, nor delegated as power to the king. All these things are called private property. . . .[1]

This was as much as Carlile ever conceded to the new analyses of the Unstamped. He did much for the freedom of the press, nothing for economic and social theory. He had no sympathy with the poor, and little sense of the lower echelons of class: he wrote for the working classes without ever asserting the cause of the oppressed.

There was one departure from this concern with religion. For a fascinating four months in 1826 Carlile was persuaded by Place and his young compositor Richard Hassell to open his columns to political economy. The change was heralded thus: 'The science of political economy is working great changes and doing much to unite all classes of politicians. It is a fair search after truth, about which, when found and exhibited, men cannot differ.' Correspondents, such as 'J. F.' and Michael Rough, immediately disagreed. They criticized Place's views on machinery even though they knew this was 'a sort of political blasphemy'; and they suggested that only those who produced should consume. For the first time in the Unstamped, manufacturers were reckoned among the parasitic and not among the productive classes, but none the less it was still taxes and not profits that kept the poor poor.[2] Carlile tried to show that taxes, like duties, dried up capital and so dried up jobs. Hassell, whose early writings were orthodox enough, now outdid even Carlile's critics. Where there were more labourers than there was capital to employ them, he wrote, labourers undercut each other, and wealth accumulated in the hands of a small body of capitalists. This was traditional enough.

But their accumulations cannot be called capital, because they are not applied to reproduction, but accumulated to be consumed. . . . The persons thus favoured by an unequal distribution, form a separate class, having but few interests in common with the rest of the community. They possess wealth; they feel their wealth to be power; and they naturally wish to make use of it . . . as their wealth enable

[1] *Gauntlet*, 1 Dec. 1833; see also 10 Feb. 1833 (O.P.Q. published a series of articles in the *Morning Chronicle* on trades unions in England and France).

[2] *Rep.*, 14, 28 July, 4, 18 Aug., 8 Sept. 1826.

them to usurp the reigns of government, it is pretty certain that they will do so. . . . Instead of governing by equitable laws, such a Government will seek only its own interests; to acquire and protect for itself exclusive privileges; and to maintain its power by keeping up its stock of wealth.'[1]

To remove such a Government, Hassell concluded, was to leave the roots of the system intact. Here for the first time in popular journalism was spelt out the interweaving of economic and political power, embedded in an orthodox Ricardian political economy. The traditional economic analysis had led to a radical political critique, but not yet to a radical economic critique. There is no hint of either Hall or Hodgskin here, nor is there any way to criticize accumulation as such, for accumulation resulted from acceptable economic laws. Hassell, a totally self-taught twenty-five-year-old, died before the end of the year; he might otherwise have rivalled O'Brien. Carlile concluded this excursion into political economy with a panegyric:

Political Economy is the science of politics, or human and social policy divested of all relations to mere political parties. It is the good divested of the evil of politics. . . . It is the interest of the public as a whole . . . it is the science of profits—the profit of labour, of rent, or exchange, and it has the harmonizing quality of seeking to equalize or to regulate the profits of all classes of industrious people or capitalists upon the basis on which the greatest aggregate and most diffusive profit can be raised. It is the science of the welfare of mankind.[2]

Then the waves closed over, political economy sank from sight and there was never another mention in Carlile's writings of the problems it posed to working-class journalists.[3] One wonders just what happened to Carlile's political sense or social sympathies during the long years in prison.

The attack on Old Corruption and Taxation, then, was the concern of the radicals of 1819; it was still being attacked by middle- and working-class radicals in the 1850s. And, to the discouragement of Hetherington and O'Brien, it remained one of the main strands of the Unstamped. Cobbett reiterated

[1] *Rep.*, 31 Aug. 1826.   [2] *Rep.*, 13 Oct. 1826.
[3] I have traced only one other reference to political economy in Carlile's writings. The *Gauntlet*, 23 Mar. 1834 reprinted the orthodox 'Working Man's Catechism of Political Economy' without comment.

the traditional account in his *Political Register*; the *Chronicler of the Times* like the *Weekly Show Up* devoted itself to taxes, church, sinecures, and fundholders. The *Working Man's Friend*, with a sure sense of its readership, reprinted many of the letters of 'Publicola' on aristocracy, pensioners, and taxes. When the National Political Union published a pamphlet, 'British Taxes Dissected', in the spring of 1833, it was reprinted in the *Gauntlet*, *Working Man's Friend*, and even in the *Destructive*. 'Pileo' in the *Man* damned trade but 'more dread, more voracious' still was taxation 'that devours our substance, and cherishes its numerous detested spawn to trample on their supporters'. Even Lovett, writing on temperance, slipped naturally into the old denunciations: 'Who are the slaves who guard the fortress of corruption, and fight the tyrants' battles?—mostly self-debased drunkards.'[1] Carlile's version of Old Corruption had put down strong roots. Dozens of letters to the *Gauntlet* were signed by 'Enemies to Priestcraft', 'Enemies to Superstition', 'No Taxation'. 'A Thorough Radical' praised the *Man* (avowedly Spencean) for 'its principles founded in *truth*' and went on: 'The time is arrived when the mystical cloke of priestcraft, and the mockery of 'kingly divinity' must be laid aside. . . .' The *Gauntlet* carried frequent editorials on corruption and taxation; and with some skill Carlile mobilized a wide public opinion behind the old rhetoric by enrolling some 3,000 Volunteers to cut government taxes from £50 million to £10 million a year. Deliberately or not, this must have undermined much of Hetherington's work with the provincial unions.[2]

[1] *Pol. Reg.*, 29 May 1830; *Chronicler*, 12 Jan. 1833; *Man*, 21 July 1833; *WMF*, 13 Apr. 1833; *Weekly Show Up*, 7 July 1832; see also *Patriot*, 27 July 1831.

[2] *Man*, 15 Sept. 1833. The Volunteers included almost every provincial agent of the unstamped and every prominent London vendor, among them Lorymer, Lee, Heins, Reeve, Pilgrim, Hancock, and Boreham. Though O'Brien dismissed taxation as a trivial evil, yet indirect taxes (mostly on food and drink) provided £35 million of the State's £50 million budget in 1832, of which in turn over half went to service the 'fundholders' of the National Debt, and half the remainder to the 'man-butchers' of the Armed Services. That is, taxation was not only regressive, but redistributed wealth upwards. R. M. Martin's solution (and O'Brien's) was not to cut taxes but to replace indirect taxation with a direct property tax. (*S.C. on Handloom Weavers petition*, 1834, qus. 3857–84).

When various London secret societies planned to use the Dorchester case in 1834 as a signal for popular revolution, the key buildings they thought to attack and hold

The attack on Old Corruption, then, was one of the most popular intellectual strands in the Unstamped. A second, and to some extent related, strand was Spencean. Paine's *Agrarian Justice* had stated that all men had a natural right to the land, but Paine, Cobbett, and O'Brien in his more cautious moods, accepted that property rights were inviolable. For the Spenceans, property was theft, an usurpation which had led to the present society of rich and poor. Private property was the enemy and land nationalization the remedy. Allen Davenport had been a friend of Spence and he contributed a thin trickle of writings on land reform through the 1820s and 1830s. Like Spence, he wanted land to revert to the parish.[1] Richard Lee, editor and proprietor of the *Man*, published the articles of 'Agrarius', who suggested that pledges extracted at the next general election should include the total repeal of primogeniture and entail, the laws of freehold, copyhold, and leasehold, and the establishment of a land office to let the land at a rent which would cover the administrative costs of the state. Former owners should receive no other reward 'than the gratification of an approving conscience'.[2] Lee steadily worked the writings of Spence and Paine together.[3] 'Agrarius', however, offered his readers a wider choice of social theories. His first leading article argued that an equality of condition which was based on the possession of land, must come before the political radicalism of equal rights and equal laws. His next move was to translate this into the language of monopoly. The landed monopoly underpinned all other ills (an umbrella phrase embracing the rhetorics of Carlile and O'Brien). The working men, he wrote, were deprived of three-quarters 'of the real value of their labour . . . under the name of *profit*, which is the parent of property, and the progenitor of monopoly and competition'. Misery, want, and national grievances originate 'in the existence of kings, lords and priests, with monopolists in land, monopolists in machinery,

---

to ransom were the Home Office, St. James Palace, the Bank of England, and the East India House, all of them architectural symbols of Old Corruption (A. Somerville, *Autobiography*, 1951 edn., p. 268).

[1] *Man*, 28 July 1833.   [2] *Man*, 21 July 1833.

[3] e.g. *Man*, 7 July 1833; cf. also *Political Penny Magazine*, 10, 17 Sept. 1836; *Truth*, 10 Feb. 1833.

and monopolists in human labour of every kind'. The following week 'Agrarius' addressed the 'priest-gull'd, king-gull'd, property-gull'd, and profit-gull'd labourers of Great Britain and Ireland'. But in his final writings he threw Carlile overboard, and came close to O'Brien. Monarchy, clergy, and aristocracy were 'trivial evils, as compared with the ravages of the monster PROPERTY—the result of profit, begotten by Fraud, aided by force on Ignorance'.[1]

Spenceanism as a strand of criticism gained extra vitality in the early 1830s from two sources: the debates in and out of Parliament on Church lands, and the debates on emigration and its domestic alternative, home colonization.[2] So Hetherington told the NUWC in a debate on Church property that 'the land was the people's farm, and he was for demanding restitution from both temporal and spiritual lords'.[3] Spenceanism was also woven into the Cobbett historiography of the Norman yoke, of the land stolen by feudal lords at the Conquest, and by an unauthorized Church at the Reformation. The version in Lorymer's *Republican* was more ominous.

Property is the produce of the soil, created by labour . . . every man has a right of property in the soil. Talk of civil rights—talk of conventional rights—talk of the law of inheritance. What right is so sacred as the right of creation—what law is so imperious as the law of necessity?[4]

From this Lorymer, Lee, Davenport, and Mee went on to argue for a National Convention to discuss the means by which land might be restored to the people; and they tapped a land hunger and an agrarian dream that passed through Owen into the various land schemes of the 1840s.

Lorymer ran Spenceanism together with an attack on Old Corruption and the aristocrats who excluded the Many from 'the Assembly where the taxes are imposed.'[5]

When the whole people is represented, we will make the tax devourers disgorge with a vengeance. Let the usurers continue their taxation. It cannot last long. The day of RETRIBUTION is not very far distant. When the real representatives of the people are deputed to the National Assembly, the plundered many shall have their own restored fourfold. Every priest, every great landowner, every cut-throat or soldier, every pensioner, and every other vulture who has been gnawing the vitals of the nation—every sloth, every glutton and every aristocrat, who has been battening on the produce of the wealth producers—every bloated hog who has been feeding on the fruits of the labour of the operatives and the peasantry, shall be made to restore the illgotten prey to the insulted, plundered owners—the industrious Many. This is our consolation for the present pickpocketism committed on the people.[1]

This was still the language of natural rights and taxes, not the language of economic analysis, though landowners have replaced priests as the main buttress of Old Corruption. None of these Spenceans discussed how the system originated nor how it was maintained; as a body of theory it was important mainly for its emphasis on land and theft. But where the attackers of Old Corruption described the poor as poor because the Government exploited them as consumers, the Spenceans, like Hall before them, thought that the poor were poor because as producers they had been dispossessed of land. Where the men of 1819 saw the model society as a fragmented bundle of individuals, the Spencean farming parish was more nearly communitarian.

The third major strand woven into the ideologies of the 1830s was Owenism. Owen's writings were coming into prominence in 1819. His *Report to the County of Lanark* in 1820 had shown a very different concern from that which had led to attacks on Old Corruption. 'The Evil for which your Reporter has been required to provide a remedy, is the general want of employment, at wages sufficient to support the family of a working man beneficially for the community.' And he stated his premises: 'that manual labour, properly directed, is the source of all wealth' and 'that, when properly directed, labour is of far more value to the community than the expense necessary to maintain the labourer in considerable comfort'. None of this was new, except perhaps that manual labour rather than productive labour was made the source of wealth. By restating it in this form, however, Owen was deliberately confronting Malthus; for if all labourers earned more than their subsistence, then any industrious labourer was entitled to subsistence, and

[1] *Rep.*, 2 July 1831.

most labourers must at present be having part of their produce appropriated.

George Mudie, rather than Owen, spread the Gospel in London by means of his paper, the *Economist*, and the Co-operative and Economical Society, of which Hetherington was a member in 1821. Like Wade, and like O'Brien later, Mudie took his diagnosis from the political economists. Wages were low because too many labourers were competing for too few jobs; and as goods were produced only for profit, the poor could not afford to consume them. 'The society requires the produce, it has lost control over the power of production.' Hall, Mudie said, had seen that poverty came from misapplying the powers of production, but this was due, not as Hall thought, to 'the waste and profusion of the rich', but to 'the decay of the social principle'. The potential wealth of the country and the potential power of machinery were 'staggering'. Competition and the inefficient flow of capital, however, strangled economic growth. Communities would bring together capital and labour, allow the artisan to retain his produce, reconcile the interest of each and all, and bring general abundance.[1]

Mudie was criticizing poverty, and not uneven wealth, exploitation, lack of land, or lack of working-class power. The rich could keep their riches, the poor would be given the opportunity to create new wealth. It was not an egalitarian society, for he had no time for 'the delusive doctrines of the Rights of Man' and property-sharing schemes. Nor was it a classless society, for, though he objected to the 'excrescences' of capital, he had no objection to capitalists and social ranking. Rather, Mudie's society was a prosperous non-political society, essentially a high wage–full employment society 'consistent with sound principles of political economy'. It was artisan and industrial, secure from the modern economic problems of wage cutting, trade fluctuations, and mechanization. As a New Society, it was meant to be a practicable alternative to the society of the political economists and not a standing refutation of it.[2]

[1] *Economist*, 3, 17 Feb., 19 May 1821.
[2] *Economist*, 7 July 1821; see also *Mr. Owen's Proposed Arrangements* . . . , G. Mudie, 1819.

The second publicist of co-operative thought was Dr. King of Brighton, whose writings recharged the co-operative movement in 1828. Where Mudie emphasized, with the political economists, that competition between labourers kept the working classes poor, King showed how this competition was aggravated by a further competition between capitalists, which brought on trade fluctuations. With Mudie, he drew out the implications of gluts, of men perishing amid plenty; and he sharpened Mudie's assertion that labour was the source of wealth by embedding it in denunciations reminiscent of Cobbett: 'The capitalists produce nothing themselves; they are fed, clothed and lodged by the working classes.'[1] He agreed with Mudie that production was limited by profits and not by need. And King did what Mudie had not done, but Richard Hassell had; he turned an economic critique into an analysis of power.

In the present form of society, the workmen are entirely in the power of the capitalists, who are incessantly playing at what is called profit and loss—and the workmen are the counters which are pitched backwards and forwards with this unfortunate difference—that the counters do not eat and drink as workmen do, and therefore don't mind being thrown aside at the end of the game. . . . But the workmen are as much in the power of the capitalists, as the counters are in that of the players; and if the capitalists do not want them, they must go to the wall.[2]

Central to King's analysis was the degradation and lack of dignity which resulted for the workman.

We claim for the workman the rights of a rational and moral agent . . . the being whose exertions produce all the wealth of the world—we claim for him the rights of a man, and deprecate the philosophy which would make him an article of mere merchandise to be bought and sold, multipled and diminished, by no other rules than those which serve to decide the manufacture of a hat.[3]

Mudie's Prosperous Society had, in King's hands, become the Moral Society. Some idea of the liberation and sense of dignity which this brought comes out in the resolutions

---

[1] *Co-operator*, Sept. 1829; see also *Lancashire Co-operator*, 11 June 1831; *United Trades Co-operative Journal*, 24 July 1830; *Magazine of Useful Knowledge*, 15 Oct. 1830.   [2] *Co-operator*, Sept. 1829.

[3] *Co-operator*, Oct. 1829; see also *Chester Co-operative Chronicle*, 10 July 1830.

of the British Association for the Promotion of Co-operative Knowledge. It was Owen 'who impressed upon our minds a conviction of our importance; who convinced us, working men, that we were the pillars of the political edifice; that we sustained the whole superstructure of society.'[1] More dramatic (if obviously literary) was a letter from 'H. D.' of Islington to the *Crisis*:

I am a poor man, Mr. Owen, and hitherto have been a most discontented one. From the hour in which I first reflected on the comparative misery of my own fate, with that of the rich and great, I have been dissatisfied . . . envious of their comforts and unmindful of my own. . . . When the painted and gorgeous carriage of the higher orders has whirled by me at the corner of the street, dashing the dirt of its wheels in the face of a poor weary man, proud even in his adversity, I will own to you that I have cursed its possessor in my heart, with a double loathing at the thought of my own wretched home, my coarse and scanty meal, my coarse and stained apparel . . . the change my whole being has undergone since I heard you, most respected Sir, advocate the people's cause, and teach him the heart reviving lesson, TO RESPECT HIMSELF. . . . As I walked from the doors of the Institution on the days of the Congress there, a noble pride swelled within me, for I had heard from some of the mouths of the labourers and neglected classes, arguments and sentiments that would have done honour to both Houses of Parliament. I said within myself 'and I also am of this order of society; I am no drone to eat the honey of the hive, and contribute nothing to the store'. I feel my own importance, and that I am equally a man with him who turns his head haughtily away, with contemptuous frowns as I civilly make way for him. . . .[2]

For twenty years, therefore, working-class theorists had recognized that there was a gap between what the labourer produced and what his wage would buy, and in turn taxation, upper-class parasites, the theft of land, and competition were held to account for it. Any more devastating critique (and a more critical attitude to political economy) was inhibited because Colquhoun, and later Owen, included the manufacturers among the productive classes. Working men were oppressed rather than exploited.

---

[1] Carpenter's *Letter to Wilmot Horton*, n.d. (end of Dec. 1830).
[2] *Crisis*, 17 May 1832.

Where the older analyses compared the value of the labourer with his spending power, Hodgskin and other 'Ricardian socialists' went further and compared the value and reward of the labourer with the value and reward of the employers of labour. The result was a class-based theory of exploitation, modified at various points by a residual attack on Old Corruption. Hodgskin on first reading MacCulloch's summary of Ricardo in the *Edinburgh Review* had written to Place that 'profits are purely and simply a portion of the product of labour which the capitalist, without any right other than that conferred upon him by law, takes for himself'.[1] The capitalist could take from the labourer more than he gave him back as wages, because the labourer was dependent on him for subsistence and was competing with other labourers for too few jobs. As a result, the labourer had to take any terms the capitalist offered him, for he could neither bargain with him nor by-pass the system. John Grey elaborated on Colquhoun's analysis and recast it as a more specifically labour theory of value. William Thompson, the third of the 'Ricardian socialists', used this as an argument for co-operation and added a concern for economic equality to Mudie's blue-print of the Prosperous Society. Hetherington, Carpenter, and O'Brien were the chief publicists of this exploitation theory in the Unstamped, and they worked it into more traditional political radicalism.[2]

So the journalists of the Unstamped drew upon four main sources of social criticism—Old Corruption, Land Theft, Competition, and Exploitation. Certain tenets were common to all of them: they agreed on the right of working men to the vote, though not always that the vote was important; those that outlined a political system made it secular and republican; and all but Carlile agreed that the working man had the right to the products of his labour. They shared either a two-tier or a three-tier social analysis in which the working classes were productive and the rest of society parasitic on their labour, and in which the working classes were oppressed and the upper classes had organized Government in their own interests. The economic and the political

---

[1] Quoted E. Halevy, *Thomas Hodgskin*, 1903, p. 120.
[2] See below, Chapter VII.

oppressions were linked in various ways—by the power of taxation, by property rights, by the power of law-making, by control of the means of subsistence, and so on. And many of the Unstamped had become critical of orthodox political economy which they saw as a class weapon defending class tyranny with immutable economic laws.

None the less, most writers presented a remarkably 'pure' version of the original critiques; each was seen as a total view of society. Only Hetherington, O'Brien, and Carpenter offered a more cumulative analysis, in which all of these sources can be traced. Their technique was to collapse the newer analysis on the old, using terms that could be translated from one level to the other. The parasites and useful classes of Old Corruption were the unproductive and productive classes of Colquhoun were the oppressors and the oppressed were the landholders and the dispossessed of Spence were the capitalists and labourers of Hodgskin. Old enemies, such as taxes, tithes, rents, and pensions appeared in the newer analysis, but as 'symptoms' and not 'causes'; the new analysis was then offered as a 'reordering of priorities'. The whole process was made easier by the flexibility of such words as Union, which had moral, economic, and political undertones, and which could embrace Carlile's Moral Bond, a political National Convention, co-operative employment, and the Grand National Consolidated Trades Union. And yet for all their superior skill, powerful writing and sophisticated analyses, and despite the deep loyalty which the *Guardian* acquired, O'Brien and Hetherington never managed to displace the old analyses.[1]

[1] See below, pp. 286–9.

VII

IDEOLOGY—THE NEW ANALYSIS

THE *Working Man's Friend* described political economy
as the law of buying cheap and selling dear. 'The
selfish may call that a science, but if it is a science,
it is only the science of trickery.' 'Agrarius' in the *Man*
remarked that political economists sought 'to prove that a
starving man is and ought to be the most contented being
in existence'. And O'Brien, when he reprinted the pamphlet,
Political Economy versus the Handloom Weaver, in which
Scrope recommended emigration and the weavers demanded
a regulated wage, commented, 'It is impossible to read these
letters without perceiving that we are on the brink of a
precipice. The statements of the two parties are so widely
opposite. . . .' Place had good reason to believe that political
economists were considered the 'bitter foe to the working
classes, enemies who deserved no mercy at their hands'.[1]
But although references to political economy in the Unstamped were almost invariably hostile, only Hetherington
and O'Brien in the *Guardian* and *Destructive*, and Carpenter for six months in his *Political Letters*, met the
doctrines of popularized political economy head-on. The
'new analysis' was compounded of the Exploitation theories
modified by the other sources of social criticism, the attack
on Old Corruption, Land Theft, and Competition; and it
was stretched and shaped in debates with popularized
political economy.

The working-class case was put by 'One of the Know-
nothings'.[2]

> Wages should form the price of goods,
> Yes, wages should be all.

[1] *WMF*, 13 Apr. 1833; *Man*, 14 July, 22 Sept., 30 Oct. 1833; *PMG*, 1 Aug.
1835; Add. MSS. 27791, f. 48; 35151, f. 100, Place to Perry, 4 Oct. 1838; f. 127,
Place to Carpenter, 24 Jan. 1839.
[2] *PMG*, 7 Jan. 1832.

Then we who work to make the goods
Should *justly have them all;*
But if their price be made of rent,
Tithes, taxes, profits all,
Then we who work to make the goods
Shall have—*just none at all.*

The questions followed easily. What did the labourer produce and why did he not receive it all? What counted as productive labour? What determined the labourer's share, and why did the capitalist receive so much more? Why were the labourers the most valuable and yet the most oppressed portion of society? And how could they remedy their lot?

(*a*) THE LABOUR THEORY OF VALUE

The Ricardians[1] accepted that labour was the source of value and that capital was stored up labour. Both they and working-class journalists agreed that the labourer did not receive as wages the full value of the goods he produced. This gap was described by middle-class economists as profits, the payment for the use of the capitalist's fixed and circulating capital, his skills as an entrepreneur, and by Scrope as the reward for abstinence.

Working-class economists objected to this version on two counts. Hodgskin put the first criticism; it was meaningless to define capital as 'stored up labour', for fixed capital such as machinery was 'dead matter' until brought into use by labour, and circulating capital was a myth, for no capitalist stored up cabbages and calico in his attic with which to pay his workers. What the capitalist did possess was the power to annex goods as they were produced, so that labourers were

---

[1] The Ricardians included Ricardo, James Mill, McCulloch, and their popularizers John Wade, Place, and Charles Knight. They were a smaller group than the classical economists, who included Nassau Senior and Poulett Scrope, forerunners of the utility school.

The following account in no sense attempts to be a comprehensive survey of middle-class political economy—it ignores such problems as rents, savings, investments, etc. It is concerned only with those tenets of orthodox political economy (often highly simplified) with which the working-class theorists of the Unstamped took issue. For an account of Ricardian theory, see M. Blaug, *Ricardian Economics*, 1958.

forced to depend upon the capitalist instead of exchanging their goods with each other. Charles Knight argued that this implied that all exchanges had to be conducted in the present, new labour with new labour, and never new labour for old. 'Labour shall be exchanged with labour, but not with the produce of labour.' Accumulation would cease, no one would work beyond his present needs, and society would retrogress.[1]

Most of the writers of the 1830s, however, brought a second criticism, simpler and more telling than Hodgskin's —if capital was stored-up labour, how came the capitalist to possess it? The answer to this was also the explanation of why the working classes were poor. The old analysis had pointed to taxes, tithes, church rates, and lawyers' fees, extracted from the working-man's pocket after he had received his wages, and used to support a corrupt Government and an established Church. The new analysis argued that the heaviest exactions were taken from the working man in the economic process itself, before he received his wages. The original theft of land had destroyed the self-sufficiency of the poor, and forced them to become wage earners and rent payers. The 'feudal aristocracy' of the land had allied with the capitalist 'aristocracy of wealth'; together they formed the propertied classes which daily exploited the producers.[2] Rent, interest, taxes, and profits, according to Grey and Thompson, deprived the labourer 'of at least half of the products of his labour. . .'. Hodgskin argued that the capitalist used his position as the middleman between exchanges to appropriate a major part of the goods.[3] O'Brien enlarged on this, and put it in popular form:

Now, since all wealth is the produce of industry, and as the privileged fraction produce nothing themselves, it is plain that they must live on the labours of the rest. But how is this to be done, since every body thinks it enough to work for himself? It is done partly by *fraud*

[1] T. Hodgskin, *Labour Defended against the claims of Capital* (1922 edn.), p. 55; *The Rights of Industry: Capital and Labour* (S.D.U.K.), 1831, p. 58.

[2] BAPCK resolutions, *Letter to Wilmot Horton*, 29 Dec. 1830; *PMG*, 24 Sept., 1 Oct. 1831; W. Thompson, *Labour Rewarded*, 1827, p. 9.

[3] J. Gray, *Lecture on Human Happiness*, 1931 edn., p. 70; W. Thompson, *An Inquiry into the Distribution of Wealth*, 1850 (edited by Pare), p. 222, pp. 125–45; Hodgskin, op. cit., pp. 71–3.

and partly by *force*. The 'property' people having all the law-making to themselves, make and maintain fraudulent institutions, by which they contrive (under false pretences) to transfer the wealth of the producers to themselves. All our institutions relating to *land* and *money* are of this kind. These institutions enable certain individuals, called *'landlords'*, to monopolize the soil, to the exclusion of the rest of society, who are thereby defrauded of their just and natural inheritance. To secure themselves in this monopoly, the landlords unite with another band of conspirators called *'capitalists'*, and from this union proceeds a *monied monopoly*, which is (if possible) a thousand times more baneful than the monopoly in land. From these two master monopolies proceed a thousand others, all working in the same way, and all tending to the same end—namely, the absorption of the annual produce of the country into the hands of the monopolists. One portion is absorbed under the name of *rent*, another under that of *tithes*, a third under that of *taxes*, a fourth under that of *tolls*, a fifth under that of *law expenses*, a sixth under that of *interest*, a seventh (which is by far the greatest) under that of *profits*, and so on with *commissions*, *agencies*, *brokerage* etc. to the end of the chapter. These and the like are the pretences under which the useful classes are plundered for the benefit of the useless.[1]

The double monopoly of land and money supported by the minor ills of Old Corruption was not the only account O'Brien gave of exploitation; sometimes his analysis was more closely Hodgskinite and he damned the middlemen who took advantage of the necessities they created. At other times, like Thompson, he turned his guns on Property and the uneven distribution of wealth that it perpetuated. 'When the aristocrat and capitalist talks of the "sacredness" of property, he means the sacredness of the right of one man to appropriate to himself, through the instrumentality of capital, the fruits of another man's industry', simply because he is powerful. When Rothschild left £5 million, he left £50,000 at 5 per cent a year for ever—that is, a power to certain men to consume other men's labour to the value of £50,000 every year.[2] Property was not just wealth; it was a claim on labour; it was the power to live off the labour of others.

---

[1] *PMG*, 26 July 1834; see also Mayhew's version in *PMG*, 30 July 1831; see also *Political Penny Magazine*, 3 Sept. 1836. 'By force and by fraud' was taken from Godwin by Thompson.

[2] *PMG*, 1 Sept. 1832; see also *PMG*, 23 Nov. 1833, 27 Dec. 1834; *Twopenny Dispatch*, 27 Aug. 1836; *PMG*, 26 Jan. 1833.

From this O'Brien could argue that he attacked not property but robbery. Private property, honestly earned and honestly saved, was the sacred and the exclusive possession of its owner. True property rights were inviolable. Socialists attacked only property wrongs, the unjust and evil powers property commanded, so that wealth became 'a sucking-pump or thumbscrew for sucking and screwing other people's produce' into another's possession. Money should not be allowed to grow money, as cabbage grew cabbage or weeds grew weeds. Property, made Power by Interest, was Theft.[1]

Not all O'Brien's correspondents thought this was the final word. P. H. G., a labourer, pointed out that O'Brien was willing to allow people to dispose of their wealth as they chose, because they would otherwise have no motive to save, but O'Brien would not allow people to *use* their wealth by loaning it at a price. As this wealth, or capital, greatly increased the productivity of the labourer, P. H. G. thought it only reasonable that the labourer should give part of his gross return back to the capitalist for the use of his capital, and in that case, working class poverty must be due to something other than profits and interest rates. O'Brien retaliated the following week with a string of questions. How did P. H. G. account for the condition of the labourer and the condition of the capitalist? Why indeed were they not the same person, 'if what the economists say be true, that "capital is only the accumulated results of former labour" '? Was the labourer better off or worse off since the growth of middlemen and machinery? Was taxation alone able to account for his lot? Finally, did capitalists favour universal suffrage? At no point, however, did O'Brien show what P. H. G. had asked him to show— how to strip wealth of power.[2]

O'Brien did claim to have shown two things. First, he had shown that taxes were a 'molehill' compared to the 'Mont Blanc' of capitalist robbery. When he had first started to write, he said, looking back over four years, the prospect had been 'dismal'. Unions, radical leaders including

---

[1] *Buonarotti's History of Babeuf's Conspiracy*, ed. J. B. O'Brien, 1836, pp. 217 f.; see also *NS*, 16 June 1838.

[2] *PMG*, 16, 23 Feb. 1833.

Cobbett and Hunt, radical journals, and the 'multitude' were all sure 'that *taxation* was the main cause of their distress'. The *Guardian* had thought very differently, and argued that the working classes were distressed because capitalists and mere middlemen appropriated the fruits of their labour. Taxation was a 'trifling evil'. Secondly, O'Brien and the *Guardian* had checked the working classes from squandering their energies in schemes to benefit their employers and oppressors. Formerly, any 'reform' scheme, 'however barren or fraudulent', could attract working-class support, whether it be the East India monopoly, Dissenters' claims, or the corn laws.

These are questions which they know can never concern them, so long as the capitalist holds them in subjection; besides, they are questions which originate with their oppressors, and whatever may have been their past stolidity, they have wit enough *now* to understand that no good can come from that quarter.[1]

O'Brien claimed that he had deflected the working-class attack away from Old Corruption, and focused it on profits and exploitation. None the less, neither he nor Hetherington were confident enough of their success to stop 'translating' from the new analysis back into the old. One of Hetherington's correspondent's explained at the end of 1831 that

Rent is the land-holders tax—*tithe* is the parsons's tax—*interest* on money is the fundholder's tax—*profits* on labour are the master's tax—and *profits* on trade are the . . . shopkeeper's tax; and those taxes amount to nearly twenty times as much as all the taxes which support the government!

In the summer of 1834, O'Brien was still embedding the sins of profit in a demonology of rent, tithes, taxes, and lawyers fees.[2] His success in substituting one rhetoric for another, was doubtful.[3]

---

[1] *PMG*, 18 Oct. 1834; see also *PMG*, 22 Feb., 22 Mar., 11 Oct. 1834, 25 July 1835; *Destructive*, 7 June 1834. O'Brien was still hammering both of these points in the 1840s. 'Before my time it was the fashion to lay all our grievances to a few, to this party in power, or the other party in power; but I have taught the people to know that their grievances do not result from a few lords, priests or Commons being in power, but from a whole class of the community being opposed to them' (*NS*, 20 Nov. 1841); and again, that the demand for the vote must not be deflected by either Attwood's currency schemes or corn law reform (*NS*, 10 Feb. 1838, 14 Nov. 1840).

[2] *PMG*, 26 Nov. 1831; see also *PMG*, 26 July 1834.

[3] See below, p. 286.

(*b*) PRODUCTIVE AND UNPRODUCTIVE LABOUR

Colquhoun had drawn an immensely fertile line between productive and unproductive classes. The productive classes, those working in 'agriculture, mines, minerals, manufactures, shipping, fisheries, commerce, and inland trade, assisted by capital, machinery and skill', created the means of subsistence or added to national wealth. The unproductive classes were those whose labour 'adds to the value of nothing', even though they included many who were 'useful'—judges, soldiers, and administrators.[1] It was a line between those who augmented national wealth and those who did not. It was explicitly neither a line between the industrious and the idle nor between the useful and the useless. However, the middle-class economists tried to broaden the notion of productiveness to include some of Colquhoun's useful but unproductive classes. The working-class economists, on the other hand, tried to exclude from the notion of productive all those who were parasitic on manual labour, including manufacturers, merchants, and shopkeepers.

Scrope, for example, argued that any exertion which had exchangeable value, including acting, writing, and soldiering, was productive. McCulloch stated more specifically that any activity augmenting the production, distribution, or exchange of goods was productive. The shopkeeper and the merchant were patronized only because they were useful. This meant that no class of 'industrious individuals' lived off any other class. Society was nothing but a series of exchanges between goods and services of equal value.[2]

Working-class writers translated Colquhoun's productive and unproductive classes into the useful and the parasites. What was in Colquhoun's hands an economic division, became now a social and then inevitably a moral division. 'Every unproductive member of society', wrote Gray, 'is a

[1] Colquhoun, op. cit., p. 104.
[2] P. Scrope, *Political Economy*, 1873 edn., p. 9; J. R. McCulloch, *Principles of Political Economy*, 5th edn., 1864, p. 65; see also J. Wade, *The History of the Middle and Working Classes*, 2nd edn., 1834, p. 175; E. Tufnell, *The Character, Objects and Effects of Trades Unions*, 1834, p. 43.

DIRECT TAX upon the productive classes. Every unproductive member of society is also a USELESS member of society, unless he gives an equivalent for that which he consumes.' By 1832 the Lancashire *Radical Reformers' Catechism*, which Hetherington reprinted in the *Guardian*, was even more explicit in its judgements.

I believe in the greedy rapacity of tithe-gorging Bishops—that the Working Classes are the only useful classes—the working bees, the honey makers; most properly speaking, the better sort of folk; while those so called are the pests of society, the worse than useless classes, and the consumers of the honey, the drones of the Hive.

The *Herald of the Rights of Industry* added that every worker had to maintain two idlers, at the very least, in luxury.[1]

On to the old idle classes of pensioners, borough-mongers, priests, lawyers, and soldiers castigated by Paine and Cobbett, and the thieving landlords of Hall and Spence, was added Hodgskin's layer of the all-devouring but parasitic middleman-capitalist and O'Brien's image of the 'shopocracy' as the servile buy-cheap-sell-dear class. The roll call of public enemies grew longer and longer.

Were society what it ought to be, we should want no priests—no lawyers—no statesmen—no hangmen—no soldiers—no stock-jobbers—no shopocrats—no slavedrivers—no literary prostitutes—no attorneys—no pickpockets—no civilians—no chicane-mongers—no mystery-mongers—no lords—no bishops—no fine gentlemen—in short no white fingered or light fingered gentry of any kind. Were society what it ought to be and (with God's blessing) what it will yet be—it would be utterly purged of the multitudinous vermin who now live by buying and selling, and trafficking, and stealing and swindling, and swaddling and smuggling, and canting, and lying, and begging, and preaching, and chicaneing, and hanging the poor, and flattering the rich and capturing the small thieves that infringe the law, and bolster-

---

[1] Gray, op. cit., p. 15; *PMG*, 1 Sept. 1832; *Herald*, 8 Feb. 1834. Asa Briggs in 'The Language of "Class" in early Nineteenth Century England' (*Essays in Labour History*, ed. A. Briggs and J. Saville, Papermac edn., 1967), pp. 49–50, suggests that there were two strands of radical language, the one of class and the other of 'industrious producers' (a functional category), that these represented different divisions in industrial society, and that the two analyses cut across each other. But on the working-class side by 1832, these were not separate views of society but one and the same; the industrious classes, the producers, the working classes—these were interchangeable words. The manufacturing class had been excluded from all these concepts. The only boundary dispute was how to label 'mental labour'.

ing up the great thieves that make the laws. All these, and ten thousand other descriptions of vermin, would vanish before the light of a real social reform.[1]

The division between the two classes, William Rider thought, was clearly marked by the Reform Act, with 'the monarchy, aristocracy, millocracy and shopocracy against the insulted, all-sustaining democracy'.[2] The one set preyed on the other, and the result, in O'Brien's words, was 'the cannibalism of artificial society'. O'Brien's study of the sub-class, shopocracy, joined the new rhetoric on to the old. Shopocrats were 'the greatest foes of the working man' because on the one hand they were the sycophants of the aristocracy, and on the other they tyrannized and exploited the poor. Their worst crime was to confine the vote to their own class and thus to maintain a system which exploited millions. 'The shopocrat makes the government— the government makes the system—the system makes the robbery, and the shopocrat pockets the booty!'[3]

O'Brien often classed shopocrat with capitalist, and together they became middlemen.

All that is mean, and grovelling, and selfish, and sordid, and rapacious, and hard, and cold, and cruel, and usurious, belongs to this huxtering race. . . . To screw all they can out of poverty and weakness, and to seduce all they can out of powerful vice, is the grand business of their lives.[4]

His technique was to work outwards from the experience shared by all working men of the ambivalent, mercenary, and competitive shopkeeper, to an analogy with the large-scale industrial capitalist, an unknown bogey to most of his readers. Both bought cheap and sold dear. The shoemakers of Saffron Hill were given a common enemy with the Norwich silkweavers and the Manchester cotton spinners. The Whitechapel shopkeeper refusing credit was the tailors' sweater, and the carpenters' garret master was the stockingers' bagman and the 'millocrat'. A number of oppressors had become an oppressive system.

---

[1] *Destructive*, 24 Aug. 1833. It was still the same roll-call in the 1850s, e.g. *FP*, 26 July 1851, *Notes to the People*, Sept. 1851.
[2] *PMG*, 20 Apr. 1833; see also *Agitator and Political Anatomist*, 1 Nov. 1833.
[3] *PMG*, 11 Jan. 1834.   [4] *PMG*, 17 Aug. 1833.

Some readers protested that not all shopkeepers ground the faces of the poor. Davenport asked, 'Who is there among the working classes that would not be a shopkeeper, or a middleman, if he had an opportunity?' Others suggested that Hetherington and O'Brien were themselves middlemen; and Helot, though he agreed that any buyer and seller had opposite interests, remarked that this was as true for the working classes buying from each other as it was for the working classes buying from or selling to the middle classes.[1]

O'Brien also needed to explain to certain readers why it was that he attacked shopkeepers and not the old enemy, aristocracy. The reasons were the same reasons he had given for attacking profits and property, rather than taxation, as the main rot in society. Not only were kings, priests, lords, and taxes *not* 'the root of the evil', but they were 'nursery tales' blinding working men to the nature of the exploitation they suffered each day.[2]

(c) THE LABOURER AND HIS WAGE

Though middle- and working-class economists disagreed in their description of the gap between the value of what the labourer produced and the return he got for it, both groups agreed that in the present system his return depended on two related things: the rate of wages and the level of employment.

Middle-class economists distinguished 'a *market* or *actual* rate of wages' from the '*natural* or *neccessary* rate of wages, or the wages required to enable the labourer to subsist and continue his race'.[3] Wages could not for long stay either above or below this subsistence level; if wages rose the birth-rate would follow, and in time wages would again be forced down; if wages fell so would the working population and wages would then rise to compete for existing labour. But working-class economists, and some middle-class economists like Nassau Senior, pointed out that the fertility of land, which on a subsistence theory determined

---

[1] *PMG*, 24 Aug. 1833; *Helot's Defence* . . ., 1834.
[2] *PMG*, 16 July 1831, 5 July 1834.
[3] McCulloch, op. cit., pp. 315–16.

the size of the population, was not necessarily declining. Wigg told the Co-operative Conference of April 1832 that there were 15 million acres of uncultivated land in England, and O'Brien quoted figures in the *Guardian* to show that England could support five times its present population.[1]

The Malthusian subsistence theory by the 1830s was being jettisoned for shorter-run accounts of the market rate of wages. Market wages were determined by the amount of capital there was available to employ labour. In McCulloch's words:

When, on the one hand, capital is increased without an equivalent increase of population, the portions of it that go to individuals, or their wages, are necessarily augmented; and when, on the other hand, population happens to increase more rapidly than capital . . . their wages or share are proportionately reduced.

Wages could rise *only* if the ratio of capital to labour improved. Labour, on this account, was subject to the same laws of supply and demand as any other 'commodity for sale'. And its price was determined not by the employed but by 'the competition of the unemployed who, rather than starve, will accept any wages on which they can barely subsist'.[2]

O'Brien did not disagree, partly because he could use the doctrines of political economy to persuade trade unions to work for the vote. Strikes, he told the unions, were effective only when labour was in demand. And even then, 'what security is there against the workman demanding more than the master can afford to give without losing his capital, and thereby destroying the very fund out of which the workman is employed?'[3]

Middle-class remedies fell into two categories: those which met the long-term problem of a surplus population, and those which met the more immediate unemployment caused by trade fluctuations and the introduction of machinery. The remedy most favoured was Malthus's prudent marriage and delayed gratification therein. This would hold off any failure of food as well as improving the

---

[1] *PMG*, 23 Apr. 1832, 30 Mar. 1833; see also the series of letters from 'Vindex' in the *PMG*, Nov. 1833–Feb. 1834.

[2] McCulloch, op. cit., pp. 316–17; see also McCulloch, op. cit., p. 320; Wade, op. cit., pp. 236, 220.

[3] *PMG*, 7 Dec. 1833; cf. *Man*, 15 Dec. 1833.

ratio of capital to labour. Some middle-class economists, among them Place, the Mills, and Wade, doubted whether the 'prudential virtues' were enough; but Malthus feared that birth control would remove 'a necessary stimulus to industry', and McCulloch agreed, adding that schemes 'for directly repressing population [are] . . . atrocious and disgusting'.[1] Working-class radicals similarly were divided by neo-Malthusianism. The *Trades Newspaper* shared Place's scepticism about prudence. 'Is it reasonable to expect that the labouring man alone should propagate on general principles, and consult the population tables every time he goes to bed?' None the less, birth control was 'detestably wicked' and not in the interests of the people. Cobbett of course denounced it as 'the horrible means of living and indulging, without the *inconvenience* . . . of being mothers'. Lovett had some sympathy with Malthusian fears, O'Brien none at all: 'in spite of the devil and Malthus, the work people are resolved to live and breed.' He never forgave Hetherington, Watson, and Cleave for circulating Dale Owen's *Moral Physiology*, Carlile's *Every Woman's Book*, and Knowlton's *Fruits of Philosophy*.[2] As a result, perhaps, of the conflict between editor and proprietor of the *Guardian*, neither Malthus nor birth control was discussed in its columns, although one letter from P. H. G. alluded to the 'propriety of limiting our numbers'. Neither O'Brien nor Hetherington commented on it.[3]

Watson told the National Union of the Working Classes of another middle-class scheme for reducing population.

Labour was reduced to the standing of a marketable commodity, and there were three remedies for the evil: either the labourers must cooperate and all have one price for their labour, or they must reduce their numbers by becoming malthusians, or they must increase their

---

[1] T. Malthus, *Essay on Population*, 1890 edn., p. 572; McCulloch, op. cit., p. 181.

[2] *Trades Newspaper*, 17, 24, 31 July, 28 Aug. 1825; *Pol. Reg.*, 15 Apr. 1826; *London Mercury*, 9, 30 Apr., 14, 28 May 1837. See also *NS*, 31 Mar. 1838: 'The question of over-population cannot be solved by any given number of inhabitants. Man has been displaced from his natural position in society, by the introduction of machinery; and if today ten millions should be considered a thin population, tomorrow, by the invention of some new piece of machinery, one million might be looked upon as a superabundant population.'

[3] *PMG*, 9 Mar. 1833.

numbers until they were compelled to export themselves to Canada or some other place.[1]

Scrope recommended the Government to sponsor emigration. Fullerton hoped young 'productive' couples would go, and McCulloch thought it was the answer to the problems of handloom weavers. Tufnell quoted approvingly the example of the Glasgow weavers who had kept up their wages by paying for one-eighth of their number to emigrate. Other voices pointed out that emigration took money which, better invested, would provide jobs.[2] Carpenter and 'Vindex' preferred home colonization on waste land, but Wade objected to farming uneconomic marginal and sub-standard land.[3] Hetherington had been a member of Wilmot Horton's class at the Mechanics Institute in 1830, but by the spring of 1831 he disapproved of emigration as strongly as did Cobbett or O'Brien: 'Let those who approved of exportation, go out of the country themselves', and he recommended bishops, nobles, and soldiers as candidates.[4]

Prudent marriages and emigration, it was hoped, would reduce the population. Charles Knight had a host of remedies for the more immediate problem of the business cycle. Like Davenport and the Revd. Bryce, Knight advised working men to become capitalists, and if they could not do that, he would have them temporarily retire to live off their savings while the 'relations between wages and labour' corrected themselves. Fullerton in the *Quarterly* stormed at this SDUK 'remedy' which would exhaust a man's savings for his old age even if they carried him through the bad times.[5] The *Westminster* suggested retraining men in depressed trades to make them more mobile, Wade and McCulloch preferred to retrain the children. Wade recom-

---

[1] *PMG*, 24 Dec. 1831.

[2] P. Scrope, 'The political Economists', *Quarterly Review*, Jan. 1831; J. Fullerton, 'The Condition of the Labouring Classes', *Quarterly Review*, Jan. 1832; McCulloch, op. cit., p. 153; Wade, op. cit., p. 271; Tufnell, op. cit., p. 96.

[3] *Political Chronicle*, 13 Jan. 1831; *Pioneer*, 8 Mar. 1834; *Letter to Wilmot Horton*, n.d. (end of Dec. 1830); *Magazine of Useful Knowledge*, 15 Oct. 1830; *PMG*, 1 Dec. 1832; Wade, op. cit., p. 255.

[4] *Rep.*, 16 Apr. 1831; see also *Political Chronicle*, 13 Jan. 1831; *Pol. Reg.*, 2 Nov. 1816; *PMG*, 29 Aug. 1835.

[5] *S.C. on Education*, 1835, vii, qus. 1023–4; *PMG*, 24 Aug. 1833; *Capital and Labour*, p. 197; Fullerton, op. cit.

mended working men to negotiate a long-term contract with their masters to cover 'the ordinary commercial cycle', and to patronize friendly societies.[1] The final safety net, Scrope, Wade, Place, and McCulloch agreed, was generous poor relief. The poor, as Wade put it, were 'an inseparable adjunct' of society, for destitution was constantly being generated by trade and seasonal cycles, disease, old age, vice, infirmity, and improvidence. Without poor laws (and relief to the ablebodied), society would be riddled by crime and mendicity; and without poor laws, the poor would have no reason to respect the social contract. Poor Laws, Scrope said, were just, charitable and expedient.[2]

O'Brien was contemptuous of Knight's schemes. Emigration out of the country was inefficient and unjust. Emigration into the upper classes was to become a parasite instead of a producer. Emigration out of the labour market was emigration into the workhouse. Savings banks were 'a hoax' to provide cheap money for the capitalist and to 'bind up the simple-hearted poor with the stability of Government'. And benefit societies pinched 'the bellies and backs of the contributors to the fund, in order to save the poor rates, that is, the pockets of the affluent classes, from the just claims of broken-down industry':[3] Some carpenters, at a meeting of the unemployed at the Rotunda in August 1831, had asked that they be allowed to construct 'some useful or ornamental public building',[4] but neither O'Brien nor the middle-class economists took up the idea of public works. O'Brien would probably have agreed that such schemes deflected capital away from productive industry. But there was never any doubt in working-class circles about the New Poor Law. Our

assailants have just perpetrated one of the most inhuman and widely devasting acts of robbery ever heard of in the world . . . 'The Poor Man's Destruction Bill.' . . . Here is an Act to rob (we might almost

---

[1] 'S.C. on the silk trade', *Westminster Review*, Jan. 1833, p. 4; Wade, op. cit., p. 264; McCulloch, op. cit., p. 153. See also R. Torrens, *Wages and Combinations*, 1834, p. 44.

[2] Wade, op. cit., pp. 352–88; Scrope, op. cit., p. 256. Wade and McCulloch both preferred the old Elizabethan to the New Poor Law.

[3] *Midland Rep.*, 14 May 1831; *PMG*, 5 May 1832, 19 Oct. 1833; *Oddfellow* 27 July 1839; *NS*, 28 July 1838.　　　　　　　　[4] *PMG*, 13 Aug. 1831.

say to murder) some three or four millions of the most desolate of mankind. The right of these poor people to parish relief is of more than two centuries' standing. It was given them in exchange for their share of the church property, of which the Reformation had despoiled them. It was their 'vested interest', in the most enlarged sense of those words, for it was not only guaranteed by the law of the land, but also by those of justice, humanity, and sound religion. Yet of this most sacred of all sacred properties have the poor been despoiled by the capitalists. . . . [It is] purely and solely the work of the middle or profit-hunting classes. . . .

The result, O'Brien prophesied with a sure sense of the intimidating, would be incendiarism, for why should the poor any longer care about property? The Act was 'frightful, inhuman, unprecedented, detestable and damnable. The country cannot bear it; the cup of sorrow is full.' If the country could not find work for the able-bodied, O'Brien and Carpenter argued, it should support them. And if workhouse conditions were *always* worse than life outside, workers were placed totally in the power of capitalists, whatever his terms.[1]

The business cycle was one reason for unemployment; machinery was another. Middle-class economists pointed out that machinery at least brought 'healing in its wings'. In Manchester and Glasgow, Malthus remarked, machinery had brought more work; and McCulloch demonstrated that cheaper goods would increase demand and with it profits, which would either be consumed and provide employment or be reinvested to provide more jobs. In Knight's words, the results of machinery were 'cheap production and increased employment'.[2]

The *Advocate*, published by the printers' protection society, was one of the few London working-class papers to challenge this. While jobs were scarce, machinery was 'a monster that devours the bread of thousands', an 'insatiable Moloch', callous to the 'emaciated form, the hollow cheek, the sunken eye'. Together with the Manchester *Union Pilot* and the *British Labourer's Protector*, it demanded that machinery be controlled, taxed, or suppressed.[3] Most of the

---

[1] *PMG*, 18 Oct., see also 8, 22 Nov. 1834; *Pol. Letters*, 6 Aug. 1831.

[2] McCulloch, op. cit., pp. 148–55; *Results of Machinery*, pp. 167, 182, 192.

[3] *Advocate*, 16 Feb. 1833; *Union Pilot*, 17 Mar. 1832; *British Labourer's Protector*, 21 Sept. 1832.

London Unstamped were sure that machinery was here to stay. No one in his right sense, said O'Brien, would willingly drudge like a carthorse, or replace the plough by the spade, merely to create enough toil for everyone. Hetherington would do all work, 'especially the hard work', by machinery if he could. The *Guardian*, the *Man*, and Carpenter agreed, that machinery was potentially an enormous power for good. But two pre-conditions were essential: working men would benefit from machinery only if their livelihood was guaranteed; and society as a whole would benefit from machinery only if consumption kept pace with production.[1]

On the first point, some writers would control the introduction of machinery by taxing it—a weapon from the armoury of Old Corruption. Others showed more concern for the victims. J. H. (presumably Julian Hibbert) would use the revenue from taxing machinery to aid those who were displaced by it. O'Brien reiterated that it was society's responsibility to take care of those thrown out of work, to give them relief, and find them other employment. 'They have a perfect right to expect it from society, seeing that society profited by their loss.' The *Herald of the Rights of Industry*, speaking for the National Regeneration Society, pressed for an eight-hour day as this would provide employment for all and allow the men to keep up their wages.[2] Charles Knight counter-attacked at the hint of restrictive practices. Working men, he wrote in his pamphlet *The Results of Machinery*, were both consumers and producers: as consumers they would benefit from cheaper goods, and as producers they would increase the demand for goods, which in time would bring further jobs. Lovett retaliated; this Society for the Diffusion of Useful Knowledge pamphlet, he told the National Union of the Working Classes, stated 'that machinery had reduced the price of goods and increased employment. (oh! oh!) It had cheapened provision, but it could not lower rent, taxes and rates, nor raise the wages of

[1] *Midland Rep.*, 14 May 1831; *PMG*, 13 Apr. 1833; *Man*, 25 Aug. 1833; *Pol. Letters*, 4 Feb. 1831.

[2] *PMG*, 5 Sept. 1835; *Magazine of Useful Knowledge*, 15 Oct. 1830; *PMG*, 29 Aug. 1835; *Herald of the Rights of Industry*, 8, 29 Mar. 1834; *PMG*, 11 Jan. 1834.

workmen; the fact that every fifth man in the kingdom was a pauper, gave a direct lie to the assertion. (hear).'[1] The *Herald of the Rights of Industry* made much the same point— if prices went up, this would hurt the drones far more than the producers. O'Brien provided the final answer to Knight:

> The capitalists, we know, will say that machinery cures the evil it creates; he will tell us that by making goods cheaper, it extends consumption, and that increased consumption causes increased employment. So it does we reply, but it is increased employment for *the machine*, not for the *workman*.[2]

This was only half the problem. Not only did machinery *not* guarantee 'increased employment' in the long run: it could not guarantee mass consumption either. Charles Knight's 'cheapened production' would bring the gluts predicted by Malthus. For years the co-operative press had argued that society must be crazy if a plethora of goods created economic distress. Warden showed why it did. The political economists in praising machinery, he told the British Association for the Promotion of Co-operative Knowledge, forgot that machines were not consumers. Only if labour were paid more, could working men afford to consume the glut of goods.[3] Carpenter developed this with some sophistication. Every time a labourer was displaced, his purchasing power was lost to the community; and as he had to be supported by others, their purchasing power was also curtailed. Goods were produced in response to demand, not need; and if nine-tenths of the population were destitute, the remaining one-tenth would have no markets for their goods. Trade would spiral down into a depression, and the capitalists themselves would become involved 'in the ruin which their folly and cupidity have produced'. Machines meant overproduction on the one side, and under-consumption on the other. A correspondent to the *Guardian* went so far as to suggest that it was in the capitalist's own interest to reduce his machinery and his profits, and to pass them on to the

---

[1] *PMG*, 24 Dec. 1831.

[2] *Herald of the Rights of Industry*, 8 Feb. 1834; *PMG*, 5 Sept. 1835.

[3] *Co-operator*, Sept. 1829; *Lancashire Co-operator*, 11 June 1831; also *PMG*, 30 Mar. 1833; *Magazine of Useful Knowledge*, 30 Oct. 1830.

working classes, for their increased spending power would in the long run increase the capitalist's total profits.[1]

Here then was a well-developed under-consumption theory. Writ large in the working-class press, it is hardly hinted at in middle-class writings. Knight's *Companion to the Newspaper* stated as a 'very simple and incontrovertible truth' that

No operations of the unions can increase consumption. In other words, they cannot give more employment to the body of workmen than they had before. On the contrary, if they raise the nominal rates of wages, they will infallibly diminish consumption. They will reduce the quantity of employment. . . .

O'Brien thought this was a fine piece of nonsense.

This absurd paragraph is based on the supposition that some men are born only to *slave*, and the rest only to *consume*, and that the existence of the *many* ought to depend on the appetites, or consuming powers of the *few*. . . . Any operation that will give the workmen increased wages, will give them increased means of consuming. . . .

He and Lovett agreed that if the problem was merely too many goods, then Cobbett had told them what to do with the suplus: give it to the poor.[2]

This working-class case was put to the Select Committee on the hand-loom weavers' petition in 1834 by many of the witnesses, including Richard Oastler and John Makin, a Bolton manufacturer.[3] They favoured a legal minimum wage, even if prices rose as a result. Oastler refused to be intimidated by the loss of foreign markets that committee members prophesied would result, on the ground that demand would be sustained at home. John Makin was asked,

---

[1] *Pol. Letters*, 4 Feb. 1831; *PMG*, 30 Aug. 1834; See also 'One of the Oppressed' in *PMG*, 14 Apr. 1832; *NS*, 10 Feb. 1838. Compare O'Connor's remarks to a London meeting: 'There is one character you working men seem proud of giving yourselves—that of being producers of wealth. At all your meetings you re-iterate this. Now, I seek to make you consumers of wealth. Production is one thing, but consumption is another. I am satisfied that machinery should be the producer so long as you can become the consumer. Machinery requires no consumption, save a few tons of linseed oil, or a few hogsheads of grease. But you require beef, bread, solid nutriment . . . ' (*NS*, 9 Oct. 1841).

[2] *Companion to the Newspaper*, Dec. 1833; *PMG*, 28 Dec. 1833; *PMG*, 25 Dec. 1831.

[3] *S.C. on Handloom Weavers Petition*, 1834, x, qus. 3783–4 (evidence of R. Oastler), qus. 4909–10 (evidence of Makin); see also qus. 628–31 (David Brook), qus. 7219–20 (William Longsom).

4909. Do you think that if they [the weavers] had that power given
them over the comforts of life, it would improve the home
market, by enabling them to consume more of the articles
which they themselves produce?—Decidedly so.

4910. Supposing the circumstances of the weaver to be much improved, would not his expenditure, in provisions, in fuel, in
clothing, in hardware, and in utensils of all sorts, contribute
very materially to revive the home market of every description?
—It would.

William Hale, a silk manufacturer, and for a long time
treasurer of the Spitalfields poor rate, pointed out that it
cost as much in charity and in poor-law relief as was saved
in low wages; and others, that the social cost of low wages
in drunkenness, ignorance, and irreligion, was incalculable.
Yet only Place appears to have offered a direct comment
on working-class under-consumption theories outside the
Select Committee. Increased wages, he said, would go on
coarse food and coarser clothing, and manufacturers and
traders in all other goods would still suffer from the general
rise in labour costs and prices.[1]

Working-class claims that higher wages were in society's
interest, had been formulated to fight the wage-fund and
scarcity-of-capital doctrines held by Knight, Brougham,
and Place, with all that they implied for men, machines,
and unions. At this point, a second tenet of middle-class
political economy was advanced: increased wages would price
English goods out of the continental market, at a time when
50 per cent of the cotton industry's goods, for example,
were exported. Increased wages, therefore, would decrease
employment in two ways—by shrinking the wage fund
and by reducing foreign, if not domestic, demand.

Some of the middle-class humanitarians replied that it
were better that 'the Continent of Europe were to be sunk
beneath the ocean than that we should be destroyed by
undue competition'. Weavers and framework knitters in
the years around 1819 had pointed out that to acquire
foreign customers by cutting wages was to gain one customer
abroad at the cost of two at home; and that manufacturers

---

[1] Loc. cit., qus. 4110, 4157 (Hale); qu. 5351 (Makin); Add. MSS. 27789, f. 215.

undersold their continental competitors only to face foreign tariff walls. Indeed, such was the scramble of English manufacturers for foreign trade, that they were undercutting not the foreigner but each other in foreign ports. Foreign competition was merely home competition abroad, not competition with foreign merchants. Keeping wages low in the name of foreign trade was either to increase capitalist profits, or to subsidize the foreign customer or to swell the tariff revenues of foreign governments, and all from the pockets of working men. 'Foreign competition means nothing more or less than home plunder', wrote the *Northern Star*. The Select Committee of 1834 took up the point with William Longson, a former weaver.

> 7098. You say that by these competitions the labouring classes have had taken from their backs and bellies very large sums; who has got them?—You have scattered them upon the Continent to the foreigners. You have undersold each other in the foreign market and in the home, and nobody has got it but the foreigners.[1]

Working-class under-consumption theories received a certain amount of sideline support from three less-orthodox schools of thought within middle-class political economy. The first of these, Thomas Attwood, had, since 1816, diagnosed under-consumption as 'the disease' and had argued for a paper currency; the resulting inflation would transfer purchasing power to the consumer. None the less, in the words of a modern commentator, 'the landlord was the strategic point at which to prime the pump of under-consumption', not the working-classes.[2] R. M. Martin, author of a text on taxation, pointed out to the Select Committee of 1834, that nearly half the working-man's wage was taken away in indirect taxation; and that to replace this with a property tax was not only more equitable but would release working-class purchasing power.[3] Torrens, political economist and M.P. for Bolton in 1833–4, thought that

---

[1] J. and B. Hammond, *The Town Labourer*, 1919 edn., pp. 298, 303; *NS*, 5 May 1838; *S.C.*, op. cit., qu. 7098 (Longson); see also qus. 3783 (Oastler), 4022 (Martin), 5758 (Halliwell).

[2] See S. Checkland, 'The Birmingham Economists 1815–1850' in *Economic History Review*, 1949, p. 9.

[1] *S.C.*, op. cit., qus. 3884, 4027.

once the Corn Laws were repealed, Britain was techno-
logically so advanced that she could sustain higher wages
or shorter hours while keeping other costs low enough to
undersell foreign competitors. Yet by 1843 he was sure that
in a country dependent on foreign trade, 'no artificial
mounds can be created for damming up money-wages above
the level determined by foreign competition'.[1] Even W.
Greg's famous pamphlet of 1842, diagnosing under-
consumption rather than overproduction as the cause of
distress, was a tract for the repeal of the Corn Laws and
free trade. Cheaper food would release more money to
spend on manufactured goods, and this would create more
employment.[2]

Middle- and working-class economists agreed, then, that
wages were low because too many men were after too few
jobs,[3] that machinery was displacing even more men, and
that there was not enough demand to absorb further
output. Working-class writers had little patience with the
middle-class remedies of prudent marriage, emigration, and
the medicinal properties of machinery. They went further,
and argued that what was seen as a problem of overproduction by middle-class economists was really one of
under-consumption occasioned by a low-wage and high-
unemployment economy. Only high wages and full employment would balance production and consumption. They
pointed out three other things: the middle-class analysis
assumed that a fixed sum would become circulating capital
(or a 'wage fund'): but it said little about the ratio of wages
to profits, or of both to prices. Secondly, they pointed out
that the middle-class analysis argued from the fact that
masters and men were dependent on each other to the un-
justified conclusion that masters and men had the same
interests. Finally, they pointed out that middle-class econo-

---

[1] See L. Sorensen, 'Some Classical Economists, *laisesr-faire*, and the Factory
Acts', in *Journal of Economic History*, 1952, p. 253 (I owe this reference to the kind-
ness of Dr. John Foster, of Cambridge). However, compare *A Letter to the Right
Hon. Sir Robert Peel . . .*, 1843.

[2] W. R. Greg, *Not Over-production but Deficient Consumption, the Source of our
Sufferings*, 1842, pp. 11, 20, 27.

[3] There was little diagnosis of 'sweating' in the Unstamped, that is, where wages
were low but employment was high, as in the Spitalfields silk trade. (See the evidence
before the *S.C.* of 1834, qu. 1058 (McKenzie)).

mists gave their premisses the dignity of laws from which political economists argued that working men and trades unions could not tamper with these laws to adjust the ratio of wages to profits. Each of these will be examined in turn.

(d) WAGES, PROFITS, AND THE HARMONY OF INTERESTS

Ricardo had stated that wages and profits were inversely related. McCulloch showed that the capitalist had only a certain sum to spend on wages, and that he wanted to buy as much labour with it as possible.

At first sight, indeed, it does appear as if their interests were opposed to those of the labourers: but such is not the case. The interests of both are at bottom identical; and it has already been seen that all the wealth of the country, applicable to the payment of wages, is uniformly, in all ordinary cases, divided among the labourers. It is true that, when wages are increased, a less portion of the produce of industry remains to the capitalist, and that profits are in so far reduced or prevented from rising. . . .

But both he and Wade preferred high wages to high profits as 'indisposing the poor to agitation' and as adding to the general happiness. Scrope appreciated that if the relation of wages to profits was an inverse one, it was difficult to show any harmony of interests. So wages, he decided, did not stand in a ratio to profits; they were a fixed cost contracted by the capitalist before he began production. Profits were therefore 'in no degree taken out of the wages of his labourers'.[1] All middle-class economists agreed that wages could not increase without an increase in capital; and as capital came from reinvested profits, it was argued that the interests of employer and workman were, in the long run, the same. 'The interests of every member of society, properly understood, are one and the same. . . .'[2]

All that middle-class economists had shown, came back the reply, was that workman and master were as interdependent as landlord and manufacturer, not that their

[1] McCulloch, op. cit., pp. 351–2; Wade, op. cit., p. 299; Scrope, op. cit., pp. 107–9; see also *Capital and Labour*, p. 191.

[2] *Capital and Labour*, p. 9; see also loc. cit., p. 63; Wade, op. cit., p. 521.

interests were the same. 'One of the Oppressed' of Manchester wrote to the *Guardian*:

When I hear master manufacturers and tradesmen say—*We must get large profits to enable us to pay you high wages*, my blood curdles within me, and I wish at once that I were a dog, or anything else, rather than a man. *Those large profits are the sole cause why wages are low.* They are got by keeping wages down. . . .[1]

Political economists had shown that an absolute growth in wages depended on an increase in capital, but they had said nothing about its growth relative to capital. O'Brien moved on to the attack.

Don't believe those who tell you that the middle and working classes have one and the same interest. It is a damnable delusion. Hell is not more remote from heaven, nor fire more adverse to water than are the interests of the middle to those of the productive classes. It is the interest of the operative to work as short time and to get as much for it as possible. The middleman's interest consists, on the contrary, in getting the greatest possible quantity of work out of the operative, and giving him as little as possible for it. Here, then, we have their respective interests as directly opposed to each other as two fighting bulls.[2]

Whatever happened to profits and prices, the working classes would gain from higher wages. If, as some middle-class economists asserted, high wages cut profits, then this must mean that prices were staying the same. If, on the other hand, higher wages were paid for not by a cut in profits but by a rise in prices, even so the idle classes would suffer more than the working classes. The gap between what the working classes produced and what they received as wages was just that amount by which they would benefit from higher prices. The *Companion to the Newspaper* was wrong when it asserted that higher wages would make everything 'so much dearer. . . . The rise of wages would be merely nominal.' Knight had also argued that higher prices would reduce demand, but if higher prices came from higher wages, the working classes would have the money to keep up demand.[3] The question for working-class writers, then, in

[1] *PMG*, 14 Apr. 1832 ('One of the Oppressed').
[2] *PMG*, 17 Aug. 1833; see also 15 Sept. 1832.
[3] *Companion to the Newspaper*, Dec. 1833; *Capital and Labour*, p. 191; *PMG*, 28 Dec. 1833. See also the evidence of A. B. to Tufnell, one of the factory commissioners, in 1833 (*P. P. England 1833*, xx, f. 757).

late 1833 and 1834, was a tactical one, whether trade-union agitation would be the most efficient way of raising wages.

Middle-class economists allowed that men could unite peacefully to resist wage cuts and to press for fringe benefits, but no union in its collective capacity must interfere with disputes, wage-rates, or work methods. Any more aggressive role was ruled out on four counts—it would be ineffectual, violent and conspiratorial, monopolistic and socially divisive, and finally it would be against the best interests of the working classes.[1] Strikes very rarely succeeded. If they did manage to raise wages above the market rate, either prices would rise and extinguish demand, or other workmen would flock into the trade and bring wages back to market level. Aggressive unions, Tufnell and Ure continued, were societies 'whose constitution is the worst of democracies—whose power is based on outrage—whose practise is tyranny—and whose end is self-destruction'. Even Wade feared that unions brought social ills, fomenting

divisions and animosities in society, arraying different classes against each other, though mostly united by common interests. Suppose this divisional spirit encouraged, the whole community might become resolved into hostile confederacies, the work-men against their masters, and the masters against the public. The result would be general anarchy.[2]

Finally, strikes defeated their own ends, for they encouraged the masters to introduce machinery or to take their trade elsewhere, as the lace masters had done, moving from Nottingham to the west country. Capital was a sensitive and timid creature, easily frightened away by turbulent, ungrateful workmen. 'The very name of union', Ure wrote, 'makes capital restive.'[3]

O'Brien, like Jones in the *Notes to the People* in the early 1850s, and like Hartwell in the *Beehive* in the 1860s, was neatly caught. The struggle of the unions was part of the uneven contest between labour and capital, productive

---

[1] Wade, op. cit., p. 280; for Place, see *S.C. on Education*, 1835, vii, qus. 824–6. Doherty claimed to agree with them, *S.C. on Combinations*, 1837–8, viii, qus. 328–31.

[2] Tufnell, op. cit., p. 125; Wade, op. cit., p. 291.

[3] Wade, op. cit., p. 281; Scrope, op. cit., p. 109; *Capital and Labour*, p. 193; A. Ure, *The Philosophy of Manufactures*, 1835, p. 41; see also P. Gaskell, *The Manufacturing Population of England*, 1833, pp. 293, 296–301, 308.

and unproductive classes; and phrases about the liberty of
master and man were so much cant when the choice for
the workman was work or starve. Lockouts, victimization,
the 'document' and the Dorchester case became fuel for
O'Brien's angry editorials. But like the middle-class economists, and for many of their reasons, O'Brien thought that
trades unions could do little and strikes nothing at all to
alter the industrial system. Unions should work for the vote.
With a deft reference to Old Corruption, O'Brien asked
how could the manufacturer possibly give the labourer 'a
fair equivalent for his labour', while he had to pay the landlords their rent, parsons their tithes, fundholders their
dividends, and placemen their pay? The *real* quarrel O'Brien
had with the masters, as he had with shopocrats and all
middlemen, was that they denied the working class the vote
and therefore the power to rectify the system. A week later
O'Brien again gave unions the same qualified support.

> We hail these coalitions as among the most glorious signs of the
> times; and to the working people of all trades and callings we accord-
> ingly say—haste!—lose no time!—marshal yourselves into Trades'
> Unions . . . and *resolve to work in future only eight hours per day, and to
> have a full day's wages (at least) for these eight hours.*

However, working men should know by now 'the utter
futility of depending upon mere *strikes for wages* as an
effective remedy for their grievances', for the masters, allied
with the propertied classes in Parliament, were invulnerable.[1]

The *Pioneer*, members of the National Labour Exchange,
and correspondents to the *Guardian* criticized this ambivalent and pessimistic attitude. A 'Unionist' was 'somewhat
surprised' that O'Brien should encourage trades unions to
become political unions when political unions contained so
many men who were against the labourer retaining the
products of his industry. 'We are certain of being able to
accomplish our object', he wrote, 'and that without the
confusion which has heretofore been the case with strikes . . .
by giving employment to the unemployed, and full employment to those who are partially employed.' O'Brien agreed
that co-operative methods were much better than strikes,
but he doubted whether they would be any more successful.[2]

[1] *PMG*, 9 Nov., 7 Dec., 14 Dec., 21 Dec. 1833.   [2] *PMG*, 28 Dec. 1833.

Both Hetherington and O'Brien supported two strands in co-operation, self-employment and wholesale trading, as they would place men beyond the grind of competition. Lloyd Jones was to emphasize that co-operative stores were the route to self-employment; and according to Holyoake, Hetherington was the first trade unionist to appreciate 'that the co-operative workshop was the bulwark of the strike'.[1] But neither Hetherington nor O'Brien had patience with the third strand of co-operation, the 'Elysiums' of community building. No aristocracy of money or land would allow its power to be demolished by letting working men acquire land and capital. This sort of economic self-help was futile if it was not protected by political power.

Middle-class economists had two other complaints against Owenism. The first was that it would mean the end of the division of labour; it was regressive since society at present, in Scrope's words, constituted one great labour exchange. The other, with which O'Brien rather agreed, was that joint stock associations required managerial skills beyond the capacity of the working classes. The numerous failures of co-operative associations seemed to suggest that they could not compete with professional concerns.[2]

If, as O'Brien seemed to indicate, neither trade unions nor communities offered working men a way to by-pass the overproduction—low wages—unemployment syndrome, what of the future? Pare and Carpenter had predicted a general slump. 'Equality', writing in the *Guardian* in the late summer of 1834, had even more dire forecasts. Working men, he argued, could never acquire land and capital while they were on starvation wages; and capitalists would never reduce their profit margins except under physical pressure. 'When the labourer knows his wrongs, the funeral knell of the capitalist has been sounded.' So he favoured strikes to increase the enmity of labourer and capitalist, as this would bring on the struggle. 'Concord' made the same prediction in the *Pioneer*.

---

[1] *PMG*, 30 Mar. 1833; see also *PMG*, 4 Feb., 1 Sept. 1832, 1 Mar. 1834; L. Jones, *The Life, Times and Labours of Robert Owen*, 1895 edn., p. 252; G. Holyoake, *60 Years . . .* , vol. ii, p. 265. O'Brien had worked with Pare in Birmingham to form co-operative societies (e.g. *Midland Rep.*, 17 Sept. 1831); and Hetherington had been a founding member of several London trading schemes in 1830.

[2] Scrope, op. cit., p. 198; Wade, op. cit., p. 486; McCulloch, op. cit., p. 367.

It behoves all classes who respect their own safety, to respect the comfort and happiness of the working mass. The capitalist is continually accumulating and the working man continually going down; and this will continue to operate, until the injured labourer, galled by intolerable oppression, shall rise with a determination, which nothing can quell, and effect a dreadful revolution. . . . I warn every accumulating capitalist that safety does not consist in individual abundance, but in a proper distribution of comfort amongst all. . . . I see that continued oppression will result in violence, and no power can stop it.[1]

McCulloch and Wade agreed. It was quite 'visionary' to imagine that there could be public tranquillity when wages were very low and most of the people very poor. No country could be 'so ripe for revolution as that where the mass of the people may hope to gain something, while they feel they can lose nothing, by subverting the existing institutions'. In their own interest, capitalists should prefer high wages to high profits.[2]

(e) ECONOMICS AND POLITICS

O'Brien, Hetherington, and Carpenter thus accepted much of the middle-class diagnosis of working-class ills. The moment that either trade unionists or philosophic Owenites had argued from this that they should bypass the political economists' society altogether, O'Brien had employed the middle-class weapons of wage fund and market rate of wages, to contain the economic critique within a political critique. The only remedy for economic ills was a political one.

Ironically, it was here that O'Brien and the middle-class economists most differed. The political economists insisted that masters and men should be free from government taxes, duties, and interference; and that the realm of government was the narrow one of protecting persons and property, and it could not and should not interfere in an economic process that was self-sufficient. Were institutions ten times more democratic, Wade wrote, the poor would have been just as distressed. When millions were out of work, government

[1] *PMG*, 30 Aug., 20 Sept. 1834; *Pioneer*, 12 Oct. 1833.
[2] McCulloch, op. cit., p. 350; Wade, op. cit., p. 247.

could neither find them jobs, nor pay them relief, nor alter the current rate of wages. As a writer in the *Edinburgh Review* expressed it:

The chief laws of political economy, however darkly they may lead to their result, are as unchangeable as those of nature; and it would be as possible to make the quicksilver in the thermometer expand beyond the temperature of its atmosphere as to fix wages at any other rate than that at which they would fix themselves, if undisturbed either by Unions or Acts of Parliament.[1]

Even McCulloch, who, like Roebuck, favoured a state system of national education, certain health measures, and some supervision of communications, nevertheless emphasized that the realms of economics and politics were distinct, and that political economists should not step from one to the other. 'The politician examines the principles on which government is founded. . . . The political economist does not take so high a flight. It is not of the constitution of government, but of its ACTS only, that he is called upon to judge.'[2] Political economists as economists should withdraw from politics.

O'Brien's position here, as usual, was summed up by the *Guardian* before he became its editor: 'There is no power, except that of Government, that can extensively affect the social state of man.'[3] Politics and economics were inseparable because both were concerned with power and both were concerned with property. Ever since the aristocracy had usurped the land, they had, on the one hand, made land or property the only qualification for law-making, and, on the other, had used their control over the means of production to monopolize all the goods created by working men. Property was rooted in economic power, and sanctioned and perpetuated by political power. They were two dimensions of the one social fact, the chasm between the haves and have-nots.

So O'Brien's analysis was in two steps: he showed how political power determined economic power for the 'upper

---

[1] Wade, op. cit., pp. 217–19; Anon., 'Trades Unions and Strikes', *Edinburgh Review*, July 1834; see also *Capital and Labour*, p. 206.

[2] J. R. McCulloch, *A Discourse on the Rise, Progress, Peculiar Objects and Importance of Political Economy*, Edinburgh, 1824, pp. 78–9.

[3] *PMG*, 26 May 1832.

classes', and how in consequence this double oppression made the working people the 'lower classes'. Working men demanded the vote, and they demanded a proper return for their labour. These were interlocking grievances, for without the first they could do very little about the second. The propertied aristocracy had the law behind them, and with the law they legitimized their control of land and capital. Without the vote, the working classes were without the legal means to remedy this. Consequently, the working class as such was oppressed because it was denied the vote; because it was denied the vote, its members were exploited each and every working day. Any working man was a member of the working classes because he daily experienced economic exploitation. What oppression was, and why it existed, therefore, were two distinct questions for O'Brien. 'One of the Oppressed' of Manchester put it neatly: '. . . the *remote* cause of your poverty is your not having seats, *personally*, in that which ought to be your house'. As a result, unlike land-stealers, merchants, manufacturers, and tradesmen, they did not make the law. 'The *immediate* cause of your poverty is the exorbitant rents, tithes, interest on money, profits on labour, and profits on trade', which the law imposed.[1]

The critique was always a double one, both political and economic. So 'class' as a concept had more to do with the modern 'status', the degradation that came from being denied both the vote and the produce of one's labour, than with either of these concepts separately.

Politics is the noble art of dividing society into two classes—*Slaves* and *Robbers*; the former including the *poor* and *ignorant*, the latter all the *rich* and *crafty*. . . . [The rich] comprises all who possess '*property*', without yielding in return for it any useful service; [the poor] comprises all who, though usefully employed in the production and distribution of wealth, are without 'property'. . . . [This robbery] has been done by politics and can only be prevented by having done with politics. Politics is the great robber. . . . By politics, then, we mean all the operations of Government, in which the people have no share. Under the existing system, all Government operations are of this kind. They are done without the people's consent—they are done in

[1] *PMG*, 14 Apr. 1832.

despite of the people—they are done to the extreme injury of the people. . . .

Repeatedly, Hetherington and O'Brien shaded one form of power in to the other. About one-seventh of the population possessed votes, O'Brien calculated, and the other six-sevenths were 'outcasts from the law'. The former 'or privileged fraction, comprise all the "property" people, the latter all the *work* people. . . '.[1] The vote and property opposed no vote and no property, for the capitalist, having 'all the law in his own hands' could make and unmake the property institutions which distributed wealth and perpetuated power. Wealth was created by labour, property was created by law. The rich were powerful because they made the laws. Because they made the laws, they were rich. It was a closed magic circle of power and property, circumscribed by law.

> By the law they can make wrong right, and right wrong—they can make bad money good money and *vice versa*, they can make blasphemy religion and religion blasphemy. They can even draught off one section of the people to slaughter the other. . . . The law, then, being our chief enemy, we should spare no efforts to obtain a mastery over it . . . [for] without a power over the *law*, we see no means of controlling the land and currency.[2]

So O'Brien demanded that the producers should be 'restored to the right of citizenship' and placed on an equal political footing with their employers and oppressors, 'so as to exert with them a coordinate authority in making or unmaking whatever laws and institutions they please'.[3]

Because there was both a political and an economic divide between the working classes and the rest of society, the enemies of the working classes were those who both denied them the vote and who appropriated their labour. O'Brien condemned 'those of all classes who are opposed to political equality, and those of no classes who are the friends of equal laws and equal rights for all the people'. Any merchant or manufacturer who supported universal suffrage was no

---

[1] *PMG*, 22 Mar. 1834; see also 26 July 1834, 23 Nov. 1833.
[2] *PMG*, 1 Mar. 34; see also *PMG*, 2, 23 Feb. 1833; *Destructive*, 24 Aug. 1833; *Pioneer*, 29 Mar. 1834; *Bronterre's National Reformer*, 7 Jan. 1837.
[3] *PMG*, 23 Nov. 1833.

enemy of the working man. A man was their enemy not because he was rich but because he opposed their rights.

At the point where the franchise is withheld [Hetherington wrote in 1831] injustice begins; that when the demand for Universal Suffrage becomes general, and not till then, the whole country will be united:—then indeed the term *classes* will merge into some comprehensive appellation, and no bloodshed will ensue, for the claims of united millions will be irresistible![1]

The primary reason for acquiring the vote, then, was to safeguard one's share of the national wealth. Other reasons for demanding the vote were drawn from the rhetoric of 1819. Universal suffrage was a right the people had lost, which should be 'restored' to them. There should be no taxation without representation. Lovett and some of the vendors of the Unstamped told magistrates that as they were without the vote, they were not accountable to society, for, in Blackstone's words, 'laws to be binding on all must be assented to by all'. And finally, Hetherington and O'Brien drew on the Paine–Carlile argument from natural rights: 'We proclaim and declare that all men are *naturally* EQUAL— entitled to equal rights and liberties—and subject to equal obligations.' Working men had as much innate ability as any other social class to distinguish right and wrong, justice and injustice, and thus to chose suitable men for Parliament. What mattered was that Parliament should be the arena for the disputes of labour and capital.[2]

James Morrison, who edited the Birmingham *Pioneer*, disagreed. 'We feel that to regulate trade, or the several branches of labour by which we live, will most speedily regulate government.' Parliament should be by-passed. There were four steps in the argument. The first was that economic activity threw up its own politics, and that as the most essential activity of government was economic, so a viable and appropriate Parliament would be a house of trades which represented 'interests'. Secondly, the *Pioneer* insisted that political skills and political knowledge were not easily

---

[1] *PMG*, 12 Oct. 1833, 3 Dec. 1831; see also 30 Apr. 33, 1 Feb. 1834.
[2] *Destructive*, 24 Aug. 1833; *Twopenny Dispatch*, 13 Aug. 1836; *PMG*, 22 Oct., 24 Sept. 1831, 21 Mar. 1835.

acquired, as O'Brien seemed to think, that honesty was no substitute for them, and that the people in their present state of education would be as 'fickle as a feather in a whirlwind . . . foreverlastingly enacting and repealing, making an external circuit of opposite extremes'. Political skills were best acquired on an apprenticeship basis within the familiar environs of a trade union; universal suffrage should begin there, 'and not, like the democratic principles of the *Guardian* and his friends, with the universal business of political legislation'.[1] Thirdly, the unions were becoming so important to national life that, once organized, they would 'gradually draw into its vortex all the commercial interest of the country'; Parliament would be displaced. Fourthly, the *Pioneer* asked O'Brien how he thought he was going to obtain universal suffrage? The *Guardian* and others 'expect it to come down as a favour from legislators, to be granted to our humiliating and degrading intercession, or petition, or extorted by our thundering or blustering threats. We expect no such thing. . . .'. The method of the *Pioneer* was dignified and sure of success. 'Social liberty must precede political liberty . . . we shall never be admitted into the legislature until our weight in society is fully felt and acknowledged.'[2]

The business of government, O'Brien replied, quoting Paine, was the simplest of things; government was only complicated at the moment because bad laws had created a number of conflicting interests, which had then to be reconciled. O'Brien next attacked the *Pioneer*'s version of universal suffrage because it was limited to members of trades unions. But the greatest weakness of the *Pioneer*'s scheme (like that of Owen) was that it attacked property, and the lawmakers would never tolerate this.[3]

Universal suffrage, O'Brien and Hetherington hoped, would usher in the New Society, an industrial, highly mechanized society of high wages, full employment, and profit-sharing. There would be no idlers or parasites in this society, for manufacturers would be paid only for their services, the nation would purchase all stock from fund-holders

---

[1] *Pioneer*, 28 Dec. 1833; 7 June, 31 May 1834.
[2] *Pioneer*, 31 May, 14 June 1834.   [3] *PMG*, 4 Jan., 7 June 1834.

and all property from the Church, and land would be nationalized (though twenty years' rent would be paid as compensation to allow the present landowners to retire, and to train their children to useful pursuits). Capitalists would continue to receive a return for the use of their machinery and their capital; but the profits would be divided among all the workers.

None would be rich because in such a state there would be neither the means nor the motives for amassing; and none would be poor because the labour of each would be more than sufficient to supply his wants, and even surround him with luxuries.

O'Brien did not object to peope saving; but he would forbid the taking of interest of any loan, and the bequest of savings to children. 'Where no individual could accumulate more than his earnings, there neither would or could be any accumulations of a dangerous character to society,'[1]

Tied in to this was a specific set of wrongs that Universal Suffrage would right—a set of wrongs about which some middle-class radicals felt as strongly as did working-class radicals. These were the wrongs that were embodied in pledges and debated in National Union meetings all over the country. Wakley, standing for Finsbury in the general election of 1832, accepted a modified version of the six points, repeal of primogeniture and entail, and the end of corn-laws, tithes, monopolies, taxes on knowledge, flogging, press gang, negro slavery, assessed taxes, and salt, malt, and soap duties.[2] The *Cosmopolite*, the *Reformer* and the *Destructive*, printed a list of proposals to be submitted to a National Convention which included the pledges Wakley accepted, together with republicanism, disestablishment, and the end of the national debt, foreign troops in England, a standing army, capital punishment, game laws, and all war; Ireland should legislate for itself, there would be laws against nuisances and adulteration of food, and a sliding scale on machinery, according to the number of men out of work; Church, Crown, and charity lands would be taken

[1] *PMG*, 28, 21, Mar. 1835.
[2] *PMG*, 17 Nov. 1832, cf. Bristol pledges *PMG*, 27 Oct. 1832; Leeds, *PMG*, 11 Aug., Macclesfield, *PMG*, 18 Aug., Tower Hamlets, *PMG*, 29 Sept., City of London, *PMG*, 27 Oct., Sabden, *PMG*, 13 Oct., Oldham, *PMG*, 29 Dec. 1832; Kenilworth, *PMG*, 23 Mar. 1833; also *PMG*, 29 Nov. 1834.

over by the people: no individual should possess more than 1,280 square acres, and anti-reformers and absentees no more than 640 acres; every soldier who co-operated with the people should receive 16 square acres free for life.[1] The details of the New Society, then, were very clearly envisaged. The radicals of the Unstamped disagreed only about its broad outlines—whether it should be primarily agricultural or industrial, organized in communities or on a profit-sharing basis within existing businesses, and whether it should be democratic or paternalistic.

(f) THE WAY TO THE NEW SOCIETY

How, then, were working men to create this New Society and acquire the vote that O'Brien promised would inaugurate it?[2] Simple physical force was rarely suggested, for, said O'Brien, millions could be mown down by guns, and soldiers had not yet made common cause with the people. The occasional talk about bringing on the struggle and buying pikes was inspired not by hopes of a revolution but by the roughness of the New Police. Even Lorymer, the rashest of writers, paused when talking about the barricades to wonder whether they would be 'omnibuses' or 'omnibi'.[3] Instead, the first way was to work the system. Some working men already had the vote, and they should demand pledges from their candidates, especially those who had been members of the old unreformed Parliament. The Unstamped, Place, and the *True Sun* circulated lists of model candidates and model pledges, strong enough to drive away 'placemen, pensioners, lawyers, and monopolists'.[4] Working men in London were encouraged to work for the return of Wakley at Finsbury, and Murphy at Marylebone. If pressure could not be put directly on the candidates, pressure in the form of organized purchasing-power could be put on those who

---

[1] *Cosmopolite*, 7 Apr. 1832; *Reformer*, 15 June 1832; *Destructive*, 27 Apr. 1833; see also *Political Investigator*, 9 June 1832; *PMG*, 1 Feb. 1834.

[2] The Chartist manifesto issued from Birmingham in the middle of May 1839 faced just this problem, '*the most efficient means*' for acquiring the Charter. It recommended a run on banks and gold, a sacred month, arms, chartist candidates at the elections, and exclusive dealing. Printed in W. Lovett, op. cit., pp. 212 f.

[3] e.g. *PMG*, 29 Mar. 1834; *Rep.* 13 Apr. 1834.   [4] See above, p. 252.

elected the candidates. The Macclesfield Political Union agreed that

We, the Unrepresented, have agreed, individually and collectively, without any evasion or mental reservation, that we will not expend one-halfpenny with any Medical Man, Grocer, Publican, Butcher, Baker, Flour Dealer, Innkeeper, Draper, Barber, nor any other person or persons whatsoever; and we further promise that we will use all our endeavours and influence with our friends and acquaintances to follow our example, in not trading directly or indirectly, with any Elector . . . who is known to aid or assist any candidate who will not give the above Pledges.[1]

Some correspondents to the *Guardian* complained that exclusive dealing was 'niggardly, paltry, pernicious, and arbitrary', but the Dudley Political Union pledged that it would use exclusive dealing to obtain its rights. Allen Davenport expressed his opinions in verse:

> The various changes that are past,
> Have all proved unavailing,
> We therefore have resolved at last,
> To try Exclusive Dealing.

> The little shops must fall in spite
> Of puffing and appealing,
> Unless their owners shall unite,
> And share Exclusive Dealing.

> And where the higher shopocrats
> Shall find their houses failing,
> They'll scamper off like other rats,
> And cry 'Exclusive Dealing'!

> Then we, like *Cousins*, may resist
> The governmental stealing,
> And those who make a stand assist
> By our Exclusive Dealing.

> Then kings, and priests, and lords must work,
> And show a kinder feeling;
> No more shall they our labour Burke—
> Our shield's Exclusive Dealing.   A.D.

---

[1] *PMG*, 18 Aug. 1832; O'Brien summarized his efforts in *PMG*, 5 Jan. 1833.

It was simple, moral, legal, and effective. It merged into co-operation. In Lowery's words, 'If properly supported and minded, it will change the face of society.'[1] It worked only in the absence of a ballot; for a ballot without universal suffrage would surrender all of government into the hands of the middle and upper classes, who would be freed from the wholesome constraints of public opinion.[2]

Working men could bring not only economic but also physical pressure to bear at elections. Processions, demonstrations, the show of hands at the poll,[3] were all outward and visible signs of working-class union, power, and self-discipline. They would win respect and recruits for the cause.

If the first form of economic pressure was turned on voters, the second form was applied to the Government itself and owed much to the methods of attacking Old Corruption. If working men abstained from such dutiable goods as alcohol, tea, coffee, and tobacco, they would impoverish the Government, enrich themselves, and improve their health. The *Black Dwarf* in 1819 had recommended herb tea, the *Medusa* a blend of coltsfoot, ivy, rose leaves, and lavender for tobacco. Mrs. Carlile had found Hunt's roasted corn breakfast powder highly profitable.[4] Similarly

---

[1] *PMG*, 14 Sept. 1833; Davenport in *PMG*, 28 Sept. 1833; *Oddfellow*, 3 Aug. 1839; R. Lowery, *'Address to the Fathers and Mothers, Sons and Daughters of the Working Classes* . . ., 1839, p. 7.

For its effectiveness, see Roebuck's use of exclusive dealing in Bath in 1837 (W. Napier, *The Life and Opinions of General Sir Charles Napier*, 1857, vol. i, p. 467); and its use by Ernest Jones and Miall at Halifax in the 1846 general election (B. Wilson, *The Struggles of an Old Chartist*, 1887, pp. 8–9). One local grocer made enough from his support of Jones and Miall to build a block of dwellings and retire. The Spitalfields weavers employed exclusive dealing so efficiently in the early 1830s that local publicans went with them in deputation to the brewers for subscriptions for their petition to Parliament (HO 64/12, 17 Feb. 1832). They collected £80 this way.

John Vincent's remark, that the non-electors had 'more influence without the vote than if they had it' does have some substance, though what mattered was the lack of the ballot not the lack of a vote. There was nothing to stop working men with the vote also employing exclusive dealing (J. Vincent, op. cit., pp. 100–6). Place, however, was scornful of all such efforts— 'pure imbecility' (Add. MSS. 27796, ff. 321–2).

[2] *PMG*, 17 Nov. 1832; see also Hancock in *Cosmopolite*, 19 Jan. 1833.

[3] Lowery triumphed over Macaulay at Edinburgh in 1841, though possibly because his supporters put up both hands (*Scotsman*, 3 July 1841).

[4] *Black Dwarf*, 17 Nov. 1819, 11 Jan. 1820; *Medusa*, 25 Sept., 9 Oct. 1819; *Pol. Reg.*, 29 Dec. 1819; *Rep.*, 22 Feb. 1822.

Cleave sold his own concoction, theobroma, as well as coffee, at his coffee shop; and Lovett told young readers of the *Guardian* that temperance 'would weaken the power of your enemy. . . . The revenue on gin greatly assists in supporting the army, even the saving on one glass of gin will buy three soldiers' muskets.' Drink also allowed working-class radicals to put pressure on publicans not only for their votes, but also for suitable newspapers and periodicals.[1]

These were ways to avoid paying indirect taxes. Radicals could also refuse to pay direct taxes. This had been urged on radicals in 1819, employed as a middle-class threat in 1832, and the Birmingham Political Union adopted this as a method to show their support for Ireland and for Attwood's currency theories in 1833. Carlile organized some 3,000 Volunteers to resist taxes in 1833, and joined Hetherington, Lorymer, Cousins, and the parochial reformers, in resisting assessed taxes, church rates, and church tithes.[2] A third source of economic pressure on the Government was the working-class version of Place's 'Go for Gold'; Goode and Kelly recommended the men of the National Union to withdraw their savings as this would destroy the national debt, while Lovett and Cleave advised a run on the banks to thwart the Irish coercion Bill.[2]

The working classes, organized as consumers, could put pressure on voters and Government. The working classes could also be organized as an 'interest' among others, competing with shipowners, bankers, and the Carlton Club for the ear of Government. It was as an 'interest' that members of the working classes signed petitions and joined deputations to Melbourne, Althorp, and Spring Rice on the stamp duties, on the fate of prisoners in Cold Bath Fields during the cholera epidemic, and on the Dorchester labourers. Hetherington and O'Brien were even prepared to welcome household suffrage, if the working classes as an 'interest' were represented. Place, Gast, and Roebuck cast unions in this role, for they might, 'if properly directed,

---

[1] *PMG*, 23 Feb. 1833; see also *PMG*, 10 Nov., 3 Nov. 1832; *Pioneer*, 10 May 1834.
[2] *Gorgon*, 8, 29 Aug. 1818; *PMG*, 1 June 1833; for the Volunteers and assessed taxes, see below, pp. 000–0.
[3] *PMG*, 25 Feb., 19 May 1832, 23 Mar. 1833; *WMF*, 16 Mar. 1833.

be rendered especially useful in watching the interests of the working men, and protecting them from injury at the hands of the Government'.[1] The unions, Place claimed, inhibited the reintroduction of the Combination Laws in 1825 and had set up the *Trades Newspaper* as watchdog; and in 1838, organized in the London Trades Combination Committee, they scrutinized the evidence fed to the Select Committee on the Glasgow Spinners. The trades 'not being represented, it behoves them to take some means of influencing the legislature' and Roebuck and O'Brien tried, though with little success, to divert unions into political activity.

The third way of organizing working-class power was around the concept of producers. Economic pressure and lobbying weight were ways to attain political leverage. This third way for the most part by-passed Parliament, and was usually the result of an analysis which did not follow O'Brien in tying economic to political power. Its advocates, such as Morrison, believed with the middle-class economists that the realms of politics and economics were distinct; exploitation was seen as an economic matter which could be redressed only by economic means. Labour exchanges, trades unions, and the various strands of co-operation were all seen in their sponsors' more idealistic moments as ways to the New Society without first having acquired the vote.[2] Benbow's National Holiday, and the National Convention (described, significantly, by the Home Office, as the 'Trades Political Union') blurred the economic and political lines.[3] O'Brien welcomed most of these schemes, for they indicated working-class activity and working-class power, though he always qualified his approval by insisting

---

[1] *PMG*, 6 June 1835; *Pamphlets for the People*, No. 7, p. 3 (J. Roebuck, 'Trades Unions . . .'). For an extension of this view, in the context of 1867, see Lord Houghton, 'On the Admission of the Working Classes,' in *A Plea for Democracy*, ed. W. Guttsman, 1967, p. 54.

[2] *Pol. Letters*, 2 July 1831; a letter from 'R. R.' in *PMG*, 15 Mar. 1834.

[3] A National Convention was first suggested by Thomas Mayhew in the early *Penny Papers* (e.g. 2 Nov. 1830) as an alternative to the unreformed House of Commons; not for another year did Benbow, Osborne, and Berthold take it up as a weapon if the Lordss hould throw out the Reform Bill (Berthold's *Political Handkerchief*, 1 Oct. 1831); after Cold Bath Fields, and with the rise of unionism, Benbow tied the idea of a National Congress specifically to trades unions (*Agitator*, Nov. 1833).

that any gains would only be protected by the vote. But if
O'Brien saw the vote as the only sure remedy for working-
class oppression and exploitation, he had vision enough to
see all these forms of working-class activity as related signs
of a self-consciousness he was deliberately trying to create:

> Let us deal with no middleman who refuses to vote or petition for
> Universal Suffrage—let us deal with no villain who is opposed to
> Trades' Unions, or in any other way hostile to our rights and privileges.
> Let us resist every attempt of the shopocrats to cut down the workman's
> wages, and uphold every effort of the men to obtain equitable advances.
> Let us support one another in all struggles against the mercenary
> combinations of slave-drivers, and encourage exclusive dealing with
> the people's friends in all lines of business. But, above all, let us as far
> as possible promote mutual exchanges of labour for labour, on the
> cooperative principle, so as to intercept the profits of trade in addition
> to the wages of labour. . . . But, meanwhile, neglect no opportunity
> of seeking Universal Suffrage, which is the grand panacea for all
> our evils.[1]

[1] *PMG*, 2 Nov. 1833; see also *PMG*, 22 Sept. 1832.

VIII

IMPACT

THE readers of the Unstamped were working class. So the owners and authors of the Unstamped had the job of developing and tying together the various working-class movements. In practical terms, this meant that they carried messages, information, and advertisements, aired grievances, and publicized and won recruits for the working-class societies to which they were allied. The provincial Unstamped, found in towns like Manchester, Birmingham, Huddersfield, and Leeds, had a narrower and smaller readership than the London Unstamped; and they took on two other tasks, that of revealing the tyranny of local cotton masters and the rapacity of clergy with 'muck-raker' thoroughness, and that of defending and interpreting working-class rights to the masters.[1] The London Unstamped were necessarily more catholic. Though they covered local parish affairs and London politics, their main concern was to mobilize working-class opinion on a host of disparate issues, and to weld it as far as possible into a coherent working-class radical stance. The *Cosmopolite* and the *Working Man's Friend* did this unobtrusively; the *Man*, Carlile's and Hetherington's papers did so explicitly. Each of these points will be examined in turn.

The pauper press carried announcements, advertisements, and messages. The 'practical' services of the Unstamped had been performed in 1819 only by the *Black Dwarf* which had reported meetings, raised funds for men imprisoned for political offences, and acted as the 'medium of communication' for Hunt's Great Northern Union.[2] A reasonably typical number of the *Guardian* in the 1830s[3] advertised Carlile's almanacs, the *True Sun* and various unstamped; the meetings

---

[1] *Herald to Trades Advocate*, 16 Oct. 1830; *Voice of West Riding*, 15 Mar. 1834.

[2] *Black Dwarf*, 14 Nov. 1821.

[3] *PMG*, 1 Dec. 1832 (*Gauntlet* and the *Man* carried very few advertisements).

of the National Union of the Working Classes, the Female Society, and one at Manchester to aid the *True Sun*; two lectures by Gale Jones; the resolutions of a Southwark meeting to examine parliamentary candidates; a plea by Lorymer to be relieved of the *Republican* because he was in bad health; and a request from the Society of United Carpenters for work, to be paid either in cash or in labour notes. The *Cosmopolite*, though it thought little of Labour Exchanges, advertised the Gothic Exchange in Marylebone, and Carlile, who thought even less of Hetherington, reported the fate of the vendors of the *Guardian*; the *Guardian*, while critical of the misguided notions of trades unions, gave their meetings due publicity.

Secondly, the Unstamped relayed local grievances. The phrases, 'the only medium through which to make our grievances known' or 'I beg to make public through the medium of your valuable publication', echoed through the columns of the London and provincial Unstamped.[1] In return they were generously praised for 'defending working class rights'.[2] Hetherington printed letters to show the cruelty of magistrates and the brutality of poor-law overseers. Carlile, equally typically, inserted a letter from a cabinetmaker of St. Luke's, complaining that trades unions victimized non-members. Doherty toured Lancashire for cases of exploitation by cotton lords to publicize in the *Poor Man's Advocate*. P. L. D. told the *Herald to the Trades Advocate*

Your paper is intended to be a channel, through which may be conveyed, to the working classes, the knowledge of rights and privileges they ought to possess; and at the same time to assist them in repelling the inroads and encroachments which are daily made by designing and unprincipled masters. . . .

Most of the radical Unstamped would have claimed with the *Guardian*,

We, the *Poor Man's Guardian*, proclaim that we represent the working, productive and useful but poor classes. . . . We proclaim that

---

[1] e.g. *Hull Portfolio*, 14 Nov. 1831; *PMG*, 5 Nov. 1831 (from Huddersfield), 3 Dec. 1831 (from Middleton); *Weekly Herald*, 4 Sept. 1836 (Norfolk labourer).
[2] e.g. *Gauntlet*, 12 Jan. 1834 (Loughborough); *Pioneer*, 21 Dec. 1833 (Wolverhampton); *Voice of the West Riding*, 5 Mar. 1834; *Cosmopolite*, 14 Apr. 1832 (Manchester); *Destructive*, 23 Nov. 1833; *WMF*, 1 June 1833; *Man*, 21 July 1833.

some hundreds of thousands of the poor have elected us the *Guardian* of their rights and liberties. . . .[1]

How effective these pretensions were, of course, is another matter. They certainly boosted sales,[2] and for more than one reason Hetherington begged his readers and his agents to forward instances of 'tyranny' for him to print. But Hetherington had not the resources to provide any sort of systematic coverage. The incidents he inserted were all very random, often taken from the stamped press, and printed rather as case studies of working-class wrongs than with any hope that publicity might remedy them. Hetherington had to rely for his local material on his ties with the NUWC, and the resolutions they forwarded to him. Carlile could do no better, and had to ask his country readers to forward their local papers to him if they wanted some incident covered, as he could not obtain provincial papers in London.[3]

The Glasgow *Herald to the Trades Advocate*[4] argued that if working men were to regain their rights and retain the fruits of their labour, they needed to unite in three ways— around an independent newspaper, in a comprehensive trade association, and in a political reform association. So, thirdly, almost all the radical Unstamped, before they turned broadsheet, were the loud-hailer of either a trade or a reform association. The stamped *Weekly Free Press* had been the main outlet of the British Association for the Promotion of Co-operative Knowledge, and its 'defection' was much lamented;[5] to some extent, Carpenter's *Political Letters* and shorter-lived periodicals like the *Magazine of Useful Knowledge* continued to cover the BAPCK. The *United Trades Cooperative Journal* and later the *Voice of the People* were established by Doherty on behalf of the National Association for the Protection of Labour, and his *Herald to the Rights of Industry* for the National Regeneration Society.

---

[1] *Herald to the Trades Advocate*, 16 Oct. 1830; *PMG*, 24 Sept. 1831; see also HO 64/12, 24 May 1832; *Gauntlet*, 7 Mar. 1834; *Penny Papers*, 2 Nov. 1830; *Poor Man's Advocate*, 27 Oct. 1832; cf. *Red Rep.*, 31 Aug., 2 Nov. 1850.

[2] See above, p. 121.   [3] *Gauntlet*, 19 Oct. 1833.

[4] *Herald to the Trades Advocate*, 22 Jan. 1831. A similar analysis was made by E. Jones in the opening numbers of the *People's Paper*, 8 May 1852, quoted Saville, op. cit., p. 123.   [5] *Political Herald*, 21 Jan. 1831.

The *Church Examiner*, edited by Carpenter and Cleave, sponsored a Society for the Extinction of Clerical Abuses, the *Cosmopolite* in its early days represented the Vendors of the Unstamped, and together with the *Working Man's Friend* covered the Irish Anti-Union Association. Around the *Gauntlet*, even Carlile built up a list of 'Volunteers' to reduce taxes from £50 to £10 million a year and on whose behalf he called meetings and toured the country in the autumn of 1833. The *Pioneer* was 'a sort of corresponding society' pulling together the lodges of the Operative Builders, though, like the *Guardian*, it became more and more catholic in its sweep. As Somerville put it,

You are the accredited organ of the trades unions; your paper is read by thousands of people who are not Unionists—by people who approve of Unions, though not immediately connected with them; by people who are wretchedly ignorant of what the Unions are, and by people who know them well and are trembling for the consequences. . . .[1]

Together with the *Crisis*, and later the *Official Gazette* it spoke for the Grand National Consolidated Trades Union. Carlile's *Union*, and the *Political Unionist* were founded expressly

to create a medium of communication between the various Unions of the Kingdom, by reporting their most important proceedings . . . and secondly to increase the number of their members and friends, by giving extensive currency to their principles and operations.[2]

The *Cosmopolite* asked for 'pithy reports of all political meetings'.[3] The Unstamped collectively spawned a number of tract and discussion societies, such as the Westminster Society for the Diffusion of Really Useful Knowledge, whose main purpose was to buy and circulate the Unstamped. Lorymer, to take one case of many, used his papers to organize London Republicanism, as Carlile, its natural leader, distrusted organization. When Hetherington was imprisoned at the end of 1832 and the original *Republican* merged with the *Working Man's Friend*, Lorymer struck out on his own. He launched a Library of Republican Books,

---

[1] *Pioneer*, 12 Apr. 1834 see also *Herald to the Rights of Industry*, 8 Feb. 1834; *Church Examiner*, 1 Oct. 1832; *Gauntlet*, 14 Apr., 25 Aug. 1833; *Pioneer*, 7 Sept. 1833.

[2] *Political Unionist*, 30 June 1832.   [3] *Cosmopolite*, 30 June 1832.

a tract society, turned his office into the Western Republican Repository, and from it published the *Bonnet Rouge* in February 1833. In July 1833 he founded the Republican Association, which linked up with small local societies, and met frequently at Theobold's Road. He wrote occasionally for the *Working Man's Friend*, sent a couple of letters to the *True Sun*, for the first of which it was prosecuted, and lectured intermittently at the Rotunda. As few copies of the later volumes of the *Republican* (formerly the *Bonnet Rouge*) survive, it is hard to estimate the impact of all this acitivity.[1]

The most important working-class political association in London was the NUWC. The *Radical* and the *Reformer* regularly carried its reports, and the *Cosmopolite* gave it a half-column. The *Man* occasionally noticed a meeting, and the *Working Man's Friend* and the *Gauntlet* advertised them. The *Guardian* was 'the principal reporter of the Union', according to Lovett. 'It therefore obtained first place in the estimation of its members.' This was surely true. But Place's remark, that to understand the NUWC, middle-class reformers should read the editorials of the *Guardian*, since the *Guardian* 'fairly represented the opinions entertained by the members of the Union, and all other Unions in correspondence with it', is far from true.[2] On the two leading issues of the day, the Reform Act[3] and the Repeal of the Irish Union, the editorial line of the *Guardian* and the main opinion within the NUWC as reported in the columns of the Unstamped, diverged quite sharply. The *Guardian* opposed both. The NUWC reluctantly supported the Reform Act and violently demanded the Repeal of the Union. However, the leading figures in the world of the Unstamped were the heroes of the NUWC. When Hetherington appeared at one meeting, in March 1832, after his unexpected release from prison, 'we were all in ecstacy. . . . We all shook Hands with

---

[1] *Rep.*, 6 Apr. 1833; *PMG*, 15 Dec. 1832; *Bonnet Rouge*, 9 Mar. 1833; *PMG*, 20 July 1833; *True Sun*, 2 May, 27 July 1833. Harney similarly used his papers to strengthen the Fraternal Democrats in the late 1840s and early 1850s, and Jones to found and publicize a number of manhood suffrage societies (*Red Rep.*, 17 Aug. 1850).

[2] Lovett, Add. MSS. 27791, f. 249; Place, loc. cit. 27796, f. 339.

[3] For the clash on the Reform Bill, see below, p. 282.

him and the greatest Ridicule took place among us on "Our Foolish Enemies" . . .'.[1] Hetherington chaired meetings and was cheered; marched off to prison amidst groans, and returned to cheers. But when he was in prison and Cleave was too busy to attend the National Union its debates went their own way.

Until the summer of 1832 both the NUWC and the *Guardian* drew heavily on current political events—the king's speech, the formation of the National Political Union, the Bristol riots—for their raw material. The *Guardian* also carried editorials on the futility of the Reform Bills while the NUWC ignored the subject. When the NUWC did debate more abstract concerns, such as working-class rights, property, capital and labour, then Cleave, Hibbert, or Watson were invariably either in the chair or the leading speakers. Left to itself the NUWC debated current wrongs in the language of Old Corruption.

From the summer of 1832 the concerns of the *Guardian* and the NUWC diverged more and more. The reasons for this lie in the history of the NUWC, and shifts in its balance of power.

Before the NUWC was formed in April 1831, the East End weavers were organized in an active and aggressive Spitalfields trade society. During the summer of 1831 its more radical members, led by Dean, Boreham, Buck, and Clemments (all by now prominent vendors of the Unstamped), formed the East End branch of the NU. It became one of the main blocs within the NUWC, providing at least a fifth of its membership, many of its leaders, and staunch support for the Unstamped.

But the Reform crisis of October 1831, the Bristol riots, and the abortive White Conduit Fields meeting which the NUWC had planned for the first week in November, provoked the Government into banning political unions on the model of the Birmingham Political Union. The NUWC was forced to reorganize itself. Branches, such as the East End and the Finsbury branch, with their own secretaries and distinct identities, were to be abolished. The NU was to become a General Union, meeting in local

[1] HO 64/12, 15 Mar. 1832.

classes under class-leaders; the central committee would decide on the resolutions for debate, and would handle all subscriptions. Members would now join the NU as separate individuals and not as a branch.[1]

By December 1831 the East End branch had grumblingly joined the General Union. In July 1832 this group, some 230 members strong, broke away from the NU and set up their own East End Political Union, drawing on the weavers and class-leaders of Spitalfields and Bethnal Green. They had resented their enforced merger and the NU had failed to back their efforts 'to get their "Own Act of Parliament" which was repealed about Six years ago repassed. . . '.[2]

Hetherington hesitated to give them separate publicity in the *Guardian* so Carlile promptly inserted their advertisements into the *Cosmopolite*, as the Political Union of the Working Classes of Tower Hamlets. The PU survived for some seven or eight months, but fell away during the winter. Dean, Yearly, and Goulburn, but not Buck and Boreham, drifted back into the main body of the NU.[3]

Within a fortnight of this split Hetherington was negotiating with the Irish Anti-Union Association, Lawless, Duffey, Leach, and Berthold, to join the NUWC and make up its depleted strength. The price was that the NU should regularly discuss Ireland and Repeal.[4] As a result, the NU debates were dominated for the next few months by the Irish question, and even before the Irish Coercion Bill hit public opinion and persuaded many Irish to join the

---

[1] HO 64/11, 29 Nov., 1, 2 Dec. 1831; see also *PMG*, 29 Oct. 1831, 28 Jan. 1832.

[2] HO 64/12, 17 Feb. 1832 ('Their own act' was of course the silk duties); see also HO 64/12, 27 July, 13 Aug. 1832.

[3] *Cosmopolite*, 18 Aug. 1832; HO 64/12, 20 Sept., 25 Oct., 7 Dec. 1832; *PMG*, 1 Dec. 1832. This would suggest that the Spitalfield weavers were very far from being the politically quietist group that D. Rowe claims they became after the repeal of the silk duties in 1824–5 (D. Rowe, 'Chartism and the Spitalfields Silk-Weavers', in *Ec.H.R.*, Dec. 1967). As well as trade and political societies, they were embroiled in a wealth of radical activity, such as extracting pledges, marching in procession in Oct. 1831, and selling the Unstamped. The silk-weavers may have been apathetic to Chartism, though whether they were relatively any more apathetic than any other group in London in these years is unclear. Even if they were, Mr. Rowe has still to account for the change between 1832 and 1839. Ragged clothes will not explain it.

[4] HO 64/12, 6, 11, 20 Sept., 2, 25 Oct. 1832; *WMF*, 29 Dec. 1832.

political unions, it was the Irish who were saving the NU from the speedy decline suffered by the NPU.

Meanwhile the *Guardian* acquired an Irish editor, O'Brien, who, though prominent in the Anti-Union Association in the spring, had become less sympathetic to repeal and more suspicious of O'Connell.[1] While the NU spent more and more time debating Ireland, the *Guardian* said less and less on the subject. Instead, O'Brien developed his critique of property relations and attacked first Owenites and then trades unions for failing to appreciate the tie of economic to political power. He studiously underplayed the increasing extravagance of the Irish speakers in the NU and their plans for a National Convention in May of 1833, though he and Carlile joined with the NUWC in deploring the police assault at Cold Bath Fields and in organizing Fursey's defence on the charge of murder.

In December 1832, however, Watson and Cleave had brought out the *Working Man's Friend*, in which, it was hoped, O'Connell, Shiel, and Lawless would write 'on the question of REPEAL'. Lawless brought out the significance of the paper in its opening number; 'This is the first time that question, so *vitally* important to both countries, England as well as Ireland, was ever made the leading topic in this metropolis of wide and general discussion. . . .' The *Working Man's Friend*, far more than the *Guardian*, spoke for the Irish-dominated NUWC. Along with the *Gauntlet* it reprinted the Irish Coercion Bill, covered parliamentary debates on it, and reported protest meetings from all over the country, from Birmingham to Edinburgh.[2] Its end in August 1833 marked the suspension of the NUWC weekly meetings, which had been thinned by the Cold Bath Fields affair and the revelations of Popay. When the NU revived meetings at the end of October, they were already beginning to lose their members to the trades unions.

Only a skeleton NU organization survived to join the Radical Association in December 1835. It was kept alive partly by the Dorchester case, but more by concern for

---

[1] See *Cosmopolite*, 24, 31 Mar., 7, 14, 21, 28 Apr. 1832, for O'Brien's appearances at the A.U.A.

[2] *PMG*, 15 Dec. 1832; *WMF*, 22 Dec. 1832, 23 Feb., 9, 16 Mar. 1833.

later victims of the Unstamped, among them James Reeve and Thomas Heins, and by the old NU pledge to repeal the taxes on knowledge. Its few classes were run by old vendors of the Unstamped, Thomas Heins at Chatham, Hassell and Huggett in Westminster, Thomas Sherman and Allen Davenport in Bishopsgate, and Harney and Simpson in Southwark.[1] The Radical Association, founded in September 1835 by O'Connor and the Marylebone radicals, devoted much of its attention to the taxes on knowledge, and got up several of the more important meetings in the spring of 1836; but the *Guardian* ignored it.

What, then, did the NUWC do for the Unstamped? The NU must have consumed many of its sales. Lorymer estimated that only fifty members of the NUWC were vendors, but great numbers of the Unstamped, according to Popay, were sold at NUWC meetings at the Rotunda, the Institution, and the Borough Chapel. A report of a branch meeting in the Infant School, Bermondsey, concluded that 'The Great Unstamped was bountifully circulated.' Popay was sure that Hetherington would have to be conciliatory to the breakaway East End group because on them depended his sales in the East End. If they grew stronger in the winter and spread to Finsbury, they would 'materially injure both the NUWC and Hetherington in his Publications'.[2] Every Quarterly Report of the NU dwelt on the 'noble work' of the Unstamped and the backing it had had from the NU. In October 1834, for example, 'Your Committee have to congratulate this Union on a continuance of the spread of the unstamped which was *first* fostered and supported against every opposition by yourselves and has already produced the noble result of the existence of a *Working Man's Press*, a thing unknown in former times.'[3] The NU regularly debated the taxes on knowledge, provided some of the more steadfast of the vendors, and, most important of all, sustained the Victim Fund.

What did the Unstamped do for the NUWC? In London

---

[1] *PMG*, 28 Mar., 18 Apr., 30 May, 6, 13 June, 1 Aug. 1835.

[2] *Radical*, 24 Sept. 1831; HO 64/11, 2 Sept., 22 Nov. 1831; HO 64/12, 12 Nov. 1832; HO 64/16, 21 Nov. 1831; *WMF*, 30 Mar. 33; HO 64/13, 13 Aug. 1832.

[3] e.g. *PMG*, 6 Oct. 1832, 20 Apr., 6 July, 19 Oct. 1833, 18 Jan., 18 Oct. 1834 (not in July 1834).

they brought the NU its members and also its publicity, with which the NU could entice leading radicals such as O'Connell and Hunt, to attend its meetings. The *Guardian* reported the meetings at Theobold's Road, the *Working Man's Friend* some of its many branch meetings. The *Gauntlet* and the later *Cosmopolite*, on the other hand, disparaged unions and the committees who lived off them, to the indignation of the rest of the Unstamped.[1] Carlile took morbid pleasure in announcing the death of any union, London or provincial.[2]

Less obviously, the Unstamped kept the NUWC transparent. Carlile again and again repeated that political and trade societies were dangerous because of their instinct for secrecy. So Lovett and Hetherington stamped on the idea of a Secret Convention, and kept committee meetings as well as the weekly meetings open to the public. Fairly full reports of NU meetings in the *Guardian* deflated the value of spy reports, as Melbourne admitted, with the result that no NUWC meeting was ever prosecuted for sedition. This transparency cut down the hunt for spies, and helped to check the sense of persecution and slight paranoia from which even Watson and Cleave suffered.[3] Probably the Unstamped toned down the violence of the NUWC. The *Guardian*, for one, refused to countenance either the extravagance of October 1831, when Benbow and Osborne tried to bluff the Government into widening the franchise, or that of the spring of 1833, when the Irish talked wildly of redress. Similarly Hetherington, according to spy reports, told a meeting on the Dorchester labourers, that he 'would resist injustice to the death. . . . He said that if the men of the Union were like him the oppressors should not exist another hour. . . . He was for physical force and settling the matter.' According to the *Guardian*, however, 'He

---

[1] *WMF*, 15 June, 13, 27 July 1833; *Gauntlet*, 9, 23 June, 4 Aug. 1833; *Man*, 8 Sept. 1833; *Cosmopolite*, 18 May 1833.

[2] e.g. of Nottingham PU, *Gauntlet*, 18 Aug. 1833; of Sheffield PU, *Gauntlet*, 2 June 1833.

[3] *Gauntlet*, 31 Mar. 1833; Watson in *Man*, 13 Oct. 1833; HO 64/11, 4, 7 July 1831; HO 64/12, 7 June, 26 July, 20 Dec. 1832; *WMF*, 23 Mar. 33; e.g. 'The Unions, themselves, think it strange that Hetherington should be allowed to carry on his proceedings with impunity' (HO 61/5, 23 Nov. 1831).

spoke in terms of indignation of the atrocity of the sentence.
. . . This transaction only confirmed him in the opinion he
had so often expressed, that no good would result by
peaceful means, without the working man having the power
to chose his lawmakers.'[1] The first sounds like Hetherington; the second was what was circulated.

The authors of the Unstamped also helped to sell the
NU the idea of political involvement, that working men
were as fit as middle-class men to take part in politics. The
mass procession and the mass meeting, they reiterated,
were not enough; NU members should also, as individuals,
employ the weapons of temperance, refusing taxes, and
exclusive dealing, not only at elections, but also to defeat
the Irish Coercion Bill and cut the Government's budgets.[2]
The Radical Association took up Roebuck's scheme, outlined in his *Pamphlets for the People*, for canvassing con-
stituencies on a ward model.[3]

The most important service the Unstamped could offer
the NUWC, however, was as 'a medium of communication'
between its eighty-six London classes and some fifty provincial unions. For their part, Cleave and Hetherington
were sharply aware of the advantages of linking the journalistic to the political crusade. The London NU, Lowery
recalled some thirty years later, sent out its delegates to
form local branches, which then established shops for the
sale of the Unstamped and joined with the shopman in
increasing their sale. Bradford, for example, sent its resolutions to the *Gauntlet*, a paper which they would 'endeavour
to promote'; and Carlile had to lecture the provincial
unions on their 'crave' to see their resolutions reported in
every Unstamped.[4] Hetherington toured Lancashire in the
late summer of 1831 as the NU delegate; in April 1832
he was on ' "Tour" through the North to employ fresh
agents for his Guardian and try to Unite all Unions with Us'.
Six months later, Hetherington and Cleave were in the
midlands, encouraging the breakaway Midland Union of
the Working Classes, establishing a union at Northampton,

---

[1] HO 64/15, 8 Apr. 1834; *PMG*, 12 Apr. 1834.   [2] See above, pp. 253–8.
[3] *Roebuck's Pamphlets*, no. 7 (On Trades Unions); James Tucker's letter to
PMG, 5 Dec. 1835.   [4] *Weekly Record*, 5 July 1856; *Gauntlet*, 2 June, 7 July 1833.

lecturing, selling the Unstamped, and recruiting further agents. In October Hetherington was at Brighton, for his health, his papers and the union. Finally, at the end of 1832 Hetherington again avoided arrest by 'a journey of business' through the northern towns.[1] Carlile, in September and October 1833, toured the south and south-west, and, like the *Guardian*, diligently reprinted provincial resolutions, as well as lists of volunteers and of subscribers to his private funds.

The intention was clear enough. Place granted that the *Guardian* spread political unions to the north and south-west, because its careful publicity of the NU

induced large numbers of the working people in the country to attribute an importance to the union it did not possess. They were misled by the advertisements in the *Guardian* of meetings to be held in some part of London, on several days in each week, these announcements made people at a distance conclude that the whole body of the workmen were confederated together, and this was a powerful inducement to them to form unions in various places. . . .

Place, indeed, thought that the reports in the *Guardian* of branch and provincial meetings of the NUWC underestimated their total number, as the *Guardian*, 'got up in a hasty careless inexpensive manner', would only print the reports and resolutions of meetings if they were 'sent up to the publisher in a form fit for publication, and no care whatever was taken to procure any information respecting them.'[2] Many meetings were therefore never reported at all.

Two provincial unions, at Blackburn and Northampton, perhaps exemplify the impact of the Unstamped and the coverage provincial unions received from it. In September 1831 the Blackburn Radical Reform Union sent an address to Hetherington backing his struggle for a free press; at the end of 1832 they recorded an address to Hunt; in April 1833 they sent Hetherington £5 and Carlile 12s. 6d. Finally, in July 1833, they protested against the Reform

---

[1] HO 64/11, 26 July 1831; 64/12, 17 Apr., 19 Oct., 30 Oct., 1 Nov. 1832; *PMG*, 17 Nov. 1832; HO 64/12, 11 Oct. 1832; *Brighton Herald*, 13 Oct. 1832; HO 64/12, 27 Dec. 1832.

[2] Add. MSS. 27791, ff. 333, 402.

Act and the Whigs, and praised Hetherington and Hunt.[1]
The Northampton PU was formed by Cleave and Hetherington on their midland tour in November 1832. In December
the Political Union sent an open letter to the *Guardian*
urging their fellow townsmen to vote for the liberal candidates. In March 1833 they protested against the Irish
Coercion Bill and in June against the outrage of Cold
Bath Fields, on which they combined 'in sentiment and
action with our brethren of the NUWC in London'.
They praised the 'truly valuable, because Unstamped'
papers, and sent money for Fursey's defence.[2] As two-
thirds of the unions were first referred to in print after the
passing of the Reform Act, their resolutions like those of
Blackburn and Northampton, centred on five topics—the
inadequacy of the Reform Act and the Whigs; pledges;
Ireland; the freedom of the press; and Cold Bath Fields.
The Reform Act and Ireland were authentic local concerns,
as possibly were pledges; but the fate of the *True Sun*,
the Victim Fund, or Cold Bath Fields were London matters
for which provincial sympathy and subscriptions were won
by the Unstamped.

Pledges were a marginal case. The Reform Act was given
the Royal Assent on 7 June 1832. Two days later the
NUWC and the *Man* took up the subject of pledges,
anticipating the middle-class radicals, W. J. Fox, Place,
Detrosier, and J. S. Mill by the best part of a month. The
Guardian suggested suitable pledges in the third week in
July which were considered by the NUWC. And for the
next six months the Unstamped carried pledges in almost
uniform language that were debated, asked for, and extracted, at meetings of electors and non-electors from
Bristol to Norwich and Oldham. The police attack at Cold
Bath Fields was strictly a London matter, but the *Guardian*
and the *Working Man's Friend* received resolutions con-
demning it from Frome in Somerset to Bolton. The *Destructive* and the *Working Man's Friend* carried subscription
lists for Fursey's defence and the £60 collected included

---

[1] *PMG*, 3 Sept. 1831, 29 Dec. 1832, 11 May, 15 June 1833; *Gauntlet*, 7 Apr.
1833.
[2] *PMG*, 17 Nov., 22 Dec. 1832, 8 June 1833; *WMF*, 9 Mar. 1833.

money from such towns as Manchester, Birmingham, Maidstone, and Leicester. Wakefield showed a nice sense of Hetherington's two concerns by concluding 'That, in order to give the foregoing Resolution due effect, Mr. Hetherington, the Champion of Union, be requested to give it publicity in the *Poor Man's Guardian* or *Destructive*.'[1]

The *Herald to the Trades Advocate* had spelt out three forms of working-class union—the independent newspaper, the political association, and the trade union. As the NUWC receded from the columns of the Unstamped in the summer of 1833, so increasing news space was devoted to the activity of the trades; to the expansion of the United Trades Association around the Labour Exchange in London, with its co-operative as well as trade-union roots; and to the growth of orthodox trade unionism outside London, as the emotions aroused by Owenism, the Operative Builders Union, factory reform, and the 'document' hardened the attitudes of both masters and men. And though many of the London Un-stamped questioned the political and economic views of the unions, as expressed by the *Pioneer* (the journal of the Opera-tive Builders Union); though the unions from late 1833 were mopping up the old NU membership; and though they had no regular weekly meetings to report, yet the Unstamped gave the unions almost as much coverage and column-space as they had given the NUWC.[2]

The *Gauntlet*'s and the *Destructive*'s efforts ended with reprinting the O.P.Q. letters from the *Morning Chronicle* on the trades unions in the autumn of 1833, and forwarding the occasional subscription. The *Man*, though it gave the unions little practical help in its columns, gave it a moral support which the *Guardian* denied, and criticized the *Guardian* for being more sympathetic to masters than to men. 'Agrarius' urged the London tailors to organize them-selves on the model of the operative builders, and pub-licized their meetings; and Lee printed two addresses to the men of Derby.[3]

---

[1] *PMG*, 8 June 1833 (Wakefield's resolution); see also *PMG*, 1, 15, 22 June 1833; *WMF*, 29 June, 6, 27 July 1833.
[2] For the debate with the *Pioneer*, see above, pp. 250–1; for the loss of NU membership, see 'Quarterly Report of the NU', *PMG*, 18 Jan. 1834; Lovett, op. cit., vol. i, p. 88.   [3] *Man*, 15 Sept., 20 Oct., 10 Nov., 1, 8, 22, 29 Dec. 1833.

The *Guardian* was the most critical of the Unstamped, for it insisted that the unions were digging their own graves if they refused to work for the vote. If the unions were not represented in Parliament, they could be wiped out by the masters whenever Parliament chose. None the less, the *Guardian* did more practical service for the unions than any other London Unstamped. It carried their advertisements, and announced their meetings. It publicized the new London unions of boot- and shoemakers, painters, Warden's saddlers and harness makers, bricklayers and masons, metalworkers, and the 'miscellaneous' lodge, as well as aiding the older societies of carpenters, Petrie's and Guthrie's tailors, O'Neill's cordwainers, and certain agricultural labourers.[1] It carried news of the cabinet-makers and joiners in Carlisle and Glasgow, of the 'tyrannical' glove-masters of Yeovil, the threatened strike of the miners of the Tyne and Wear, the efforts of the mayor of Exeter to suppress unions; and it reported the Nottingham silk-hose union, the smiths and shoemakers of Northampton, the strikes of the Reading stonemasons, Aberdeen operatives, and Gloucester weavers, the threatened strike of the Oldham power-loom weavers, and the failure of the Leeds trade union.[2] In London the *Guardian* covered the coopers' strike in some detail and warned journeymen coopers from the country not to undertake black-leg work.[3] It detailed the fortunes of the London bricklayers from their swift increase in November 1833, their meetings at Fishmongers' Hall in March 1834, to the masters' wage-cutting in May, the strike of July, and their public meetings on Islington Green and at the Mechanics Institute.[4] And gave the tailors similar coverage and publicity, from Guthrie's meetings in January 1834, to the strike in May, and their attempts to set up in business independent of their masters.[5]

Above all, the *Guardian* and its circle raised money, meetings, and sympathy for the Leicester unions in October and November 1833 who were refusing the 'document',

[1] *PMG*, 23, 30 Nov. 1833, 4, 11 Jan., 8 Mar., 25 Apr., 26 July 1834.

[2] *PMG*, 23, 30 Nov., 7, 14, 21, 28 Dec. 1833, 4, 11, 18 Jan., 8 Feb., 8, 15 Mar., 21 June 1834.   [3] *PMG*, 1, 15 Mar., 31 May 1834.

[4] *PMG*, 23 Nov., 8 Mar., 31 May, 26 July, 23, 30 Aug., 6, 13, 20 Sept. 1834.

[5] *PMG*, 4 Jan., 3, 10, 31 May 1834.

for the Derby silk-weavers' strike in November, and for the Dorchester men. A public meeting to raise funds for Derby was held at the Equitable Labour Exchange, with Thomas Heins as secretary and Cleave and Lee among the speakers. Hetherington even opened a subscription for Derby 'on my own responsibility' and forwarded £5. 10s. Artisans of Norwich, Winchester, Hertford, and Bristol sent their 'mite' to Derby via the *Guardian*. Hetherington reported provincial meetings on behalf of the strikers, and copied from the *Pioneer* the names of the blacklegs who were setting out from London to break the strike.[1] On the Dorchester case, London working men both joined with the middle-class radicals and worked on their own. Issue after issue deplored 'The Horrible Sentence', publicized the mass procession and raised £21. 10s. (independent of the Dorchester Central Committee Fund) which Hetherington personally distributed to the Dorchester families.[2]

Symptomatically, the *Destructive* changed its name to the *People's Conservative and the Trade Union Gazette*. Watson republished the 'Address to Trades Unions' by a Journeyman Bootmaker, and the columns of the *Guardian* were filled with letters criticizing and defending the unions.[3] The *Guardian* of 28 December 1833, for example, included an editorial on trade unionism, a defensive article on the *Guardian* and trade unionsim; a report of a meeting to aid Derby; a long letter from a unionist; and a one column extract from the *True Sun* on trades unions and the need for a wider franchise: all this in one issue. From November 1833 to February 1834 nine of the *Guardian*'s thirteen editorials were on trades unions, and, of the four that were not, two were devoted to Hetherington's prosecution. From the end of March nine of the next eleven editorials were again devoted to trade unionism, Leeds, Dorchester, and the *Pioneer*; in September the *Guardian*'s editorials were on the builders. It is hard to see what more the *Guardian* could have done.

---

[1] *PMG*, 4, 18, 25 Jan., 15 Feb. 1834.
[2] *PMG*, 29 Mar., 5, 12, 19 Apr. 1834, 4 Apr. 1835.
[3] *Destructive*, 14 Dec. 1883. The '*Address*' was originally published in 1827 and was to reappear in 1839.

The Unstamped, then, carried messages and advertisements, relayed local grievances, and were the loudhailers of political associations and trade unionism. They also had the more intellectual function of creating and co-ordinating a working-class public opinion both in and out of London. O'Brien, before he became editor of the *Guardian*, had written to Owen, that governments, republican or monarchical, stood or fell by public opinion. 'It is therefore of vital importance to gather up this Public Opinion—concentrate it on the Social System, and make it bear irresistibly on the Government, by the weight, unity of direction and simultaneous action of all its parts.'[1]

Some subjects on which the Unstamped elaborated were already well aired. Hatred of the press gang, the standing army, flogging, the national debt, and the New Police, were all part of the baggage of the 'free-born Englishman', working or middle class. What O'Brien, Hetherington, and Carlile where possible, tried to do was to make these issues a case study of the wrongs done to the working class. Flogging, for example, had been debated in the National Union and attacked in the *Guardian* before Somerville's case turned it into a national issue. The debate quickly widened. Somerville, probably coached by Carlile, told the NU that only the lash kept soldiers from demanding their political rights; O'Brien told his readers that a standing army existed simply to protect property.[2] The national debt, like taxation, in O'Brien's hands was not just a simple robbery of the poor by the rich, but part of the wider mechanism of exploitation. Corn Laws, State Church and tithes, monopolies like the East India Company and the Bank of England, hang-happy judges, and insolent magistrates, all were examined by the *Guardian* and the analysis deflected from a piecemeal attack on Old Corruption into a comprehensive attack on property.

On other subjects the *Guardian* tried less to deflect the analysis than to widen the basis of public opinion. Lovett, for example, refused to serve in the militia or to pay for a

---

[1] *Owen Collection*, 27 May 1832, f. 546.
[2] *PMG*, 16 July, 26 Nov. 1831, 7 July, 13 Oct. 1832, 30 Nov., 7 Dec. 1833, 26 July 1834.

substitute. Carpenter and Hetherington publicized his No Vote—No Musket scheme and 'a number of persons' followed Lovett's examples. When £30 of Lovett's goods were seized in lieu, Hetherington set up a fund in the *Guardian* and by August 1832 over £17 had been collected, most of it in pennies and half-pennies, from Birmingham, Manchester, and Winchester as well as London.[1]

Assessed taxes, tithes and church rates, to take another example, were primarily the grievance of the small shopkeepers, the Rogers, Potters, and Murphys who overlapped both the NU and the NPU; and they were, after all, direct, not indirect, taxes. None the less, the leaders of the Unstamped broadened the basis of resistance to include working-class men and working-class interests. Lee, Hetherington, Carlile, Lorymer, Cousins, Savage, and Baume (most of them property owners) refused to pay. All the Unstamped reported cases of resistance, such as Savage's or Cousins's in the autumn of 1833, and covered the parliamentary debates and public meetings in Marylebone, St. Pancras, Westminster, and Lambeth on the subject. The NUWC debated the value of aiding 'the middling classes' to resist the taxes, and Jackson, one of the few proponents of O'Brien's views in the NU, pointed out that this was a way to detach the middle classes from the aristocratic embrace. O'Brien, unusually austere, insisted that the taxes should be widely resisted because they were unjust—they were war taxes which should have long since disappeared, they were uneven in their incidence, and they hampered the registration for the vote. The *Man* reported every meeting on the subject, but this may have been because its circulation in Marylebone depended on it. Carlile's concern was simple and didactic; he reduced the attack on assessed taxes to an attack on taxation and Old Corruption. 'This is now the profitable working of the reform question', he wrote in the *Gauntlet*, in December 1833, 'because all tyranny turns on the pounds, shillings and pence for extravagant expenditure, so all the reform must be made on that head.' His move was to enroll Volunteers who pledged themselves to reduce taxes from £50 million to £10 million a year; almost every

[1] *Penny Papers*, 29 Jan. 1831; *Lovett*, vol. 1, p. 66; *PMG*, 25 Feb. 1832.

prominent vendor of the Unstamped enlisted himself, and he printed over 3,000 names in the *Gauntlet* as well as dozens of letters on the subject.[1]

All this activity spilt over into local politics, parochial reform, and a scrutiny of vestries and poor-law overseers. Hetherington and Cleave marshalled NU votes, meetings, and money for Wakley at Finsbury and Murphy in Marylebone at the cost of neglecting their papers. The proprietors of the Unstamped joined deputations to Melbourne on parish matters. And outside London James Acland used his unstamped papers to castigate the municipal corporations first of Bristol and then of Hull; and Unstamped in Huddersfield, Manchester, Glasgow, and Liverpool did likewise.[2]

The Assessed Taxes campaign incorporated working men into a primarily middle-class campaign. The moves to save the *True Sun* (like the funds to defend Fursey) incorporated provincial opinion into an obscure London matter. The *True Sun*, established in March 1832 by Grant and edited by John Bell and Carpenter, was never adequately financed and failed to win a stable circulation outside London; but after the demise of Wakley's *Ballot* in July 1832, and until Beaumont's *Radical* in March 1836, it was the only stamped paper to share the concerns of the Unstamped. So the Unstamped encouraged the political unions, and their coffee- and reading-rooms to take the *True Sun* to the exclusion of other stamped papers, and to coerce public houses into doing the same; and they worked for the success of the meeting of October 1832 where 3,000 people heard Wade, Carpenter, O'Brien, and Hetherington ask for £5,000 and regular orders to keep the paper afloat. Further meetings, and a subscription (whose secretary was Grady of the Anti-Union Association) followed; and Manchester, Birmingham, Stratford, Leicester, and Northampton pledged themselves to circulate the *True Sun*.[3]

---

[1] *Rep.*, 6 Apr. 1833; *Cosmopolite*, Sept., Oct. 1833; *PMG*, 2, 9 Nov. 1833; *Destructive*, 2 Nov. 1833; *Man*, 25 Aug., 1, 22, 29 Sept. 1833; *Gauntlet*, 12 May, 19 Oct., 1 Dec. 1833.

[2] HO 64/12, 5 Dec. 1832; *PMG*, 8 Dec. 1832; *PMG*, 24 Aug. 1833, 8 Mar. 1834.

[3] *PMG*, 2 Nov. 1832; broadsheet in HO 64/18; *PMG*, 10 Nov., 8 Dec. 1832; *Man*, 22 Sept. 1833; HO 64/12, 5 Dec. 1832.

Other topics were new, and here the task of the Unstamped was to familiarize their readers with self-evident wrongs. Infant Slavery and the Northern Short-Time Movement emerged in the columns of the Unstamped and the debates of the NU when Sadler introduced his Bill into the Commons. Cleave and Hetherington lectured the NU in March 1832 with evidence from Sadler's committee, but the tone was cool and the subject obviously foreign. Hetherington declared only that 'in this subject he took a deep interest'. Cleave, however, toured the northern factories before steering the NU on to a second round of debates when Ashley's Bill was defeated in the summer of 1833. By now the tone was indignant, the sufferings shared and the subject thoroughly familiar. Between these two rounds of debates, all the Unstamped had carried excerpts from Sadler's evidence, had critized the grant of £20 million to the West Indian slave-owners, had elaborately compared black and white slavery, and had shown that one set of slaves were being robbed to free others. Carlile, with his usual claim on history, asserted that he was the first to publicize the issue when he printed, in the *Lion* of 1828, the life of Blincoe, a deformed factory child; now he covered meetings and parliamentary debates. The *Guardian* carried nearly a dozen editorials on the subject, and the indictment gradually widened. The early editorials relied on Sadler's evidence, and argued like the *Working Man's Friend* that the lot of the negro was preferable to that of the white slave. The later editorials in the *Guardian* and *Destructive*, now written by O'Brien, wove 'infant slavery and adult degradation' into a violent attack on the manufacturing system in which parents were forced to mortgage the 'sweat, sinews and bones' of their children to the owners of land and capital.[1]

Thus Hetherington and O'Brien always tried to turn isolated issues into a coherent public opinion, not just by broadening the basis of their class or regional support but also by meshing them into a wider ideological analysis.

[1] *PMG*, 10, 31 Mar. 1832; *WMF*, 12 Jan., 2 Feb., 2 Mar., 29 June, 13, 27 July 1833; *Man*, 4 Aug. 1833; *Gauntlet*, 3 Mar., 14, 28 Apr., 1 Sept. 1833; *PMG*, 17 Mar., 5 May, 9 June, 17 Nov., 1 Dec. 1832, 26 Jan., 15 June, 10, 17 Aug. 1833; *Destructive*, 13 Apr., 8 June 1833; *Truth*, 24 Feb. 1833.

Two other topics, Ireland and foreign liberalism, extended working-class sympathies yet further. On Ireland, the *Guardian* even with its Irish editor, did less than most of the Unstamped and was outpaced by the *Cosmopolite* which regularly reported the meetings of the Anti-Union Association, by the more generous spread to Irish matters and Irish meetings (especially resistance to tithes) given by the *Gauntlet* and *Man*, and particularly by the *Working Man's Friend*, which concerned itself primarily with Irish affairs. Ireland accounted for nearly a fifth of the NU debates but only five of the *Guardian*'s 238 editorials. This did not stop O'Brien from giving Irish matters his own indelible mark. Carlile, for example, deplored the Irish Coercion Bill as so much evidence that Ireland was ruled in the interest of kingcraft and priestcraft, and complained of the 'feudal nonsense of foreign rule'. Equally typically, O'Brien and Hetherington objected to Irish Repeal. Church Establishment was to be deplored, especially when tithes had to be collected by force. But the Irish poor were priest-ridden, lawyer-stricken, backward, rack-rented, and famished. For them 'Repeal would be of little use *just now*.' Far worse than the exploitation of the Irish by the English was that of the poor by the Irish middle and upper classes; and the remedy for that was universal suffrage, not repeal.[1] The *Guardian* may well have been reticent about such an unpopular line.

To some extent, internationalism was an extension of the concern for Ireland, 'English Poland'.[2] Its real roots of course lay in the French revolutions, the second of which, in July 1830, Harney was sure had fanned the Unstamped into life. This interest in the Continent was formalized in the Unstamped by the customary column of foreign news, which described the struggles in Belgium, Poland, and Germany. O'Brien tapped it when he printed his notorious apologia for Robespierre in the autumn of 1832, and again in the spring of 1834 when he headlined 'The Conspiracy of the European Despots to crush the honest portion of the Press'. The Whigs, prosecuting the Unstamped, were the

---

[1] *Gauntlet*, 24 Feb., 8 Dec. 1833; *PMG*, 25 Dec. 1831, 6 Oct. 1832, 2, 23 Mar. 1833, 3, 10 May 1834.
[2] Osborne in NU reported *PMG*, 25 Aug. 1832.

French Government imprisoning Cabet, editor of the republican *Populaire*.[1]

The international comparison that sprang always to mind was with America, whose republicanism meant a broad franchise, non-intervention, economy, low taxes, and no great amassing of property. Hibbert in the NU, the *Guardian*, *Man*, and the *Gauntlet* freely compared the King's Speech with that of the President of America, and the doings of Congress with that of Parliament. From July 1834, however, Jackson's struggle with the American banks led to a fresh twist in the comparison; Jackson's struggle according to O'Brien was on behalf of labour against capital, and showed that universal suffrage, without further social reform, was valueless. None the less, in America the working class *did* have the vote and did have the power to rectify the situation. In Ireland as in England, in France as in America, O'Brien refused to employ the natural language of Old Corruption. Always he insisted that it was the middle classes in control of property who oppressed the Irish poor, took from the English labourer three-quarters of his industry, had ruined Robespierre's finest plans, pressed the French Government to imprison Cabet, and tried to thwart Jackson's work in America.[2]

On most of these issues mere publicity was enough. Flogging or the New Police were widely hated, and the Unstamped (that is, the *Guardian*) had only to add colour and weave the issue into the wider analysis. On newer crusades, the Unstamped had merely to spell out infant slavery to London readers or the plight of the Spitalfields weavers to provincial readers, to develop a common attitude or 'consensus of opinion'. On other causes, the leaders of the Unstamped and the NUWC tried to widen working-

---

[1] *Democratic Review*, Mar. 1850 (Hetherington, Cleave, Lorymer, and O'Brien spent some time on the Continent). HO 61/2, 20 Oct. 1830; *PMG*, 23, 30 July, 24 Sept., 8 Oct. 1831, 25 Aug. 1832 (Poland, Belgium, and Germany). *PMG*, 24 Nov., 8, 15 Dec. 1832 (Robespierre); 8 Mar. 1834 (Cabet). Somerville sketched the impact the Lyons rising of April 1834 had on the Dorchester secret committees in his *Autobiography*, 1951 edn., pp. 266–7.

[2] *Cosmopolite*, 10 Mar. 1832; *PMG*, 22 Oct., 2, 17 Dec. 1831, 7 Jan., 29 Sept. 1832; *Man*, 11 Aug. 1833; *Gauntlet*, 14 Apr., 17 Nov. 1833; *PMG*, 5 July, 16 Oct., 1 Nov. 1834, 17 Jan. 1835. See also, O'Brien's edition of *Buonarotti's History*, 1836, xv, p. 55.

class attitudes by involving them in more remote wrongs—
assessed taxes, the fate of the *True Sun*, and foreign news.
But there was a final category of causes which were less
straightforward. The Reform Act, machinery, the ballot,
temperance, Methodism and nonconformity, education,
SDUK literature, the repeal of the Union, foreign inter-
ventionism, free trade, poor rates: all these issues were
double-edged. Either they cut across the working class,
or, if they benefited the working class, they benefited the
middle class even more.

Machinery[1] and free trade divided the working classes
into a minority of producers and a majority of consumers.
The repeal of the Irish Union would in O'Brien's eyes ally
Irish labourer to Irish priest instead of Irish labourer and
English labourer in the demand for the vote. Carlile won the
enmity of his sons, O'Brien lost readers, and the *Slap at the
Church* raised 'a great outcry' for their attacks on the quietism
of religion. The working classes, O'Brien wrote to Owen,
'are *frightfully sensitive* and, if you like, *insane*' on religious
questions.[2] The usual approach in such cases was to distinguish between the use of a thing and its abuse: capital,
machinery, free trade were good servants but bad masters;
'pure' Christianity was noble but the Church and Chapel
needed reform. Then there were those issues from which the
working class would benefit, but the middle or governing
classes even more. Hetherington, Cleave, and Watson were
all abstainers, and Lovett wrote frequently in the Unstamped that drink was expensive and degrading. But John
Hawkins, also a cabinet-maker in the NU, retorted that
drink was the result of poverty not the cause of it. 'That
the base-minded, grasping and greedy portion of the
"masters" should praise the war-cry of drunkenness against
the men upon whose toil they live, I can understand and
pardon', but in Lovett it was unforgiveable.[3] Similarly,
education was knowledge was power, but that given in
schools and the Mechanics Institutes or offered by the SDUK
was sponsored and managed by middlemen in their own

---

[1] See above, pp. 234–5.
[2] O'Brien to Owen, *Owen Coll.*, 27 May 1832, f. 546; *Church Examiner*, 9 June
1832.   [3] *WMF*, 27 Apr. 1833; see also *WMF*, 6, 13 Apr., 18 May 1833.

interests. The Belgian liberals were being suppressed, yet if the Government were to intervene to help them Paine had shown that it would be the aristocracy, and not the working classes, who would ultimately benefit.[1] Poor relief was a sacred and inalienable right, but heavy poor rates did depress the working man struggling to be independent.

The Reform Act was perhaps the most striking of these double-edged issues. The NU, like many in the NPU, considered it inadequate, irrelevant to working men, but acceptable as a first step. The *Cosmopolite* agreed. Hetherington, Hunt, and Hibbert opposed the Act but Hunt was seldom at the NU, and Hetherington was in prison for the formative six months. Neither Lovett nor Cleave opposed it, Doherty came to support it, and Carpenter, Davenport and Osborne actively worked for its success. O'Brien, though not 'warm' for it, said he was prepared to 'labour' for it, and he criticized Hunt's stance. Not until May 1832 did O'Brien denounce the 'mean, jealous, niggardly, aristocratic whiggish bill'. It was only Hetherington who systematically opposed the Bill both in the NU and in the *Guardian*; as a result, perhaps, the NU refrained from debating it more than three times in twelve months, while the *Guardian* carried nearly a dozen leading articles, as well as countless short pieces, criticizing the Bill, as 'a mere trick', 'an additional barrier to the people's rights', and so on. When O'Brien joined the *Guardian* in the summer of 1832, Hetherington drew him into denouncing the Reform Act and any scheme for the ballot without universal suffrage; though this did not apparently stop O'Brien joining Carpenter and Major Revell in the Southern Metropolitan Union to give the Reform Bill 'a fair trial'.[2] Hetherington's line was not well received though he made some impression, if his correspondents' letters are at all representative. But from the winter of 1832 Hetherington and O'Brien, with some malice, were able to print letters from correspondents and provincial unions, confessing they had been deceived by the Act.

---

[1] *PMG*, 25 Aug., 6 Oct., 1 Dec. 1832 (reports of the NU).

[2] *Cosmopolite*, 5 May, 9 June 1832; *Midland Rep.*, 4 June 1831, 24 Apr., 12 May 1832; *PMG*, 4 Mar., 30 July, 1 Sept. 1832; *True Sun*, 16 Oct. 1832.

The Unstamped, then, performed the 'practical' services of carrying messages and advertisements, airing local grievances, and acting as the spokesman and fund-raiser of political societies such as the NUWC and the trades unions. They also had the more intellectual function of raising up and co-ordinating working-class opinion, extending it to include topics formerly alien to it, and of underpinning it with an ideological base, in Carlile's writings that of Old Corruption buttressed by the priesthood, in O'Brien's writings that of property, power, and exploitation.

Is there any way of judging the success of the Un-stamped? Three ways seem open. The first is to map the coverage, sales, and distribution of the Unstamped;[1] but this geographical approach will reveal nothing about the geology of the Unstamped's impact. The second is to measure influence 'in depth', by studying the vocabulary of pledges, the money sent to working-class causes, the receptions given to heroes of the Unstamped. But two difficulties follow; it is hard to assess other sources of influence such as the local stamped paper read in the public house, or the battered copy of Paine on the shelf of an old radical; and it is equally hard to know what would count as success. How much of the rhetoric? How much money? How large a reception? The third way is to relate the Un-stamped to the general development of working-class radicalism, and in particular Chartism. But in the absence of a 'control group', the methodological problem seems in-superable. Each of these dimensions will be examined in turn.

A host of small incidents suggest the Unstamped's coverage and the breadth of their influence. A Preston meeting criticized the NUWC for calling off the mass meeting at London's White Conduit Fields in November 1831. A Manchester meeting to denounce the Nottingham and Bristol trials spotted Joseph Swann, 'languid and for-lorn', in a crowd of 10,000 and put him on the hustings to talk of his sufferings for unstamped knowledge. A letter from Coventry, a town censured by Hetherington and Cleave as being demoralized by its cheap beer and cheaper charities, began 'As your valuable paper has a most extensive

[1] See above, Chapter IV, for sales and distribution of the Unstamped.

circulation in and near Coventry, I think it will be doing good to record within its pages the progress of liberal principles in that ancient city'. When the agricultural labourers of east Sussex received money from Brighton trades unions, they were asked to acknowledge it in the *Guardian*; when Wastneys, the Newcastle vendor, received aid from Darlington, he was asked to acknowledge it in the *Gauntlet*. Brighton contributed pound after pound to the Victim Fund; and Carlile received £30 in 325 subscriptions of a penny upwards from Bath.[1] A correspondent from Ashton under Lyne suggested that the agents of the Unstamped should collect money for the Short Time movement. Members of the Birmingham Non-electors (which were to become the Midland Union) established two 'law-defying political publications . . . after the plan of the *Poor Man's Guardian*'. Carlile was thanked by a Nottingham writer for his defence of Fursey, and Hetherington by 'a little weaver' who lived '200 miles off' for providing him with all the political knowledge he had. Uxbridge NU described the *Destructive* and the *Guardian* as

two such valuable papers, wherein the highly talented Editor points out the oppressed condition of the working classes of society in such plain terms as to come within the comprehension of men of the humblest abilities.

Carlile attended 'divine service' in Birmingham where the leading article of the *Guardian* was part of the sermon. C. Morris wrote from Swansea

It gives me much pleasure to bear testimony to the gradually-increasing distribution of your invaluable work in this neighbourhood, and the avidity with which many, (hitherto in a state of political darkness), seek it and read it. . . [it will] eventually tend to dispel the almost impenetrable mists and fogs that have so long clouded the political hemisphere in this neighbourhood.[2]

All these examples could be multiplied. Whether cumulatively this represented success for the Unstamped is very

[1] *PMG*, 3 Dec. 1831 (Preston); *PMG*, 28 Jan. 1832 (Swann); *PMG*, 17 Nov. 1832 (Coventry); *PMG*, 22 Aug. 1835 (labourers); *Gauntlet*, 23 Feb. 1834 (Wastneys); *Gauntlet*, 17 Nov. 1833 (Bath).

[2] *PMG*, 28 July 1832 (Ashton under Lyne); *PMG*, 1 Sept. 1832 (Birmingham) cf. *Salford Patriot*, 16 Feb. 1833; *Gauntlet*, 11 Aug. 1833 (Nottingham) cf. 18 Aug.; *PMG*, 16 Nov. 1833 (weaver); *Destructive*, 23 Feb. 1833 (Uxbridge) cf. *PMG*, 14 June 1834; *Gauntlet*, 6 Oct. 1833 (Birmingham); *PMG*, 13 June 1835 (Swansea).

hard to assess. Resolutions and pledges were common to many London and provincial meetings, but how often do they have to be repeated? Money was sent to the Victim Fund, for Lovett's militia seizure, for Carlile, and to the unions on strike; yet how much would have to be sent for the Unstamped to claim success? The London men were given large receptions on their northern tours, but how large do they have to be, and how much is to be discounted for the lack of any other entertainment? Carlile enrolled 3,000 Volunteers: could he have expected more than 1,000 or should he have enlisted 10,000? London and provincial protests against the Irish Coercion Bill, flogging, or Cold Bath Fields, filled the columns of the Unstamped; but how much should be allowed for the influence of other sources of opinion including the stamped newspapers? There is the testimony of individual correspondents, but that will help to get their letters published. There are the resolutions of provincial unions, designed to be sent to the Unstamped, but Place pointed out that this was all very random. There are the complaints of middle-class observers, but Place, one of the most prolific, never left London. There is the vigilance of the Home Office, but the reports of its spies and provincial military commanders were concerned with popular unrest and only incidentally with the popular press.[1] Sales, and the length of time a paper survived, seem to be a surer way of estimating the success of the Unstamped; yet the great leap in sales that followed the Unstamped, when they turned broadsheet,[2] suggests that the Unstamped were read and sold less for their political and economic doctrines than for their cheap news. How, today, would one measure and compare the influence of any two leading papers if one had only the newspapers themselves, a few scattered memoirs and some libel material tucked away in the Home Office, to go on?

All this is difficult enough. Even harder is the task of assessing the 'didactic' success of the Unstamped. Time and again the phrases of the *Guardian* occur in working-class meetings all over the country in the 1830s and 1840s— 'equal rights and equal laws', 'right against might', 'by force and by fraud', 'the rights of property are the wrongs of

---

[1] See above, pp. 29 f.   [2] See above, pp. 122 f.

labour', middlemen 'buy cheap and sell dear', 'shopocrats and usurers' and so on—yet this may be due more to the quarrying of O'Brien's sources, Paine, Spence, and Hodgskin, than to echoing the *Guardian*. No content analysis of the *Northern Star*, for example, could isolate the lingering influence of the *Guardian* as distinct from that of Owenism or Paine or the missionary work of the NU and LWMA delegates. More specifically, the *Guardian* from 1831 to 1835 sought to deflect the working-class analysis away from an attack on taxation and Old Corruption and on to Property and Power, the oppression of capital and the exploitation of labour. Carlile, first in the *Prompter* and then in the *Gauntlet* and in later issues of the *Cosmopolite*, met this with a restatement of Old Corruption, for which he skilfully won adherents by establishing a list of Volunteers. The *Guardian* never succeeded in edging out the old analysis; at best, working-class speeches and letters were a somewhat undigested mixture of both attacks.

Carlile, for example, received this letter from Rotherham.

By the fearless exercise of your powerful talents, you have done more to establish the permanent freedom of the press, and to promote the cause of free discussion, than any man who ever existed. You are detested and dreaded by a haughty and ignorant aristocracy, and a proud, hungry and hypocritical priesthood and their credulous dupes, who very well know that superstition, which is the mainstay of tyranny and oppression, can never bear free discussion. . . .[1]

Few of the letters the *Guardian* received were ever as 'pure' as this. This next letter from Winchester typically embraced both 'wealth producers' (Owenite or the *Guardian*?) and the 'drones' of the older analysis. We

wish to inform your readers, through your most valuable paper, that although you are in a dungeon, your spirit is abroad, and in Winchester, as firm as it can be, in a small number; but our numbers increase daily, and that they will increase, is the prayer of your constant readers here.... The Mayor says that they are dangerous; but we know who it is dangerous to—not to the wealth-producers, but to the drones in society, who suck the very marrow from our bones, and then tell us it is dangerous to question their right to do so. . . .[2]

---

[1] *Gauntlet*, 13 Oct. 1833; see also a letter from Wigan, 18 Aug. 1833.
[2] *PMG*, 5 Nov. 1831.

Similarly Seal, the Leicester agent, complained to the *Gauntlet* that a swarm of aristocrats, bastards, and clerical locusts lived off the wealth producers. John Brooks, the secretary of the Brighton PU wrote

the flame which would rise from the ruins of Old Mother Church, of the privileges and usurpation, and the unnatural plunder of the proud and pampered monster Aristocracy, would light the poor, plundered, insulted millions to wealth, acquired by industry, liberty, happiness and prosperity.

All this would come from republicanism. The aristocrats would no longer 'fatten' on the toil of the working classes. 'The working men are the *wealth-producers*!—the oligarchy cannot deny that. Let us assume our proper station then, and claim *precedence* in society. . . .'[1] The NU, steered by Watson, agreed that the resolutions to be put to the White Conduit Fields meeting in November 1831 would include the Six Points and a declaration that 'these principles' were 'essential to our protection as WORKING MEN—and the only sure guarantees for securing to us the proceeds of our labour. . . .'[2] Hetherington and O'Brien could have found nothing to complain of in this. The NUWC of 4 February 1833, however, met and agreed that till the laws of property were thoroughly understood, the working classes would stay wretched. Mr. Plummer explained to the meeting that the present possessors of landed property acquired it at the Norman conquest, and the holders of funded property by theft. Mr. Jackson pointed out that property laws oppressed working men and that 'till they were removed, till every man had his right to the soil in which he was born, he could never enjoy the fruits of his own labour (hear)'. The unproductive classes were living off the working classes. Yearly concluded the debate by observing 'that kings had been murderers, that lords were thieves, and parsons rogues and hypocrites (cheers)'.[3] Carlile and O'Brien, Cobbett, Spence, and Hodgskin were all arrayed in the market-place, all cheered, and presumably all thought to be saying the same thing. O'Brien knew this, and time again he and Hetherington sought to 'translate' from one set of terms to another, to overlay the old analysis with the new.

[1] *Gauntlet*, 30 June 1833 (Seal); *PMG*, 4 May 1833 (Brooks).
[2] *PMG*, 29 Oct. 1831.   [3] *PMG*, 9 Feb. 1833.

But the columns of the *Northern Star* showed that success was a long way off. A hundred and two radical associations in 1838, to take one example out of many, stated that wars and monopolies were impoverishing a nation of gentry, peasants, and yeomen. Benbow's defence at the Chester Assizes in spring 1840 was littered with references to a haughty and unprincipled aristocracy and its tools. W. Serle in 1842 would have Chartists go a-Christmas-boxing for the Victims Defence Fund, 'just as did placemen, pensioners, churchmen, policemen, beadles and all other black beatles and leeches'. Henry Vincent from prison and Robert Lowery on the platform ascribed the country's ills to taxes, corn laws, and an established church. O'Connor himself in 1847 was still listing a bloated aristocracy, Ministeral menials, a well-fed standing army, a gorged church, pensioned paupers, drones, and overgrown bankers.[1] Even Ernest Jones bothered to turn his guns on parsons, placemen, and pensioners, and Harney, who, as O'Brien's pupil, should have known better, and who added the word 'proletarian' to the radical language, devoted column after column to exposing priestcraft. Predictably, therefore, a 'Democrat' from Glasgow wrote to Harney's *Red Republican* that 'We British proletarians' had too long endured the 'grinding persecutions of Cotton Lords, and the dastardly tyranny of a besotted Aristocracy, and a bloated Church.'[2]

O'Brien, Hetherington, and Carpenter had a very real job to do when they attempted to innovate on this older rhetoric. It was not just that this language of 1819 was out of place; by 1850 it was also without meaning and emotion. Even in the *Prompter* of 1830 the language of Old Corruption had been flexible enough to carry natural speech rhythms and analytical enough to be a language of debate. Carlile and O'Brien could still *argue* in the early 1830s, though this was becoming increasingly difficult. By 1850 it was almost

[1] *NS*, 3 Nov. 1838, 25 Apr. 1840 (Benbow); 3 Dec. 1842 (Serle); 12 Dec. 1840 (Vincent); R. Lowery, *An Address to the Fathers and Mothers* ... 1839; *NS*, 23 Jan. 1847 (O'Connor). See also 'Democrat' in *Southern Star*, 3 May 1840; 'Republican' in *NS*, 20 June 1840; J. Knight in *NS*, 6 Jan., 14 July 1838; A Woolwich cadet in *NS*, 17 July 1841; A. Beaumont in *Northern Liberator*, 28 Apr. 1838. For a splendidly feudal version of the ideal society, see *NS*, 27 June 1840.

[2] *Notes to the People*, Sept. 1851 (Jones); *Red Rep.*, 13 July 1850.

impossible. What had been an analysis in 1819, and was a rhetoric by 1832, had become an etiquette by 1850. The Church was bloated or gorged, the aristocracy bloated, besotted, haughty, or insolent. The enemies were ritual enemies, the attacks formalized protests. There could be no call to a self-conscious working class in such an all-too-easy language.

But if O'Brien and Hetherington failed to displace the old analysis, at least elements of the new analysis became an accepted and important part of working-class radicalism. Alexander Yates of Coventry had been one of Hetherington's agents in 1832. His letter to the *Red Republican* in 1850 reveals three generations of radical language, that of Carlile, that of O'Brien, and that of Harney, one on top of the other.

The principles enunciated in the *Red Republican* are just what the mass of the people require to be made thoroughly acquainted with, and without which I verily believe that if this country were to be revolutionized tomorrow, in twelve months hence our position would be little, if anything, superior to that which the brave but too confiding Proletarians of France is at the present time. The lords of the soil, the lords of the tall chimneys, the swindling usurers, profit-mongers, and priests, would combine and resort to any and every stratagem to cheat us out of the fruits of our victory. . . . The people have been so long accustomed to part with four-fifths of their earnings to tax-eaters and profit-mongers, that now they appear to bear it with the same indifference that a Jersualem pony bears his burden; but once let their minds be stored with a knowledge of the evils under which they labour, and the remedies necessary to be applied, and the funeral dirge of kingcraft, priestcraft, lordcraft, and all the other devilish crafts that stand in the way of human progression, will speedily be sung. . . .[1]

When Hetherington and O'Brien analysed profits and power, instead of invoking priests and pensions, they forced their readers to reconsider their rights and their wrongs, and not merely to repeat them. Countless grateful letters to the *Guardian* claim that their writers had had their 'eyes opened'. Some readers, but not very many, took over O'Brien's arguments and language wholesale. Much more

---

[1] *Red Rep.*, 7 Sept. 1850.

often, a phrase such as Yates's 'profit-mongers' or Seal's 'wealth-producers' show that some intellectual reordering had taken place. And this was a sizeable achievement. If few letters to the *Northern Star* were wholly free of the language of 1819, most contained a phrase or two of the new analysis. Some of this, though by no means all of it, was due to the Unstamped.

Roebuck in 1835 commented in his *Pamphlets*, 'New ideas cannot be introduced by any sudden or singular effort, however powerful or well-directed. . . . It is by the dropping of water on the stone, the line upon line, the precept upon precept, that brings about important changes.'[1] Hetherington and O'Brien did not manage to displace the old language —it took fifty years to erode it—but they did manage to add to it. As a result, whatever the shortcomings of their own critique, they stretched working-class radicalism, keeping it first-hand and flexible; and they did force some intellectual content into it. But this sort of success cannot be precisely measured.

The third way of testing the success of the Unstamped would be to study the effect of the papers on working-class radicalism, particularly Chartism. Yet for two reasons this is no easier to assess than the other methods. First, to isolate the impact of the Unstamped on Chartism, one would have to try a sociological experiment along modern lines. One would need to compare two very similar towns or areas, one of which had been deluged with the Unstamped, and the other of which had not. These two towns must next have had the same 'exposure' to Chartism, and some of the differences in the response of the two towns or areas might then be attributed to the Unstamped.

But this cannot be done. The main catchment areas of the Unstamped correlate so closely with the later strongholds of Chartism, that no 'control' groups exist.[2] The second difficulty lies in the very nature of the correlation. Even if the Unstamped did correlate so exactly with Chartism that it

---

[1] J. Roebuck, 'The Stamped Press of London and its Morality', *Pamphlets for the People*, No. 3, p. 1.

[2] Compare the map of distribution (at end), for example, with the strongholds of the National Charter Association in 1842 (*NS*, 23, 30 Apr. 1842).

suggested a relationship between the two, it would not necessarily have been the Unstamped which made working men
respond to Chartism, but a third factor, such as a local
radical tradition, which made men respond to both Chartism *and* the Unstamped. The correlation would then be
technically spurious, and the Unstamped would only be
indicating, and not creating, pockets of radicalism. On this
basis all the Unstamped could have done would have been to
sustain working-class radicalism through the years after the
Reform Act.

Yet certain things can still be said. Provincial names that
were later to be prominent in Chartism—William Rider,
Joshua Hobson, Peter Bussey, Lawrence Pitkeilthy, Robert
Lowery, and John Hanson, to name but a few—first appeared
in print as correspondents to, or agents of, the Unstamped,
even though they would probably have emerged in Chartism
in any case. O'Brien and Carpenter, and to a lesser extent
Lee and Lorymer, had been made by the Unstamped, and
they continued to publish radical papers, the *National
Reformer*, the *Operative*, the *Charter*, the *Southern Star*,
and the *London Democrat*, into the 1840s. O'Connor and the
young Henry Vincent were the only prominent journalists
of Chartism who did not come up through the Unstamped.
Hetherington, Cleave, Carpenter, Bell, O'Brien, Lee,
Hobson, Hartwell, and Harney all served their trade with
the pauper press.

The Unstamped established Hetherington's name as
a household word, according to Gammage, the historian
of Chartism; and Holyoake was sure that the names of
Hetherington, Watson, and Cleave 'were in the mouths of
every newsvendor and mechanic in the three kingdoms,
Hetherington's always being mentioned first'. When the
Revd. Henry Solly, founder of a network of boys' clubs,
wrote his fictional biography of James Woodford, a carpenter,
in 1881, he made Woodford visit the London Working
Men's Association, where he met Hetherington, Cleave,
and Watson, the 'mighty champions of the Unstamped'.[1]

---

[1] R. Gammage, *The History of the Chartist Movement*, 1894 edn., p. 7; G. J.
Holyoake, *60 Years* . . ., vol. ii, pp. 264–5; H. Solly, *James Woodford, Carpenter
and Chartist*, 1881.

Hetherington's name had become so well known that when Frost was reprieved for his part in the Newport rising, the announcement was sent to Hetherington's shop in the Strand to cool popular excitement. Thomas Cooper, the Leicester Chartist, when he left prison in 1845, paid a pilgrimage to 'the little shop in Shoe Lane whence John Cleave issued so many thousands of sheets of Radicalism and brave defiance of bad governments, in his time. . . '.[1]

Not only did the Unstamped create one generation of radical journalists, but it inspired a second. W. J. Linton was introduced to radical journalism and radical politics when he worked with Watson to produce a *People's Library* in 1838 and with Hetherington to edit his *Oddfellow* for him in 1841. Thomas Frost, a provincial journalist and Owenite, sent his first 'essay in authorship' at the age of eighteen to Hetherington, 'famous' as the champion of the Unstamped. Hetherington tactfully turned it down. James Watson was Holyoake's first publisher, and helped both Holyoake and Ernest Jones to survive the lean years of the 1850s. Holyoake took over Watson's business when he retired.[2] Robert Hartwell, compositor and friend of Hetherington, spanned several decades of radical activity, selling the Unstamped in the 1830s, editing the *Beehive* for George Potter in the 1860s.

The Unstamped made journalists; it also made businesses. The most successful of these was undoubtedly Abel Heywood's in Manchester, who by 1851 handled 10 per cent of the country's newspaper trade. In his speech in 1888 to the Manchester city council after fifty years of municipal service, and again in 1891 when he received the honorary freedom of the city, he referred with pride to the early days when 'I worked and suffered in the struggle' for an unstamped press. His son, several years later, compiled a pamphlet on illegal almanacs on the strength of his father's memories.[3]

---

[1] W. J. Linton, *James Watson, a Memoir*, 1879, p. 49; T. Cooper, *Life*, 1872, p. 276.

[2] T. Frost, *Forty Years Recollections*, 1880, p. 8; *Reminiscences of a Country Journalist*, 1886, p. 39; Holyoake, op. cit., vol. i, p. 102; vol. ii, p. 267.

[3] *Abel Heywood and Son, 1832–1932*, pp. 4–5; A. Heywood, jun., *Three Papers*, 1904.

So, if the influence of the Unstamped cannot be quantitatively measured, this is not to say that it was not extensive or profound. James Grant recalled 'one of the parties connected with it saying to me in exulting tones, in 1833, "O, Sir, the *Guardian* is rapidly tearing up society by the roots" '. James Tucker, an informed observer, told the *Guardian* that its influence with working men surpassed that of any other journal in existence. And Thomas Goldspink, a loyal NUWC member, wrote in to the penultimate number of the *Guardian* that he wanted

to express my gratitude to you as a political and moral preceptor, from whom I have derived much of the information I possess. . . . I am sure, Sir, that the *Poor Man's Guardian* will be preserved by many of the industrious classes, and it is highly desirable that it should be. It will be resorted to, in after times, as a corrective of the histories that will be written, by hireling scribes, of the doings of the basest faction that ever scourged a nation, namely, the Whigs. . . .[1]

A letter from Exeter in the winter of 1836 told Hethering-ton that its authors

have for a long time taken into this ward your unstamped newspapers, and not only yours but various others of the above; in fact, we took in all the unstamped we could get; for we were certain that the whole of you gentlemen connected with the Unstamped was obliged to make a vigorous struggle to keep the field. . . .

They would like to take Hetherington's *Dispatch* 'did we know how to get it. We should like to have a London paper regularly every week.'[2]

It was the *Guardian*, the longest lived of the Unstamped, which above all captured working-class loyalty. Thomas MacConnell, a radical lecturer, wrote to the *National Reformer* that had O'Brien described himself in it as the late editor of the *Guardian*, 'great numbers' would then have hailed the *Reformer* 'as that of an old friend'. John Ward of Barnsley had read the *Guardian* from its very first number, and owed to O'Brien 'whatever knowledge I may possess in politics'.[3] With good reason Oastler wrote to

---

[1] J. Grant, op. cit., pp. 298–301; *PMG*, 14 Jan. 1832, 19 Dec. 1835; see also Vincent in *London Democrat*, 17 Sept. 1836.

[2] *London Dispatch*, 27 Nov. 1836.

[3] *National Reformer*, 28 Jan., 18 Mar. 1837.

J. R. Stephens, 'Tell O'Brien to put the *Poor Man's Guardian's* soul into the *Star*.' And with good reason O'Brien and Hetherington floated a second *Poor Man's Guardian and Repealer's Friend* in 1843, hoping 'that all old friends and supporters of the *Guardian* will rally round it'.[1]

Perhaps the real achievement of the editors and publishers of the Unstamped was not their efforts to co-ordinate a variety of working-class movements, nor their old and new analyses of working-class wrongs, but that they led a working-class movement in its own right. Lovett was sure that it was 'one of the most important *political movements* that I was ever associated with'.[2] When the Reform agitation and anger at the Irish Coercion Act died away in the summer of 1833, it was the campaign for an unstamped press that kept an attenuated NUWC alive during the trade union revival. And after the Dorchester case, the Unstamped press became the focal concern of London working-class radicalism. Between 1831 and 1836 nearly 750 people in London alone were brought before the courts for selling the Unstamped. More money was collected for the Victim Fund than for any other London cause in these years. Prominent working-class leaders, who earlier had been trade unionists or co-operators, and later were Chartists, for these years were primarily the organizers and heroes of the Unstamped. The later leaders of London Chartism and the authors of the Charter had put out the Unstamped; they were leaders partly *because* they had put out the Unstamped; and they continued to talk in the language of the Unstamped.

---

[1] G. J. Holyoake, *Life of J. R. Stephens*, 1881, p. 86 (I owe this reference to the kindness of Mrs. D. Thompson, University of Birmingham); *PMG and Repealers' Friend*, no. 11.

[2] Lovett, op. cit., vol. i p. 60 (my italics).

CONCLUSION

THE campaign for the repeal of the stamp duties on newspapers in London between 1830 and 1836 is important in at least five ways. First, it was yet one more arena for the battle over popular education.[1] The more out-spoken of the tories continued to deplore 'teaching their heads to reason rather than their hands to work'.[2] The middle-class radicals continued to defend the right of the working man to cheap news, as they had defended his right to cheap books and the right of his children to national schools. They argued that an educated people was a sober and a responsible people; and that, as the working classes were determined to obtain information somehow, it was essential that they should have access to 'suitable' knowledge. If working men were to be educated, then cheap newspapers were the only means of doing it: Mechanics Institutes were too few and formal, cheap books and public libraries were for the converted, schools were for children, and lectures were of too limited an influence. Newspapers, on the other hand, were the adult counterpart of national schools. They would give working men the mechanics of literacy; the 'useful knowledge' which would allow them to live in comfort and security under the laws; and, hedged with suitable precautions, cheap newspapers could allow working men to think, reflect, and free themselves from deference, demagogues, and drudgery.

Behind this lay two articles of belief. The first was paternalistic. Middle-class radicals hoped, but were not quite sure, that working men would chose good literature rather than bad, and sound opinions in preference to subversive. Middle-class men wanted a free market in which the options were none the less weighted and the choices none the less guided. They did not trust working men to

[1] See above, Chapter I.
[2] *PP Report of the Commissioners of the Poor Laws*, 1834, xxxiv, Reply from Stiffkey, Norfolk.

throw up a sound literature of their own. Place was asked by the Select Committee on Drunkenness in 1834: 'Might not the writers of the atrocious penny publications then become editors of the newspapers and publish the same atrocious matter?' 'They could not get readers if better material were offered.'[1] By 1840 the *British and Foreign Review* found that the wholesome were a little more numerous than the immoral. The *Quarterly Review* in 1849 found on the contrary that immoral and seditious papers were very much on the increase 'both in numbers and malignity'. Two years later the Select Committee on Newspaper Stamps appeared to justify the educationalists' faith. Witness after witness testified to the improvement in public taste and general knowledge. Working men were reading sound opinions and good literature.[2]

The second article of belief shared by working men as well as middle-class men has been well described as the 'rationalist illusion'.[3] The only bar to the diffusion of knowledge was technical, low literacy rates, bad communications, expensive newspapers; and the attaining of knowledge was a mechanical process, in which each item of knowledge worked its effect on the mind as each of Morrison's pills worked on the body. The SDUK counted its success by the number of pamphlets it sold. So did Carlile. Carlile's very image of the Multiplication Table[4] could have come from the columns of the SDUK. At its most philistine, this acquisition of knowledge became a magpie collection of items of information, found in the *Penny Magazine* and in Miscellanies in the Unstamped. At its most liberating, knowledge was seen as the supreme right and heritage of man. Joseph Hickin of Walsall wrote to Carpenter, that repealing the taxes on knowledge would

free the immortal mind. I need not describe to you, who feel the intellectual flame, the burning and intense desire of attaining knowledge, which every man must feel and experience who has tasted its sweetness. . . . We are here obliged to submit to receive it drop by drop,

[1] *S.C. on Intoxication*, 1834, qu. 2057.
[2] *British and Foreign Review*, 1840, pp. 223–46; *Quarterly Review*, 1849, lxxxv, p. 309.
[3] E. P. Thompson, op. cit., p. 733.   [4] See above, p. 208.

which, like the imaginary appearance of water in the burning sandy desert, only increases the thirst.[1]

Secondly, these middle- and working-class efforts to circulate cheap knowledge opened up a new field in cheap literature for the masses. It was as a phenomenon of cheap literature that the Unstamped were reviewed by the *Tatler* in June 1832, counted by the *Christian Reformer* in the summer months of 1832, deplored by the *New Monthly Magazine* in 1833 and 1834, investigated by the Manchester Statistical Society in 1835, and recalled by the Manchester Literary Club in 1876.[2] Such diverse witnesses as Charles Knight, the publisher of cheap books, Fox-Bourne, the historian of newspapers, and William Lovett, the founder of the National Association, agreed that the Unstamped, in Lovett's words,

originated the cheap literature of the present day—for few publications existed before they commenced—and the beneficial effects of this cheap literature on the minds and morals of our population are beyond all calculation. For many of the cheap literary and scientific publications that were published during that period were started with the avowed object of 'diverting the minds of the working classes away from politics' and of giving them 'more useful knowledge'. In fact a new class of literature sprang up for the first time in England avowedly for the millions, and has gone on increasing and extending its beneficial influence from that period to the present. To this cheap literature, and the subsequent cheap newspapers that resulted from our warfare, may also be traced the great extension of the coffee-rooms and reading-rooms of our large towns, and the mental and moral improvement resulting from their establishment.[3]

Thirdly, the reduction of the newspaper stamp was the result of two campaigns, middle-class and working-class. The middle-class campaign was worked by a pressure group

[1] *Political Observer*, 16 Apr. 1831; cf. W. Lovett, op. cit., vol. i, p. 36; and Collins's and O'Neill's letter to the *NS*, 20 Feb. 1841.

[2] *Tatler*, 1832, pp. 315–17, 328, 344; *Christian Reformer*, May 1832, p. 219, July 1832, p. 307, Aug. 1832, p. 369, Sept. 1832, p. 434; *New Monthly Magazine*, 1833, vol. xxxix; 1834, vol. xl; T. Ashton, *Economic and Social Investigations in Manchester*, 1934; *Papers of the Manchester Literary Club*, vol. ii, 1875–6, pp. 39–58.

[3] W. Lovett, op. cit., vol. i, p. 64; see also *S.C. Public Libraries*, 1849, xvii, qus. 2785, 2819; H. Fox-Bourne, *English Newspapers*, 1887, vol. ii, pp. 58–9; C. Knight, *Passages of a Working Life*, 1864, vol. ii, ch. 6; *The Old Printer and the Modern Press*, 1854, pp. 242 f.

in and out of Parliament.[1] The cause had been more important in 1831; the pressure was to be more skilfully organized and more widely based in the 1840s. But as a London campaign which sought to change one law, it developed and refined techniques which were later to be commonplace. It employed three forms of action, the lobby, the debate, and the pressure of an organized public opinion, which was fed on a journal (Roebuck's *Pamphlets for the People*) and numerous circulars, marshalled in a Society for the Repeal of the Stamp Duties, which cut across class lines, and focused in public meetings, petitions, and deputations. As a campaign it had a certain degree of success; but it did not succeed in abolishing the stamp duty altogether, partly because not all the radicals shared Place's conviction that the last penny was the worst penny, and partly because many of those who were convinced of the iniquity of the penny stamp lost their political nerve. Hume, Grote, and Warburton believed that ministerial goodwill and certainly the Whig Government were too insecure and too valuable to be jeopardized for just one radical cause.

Fourthly, the campaign to repeal the taxes on knowledge by flouting the law and flooding the market with Unstamped newspapers, was a working-class campaign in its own right.[2] It had its martyrs and its heroes, it was led by men of the working class and financed within the working class. Few proprietors of the Unstamped demanded the classical liberties of the press, though Cleave did reprint the *Areopagitica*; but most of them said explicitly that the working classes must first have cheap news and cheap knowledge if they were to obtain the vote and the produce of their labour. According to whether or not their campaign was a success depended whether the next move was a National Convention or a National Association. Lovett's New Move in 1840 was in many ways an extension of the Unstamped, and to that extent a confession of its failure. And yet the Unstamped press did compel a change in the law. Reckoned by middle-class criteria, it was perhaps the most successful working-class campaign of the decade.

[1] See above, Chapter III.
[2] See above, Chapters IV, V, VIII.

Finally, the Unstamped press in the hands of Carpenter and O'Brien, developed working-class political, economic, and social theory.[1] The old rhetoric of 1819, a language common to both working- and middle-class radicals, was in their hands overlaid with the new analysis of property, power, and exploitation. Hetherington and O'Brien repeated time and again that the main line of cleavage in society was simultaneously economic and political. All those on the wrong side of that line shared a common enemy, were in common denied their rights, and had enough common interests to make possible a working-class crusade to regain their lost rights and their due status.

Their analysis looked towards Marx, but differed in many profound ways. Marx's concept of class in *The Eighteenth Brumaire* was strict.

In so far as millions of families live under economic conditions of existence that separate their mode of life, their interests and their culture from those of the other classes, and put them in hostile opposition to the latter, they form a class. In so far as there is merely a local interconnection among these small-holding peasants, and the identity of their interests begets no community, no national bond and no political organization among them, they do not form a class.[2]

A functional or occupational group, defined in economic terms, became a class when it was aware of itself as a class and its interests as opposed to those of other classes. By this account O'Brien did not operate a 'pure' sense of class, but then neither did Harney, even though he made 'proletariat' fashionable, nor Ernest Jones, although he was a colleague of Marx.

Jones wrote, as O'Brien could have done, that 'An amalgamation of classes is *impossible where an amalgamation of interests is impossible also.*' Those who did share similar interests, according to Jones, were working men, small shopkeepers, smaller farmers, soldiers, and policemen. Opposed to them were factory and mine owners, landlords, bankers, parsons, placemen, and pensioners. 'These two portions of the community must be separated, distinctly,

[1] See above, Chapter VII.
[2] *Marx Engels Selected Works*, 1962 edn., vol. i, p. 334, Marx employed a much weaker version than this in the *Manifesto*.

dividedly, and openly from each other—CLASS AGAINST CLASS —all other mode of proceeding is mere moonshine.'[1] Jones, like O'Brien, was using both economic and political categories, and hitting out at both old and new enemies.

Small shopkeepers, mill-hands, and smallholders, on this account, formed a class. But they were patently not a proletariat with common 'economic conditions of existence'. Nor did pensioners and landlords form a bourgeosie. Jones, like O'Brien, was pitting the labouring classes against the parasites, the useful against the useless, the politically excluded against the politically dominant. What mattered was not the degree of homogeneity within the respective parties, but the size of the gap between them. It was a We-They diagnosis, not specifically economic, in which the gap gave coherence to the parties on either side of it. What was 'made' during the 1830s, was not a class but class-consciousness: the gulf between We and They was more important and more imminent than the divergences and conflicting interests within the working classes. And the gulf was marked by the vote. In a very real sense, politics, not economics, established class. Its implications, of course, were worked out in the economic field.

Because O'Brien and Hetherington attached so much importance to the vote, they could employ a Marxian sense of class-consciousness without a Marxian use of class. For the same reasons, their account of the processes of social change differed from that of Marx. The New Society might have to be obtained by working-class revolution if working men were denied the vote. But if the ruling classes had any sense and the radicals obtained a free press, then the New Society would be the gradual and peaceful result of universal suffrage. There was no hint of a dialectic in the London pauper press.

Recent authors have suggested that the Unstamped divided the radical world by their violent attacks on political economy, and that Chartism drew on this class-hostility.[2]

---

[1] *Notes to the People*, Sept. 1851.

[2] Thompson, op. cit., p. 727: 'To some degree (although by no means entirely) they [*The Times* and Lord Brougham] carried the Radical middle-class with them—the schoolmasters, surgeons, and shopkeepers, some of whom had once supported

But this account is hardly complete: it underestimates the considerable overlap in the content of middle- and working-class radicalism, and it ignores those groups and those individuals who belonged to both radical worlds. To say that there were radical working men and that there were radical middle-class men suggests only that radicalism was not limited to one class, not that there were two kinds of radicalism, and two radical and hostile publics.

First, to pit two radicalisms against each other is to concentrate exclusively on the new rhetoric of the Unstamped, and to rely far too heavily on the educational neuroses of Francis Place. Certainly the new rhetoric denounced middlemen and abhorred existing property relations. Certainly—and mistakenly—Place projected the editorials of the *Guardian* on to the members of the National Union of the Working Classes. In 1832 to 1833, the new rhetoric was to be found in four important papers with an estimated circulation of 25,000.[1] But at least another 25,000 papers were circulated each week which ignored political economy. The *Gauntlet* denounced the foe as kingcraft, priestcraft, lordcraft. The *Cosmopolite* and the *Political Soldier* demanded radical reform without invoking socialist critiques of property. Cobbett until his death in 1835, hammered away at Old Corruption. Lorymer turned all his invective upon servile minions and man-butchers. Cleave and Carpenter, in *Slap* and the *Church Examiner*, mocked a corrupt church, while Lee blasted indolent landlords.

And this older style of denunciation merged into—and was strengthened by—the more genteel middle-class criticisms of aristocracy, monopoly, and corruption in high places.

Cobbett and Wooler—so that by 1832 there were *two* Radical publics: the middle-class, which looked forward to the Anti-Corn Law League, and the working-class, whose journalists (Hetherington, Watson, Cleave, Lovett, Benbow, O'Brien) were already maturing the Chartist movement. . . . The dividing-line came to be, increasingly, not alternative "reform" strategies (for middle-class reformers could on occasion be as revolutionary in their tone as their working-class counterparts) but alternative notions of political economy.' See also R. K. Webb, op. cit., p. 163; M. Hovell, *The Chartist Movement*, 1966 edn., pp. 51–3.

Holyoake, after all, who had an acute sense of class, thought political economy 'a science of sense and mercy', but widely detested because of the New Poor Law. See G. J. Holyoake, *The Life of J. R. Stephens*, 1881, p. 61.

[1] See above, Chapters VI and VII.

The punishment of the Bristol and agricultural rioters, infant slavery, flogging, the fate of the *True Sun*, primogeniture, the condition of the Spitalfields weavers, the national debt, taxes, and the septennial act were fed by middle- and working-class writers alike to middle- and working-class radicals alike. O'Brien's conceptual framework was very different from that of Fonblanque, editor of the *Examiner*. But it was also very different from that of Cobbett and Carlile. One of the main reasons, after all, why O'Brien failed to displace the older analysis, and could at best add only another layer or dimension to it, and one of the main reasons why he and Hetherington had to 'translate' between rhetorics, was that the older analysis was reinforced by middle-class rhetoric. The 'socialist' authors were a mainstream in working-class radicalism. But they did not create or manipulate a working-class radical public. They were one group among many clamouring for hearers.

And just as O'Brien, Hetherington, and Benbow cannot be considered representative of working-class thought, neither was the middle-class radicalism which they confronted any more 'pure' or homogeneous. The poor laws, trades unions, Malthusianism, the wage fund, the harmony of interests and the role of the state provoked almost as much disagreement within the ranks of the middle class, between parliamentary radicals, the Society for the Diffusion of Useful Knowledge and the political economists, as they did between middle- and working-class radicals. McCulloch, Wade, and Place, for example, agreed that men should always resist wage cuts. Place and John Stuart Mill joined Watson and Hetherington in circulating birth-control literature. Roebuck publicly questioned whether there could still be said to be a harmony of interests between masters and men, Nassau Senior whether the fertility of land was declining and thus whether a subsistence theory of wages made any sense. The *Westminster* would have the Government responsible for the plight of the handloom weavers, McCulloch and Roebuck for a system of national education. Napier roundly denounced an industrial system which forced masters and men into hostile camps. Even the New Poor Law, the harshest exercise in political economy, was opposed by McCulloch, Wade, and Wakley. Attitudes did cluster; but if political economy was the *casus belli* of Chartism, then the trenches were far from straight and there was much fraternization between the rival troops.

From 1834 and the coming of the unstamped broadsheets, the notion that there were two radical publics each with its own press and divided by political economy, is even less valid. These broadsheets were widely read within the middle class. They were 'respectable', they had dropped much of their political comment in favour of police-court news, and were making money rather than Chartism. Hetherington, a man of considerable integrity, after all, not only sold his former unstamped broadsheet, the *Dispatch*, to Place's circle of friends in early 1837 but, despite O'Brien's sneers, wrote in it and used his good name to make it sell.

Secondly, to argue that the Unstamped sharpened the divide between two radical publics, or increased class-hostility, is to ignore all those men who touched both the world of the ragged street seller and the world of the parliamentary question. It ignores men like Carpenter (one of the leading 'socialist' writers) and Lovett, who were on the committee of the NUWC and the council of the National Political Union, or men like Major Beauclerc who worked within the NPU for closer co-operation with the NUWC. It ignores those three radical members of Parliament, who were not averse to speaking the language of Paine—that is, Wakley, Roebuck, and Thompson. It ignores that most important group, the parochial reformers (the Savage brothers, Rogers, Murphy, and Potter), who spoke at the Rotunda, elected each other on to the council of the NPU, who helped Hetherington with his press, introduced Wakley into politics, provided O'Connor with his early support in London, and who were backed by Hetherington, Carlile, and Lee in their campaigns for parish reform and the abolition of assessed taxes. It ignores the Irish, who reached to Hunt on the one side through his former Civil and Religious Liberty Association, and O'Connell on the other, and who were the mainstay of the NUWC from the summer of 1832 on. And finally it ignores those self-appointed schoolmasters, Place, Dr. Black of Kentucky, and Dr. Birkbeck (who knew Hetherington well enough to visit him when he was in hiding), who were willing to write for the radical broadsheets after 1834.

Far from the Unstamped aggravating class differences, the campaign for the repeal of the taxes on knowledge served to bring certain middle-class reformers, and the leaders of the London working class, into a hesitant but genuine alliance. The working-class leaders could always count on the middle-class radicals for anything within the law. Hume, Bulwer, and others presented petition after petition from the victims, complained in Parliament of selective prosecutions, demanded returns of all those imprisoned. They shared platforms with the NUWC men and went in deputation with them to Melbourne, Althorp, and Spring Rice. From late 1834 on, when Place helped Cleave to edit his *Gazette* from prison, and Black probably assisted Hetherington in the same way; when working men worked with and for the middle-class society for promoting a cheap and honest press to create a national public opinion; thereafter, the two campaigns, middle- and working-class, merged into each other. Hetherington acknowledged this when he challenged O'Connor's claim to have reduced the stamp duty single-handed.

I think your readers must have laughed outright when they read your claim to the honour of repealing the Fourpenny Stamp duty on Newspapers. So then Watson, Hetherington, Cleave, Dr Black, Mr Place, Mr John Travers, Dr Birkbeck, and many others, who expended time and money in upholding the cause in every possible way, are to yield the palm of victory to Feargus O'Connor. These good men, who paid the expense of public meetings, headed deputations, and Watson, Cleave and Hetherington, who sustained repeated fines and imprisonments, and ruinous seizures, till victory crowned our efforts, are all to be thrust aside. . . .[1]

Unless middle-class men were expected to join the ranks of the victims, it is hard to see what more they could have done. Certainly the techniques of the two campaigns were distinct. Certainly O'Brien (and O'Brien alone) was

[1] *NS*, 12 June 1841.

reluctant to work with middle-class men. Certainly the
Unstamped sought to make working men conscious of their
distinct class identity, their rights, and their dignity. Yet a
corporate sense of class does not have to entail a stance of class
war, but only a sense of the class gulfs. What hampered
class co-operation in the 1830s was not so much class
hostility as a feeling shared by both middle- and working-
class men that politics and pressure groups were middle-
class activities not suitable for working men. Robert Lowery
and Thomas Carter (hero of Charles Knight's *Memoirs of a
Working Man*) felt this strongly in the 1830s, and Herbert
Gladstone was having great difficulty in persuading Liberal
caucuses to accept working-class candidates in the 1890s.

Radicals of all classes believed that a free press and a wide
franchise were inseparable.[1] The alliance of working- and
middle-class men, found in the Society for Promoting
a Cheap and Honest Press (which became the London
Working Men's Association), was echoed in the People's
Charter Union of 1848 which, significantly, became the
Association for the Repeal of the Taxes on Knowledge in
1849. The taxes on knowledge formed one of those many
causes, like temperance, foreign refugees, the health of
towns, the ballot, corn laws, and land reform, which co-opted
working men under liberal banners, and which allowed
several of the leaders of the Unstamped in the 1830s to
become the Liberals of the 1860s.

In this sense, then, both John Stuart Mill and Engels
missed the point. In Mill's political model, the State confronted the individual and his voluntary associations.[2] The
way to preserve liberty was to check the State from encroaching on the private. But this ignores the social fact that many
of those same voluntary associations were also pressure
groups, encroaching on the function of the State. These
radicals were not fighting *off* the State but fighting for
access *to* the State. Engels, on the other hand, suggested
that Chartism so frightened the Victorian middle class,

---

[1] 'The Political Creed of the *Northern Liberator* may be thus abridged:
freedom of the press
universal suffrage.'
See *Northern Liberator*, 9 Dec. 1837.
[2] J. S. Mill, 'Centralization', in *Edinburgh Review*, Apr. 1862, p. 325.

that it bought 'a prolonged armistice at the price of ever-repeated concessions to the working-people'.[1] Yet to extend the vote to those already engaged in politics was to stabilize the system. The larger the political community, the greater the area that was subject to the divide and rule of politics. For politics in the realm outside Parliament entailed pressure groups, and pressure groups cut across class.

The Unstamped press [wrote Lowery, looking back after twenty years] had freely reported the meetings and discussions of the working men's association, and thus it might be said they were the means by which the people were admitted to the press, for from that time their influence grew stronger, and their wants and wishes were more and more inquired into by the standard press and by Parliament. They thus became a recognized portion of public opinion. . . .[2]

To become a 'recognized portion of public opinion' was to become paid-up members of the political community.

[1] F. Engels, 'Trades Unions', 1881, in *Marx Engels on England* (1926 Moscow edn.), p. 514.
[2] *W.R.*, 19 July 1856.

APPENDIX

BIOGRAPHICAL NOTES ON THE LEADING PUBLISHERS AND AUTHORS OF THE LONDON UNSTAMPED

JOHN BELL

Mar. 1832–5 edited stamped *True Sun*.

Oct. 1835 edited *New Political Register* (unstamped), printed by Lee.

Jan. 1836 launched unstamped *New Weekly True Sun*, which in Apr. 1836 became the *Mirror for Magistrates*.

Sept. 1836 edited the stamped *London Mercury*, to which O'Brien contributed, and allied with Bernard's currency schemes.

Place's comment, 'a tall dark well dressing man, had the air of a man of fashion but not much of the demeanour of a gentleman'. Add. MSS. 27819, f. 50.

WILLIAM BENBOW 1784–

1816 a Manchester shoemaker, friend of Bamford; 1817 imprisoned.

1822 indicted by Vice Society for publishing obscene books [French novels] for which acquitted.

In business as a bookseller at Castle St.; member of the NUWC and on committee.

Jan. 1832 wrote 'Grand National Holiday and the Congress of the Productive Classes'.

March 1832 arrested for taking part in the Fast Day disturbances, published 'The Trial of William Benbow and Others'.

Hired Theobold's Road Institution which he let out to the NUWC when they left the Rotunda. A co-operator but not an Owenite.

May 1832 wrote 'The Delusion, or Owenism Unmasked'.

June 1832 edited *The Tribune of the People*, printed by Lee.

Ran the Commercial Coffee House at Temple Bar until Mar. 1832.

Sept. 1832 ran the Temple of Liberty, King's Cross, as a meeting-place for co-operators and the Female Society.

Nov. 1833 edited *Agitator and Political Anatomist*.

Aug. 1839 imprisoned for 16 months for seditious language.

(Rüter, *International Review for Social History*, 1936.)

G. BERGER

Printer, radical publisher and bookseller of Holywell Street, Strand. Published for Benbow as well as numerous small Unstamped.

In 1839 employed 2 men and 2 boys.

Became largest newsagent in London until the coming of W. H. Smith. (L. James, op. cit., p. 19.)

HENRY BERTHOLD 1800–

Born in Saxony, came to England 1824. (HO 40/29, f. 435.)

July 1830 launched tricoloured *National Guardian*, for which the first vendors of the Unstamped were imprisoned.

Jan. 1831 brought before Murray of Union Hall for selling *National Guardian*; imprisoned for 3 months in Kingston Gaol.

Dec. 1831 again in prison in Kingston Gaol.

Aug. 1832 launched *Regenerator*.

Charged with stealing a boa from a warehouse; Hibbert testified on his behalf and caught the chill from which he died. (*Gauntlet*, 2 Feb. 1834.)

RICHARD CARLILE 1790–1843

Writer, bookseller, and lecturer.

1817 selling periodicals in Devon and then in London.

1819–26 edited *Republican*.

1819–25 Dorchester Gaol. Moved to 62 Fleet St.

Jan. 1828–Dec. 1829 edited the *Lion*, in which he patronized the Revd. Robert Taylor.

Jan. 1830 launched his *Journal* 'to test the real state of liberty of the press'.

May 1830 hired the Rotunda, though highly critical of the societies that met there.

Nov. 1830 launched the *Prompter*, for which in Jan. 1831 sentenced to 2 years.

Nov. 1831 publishing *Union*.

Feb.–Dec. 1832 published *Isis*; entered into a 'moral marriage' with Eliza Sharples.

July 1832 controlling *Cosmopolite*.

Feb. 1833 launched *Gauntlet*; released from prison Aug. 1833.

Sept., Oct. 1833 touring country to Jan. 1834, recruiting 'Volunteers'.

Oct. 1834 launched *Scourge*.

1838 and 1839, editing *Church*, *Phoenix*, *Political Register*.

Nov. 1842 tried and failed to become a lecturer for the Anti-Corn Law League.

WILLIAM CARPENTER 1797–1874

Former bookseller and 'sectarian preacher.'

c. 1828 to summer 1830 edited stamped *Trades Newspaper* and *Weekly Free Press*.

Co-operator and disciple of Thompson; prominent at the Co-operative Congresses.
Oct.–Nov. 1830 edited *Magazine of Useful Knowledge and Co-operative Miscellany.*
Oct. 1830–May 1831 launched unstamped *Political Letters.*
May 1831–Dec. 1831 imprisoned King's Bench.
June–August 1831 edited stamped *Political Letter.*
Sept. 1831–July 1832 edited monthly unstamped *Political Magazine.*
Jan.–Nov. 1832, edited with Cleave the *Slap at the Church,* and the *Church Examiner.*
1832–5 sub-editor of the stamped *True Sun;* published various Addresses and pamphlets.
Member of the NUWC, and council member of the NPU.
Feb. 1836 published *Carpenter's London Journal.*
1838–40 edited *Charter.*
Feb. 1839 represented Bolton at the Convention.
1840 with O'Brien edited the *Southern Star;* moved into orthodox journalism.
1847 associated with People's International League.
Place: 'a shrewd cunning voluable fellow, precise, plausible and persuasive'. Add. MSS. 27795, f. 165.

JOHN CLEAVE *c.* 1790–*c.* 1847

Been a sailor, and a Baptist; probably Irish. 'Freeman and House-holder of the City'.
1828 with Hetherington in the Civil and Religious Association.
1829–30 Carpenter's 'errand boy' (Carlile) on *Weekly Free Press* and then on *Political Letters.*
Ran the Hope Coffee House, Snow Hill, and then added a bookshop in 1 Shoe Lane in Mar. 1833.
One of the leading figures of the NUWC, and on Council of NPU.
Jan.–Nov. 1832 working with Carpenter on *Slap at the Church,* and the *Church Examiner.*
Dec. 1832–Aug. 1833 with Watson publishing *Working Man's Friend.*
Late 1833 working with Penny on the *People's Police Gazette.*
Feb. 1834–Oct. 1836 launched his own broadsheet *Weekly Police Gazette.* Registered a Press.
Apr. 1834, fined but Hibbert insisted on paying fines.
May 1834 sentenced to 3 months at Giltspur St., Compter, for selling *WPG.*
June 34 fined £100 in Court of Exchequer prosecution; Aug. 1835, presses seized.
Feb. 1836 charged with fines of £600.

Mar. 1836 imprisoned for portering the Unstamped; freed April because of Exchequer prosecution.

1839 London delegate.

Mar. 1842 treasurer Convention Fund, NCA, and agent for NCA journals.

BENJAMIN COUSINS

Printer and publisher of the Unstamped, 18 Duke St., Lincolns Inn Fields.

Dec. 1831 fined £10 for selling cotton almanacs.

Sept. 1833 goods seized for assessed taxes.

Nov. 1833–July 1834, printing and publishing London edition of *Pioneer*.

Launched *Political Register*, c. July 1834–Aug. 1835.

Apr. 1835 fined £20 for selling *Register*.

Aug. 1835 registered a press.

Mar. 1836 accused of inciting a mob to attack the informer, Dean.

July 1836 launching broadsheet *Weekly Herald* and *Weekly Chronicle*. Alive in 1876.

C. COWIE

Printer and publisher of the Unstamped, 312 Strand. Registered a press 1822.

Published *Slap*, and *Church Examiner*, Jan.–Nov. 1832.

Fined £20 for selling *Church Examiner*, June 1832.

Apr. 1834 member of the Society for the Protection of Booksellers.

ALLEN DAVENPORT –1847

1804 a friend of Spence.

Writing verses, pamphlets, articles in Unstamped, especially for *Man*, *Guardian*, *Prompter*, and *Bonnet Rouge*.

Supporter of Lovett's New Move.

GEORGE EDMONDS of 2 Tavistock Road, Covent Garden

A free-lance contributor to the Unstamped, writing for the quarto *Bonnet Rouge*, 1833, and the broadsheet *People's Weekly Police Gazette* and *Weekly Herald* in 1836.

Edited the later numbers of *Cab*.

1831 wrote 'The English Revolution', which the chief magistrate of Bow St. described as 'execrable trash'. Registered a press May 1832.

1836 wrote 'An Appeal to the Labourers of England . . .'.

An advocate of St. Simonianism in the NUWC, and a lecturer for it.

HENRY HETHERINGTON 1792–1849

Printer, publisher, and bookseller, of 27 Kingsgate St., Holborn.

Son of a Soho tailor, apprenticed 1805 to Luke Hansard; 1812 to
  c. 1815 working in Belgium.
1821 joined first co-operative printers society in London, and Mudie's
  discussion circle.
1822 registered his own press.
1824 on committee of Mechanics Institute.
Member of Freethinking Christians from which he and the Savage
  brothers were expelled in 1828.
1828 joined Civil and Religious Liberty Association, which became
  the Radical Reform Association and then the Metropolitan Political
  Union.
Joined First London Co-operative Trading Association, which in
  1829 became the BAPCK.
Helped to launch the Metropolitan Trades Union which became the
  NUWC Apr. 1831.
Oct. 1830 started the *Penny Papers*, which in July 1831 became the
  PMG.
Mar. 1831 published *Republican*, edited by Lorymer.
June 1831 tried for selling *Republican*; toured the country.
Aug. 1831 published *Radical*, edited by Lorymer.
Sept. 1831–Mar. 1832 imprisoned in Clerkenwell.
Nov. 1832 touring midlands.
Dec. 1832–June 1833 imprisoned in Clerkenwell.
Feb. 1833 launched *Destructive*, edited by O'Brien.
May 1833 prosecuted for 'Palafox' letter which became the Court of
  Exchequer trial of June 1834, in which the *PMG* was declared to
  be not a newspaper, but in which he was fined for the *Destructive*.
May 1834 moved from Kingsgate St. to 126 Strand.
Aug. 1834 fined £40 for selling the *Twopenny Dispatch*.
For much of 1835 hiding in the country.
Aug. 1835 presses seized in lieu of fines.
Feb. 1836 imprisoned until fines paid in May 1836.
Continued the *London Dispatch* until the end of 1837; published the
  Oddfellow and other papers. Represented London and Stockport
  at the Chartist Convention. Supported Lovett's New Move;
  attended the Complete Suffrage conferences in 1842. Became
  prominent at John's Street Institution, became a Guardian of the
  Poor.
Died of cholera.

JULIAN HIBBERT *c.* 1800–34
Radical philanthropist, and Greek scholar, of 35 Upper Norton St.,
  Fitzroy Sq.

Second of three brothers whose fortunes were made in the West Indies; Catholic; educated at Eton and Cambridge. Befriended Watson in 1826.

Supposed to have spent upwards of £5,000 helping Carlile from 1825 on.

Main prop of Victim Fund; subscriber to the *True Sun*; a class leader of the NUWC.

Author of notorious 'Palafox' letter to the *PMG*, May 1833.

His private papers burnt at his death. In his will, left Hetherington and Watson 450 gns. each, and paid Cleave's fines.

The one wealthy man in the world of the Unstamped.

RICHARD LEE 1809–   of 31 Marylebone Lane

Printer (who worked with a hand press in his own house), co-operator and member of the NU.

June 1832 printed Benbow's *Tribune*; summoned for publishing Petrie's 'Equality.'

May 1833 prominent at Cold Bath Fields affray. Wrote 'A Whisper to the Whigs, or what is Treason'.

July 1833–Aug. 1834 edited and printed *Man*.

Mar. 1834 launched broadsheet *People's Hue and Cry*.

Apr. 1834 member of Society for Protection of Booksellers.

June 1834 sentenced to six months in Clerkenwell for the *Man*.

1839–41 London correspondent to the *Northern Star*; printed *English Chartist Circular*.

1840 looked after Cleave's business during his imprisonment.

1836 registered a press at 6 Catharine St., Strand.

Dec. 1849 registered a press in Drury Lane.

JAMES BADEN LORYMER of 14 Melton Place, Euston Sq.

'Quite a young man of respectable appearance' (HO 64/11, 7 July 31) and thought to have been a barrister. Writer: pen name 'Ichneumon Scrutator'.

Mar. 1831 edited Hetherington's *Republican*.

Aug. 1831 edited *Radical*. Summer 1831 suspected of being a spy.

Member of the NUWC from its commencement.

Aug. 1832 edited *Laughing Philosopher*.

Oct. 1832 'the agent of Lord Kinnoull' of Perthshire. (*Rep.*, 27 Oct. 1832)

Dec. 1832 established Society for Promotion of Republican Knowledge, tract and reprint society.

Feb. 1833 edited *Bonnet Rouge* from 336 Strand.

Spring 1833 published *Reformer*, a 4d. evening newspaper.

May 1833 represented as bookseller and publisher of 5 Brydges St.

Refused to pay church rates, assessed taxes; advocate of National Convention.

His *Republican* circulating into the summer of 1834.

July 1833 established Republican Society for which lectured; office at 378 Strand.

1838 translated Lamennais's 'Book of the People', which he was selling at 188 Strand.

May 1839 writing to the *London Democrat* on the Charter.

THOMAS CHARLES WILSON MAYHEW *c.* 1808–34

Writer. As a 'young law student at Lincoln's Inn' wrote in 1828, 'A Complete History of an Action at Law . . .', of which Hetherington purchased the copyright, and whereby he came to Hetherington's notice. (*Penny Papers*, 7 Oct. 1830.)

Oct. 1830 edited *Penny Papers*.

July 1831 edited *PMG*, probably till Dec. 1831 when he may have joined Gilbert A'Beckett in publishing *Figaro in London*; collaborated with A'Beckett on other popular works such as the Diamond Shakespeare, etc.

Oct. 1834 committed suicide when he was unable to meet a printer's bill.

Probably the eldest of the Mayhew brothers.

(C. H. Timperly, *Encyclopedia of Literary and Typographical Anecdote*, 1842; Vizetelly, p. 218; *Scourge*, 31 Dec. 1834.)

JAMES BRONTERRE O'BRIEN 1805–64 of Arundel St., Strand

Writer. 1822 Trinity College, Dublin; 1830 Grey's Inn.

1830 contributing to Carpenter's *Letters*.

Nov. 1830 attending Rotunda as 'an Attorney's assistant'. (HO 64/11, 29 Nov.)

1831–summer 1832 edited *Midland Representative*; worked with Pare in Birmingham co-operation. Late summer possibly worked on the *True Sun*.

Sept. 1832 edited *PMG*; from Feb. 1833 edited *Destructive*.

Oct. 1832 member of S. Metropolitan Political Union.

Sept. 1836 writing for Bell's *London Mercury* as finally quarrelled with Hetherington.

Published a series of papers through the 1840s and 1850s including the *Operative*, *Southern Star*, the *National Reformer*, etc.

Prominent in all stages of Chartism.

(G. D. H. Cole, *Chartist Portraits*, 1966 edn.)

CHARLES PENNY of 110 Chancery Lane.

Stationer and publisher.

1833–May 1834 published *People's Police Gazette*.
Feb. 1834 fined £120; goods levied in lieu May 1834.
Apr. 1834 member of Society for Protection of Booksellers.
1835 published *Weekly Times*.

GEORGE PETRIE 1792–1836

Writer. Scots tailor, served in Peninsula war under Wellington, where wounded.
Republican Owenite, and part-Spencean.
Summer 1832 lecturing at NU; published 'Equality' and other poems.
Spring 1833 advocating National Convention.
From July 1833 writing regularly for *Man* as 'Agrarius'.
Winter 1834 working with Robert Guthrie on behalf of the tailor's unions.
Mar. 1834 missionary for GNCTU.
July 1834 tried to rescue *Man* when Lee imprisoned.
Sept. 1834 registered a press of his own.
Unstable and probably became insane. 'One of the most violent of the members.' (Add. MSS. 27797, f. 15.)

BENJAMIN STEILL

Publisher and printer, of 20 Paternoster Row.
1817 published Wooler's *Black Dwarf*, and had to give recognisances for good behaviour.
1820 registered a press; registered a second press in 1828.
Published numerous small Unstamped in the 1830s.
1848 paid T. Cooper £2 p.w. to write and edit the *Plain Speaker*.

WILLIAM STRANGE

Bookseller and publisher, of 21 Paternoster Row.
Registered a common press with Cowie and Clements in 1822; registered again in 1835.
Worked with Carpenter.
Apr. 1834 member of Society for Protection of Booksellers.

JAMES WATSON 1799–1874

Bookseller, printer, and publisher, of 33 Windmill St., Finsbury Sq.
Yorkshireman who came to London in 1822 as one of Carlile's shopmen.
April 1823 sentenced to Cold Bath Fields.
1824–5 working as compositor for *Republican*.
1826–8 seriously ill with cholera and typhus, rescued by Hibbert who employed him in printing his Greek books.

Co-operator and in 1828 storekeeper at Red Lion Sq., 1829 storekeeper at Jerusalem Passage.

1830 touring north for co-operative movement. Moved to Finsbury
Sq. where used Baume's Optimist chapel for radical meetings.

1831 printer and publisher when Hibbert gave him his presses;
registered them.

Leading member NUWC.

Dec. 1832–Aug. 1833 launched *Working Man's Friend* with Cleave.

Feb. 1833–Aug. 1833 in Clerkenwell for selling *PMG*.

End 1833 moved to Hall of Science, City Rd., of which became
custodian.

Bookseller.

Aug. 1834–Jan. 1835 in Clerkenwell for selling *Destructive*.

1836–9 working with WMA.

Aiding Jones, Cooper, and Holyoake in 1840s and 1850s. Retired
as bookseller 1854.

Working with refugees, friend of Mazzini, Cowen, W. E. Adams, etc.

(W. J. Linton, *James Watson* . . . 1879.)

BIBLIOGRAPHY

MANUSCRIPTS

Birmingham Public Library, *Lovett Collection*
Bishopsgate Institute, *Howell Collection*
British Museum, *Place Papers*, Additional Manuscripts, 27789, 27790,
  27791, 27792, 27793, 27794, 27795, 27796, 27797, 27809, 27810,
  27819, 27820, 27821, 27822, 27823, 27824, 27827, 27835, 27844,
  35145, 35146, 35147, 35148, 35149, 35150, 35151, 35154, 37949,
  37950
British Museum, Place Newspaper Collection, Sets 17, 57, 61, 65, 70, 75
Cooperative Union Library, Manchester, *Owen Collection*
Cooperative Union Library, Manchester, *Holyoake Collection*
Huntington Library, San Marino, California, *Carlile Collection*
Public Record Office, *Russell Papers*
St. Bride's Collection, London
University of London, *Pare Collection*
University College, London, *Brougham Collection*
  Chadwick Collection
  S.D.U.K. Papers

PUBLIC RECORD OFFICE PAPERS

HOME OFFICE
*HO 40/25, 27, 29, 30, 31, 32, 33, 34 (in-letters, civil disturbance)
HO 41/8, 9, 10, 11, 12, 26 (London out-books)
HO 43/43 (exit books to rural areas)
HO 49/7 (law officers 1817–34)
HO 59/3, 4, 5, 6, 7 (courts—pensions, reports, appointments)
HO 60/2 (copy book, exit letters)
HO 61/2, 3, 4, 5, 6, 7, 8, 9, 10, 11, 12, 13, 14, 15, 16 (police—metropolitan
  correspondence)
HO 62/7, 10 (printed daily police reports)
*HO 64/3, 4, 5, 6, 8, 11, 12, 13, 14, 15, 16, 17, 18, 19 (secret service,
  including seditious publications)
HO 65/11, 12 (exit copy books on police organization)
HO 75/5, 8 (*Hue and Cry*)
*HO 79/4 (exit copy book, civil disturbance)
HO 119/16, 17 (law reports on special cases)

METROPOLITAN POLICE PAPERS
Mepol 1/44, vol. 1 (Commissioners')

* Most useful.

Mepol 1/49, 50 (Bow St.—H.O. correspondence)
Mepol 2/59 (meetings and demonstrations)
Mepol 2/70 (general correspondence)

TREASURY PAPERS
T22/20, 26, 27

PUBLIC RECORDS

Corporation of London Record Office, Printers Notices
                                    Giltspur Street prison records
                                    Southwark Compter records
Guildhall Library, Mansion House charge books, 1832–3
Guildhall Library Muniment Room, Cold Bath Fields gaol delivery, 1832
Middlesex County Record Office, Printers Notices
Somerset House, Hetherington's will
Stationers' Hall, Apprentices' Register, Masters and Apprentices Calendar
    1763–1807
Surrey County Record Office, Kingston House of Correction records

PARLIAMENTARY PAPERS

Hansard
Accounts and Papers 1831–2 xxxiv   (press prosecutions)
                      1833   xxix   (,,   ,,   )
                      1834   xlvii   (,,   ,,   )
                      1835   xlvi   (case of Joseph Forster)
                      1836   xli   (press prosecutions)
                      1831–2 xxxiv   (newspaper stamps)
                      1833   xxxii   (London newspaper stamps)
                      1840   xxix   (newspaper stamps)
                      1842   xxvi   (,,   ,,   )
                      1851   xvii appx. 4 (,,   ,,   )
Reports
Select Committee on Cold Bath Fields meeting   1833   xiii
Select Committee on the Stationery Contract   1833   xvi
Select Committee on the petition of Frederick Young
    and others . . . (Popay case)   1833   xiii
Royal Commission on Factories   1833   xx
Commissioners of the Poor Laws   1834   xxxiv
Select Committee on Intoxication   1834   viii
Select Committee on the Handloom Weavers' Petition   1834   x
Select Committee on the Police of the Metropolis   1834   xvi
Select Committee on Education   1835   vii
Select Committee on the Education of the Poorer Classes 1837–8 vii
Select Committee on Fourdrinier's Patent   1837   xx
Select Committee on Combinations   1837–8 viii

Asst Commissioners on the Handloom Weavers	1840	xxiii
Asst Commissioners on the Handloom Weavers	1840	xxiv
Select Committee on Public Libraries	1849	xvii
Select Committee on Newspaper Stamps	1851	xvii

PERIODICALS

Published in London unless otherwise stated.

Located in the *British Union Catalogue of Periodicals*, unless otherwise located within square brackets [ ].

The unbracketed dates are those issues which have been consulted.

Description:

Br.	broadsheet		O	Owenite
C	co-operative		P	parliamentary
Cr	crime reporter		R	radical
D	attacked established church		T	theatrical
	and established religion		TU	trade union, NAPL, etc.
H	humorous		U	useful knowledge
L	literary		X	religious

THE PAPERS OF 1819

Black Dwarf (Wooler)	4*d*., 6*d*.	28 Jan. 1817–5 Nov. 1823	R
Cap of Liberty (James Griffin)	2*d*.	8 Sep. 1819–4 Jan. 1820	R
Gorgon (John Wade)	1*d*.	23 May 1818–Apr. 1819	R
Medusa (T. Davidson)	1*d*.	20 Feb. 1819–7 Jan. 1820	R
Register (Cobbett)	2*d*., 6*d*.	12 Oct. 1816–29 July 1820 1 Dec. 1827–1 Dec. 1835	R
Republican (Carlile and Julian St. John 1819–20)	2*d*., 6*d*.	24 Sept 1819–29 Dec. 1826	R; D
Shadgett's Weekly Review	4*d*.	1 Feb. 1818	Tory
White Dwarf (Merle and Shadgett)	4*d*.	29 Nov. 1817–28 Apr. 1818	Tory
Wooler's British Gazette	8½*d*.	31 Jan. 1819–29 Aug. 1819	R

PAPERS OF THE 1820S

Associate [Bishopsgate Institute]	1*d*.	1 Jan. 1829–1 Jan. 1830	C
Birmingham Co-operative Herald	1*d*.	1 Apr. 1829–1 Sep. 1829	C
Co-operator (King of Brighton) [Bishopsgate Institute]	1*d*.	1 May 1828–1 Aug. 1830	C
Economist (G. Mudie)	3*d*.	27 Jan. 1821–1 Dec. 1821	C; O
Lion (Carlile)	6*d*.	4 Jan. 1828–25 Dec. 1829	R; D
Mechanics Magazine (Robertson; Hodgskin)	3*d*.	30 Aug. 1823–18 Sept. 1824	R; TU

Trades Newspaper   7d.   17 July 1825–
  (Became *Trades Free*   7d.   29 July 1827–
    Press)
  (Became *Weekly Free*   7d.   23 Aug. 1828–19 Mar. 1831   R; C; TU
    Press (ed. Carpenter))

UNSTAMPED PAPERS 1830–6

Though this list attempts to cover all London radical papers, it excludes many provincial and 'useful knowledge' or literary papers.

Very many of the papers listed in the *British Union Catalogue of Periodicals* as held by the British Museum were destroyed during the war.

Advocate or Artizans and   1d.   16 Feb. 1833–20 Apr. 1833   TU
  Labourers Friend (ed. J.
  Williams, for the
  Printers Protection
  Society)
Agitator (Glasgow)   1d.   9 Mar. 1833–13 Apr. 1833   R
Agitator and Political   1d., 2d.   ? Nov. 1833–? Dec. 1833   R
  Anatomist (Benbow)
Annals of Crime   1d.   24 Aug. 1833–7 Sept. 1834   Cr
Antichrist (the Revd. J.   3d.   1832–3   D
  Smith)
Antiquarian   1d.   26 May 1832   U
Argus   1d.   6 Oct. 1832–13 Oct. 1832   L

Barber's Journal   1d.   4 Apr. 1835   R; H
Bee (Falvey and Finch,   1d.   22 Dec. 1832   R
  Liverpool)
Benefit Societies Magazine   3d.   1 Nov. 1834–1 Dec. 1834
Benefit Societies Penny   1d.   17 Nov. 1832
  Magazine
Berthold's National   ?   July 1830   R
  Guardian [HO 64/17]
Berthold's Political   4d.   5 Sept. 1831–15 Oct. 1831   R
  Handkerchief [HO 64/17]
Birmingham Labour Ex-   1d.   16 Jan. 1833–9 Feb. 1833   O; TU
  change Gazette
Bonnet Rouge (Lorymer)   1d.   2 Feb. 1833–30 Mar.   R
  [first number in Cole   (to 13 Apr. 1833)
  Coll., Oxford]
Brazen Head (Liverpool)   1d.   15 Feb. 1834   R; T
Brazen Mask   1d.   1 Mar. 1833   D
Bristol Job Nott   1½d.   15 Dec. 1831–26 Dec. 1833   X; tory
Bristol Policeman   1½d.   6 Aug. 1836–4 Feb. 1837   Cr
British Labourer's Pro-   ½d.   21 Sept. 1832–19 Apr. 1833   R; TU
  tector and Factory
  Child's Friend (Leeds)
  [Cole Coll., Oxford]
British Mirror   1½d.   4 Apr. 1836   L

Cab (publ. Berger, Cowie; later numbers ed. G. Edmonds) [Birmingham Public Library]	½*d.*	3 Mar. 1832–21 Apr. 1832 (to 7 July 1832)	R; H
Calendar of Crime	1*d.*	17 Mar. 1832	Cr
Carlile's Cotton Handkerchief	3*d.*	Dec. 1831	R
Carlile's Journal	?	1–21 Jan. 1830	R
Carpenter's London Journal	2*d.*	13 Feb. 1836 (to Mar. 1836)	R
Carpenter's Political Magazine	?	1 Sept. 1831–1 July 1832	R
*Chambers' Edinburgh Journal	1½*d.*	4 Feb. 1832–30 Jan. 1836 (to 1854)	U
Chambers' Historical Newspaper (Edinburgh)	1½*d.*	2 Nov. 1832	U
Chester Co-operative Chronicle [Bishopsgate Institute]	1*d.*	10 July 1830–1 Oct. 1830	C
Christian Corrector (ed. T. Parkin) [HO 64/18]	1½*d.*	(*c.* Apr. 1831)–2 May 1832	R; D
Christian Investigator (ed. E. Gotch)	1*d.*	1 July 1833	X
Christian's Penny Magazine	1*d.*	9 June 1832	X; U
Chronicler of the Times (ed. H. Record)	1*d.*	12 Jan. 1833	R
Church and State	2*d.*	16 Jan. 1836	R; D
Church Examiner see *Slap at the Church*			
Cleave's Weekly Police Gazette [incomplete; cuttings in Place Newspaper Coll.]	2*d.*	(Spring 1834)–1 Oct. 1836	R; Br
Cobbett's Twopenny Trash	2*d.*	July 1830–June 1832	R
Comet (Falvey of Liverpool)	1*d.*	4 Aug. 1832–8 Sept. 1832	R; L
Common Sense (A. Poplett) [HO 40/25]	2*d.*	20 Nov. 1830–25 Dec. 1830	R
Companion to the Newspaper	2*d.*	1 Mar. 1833–1 Apr. 1836	U
Conductor (ed. T. Macconnell)	1*d.*	17 Sept. 1836	R
Corn Law Magazine (publ. Steill)	1*d.*	4 Jan. 1834	
Cosmopolite (vendors; Carlile) [HO 64/19 and Newcastle C. L.]	1½*d.*	10 Mar. 1832–23 Nov. 1833	R
Crisis (Owen; the Revd. J. Smith)	1*d.*, 1½*d.*	14 Apr. 1832–23 Aug. 1834	O
Critical Figaro of Paris and London (publ. Steill)	3*d.*	21 Jan. 1832–4 Feb. 1832	R; H

* Most important papers.

Daily Politician	1*d.*	25 Jan. 1836 (to 25 Apr. 1836)	P
*Destructive (ed. O'Brien; publ. Hetherington)	2*d.*	2 Feb. 1833–	R
(Became) *People's Conservative and Trade Union Gazette*		14 Dec. 1833–	
(Became) *Twopenny Dispatch and People's Political Register* [incomplete; cuttings in Place Newspaper Coll.]		14 June 1834–	Br.
(Became) *London Dispatch* [St. Bride's]	3½*d.*	17 Sept. 1836	
Devil in London [HO 64/18]	1*d.*	29 Feb. 1832–	R; H
(Became) *Ashmodeus*	1*d.*	12 May 1832–	
(Became) *Ashmodeus in London*	1*d.*	–10 Nov. 1832	
Devil's Menagerie (W. Chubb)	1*d.*	n.d. 1832	R
Devil's Pulpit (the Revd. Robert Taylor; Carlile) [HO 64/18]	2*d.*	4 Mar. 1831–20 Jan. 1832	D
Devil's Walk (publ. Steill)	1*d.*	17 Feb. 1832	R; H
Dibdin's Penny Trumpet	1*d.*	20 Oct. 1832–27 Oct. 1832	H
Dicky Sam (Liverpool)	1½*d.*	26 Feb. 1835–26 Mar. 1835	H; tory
Doctor	1*d.*	1832–7	U
English Figaro (publ. Berger)	1*d.*	21 Jan. 1832–28 Jan. 1832	R; H
Entertaining Press [HO 64/18]	1*d.*	Nov. 1831–1 Feb. 1832	P
Episcopal Gazette (publ. Strange)	2*d.*	1 Mar. 1832	D
Evangelical Penny Magazine	1*d.*	13 Oct. 1832 (to 15 Dec. 1832)	X
Everyman's Paper of Useful and Entertaining Knowledge	3*d.*	14 July 1832	U
Figaro	1*d.*	23 Jan. 1836	R; H
Figaro in Liverpool (J. Pannell)	1*d.*	14 Jan. 1833	H
Figaro in London (G. A'Beckett, possibly Th. Mayhew and later Henry Mayhew)	1*d.*	10 Dec. 1831–19 Oct. 1832 (to 1839)	
Figaro in Sheffield	1*d.*	(1832–8)	R; H
Figaro's Life in London	2*d.*	26 Mar. 1836	R; H
Fly (printed Hetherington)	2*d.*	28 Oct. 1832	H
*Gauntlet (Carlile)	3*d.*	10 Feb. 1833–30 Mar. 1834	R; D
Giovanni in London (publ. Steill)	1*d.*	18 Feb. 1832–24 Mar. 1832	R; H

* Most important papers.

God's Revenge against Murder	1*d.*	27 Apr. 1833	L; X
Halfpenny Library	½*d.*	4 May 1832–26 June 1832	U
Halfpenny Magazine	½*d.*	5 May 1832–9 June 1832	L
Halfpenny Magazine and Witness (Leeds)	½*d.*	1 July 1832–25 Dec. 1832	X
Herald of the Rights of Industry (Manchester, ed. Doherty)	1*d.*	8 Feb. 1834–24 May 1834	TU
Herald to the Trades Advocate (Glasgow)	2*d.*	25 Sept. 1830–28 May 1831	TU; R
Hoxton Sausage		1–2 n.d. (Aug. 1832 ?)	R; TU
Hull Portfolio (James Acland) [Hull P.L.]	2*d.*	20 Aug. 1831–Dec. 1832	R
Hunt's Addresses [HO 64/18]	?	20 Oct. 1831–9 Jan. 1832	R
Idler (publ. Strange)	1*d.*	24 May 1832	L
Illuminator (Liverpool)	1½*d.*, 2*d.*	7 Jan. 1835–23 Mar. 1836	X
Isis (E. Sharples; Carlile)	6*d.*	11 Feb. 1832–15 Dec. 1832	R
Kidd's London Journal (W. Kidd)	1½*d.*	23 May 1835	R; L
Lancashire and Yorkshire Co-operator [Bishopsgate Institute]	1*d.*, 2*d.*	11 June 1832–1 Nov. 1832	C
Lancashire Conservative (Manchester)	2*d.*	30 July 1836	Tory
Lancashire Omnibus (Liverpool)	1*d.*	8 Mar. 1832	L
Laughing Philosopher (Lorymer)	1*d.*	28 July 1832 (to 25 Aug. 1832)	R; H
Lawyer	1*d.*	26 Jan. 1833 (to 16 Mar. 1833)	U
Leporello in Liverpool	2*d.*	24 Dec. 1835	L
Liar (J. Ward)	1*d.*	6 Aug. 1836	R; H
Life in London	1*d.*	1–2 n.d. (Mar. 1832 ?)	R; H
Literary Beacon (publ. Steill) [St. Bride's]	3*d.*, 6*d.*	(18 June–24 Sept. 1831)	L
Literary Guardian	2*d.*	1 Oct. 1831 (to 28 July 1832)	L
Literary Test (publ. Steill)	2*d.*	1 Jan. 1832 (to 28 Jan. 1832)	L; R
Liverpool Thesbian Register	1*d.*	15 June 1836	T
London Penny Journal (N. Burney; publ. Strange)	1*d.*	12 May 1832–7 July 1832	U
London Policeman (publ. C. Penny)	1*d.*	6 July 1833 (to 28 Dec. 1833)	R; Cr
London Spy (publ. W. Chubb)	2*d.*	(14 May 1831)–24 Nov. 1832	L; U

London Star (publ. James Reeve) [Cole Coll.]	?	20 Apr. 1834	R
London Telegraph (publ. Steill)	2*d*.	17 Aug. 1832	U
Lord Mayor's Fool	1½*d*.	25 July 1835	R; H
Magazine of Interest	1*d*.	31 Aug. 1833	U
Magazine of Useful Knowledge and Co-operative Miscellany (Carpenter)	2*d*.	1 Oct. 1830–13 Nov. 1830	C
Magnet (publ. Berger)	1*d*.	14 July 1832	U
*Man (R. Lee) (in 1834, Br.) [HO 64/19; HO 64/15]	1*d*., 2*d*.	7 July 1833–13 July 1834	R
Mirror for Magistrates (John Bell)	2*d*.	16 Apr. 1836	R; Br
Modern Times	1*d*.	24 Mar. 1832	R
Monthly Political Register (John Bell)	2*d*.	2 Apr. 1836	R; Br
National Magazine (publ. Steill)	1*d*.	5 Oct. 1833 (to 1834)	U
National Omnibus (ed. F. Bayley)	1*d*.	1 Apr. 1831–18 Oct. 1833	U
New Casket (publ. Strange)	1*d*.	(*c.* 1831–*c.* 1834)	L
New Entertaining Press [St. Bride's]	1*d*.	25 Jan. 1832–3 Oct. 1832	U
New Figaro	1*d*.	17 Mar. 1832–31 Mar. 1832	R; H
New Moral World and Manual of Science (ed. Owen)	1*d*.	1 Nov. 1834–8 July 1837 (to 1845)	O
New Moral World and Official Gazette (publ. Cousins)	1½*d*.	30 Aug. 1834	O
New Penny Magazine (publ. Strange)	1*d*.	22 Sept. 1832	U
New Political Register (John Bell)	2*d*.	17 Oct. 1835–7 Nov. 1835	R; Br
New Weekly True Sun (John Bell)	2*d*.	16 Jan. 1836–2 Apr. 1836	R
Official Gazette of the Trades Unions [HO 64/19]	1½*d*.	7 June 1834–28 June 1834	O; TU
Old Bailey Reporter (ed. Curtis)	2*d*.	22 Sept. 1832	Cr
Olio (J. Shackell)	1*d*.	1832 ?	U
Original (publ. Cowie)	3*d*.	3 Mar. 1832 (to 28 July 1832)	L

* Most important papers.

Original (Th. Walker) [Newcastle C.L.]	3*d.*	20 May 1835–19 Aug. 1835	U
Paddy Kelly's Budget (Dublin)	1*d.*	14 Nov. 1832–*c.* Aug. 1833	H
*Pamphlets for the People (J. Roebuck) [Cole Coll.]	1½*d.*, 2*d.*	8 June 1835–*c.* Feb. 1836	R
Parnassus (Liverpool)	1*d.*	4 July 1832	U
Parochial Herald	1*d.*	16 Jan. 1836	Tory
Parrot	2*d.*	14 Jan. 1832–2 June 1832	U
Patriot	2*d.*	27 Aug. 1831; 4 Feb. 1832	R; L
Penny Lancet (publ. Berger)	1*d.*	3 Oct. 1832–24 Oct. 1832	U
*Penny Magazine (Ch. Knight)	1*d.*	21 Mar. 1832–Dec. 1836 (to 1845)	U
*Penny Papers for the People (Th. Mayhew; publ. Hetherington) [Bishopsgate Institute; HO 64/11; HO 64/17; 40/25]	1*d.*	1 Oct.–23 Nov. 1830; 25 Dec. 1830–2 July 1831	R
Penny Satirist (Dublin) [Rylands L., Manchester]	1*d.*	2 Jan. 1835–8 Jan. 1836	U
Phrenologist	2*d.*	16 Feb. 1833	U
People's Hue and Cry (Lee) [HO 64/15]	1*d.*	(Mar. 1834)–13 July 1834	R; Br
People's Parliamentary Reporter [Cole Coll.]	2*d.*	19 Apr. 1834	P
People's Police Gazette (C. Penny) [HO 64/19]	2*d.*	(1833)–3 May 1834	R; Br
People's Press (ed. Ch. Riley) [HO 64/18]	4*d.*	(11 Dec.)–17 Dec. 1830	P
People's Weekly Dispatch [HO 40/33]	2*d.*	(1835)–Nov. 1835; May 1836	R; Br
People's Weekly Police Gazette (publ. Cousins)	2*d.*	(1834)–Dec. 1835; May 1836	R; Br
Physician	1*d.*	3 Nov. 1832–10 Nov. 1832	U
*Pioneer (James Morrison, Birmingham)	1*d.*	7 Sept. 1833–5 July 1834	O; TU
Police Gazette or Hue and Cry (Stafford) [HO 75]	4*d.*	1830–6	
Political Anecdotist (Carpenter)	2*d.*	18 June 1831–9 July 1831	R
Political Investigator	2*d.*	9 June 1832–7 July 1832	R
*Political Letters (Carpenter)	4*d.*	9 Oct. 1830–14 May 1831	R
Political Penny Magazine [Cole Coll.]	1*d.*	3 Sept. 1836–17 Sept. 1836	R
Political Register (Cousins) [HO 40/33]	2*d.*	–Aug. 1835–	R; Br

* Most important papers.

Political Soldier (Somerville; Carlile) [HO 64/19]	1½*d*.	7 Dec. 1833–14 Dec. 1833	R
Political Unionist (ed. Carpenter; publ. Strange)	2*d*.	30 June 1832–7 July 1832	R
Poor Man's Advocate (Doherty, Manchester)	1*d*.	21 Jan. 1832–8 Dec. 1832 (to 5 Jan. 1833)	R; TU
*Poor Man's Guardian (ed. Thomas Mayhew; Phipps; O'Brien; publ. Hetherington)	1*d*.	9 July 1831–26 Dec. 1835	R
Poor Richard's Journal	2*d*.	24 Nov. 1832–8 Dec. 1832	U
Prodigy	1*d*.	2 Aug. 1833	U
*Prompter (Carlile)	3*d*.	13 Nov. 1830–12 Nov. 1831	R; D
Public Communicator and General Advertizer	3*d*.	14 Jan. 1832	U
Punch in London (D. Jerrold)	1*d*.	14 Jan. 1832–14 Apr. 1832	R; H
Punchinello (Th. Hood)	1*d*.	20 Jan. 1832–*c*. Mar. 1832	L; H
Quartern Loaf	1*d*.	4 Jan. 1834	Anti-corn law
Quiz	1*d*.	4 Feb. 1836	H
Quizzical Gazette (ed. J. Mitford)	1*d*.	27 Aug. 1831–14 Jan. 1832	H
*Radical (Hetherington; Lorymer)	1*d*.	20 Aug. 1831–	R
(Became) *Radical Reformer*		15 Oct. 1831–12 Jan. 1832	R
Radical Register (Liverpool)	1*d*.	20 Feb. 1835	R
Rationalist (Hetherington; Cousins)	1*d*.	1–2 (1830)	D
Reformer (Liverpool)	2*d*.	6 Aug. 1835	R
Reformer or Schoolmaster Abroad (Berger)	2*d*.	2 June 1832–15 June 1832	R
Reformer (Lorymer)	1*d*.	–15 Mar. 1833–	R
Reformer (Lorymer) [HO 64/19; HO 64/15]	4*d*.	12 May 1833 (to Feb. 1834)	R
Regenerator (Berthold)	?	1 Aug. 1832	R
*Republican (Lorymer; Hetherington)	½*d*.	26 Mar. 1831–1 Feb. 1832	R
(Became) *Republican and Radical Reformer*	1*d*.	–27 Oct. 1832–	R
Republican (Lorymer) [HO 64/19]	1½*d*.	–Apr. 1833; Apr. 1834	R
Rover	2*d*.	7 Dec. 1833–26 Apr. 1834	L
Salford Patriot (B. Hackett)	1*d*.	16 Feb. 1833–23 Feb. 1833 (23 Mar.)	R
Satchel	1*d*.	5 Mar. 1831–30 Apr. 1831	H

* Most important papers.

Saturday Magazine	1*d.*	June 1832 (to 1844)	X; U
Schoolmaster at Home (publ. Steill)	1*d.*	9 June 1832–14 July 1832	R
Scourge (Carlile) [Manchester P. L.]	1*d.*	4 Oct. 1834–21 Feb. 1835	R
Scourge or Public Censor (publ. Berger)	1*d.*	22 June 1833	L
Scrap Book	1*d.*	23 Apr. 1831–18 Aug. 1832	L
Shepherd (the Revd. J. E. Smith)	1*d.*	30 Aug. 1834 (to 1838)	D
Sketch Writer (publ. Strange)	1½*d.*	20 July 1832–3 Aug. 1832	L
Slap at the Church (Carpenter, Cleave; Cowie)	1*d.*	21 Jan. 1832–	R; D
(Became) *Church Examiner* [HO 64/18]	1*d.*	19 May 1832–1 Nov. 1832	R; D
Spirit of the Press (publ. Berger)	1*d.*	12 May 1832	U
Squib (Cowie, Strange)	1*d.*	13 July 1832–20 July 1832	R; H
Stage	1*d.*	1 July 1833	T
Sunday Chronicle	1*d.*	15 July 1832	L
Sunday Herald (publ. Cowie)	1*d.*	15 July 1832	R
Tartar	1*d.*	12 Dec. 1835	Tory
Tatler	1*d.*; 3*d.*	4 Sept. 1830–6 Oct. 1832	L
Thief [HO 64/18)	2*d.*	21 Apr. 1832–5 May 1832 (–Nov. 1833)	L
Tickler or Dramatic Intelligencer	1*d.*	28 Oct. n.d.	T
True Halfpenny Magazine	½*d.*	4 May 1832–13 July 1832	U
Truth (pr. Hetherington, publ. Strange)	1*d.*	22 Aug. 1832–29 Aug. 1832	R; L
Union (Carlile)	2*d.*	26 Nov. 1831–28 Jan. 1832	R
Union Pilot (Manchester)	1*d.*	(*c.* Jan. 1832)–5 May 1832	R; TU
United Trades Cooperative Journal (Doherty of Manchester) [HO 64/18]	2*d.*	6 Mar. 1830–24 July 1830	R; TU
Voice from the Commons (Th. Wakley)	2*d.*	23 Apr. 1836–28 May 1836	R
Voice of the West Riding (Joshua Hobson of Huddersfield) [HO 64/19; HO 40/32; /31]	1*d.*	1 June 1833–12 Apr. 1834	R; TU
Walker's Political Touchwood [HO 59/3]	?	Feb. 1832	R
Wanderer (publ. Cousins)	1½*d.*	1 Dec. 1832	L
Wasp (Birmingham)	1*d.*	14 July–13 Oct. 1832	R

* Most important papers.

Watchman's Lantern (Manchester)	1½*d.*, 2*d.*	17 Dec. 1834–9 Sept. 1835	X
Weekly Chronicle (Cousins)	3*d.*	–19 Sept. 1836	R; Br
Weekly Herald (Cousins)	2½*d.*, 3*d.*	3 July 1836–4 Sept. 1836	R; Br
Weekly Miscellany	1*d.*	7 July 1832 (–Aug. 1832)	U
Weekly Show-Up	1*d.*	30 June 1832–4 Aug. 1832	R; H
Weekly Times (C. Penny)	2*d.*, 2½*d.*	27 Dec. 1835–11 Sept. 1836	R; Br
Weekly Visitor	1*d.*	7 Jan. 1832 (–Apr. 1832)	L
Whig Dresser (publ. Cowie)	1*d.*	5 Jan. 1833–26 Jan. 1833	R
Working Man's Advocate	1*d.*	27 June 1835–8 Aug. 1835	R
*Working Man's Friend (Cleave, Watson)	1*d.*	22 Dec. 1832–3 Aug. 1833	R
Workman's Expositor (Doherty; Manchester)	2*d.*	7 Jan. 1832–14 Jan. 1832	R; TU

STAMPED NEWSPAPERS

(this ignores local papers consulted for specific events)

Ballot (ed. Wakley)	2 Jan. 1831–29 July 1832	R
London Dispatch (publ. Hetherington)	17 Sept. 1836–3 Sept. 1837	R
London Mercury (Bell, O'Brien)	18 Sept. 1836–13 Aug. 1837	R
Midland Representative (O'Brien)	23 Apr. 1831–2 June 1832	R
Morning Chronicle	1830–6	
Morning Herald	1830–6	
Northern Star (O'Connor; Leeds, London)	1837–48	R
Oddfellow (ed. J. Cooke, W. Linton, publ. Hetherington)	5 Jan. 1839–29 May 1841	R
Political Letter (Carpenter)	4 June 1831–13 Aug. 1831	R
Radical	5 June 1831–19 June 1831	R
(Became) *Reformer*	26 June 1831–17 July 1831	R
Radical (ed. A. Beaumont)	13 Mar. 1836–17 July 1836	R
Satirist	Summer 1831	
The Times	1830–6	
True Sun (Bell, Carpenter)	14 Mar. 1832–25 July 1836	R
Truth	10 Feb. 1833–10 Mar. 1833	R
Voice of the People (Doherty; Manchester)	1 Jan. 1831–24 Sept. 1831	R; TU

PERIODICALS (post 1836)

Bronterre's National Reformer	1*d.*	7 Jan. 1837–18 Mar. 1837	R
Carlile's Political Register	2*d.*	19 Oct. 1839–14 Dec. 1839	R
The Charter (ed. Carpenter)	6*d.*	1839–40	R
Chartist	2½*d.*	1839	R

* Most important papers.

Democratic Review (Harney)		June 1849–Mar. 1850	R
Friend of the People (Harney)	1*d.*	7 Dec. 1850–26 July 1851	R
London Democrat (Harney)		4 May 1839–29 June 1839	R
National Reformer (O'Brien)		3 Oct. 1843	R
Poor Man's Guardian and Repealers' Friend (O'Brien, Hetherington)	1*d.*	3 June 1843–26 Aug. 1843	R
Reasoner (Holyoake)		1849–50	R
Red Republican (Harney)	1*d.*	22 June 1850–30 Nov. 1850	R

PRINTED SOURCES—PRIMARY SOURCES
(Published in London unless otherwise stated)

Address to the members of trades unions and to the working classes generally, by a journeyman bootmaker. Reprinted 1833.

The Association of Working Men to procure a cheap and honest press, An Address, 1836.

Bee, 'The present taste for cheap literature', 16 Mar. 1833.

W. BENBOW, *The grand national holiday and congress of the productive classes*, 1831.

—— *The trial of William Benbow and others*, 1832.

H. BROUGHAM, 'Cheap literature for the people', an address to the National Association for the Promotion of Social Science, delivered 12 Oct. 1858.

—— *Practical observations on the education of the people*, 1825.

—— 'Progress of the people', *Edinburgh Review*, Apr. 1833, pp. 239–48.

—— 'Taxes on knowledge', *Edinburgh Review*, Oct. 1835, pp. 126–32.

—— *Taxes on knowledge. Stamps on newspapers. Extracts from the evidence of the Right Honourable Baron Brougham and Vaux, Lord Chancellor, before the Select Committee of the House of Commons on libel law, 14 June 1834*.

—— 'The newspaper tax', *Edinburgh Review*, Apr. 1835, pp. 181–5.

—— 'The Society of Useful Knowledge', *Edinburgh Review*, Oct. 1829.

E. L. BULWER, *Letter to a late Cabinet Minister on the present crisis and a letter from Lord Brougham to Mr. Bulwer, 1834*.

—— 'Journalism', *New Monthly Magazine*, Nov. 1831.

REVD. C. BURGES, *An address to the misguided poor . . .*, 1830.

R. CARLILE, *An address to reformers on the political excitement of the present times*, 1839.

E. CHADWICK, 'The taxes on literature', *Westminster Review*, July 1831, pp. 416–29.

C. G., 'Cheap periodical literature', *Christian Reformer*, vol. xviii, 1832.

P. COLQUHOUN, *A treatise on the population, wealth, power and resources of the British Empire*, 1814 edn.

'The condition of the working classes and the Factory Bill', *Westminster Review*, April 1833.

JOHN CRAWFURD, *A financial and historical review of the taxes which impede the education of the people*, 1836.

JOHN CRAWFURD, *The newspaper stamp and newspaper postage compared*, 1836.
—— 'Democracy', *Quarterly Review*, 1849, vol. lxxxv.
J. DERISLEY, *An address to the National Union of the Working Classes*, 1832.
C. EDMONDS, *An appeal to the labourers of England, an exposure of aristocratic spies, and the infernal machinery of the Poor Law Murder Bill*, . . . 1836.
W. EMPSON, 'Miss Martineau and political economy', *Edinburgh Review*, April 1833, pp. 1–39.
W. J. FOX, *On the parliamentary pledges to be required of candidates at the ensueing elections*, 1832.
J. FULLERTON, 'The condition of the labouring classes', *Quarterly Review*, Jan. 1832, pp. 349–89.
P. GASKELL, *The manufacturing population of England* . . ., 1833.
JOHN GRAY, *A lecture on human happiness*, 1825 (L.S.E. reprint, 1931).
—— *The social system; a treatise on the principle of exchange*, Edinburgh, 1831.
Helot's defense of himself, O'Connell and Catholic emancipation . . ., 1834.
H. HETHERINGTON, *Cheap salvation, or an antidote to priestcraft*, 1833.
—— *Principles and practice contrasted; or, a peep into 'The only true Church of God upon earth', commonly called Freethinking Christians*, 1828.
C. H., 'The penny press', *New Monthly Magazine*, vol. xl, 1834.
W. HICKSON, 'Taxes on knowledge. Reduction or abolition of the Stamp Duties on newspapers', *London Review*, Jan. 1836, pp. 336–55.
T. HODGSKIN, *Labour defended against the claims of capital* (1825), 1922 edition, edited by G. D. H. Cole.
—— *Popular political economy* . . ., 1827.
K., *A fable for the times* (1830?).
—— *The working of capital* (1830?).
C. KNIGHT, *An address to the labourers on destroying machinery*, 1830.
—— *The newspaper stamp and the duty upon paper viewed in their relation to their effects upon the diffusion of knowledge*. 1836.
—— *The results of machinery*, 1831
—— *The Rights of industry: capital and labour*, 1831.
R. E. LEE, *Victimization or Benbowism unmasked*, 1832.
'Licentiousness of the press', *Livesey's Moral Reformer*, vol. iii, 1833.
J. B. E. LORYMER, *Brittania's cat o'nine tails*, 1833.
—— *A national convention, the only proper remedy*, 1833.
—— (transl.) Lamennais, *The book of the people*, 1838.
J. R. MCCULLOCH, *A discourse on the rise, progress, peculiar objects, and importance of political economy*, Edinburgh, 1825.
—— *The principles of political economy*, 5th edn., 1864.
—— 'The proposed taxes on property and income', *Edinburgh Review*, Apr. 1833.
—— 'The taxes on literature', *Edinburgh Review*, June 1831.
T. MALTHUS, *An essay on the principles of population*, 1890 edn.
K. MARX and ENGELS, *Selected works*, 2 vols. (Moscow, 1962).
K. Marx and Engels on England (Moscow, 1962).
T. MAYHEW, *Complete history of an action at Law* . . . *proving the present practice of the Courts of Law to be extravagant and unjust*, 1828.
The mayor of Manchester and his slanderers, 1877, Manchester.

A memorial of certain inhabitants of the City of London to the Chancellor of the Exchequer, 6 May 1835.

G. MERLE, 'Journalism', *Westminster Review*, Jan. 1833.

J. S. MILL, 'Centralization', *Edinburgh Review*, Apr. 1862.

—— 'Manifesto of the Chancellor of the Exchequer against the moral interests of the productive classes', *Monthly Repository*, vol. x, 1836.

—— 'The taxes on knowledge', *Monthly Repository*, vol. viii, 1834.

Moral and political evils of the taxes on knowledge, 1830.

The Newspaper Stamps. A deputation to Viscount Melbourne, to procure the total repeal of the Stamp Duties on Newspapers, 1836.

The Newspaper Stamp Abolition Committee to the parliamentary and financial reformers of the United Kingdom, 1849.

'Newspapers and the stamp question', *British Quarterly Review*, 1852.

'Notes on newspapers', *Monthly Repository*, vol. viii, 1834.

'Notes on periodicals', *New Monthly Magazine*, vol. xxxix, 1833.

'Notes on the newspaper stamp', *Frazer's Magazine*, vol. xliv, 1851.

J. BRONTERRE O'BRIEN ed., *Buonarotti's History of Babeuf's Conspiracy*, 1836.

Observations on the duty on paper, 1836.

F. PLACE, *A letter to a Minister of State*, 1831.

—— *The Stamp Duty on newspapers*, 1836.

The poor man's book of the Church, 1831.

'Popular literature of the day', *British and Foreign Review*, 1840, pp. 223–46.

J. A. ROEBUCK, *A history of the Whig Ministry of 1830, to the passing of the Reform Bill*, 2 vols., 1852.

P. SCROPE, *Political economy*, 1873 edn.

—— 'The political economists', *Quarterly Review*, Jan. 1831.

—— 'The rights of industry and the banking system', *Quarterly Review*, July 1832.

J. KAY SHUTTLEWORTH, *Four stages of public education, as reviewed in 1832, 1839, 1846, 1862*, 1862.

REVD J. E. SMITH, *The Anti-Christ or Christianity reformed*, 1832.

J. T. SMITH, *Local self-government and centralization*, 1851.

R. SOUTHEY, 'New distribution of property', *Quarterly Review*, July 1831.

—— 'The moral and political state of the British Empire', *Quarterly Review*, Jan. 1831.

T. SPRING RICE, 'The financial measures of the Government', *Edinburgh Review*, Oct. 1833.

'Taxes on literature', *Westminster Review*, Apr. 1830.

'Taxes on necessities against taxes on knowledge', *New Monthly Magazine*, vol. xliv, 1835.

W. THOMPSON, *An inquiry into the principles of the distribution of wealth most conducive to human happiness*, edited by W. Pare, 1850.

—— *Labour rewarded. The claims of labour and capital conciliated* . . ., 1827.

—— *Practical directions for the speedy and economical establishment of communities* . . ., 1830.

R. TORRENS, *A letter to the Right Hon. Sir Robert Peel . . . on the condition of England and on the means of removing the causes of distress*, 1843.

—— *On the wages of labour*, 1832 edn.

'Trades unions and strikes', *Edinburgh Review*, July 1834.

'The trammels of the Press', *Westminster Review*, Apr. 1833.

E. Tufnell, *The character, objects and effects of trades unions*, 1834.

'Unstamped Press in London', *Tait's Edinburgh Magazine*, Oct. 1834.

A. Ure, *The philosophy of manufactures; or an exposition of the scientific, moral, and commercial economy of the factory system of Great Britain*, 1835.

M. Volney, *The ruins, or a survey of the revolutions of empire*, 5th edn., 1811.

J. Wade, *A history of the middle and working classes . . .*, 2nd edn., 1834.

E. G. Wakefield, *Householders in danger from the populace*, 1831.

T. Wakley, *A letter to the people of England on the proposed new laws for gagging the press*, 1836.

C. M. Westmacott, *Serious considerations on the proposed alteration of the newspapers*, 1836.

CONTEMPORARY MEMOIRS

A. W. A'Beckett, *The à Becketts of 'Punch'*, 1903.

W. E. Adams, *Memoirs of a social atom*, 2 vols., 1903.

J. Amphlett, *The newspaper press, in part of the last century, and up to the present period of 1860*, 1860.

A. Andrews, *The history of British journalism*, 2 vols., 1859.

Sir J. Arnold, *The life of Thomas, first Lord Denman*, 2 vols., Boston, 1874.

Autobiographical fragment of Dr. John Bowring, 1877.

A. Bain, *James Mill*, 1882.

Samuel Bamford, *Passages in the life of a Radical*, 2 vols., 1893.

J. Bertram, *Some memories of books, authors and events*, 1893.

H. R. Fox Bourne, *English newspapers*, 2 vols., 1887.

J. W. Brooke, *The democrats of Marylebone*, 1839.

H. Brougham, *Life and times of Lord Brougham, written by himself*. 3 vols., Edinburgh, 1871.

E. L. Bulwer, *England and the English*, 1833.

J. D. Burn, *The autobiography of a beggar boy*, 1855.

T. C. Campbell, *The battle of the press, as told in the story of the life of Richard Carlile*, 1899.

T. Carter, *Memoirs of a working man*, 1845.

W. Chambers, *The story of a long and busy life*, Edinburgh, 1882.

G. L. Chesterton, *Revelations of prison life*, 2 vols., 1856.

C. D. Collet, *The history of the taxes on knowledge*, 1933 edn.

T. Cooper, *The life of Thomas Cooper. Written by himself*, 1872.

—— *Thoughts at four score, and earlier*, 1885.

H. Curwen, *History of booksellers*, 1873.

T. A. Devyr, *The odd book of the nineteenth century, or 'Chivalry' in modern days . . .*, New York, 1882.

G. Dodd, *Days at the factories*, 1843.

S. Dowell, *A history of taxes and taxation in England from the earliest times to the present day*, 4 vols., 1884.

T. Escott, *Masters of English journalism*, 1911.

A. Fonblanque, *England under seven administrations*, 1837.

T. Frost, *Forty years recollections: literary and political*, 1880.

—— *Reminiscences of a country journalist*, 1886.

R. G. Gammage, *The history of the Chartist Movement, 1837–1854*, Newcastle upon Tyne, 1894.

H. Goddard, *Memoirs of a Bow Street Runner*, edited by P. Pringle, 1956.

G. L. Gomme, *London in the reign of Victoria, 1837–1897*, 1898.

J. Grant, *The newspaper press: its origin, progress, and present position*, 3 vols., 1871–2.

—— *Sketches in London*, 1838.

H. Grote, *The personal life of George Grote*, 1873.

T. C. Hansard, *Treatises on printing and typefounding. From the 7th edition of the Encyclopaedia Britannica*. Edinburgh, 1841.

J. Hatton, *Journalistic London . . .*, 1882.

A. Heywood and Sons, 1832–1899, Manchester, 1899.

A. Heywood, *Three papers on English printed almanacks*, Manchester, 1904.

C. Hindley, *The history of the Catnach Press*, 1886.

R. Hoe & Co., *Manufacturers of single and double cylinders and type-revolving printing machines*, New York, 1853.

G. J. Holyoake, *Bygones worth remembering*, 2 vols., 1905.

—— *The history of cooperation*, 1906 edn.

—— *The life and character of Henry Hetherington, from the éloge by T. Cooper . . .* 1849.

—— *The life and character of Richard Carlile*, 1870.

—— *The life of Joseph Rayner Stephens . . .*, 1881.

—— *The logic of death, or, why should the atheist fear to die?* 1870.

—— *Sixty years of an agitator's life*, 2 vols., 1892.

F. K. Hunt, *The fourth estate: contributions towards a history of newspapers, and of the liberty of the press*, 2 vols., 1850.

Leigh Hunt, *The autobiography of Leigh Hunt, with reminiscences of friends and contemporaries*, 1860.

N. Hunt, *Then and now, or fifty years of newspaper work*, Hull, 1887.

Lloyd Jones, *The life, times and labours of Robert Owen*, 1895.

C. Knight, *Passages of a working life during half a century*, 2 vols., 1864.

—— *The old printer and the modern press*, 1854.

Knight's Cyclopedia of London, 1851.

R. E. Leader, *The life and letters of J. A. Roebuck, with chapters of auto-biography*, 1897.

J. B. Leno, *The aftermath*, 1892.

W. J. Linton, *James Watson, a memoir of the days of the fight for a free press in England, and of the agitation for the People's charter*, 1879.

—— *Memories*, 1895.

W. Lovett, *The life and struggles of William Lovett in his pursuit of bread, knowledge and freedom* (1876), 1920 edn.

H. Martineau, *The history of the thirty years peace*, vols. ii and iii, 1877.

H. Mayhew, *London labour and the London poor* (vol. i, 1851, vol. ii and iii, 1864 edn.).

H. Mayhew and J. Binney, *The great world of London*, 1862.

D. LE MARCHANT, *Memoir of John Charles, Viscount Althorp, Third Earl Spencer*, 1876.

Lord Melbourne's papers, edited L. C. Sanders, 1889.

W. NAPIER, *The life and opinions of General Sir Charles Napier*, 4 vols., 1857.

The correspondence of Daniel O'Connell edited with notices of his life and times by *W. J. Fitzpatrick*, 2 vols., 1888.

J. OVERS, *The evenings of a working man, being the occupation of his scanty leisure*, 1844.

Papers of the Manchester Literary Club, vol. ii, 1875–6.

C. PEBODY, *English journalism and the men who have made it*, 1882.

Questions for a reformed Parliament, 1867.

C. REDDING, *Fifty years recollections, literary and personal*, 1858.

―――― *Yesterday and today*, 3 vols., 1863.

ROLLO RUSSELL ed., *Early correspondence of Lord John Russell, 1805–1840*, 1913.

W. SAVAGE, *A dictionary of the art of printing*, 1841.

H. SOLLY, *James Woodford, carpenter and chartist*, 1881.

―――― *'These eighty years', or, the story of an unfinished life*, 2 vols., 1893.

A. SOMERVILLE, *The autobiography of a working man*, 1848.

C. MANBY SMITH, *The working man's way in the world, being the autobiography of a journeyman printer*, 1853.

C. THOMPSON, *The autobiography of an artizan*, 1847.

C. H. TIMPERLEY, *The encyclopedia of literary and typographical anecdote*, 1842.

W. TINSLEY, *Random recollections of an old publisher*, 2 vols., 1905.

'The Unstamped Press', *Notes and Queries*, 1872, vol. ii, pp. 415–16.

H. VIZETELLY, *Glances back through seventy years; autobiographical and other reminiscences*, 2 vols., 1893.

B. WILSON, *The struggles of an old Chartist*, 1887.

J. F. WILSON, *A few personal recollections. By an old printer*, 1896.

SELECTED LIST OF SECONDARY SOURCES

G. ALDRED, *Richard Carlile, agitator: his life and times*. 1923.

―――― *The 'Devil's Chaplain': the story of the Revd. Robert Taylor, M.A., M.R.C.S. (1784–1844)* [*sic*], Glasgow, 1942.

R. D. ALTICK, *The English common reader: a social history of the mass reading public 1800–1900*, Chicago, 1957.

W. ARMYTAGE, *Heavens Below: utopian experiments in England, 1560–1960*, 1961.

T. ASHTON, *Economic and social investigations in Manchester, 1833–1933*, 1934.

A. ASPINALL, *Lord Brougham and the Whig Party*, 1939.

―――― *Politics and the Press 1780–1850*, 1949.

―――― 'The circulation of newspapers in the early nineteenth century', *English Historical Review*, 1948, pp. 201–32.

―――― 'Some statistical accounts of London newspapers in the eighteenth century', *English Historical Review*, 1949, p. 205.

―――― 'Some statistical accounts of London newspapers 1800–1836', *English Historical Review*, 1950, p. 223.

334 BIBLIOGRAPHY

A. G. BARKER, *Henry Hetherington, 1792–1849*, 1938.
J. BARNES, *Free trade in books, a study of the London book trade since 1800*, Oxford, 1964.
H. BEALES, *The early English socialists*, 1933.
M. BEER, *A history of British socialism*, 2 vols., 1953 edn.
S. BEER, 'The representation of interests', *American Political Science Review*, 1957.
A. E. BESTOR, *Backwoods Utopias. The Sectarian and Owenite phases of communitarian socialism in America, 1663–1829*, American Historical Association, 1950.
—— 'The evolution of socialist vocabulary', *Journal of the History of Ideas*, 1948.
M. BLAUG, *Ricardian economics, an historical study*, Yale, 1958.
M. BOWLEY, *Nassau senior and classical economics*, 1937.
A. BRIGGS, ed., *Chartist studies*, 1962 edn.
—— 'The language of "class" in early nineteenth century England', in *Essays in Labour History*, pp. 43–73, ed. A. Briggs and J. Saville, 1960.
C. BROOK, *Battling surgeon* [a life of Thomas Wakley], Glasgow, 1945.
L. BROWN, *The Board of Trade and the Free Trade Movement 1830–1849*, Oxford, 1958.
S. CHECKLAND, 'The Birmingham economists 1815–1850', *Economic History Review*, 1948.
R. V. CLEMENTS, 'Trades unions and popular political economy 1850–1875', *Economic History Review*, 1961.
G. D. H. COLE, *Attempts at general union: a study in British trade union history, 1818–1834*, 1953.
—— *Chartist portraits*, 1941.
—— *The life of William Cobbett*, 1924.
D. C. COLEMAN, *The British paper industry, 1495–1860*, 1958.
S. COLTHAM, 'The "*Beehive*" newspaper: its origins and early struggles', in *Essays in Labour History*, pp. 174–204, ed. A. Briggs and J. Saville, 1960.
—— 'George Potter and the "Beehive" newspaper' (Oxford University D.Phil. thesis 1956).
W. F. CONNELL, *The educational thought and influence of Matthew Arnold*, 1950.
B. A. CORRY, *Money, saving and investment in English economics, 1800–1850*, 1962.
G. A. CRANFIELD, *The development of the provincial newspaper, 1700–1760*, Oxford, 1962.
R. DAHRENDORF, *Class and class conflict in industrial society*, 1959.
Dictionary of national biography.
S. FINER, *Life and times of Sir Edwin Chadwick*, 1952.
R. GARNETT, *The life of W. J. Fox, public teacher and social reformer 1786–1864*, 1910.
N. GASH, *Reaction and reconstruction in English politics, 1832–1852*, Oxford, 1965.
E. GLASGOW, 'The foundation of the '*Northern Star*', *History*, 1954.
J. GODARD, *George Birkbeck, pioneer of popular education*, 1884.

A. GRAHAM, 'The Lichfield House compact, 1835', *Irish Historical Studies*, 1961, pp. 209–25.

SIR A. GRAY, *The socialist tradition, from Moses to Lenin*, 1946.

M. GROBEL, 'The Society for the Diffusion of Useful Knowledge 1826–1846' (London University Ph.D thesis 1932).

W. GUTTSMAN, ed., *A plea for democracy*, 1967.

E. HALEVY, *Thomas Hodgskin 1787–1869*, 1903.

J. HAMBURGER, *Intellectuals in politics: John Stuart Mill and the philosophic radicals*, Yale, 1965.

J. and B. HAMMOND, *The town labourer, 1760–1832*, 1917.

J. F. C. HARRISON, *Learning and living, 1790–1960, a study in the history of English adult education*, 1961.

History of the Times, 'The Thunderer in the Making', *1785–1841*, 1935.

M. HOVELL, *The Chartist Movement*, 1918.

L. JAMES, *Fiction for the working man, 1830–1850*, 1963.

H. JEPHSON, *The platform, its rise and progress*, 2 vols., 1892.

L. G. JOHNSON, *General T. Perronet Thompson*, 1957.

T. KELLY, *George Birkbeck, pioneer of adult education*, Liverpool, 1957.

W. KENNEDY, 'Lord Brougham, Charles Knight, and "The rights of industry"' *Economica*, 1962, pp. 58–71.

W. KENT, *London for heretics*, 1932.

E. LOWENTHAL, *The Ricardian socialists*, New York, 1911.

S. MACCOBY, *English radicalism 1832–1852*, 1935.

N. McCORD, 'Some difficulties of parliamentary reform', *Historical Journal*, 1967.

F. C. MATHER, *Public order in the age of the Chartists*, Manchester, 1959.

D. C. MOORE, 'The other face of reform', *Victorian Studies*, 1961.

—— 'Social structure, political structure and public opinion in mid-Victorian England', in *Ideas and Institutions of Victorian England*, ed. R. Robson, 1967.

M. G. MOORE, 'The history of the agitation against the stamp duty on newspapers' (London University M.A. thesis 1935).

A. MUIRHEAD, 'Introduction to a bibliography of William Cobbett', *Library*, 1940.

C. NEW, *The life of Henry Brougham to 1830*, Oxford, 1961.

W. OLIVER, 'The organization and ideas behind the efforts to achieve a general union of the working classes in the early 1830's' (Oxford University D.Phil. thesis 1954).

R. PANKHURST, *William Thompson (1775–1833), Britain's pioneer socialist, feminist and cooperator*, 1954.

M. V. PATTERSON, *Sir Frances Burdett and his times 1776–1844*, 2 vols., 1931.

M. PLANT, *The English book trade*, 1939.

A. PLUMMER, 'The place of Bronterre O'Brien in the working class movement', *Economic History Review*, 1929, pp. 65–80.

G. POLLARD, 'Notes on the size of a sheet', *Transactions of the Bibliographical Society*, 1941.

I. PROTHERO, 'London working class movements, 1825–1848' (Cambridge University Ph.D. thesis, 1967).

A. Pulling, *The laws, customs, usages, and regulations of the City and Port of London*, 1854.

L. Radzinovitz, *History of criminal law*.

D. Read, *Press and people 1790–1850: opinion in three English cities*, 1961.

L. Robbins, *The theory of economic policy in English classical political economy*, 1952.

J. M. Robertson, *A history of freethought in the nineteenth century*, 1929.

E. Roll, *A history of economic thought*, 1953 edn.

J. Holland Rose, 'The Unstamped Press', *English Historical Review*, 1897, pp. 711–26.

D. J. Rowe, 'Radicalism in London, 1829–1841' (Southampton University M.A. thesis, 1965).

—— 'Chartism and the Spitalfields silk weavers', *Economic History Review*, 1967.

A. J. C. Rüter, 'William Benbow as publisher', *Bulletin of the International Institute for Social History*, 1940, pp. 1–14.

—— 'William Benbow's "Grand National Holiday and Congress of the Productive Classes" ', *International Review for Social History*, 1936, pp. 271–56.

J. Saville, *Ernest Jones, Chartist*, 1952.

A. R. Schoyen, *The Chartist challenge*, 1958.

L. Shepard, *The broadside ballad: a study in origin and meaning*, 1962.

F. Sheppard, *Local government in St. Marylebone, 1688–1835*, 1958.

K. Smith, *The Malthusian controversy*, 1951.

B. Simon, *Studies in the history of education, 1780–1870*, 1960.

L. Sorenson, 'Some classical economists, *laisser-faire*, and the factory acts', *Journal of Economic History*, 1952.

S. Sprigge, *The life and times of Thomas Wakley*, 1897.

E. P. Thompson, *The making of the English working class*, 1963.

K. R. Tonneson, The 'Babouvists', *Past and Present*, July 1962, pp. 60–77.

J. Vincent, *The formation of the Liberal Party, 1857–1868*, Cambridge, 1966.

C. H. Vivian, 'Radical journalism in the 1830's, the *True Sun*', *Modern Language Quarterly*, 1954.

G. Wallas, *The life of Francis Place 1771–1854*, 1918.

R. K. Webb, *The British working class reader 1790–1848*, 1955.

—— *Harriet Martineau, a radical Victorian*, 1960.

—— 'Working class readers in Victorian England', *English Historical Review*, 1950, pp. 333–51.

J. M. Wheeler, *A biographical dictionary of freethinkers of all ages and nations*, 1889.

W. H. Wickwar, *The struggle for the freedom of the press, 1819–1832*, 1928.

J. Wiener, 'The movement to repeal the "Taxes on Knowledge" 1825–1840: a study in British working class radicalism' (Cornell University Ph.D. thesis, 1965).

G. M. Young, ed., *Early Victorian England*, vol. ii.

INDEX

INDEX

347

PRINTED IN GREAT BRITAIN
AT THE UNIVERSITY PRESS, OXFORD
BY VIVIAN RIDLER
PRINTER TO THE UNIVERSITY